GOSPEL INTERPRETATION

NARRATIVE-CRITICAL & SOCIAL-SCIENTIFIC APPROACHES

EDITED BY

Jack Dean Kingsbury

TRINITY PRESS INTERNATIONAL
Harrisburg, Pennsylvania

The symbols of the four evangelists on the cover and the part-opening pages are taken from a title page by Hans Holbein the Younger, from the print shop of Adam Petri, Basle, ca. 1524, plate 61 in Albert Fidelis Butsch, *Handbook of Renaissance Ornament* (New York: Dover Publications, 1969). The illustration for the part opening of "The Historical Jesus" is from "Christ Taking Leave of His Mother," ca. 1505, by Albrecht Dürer, in Willi Kurth, ed., *The Complete Woodcuts of Albrecht Dürer* (New York: Dover Publications, 1963).

Trinity Press International, P.O. Box 1321, Harrisburg, PA 17105
Trinity Press International is a division of the Morehouse Group

Library of Congress Cataloging-in-Publication Data

Gospel interpretation : narrative-critical & social-scientific approaches / edited by Jack Dean Kingsbury.
p. cm.
Includes bibliographical references and index.
ISBN 1-56338-214-8 (alk. paper)
1. Bible. N.T. Gospels – Criticism, Narrative. 2. Bible. N.T. Gospels – Social scientific criticism. I. Kingsbury, Jack Dean.
BS2555.2.G58 1997
226′.066 – dc21 97-28264
CIP

Printed in the United States of America

97 98 99 00 01 02 10 9 8 7 6 5 4 3 2 1

To

Mary T. Atkinson

Contents

Abbreviations

AB	Anchor Bible
ABRL	Anchor Bible Reference Library
AGJU	Arbeiten zur Geschichte des antiken Judentums und des Urchristentums
ATJ	*Asbury Theological Journal*
ATR Sup.	*Anglican Theological Review* Supplement
BETL	Bibliotheca ephemeridum theologicarum lovaniensium
BJRL	*Bulletin of the John Rylands Library*
BLS	Bible and Literature Series
BS	*Bibliotheca Sacra*
BTB	*Biblical Theology Bulletin*
BZ	*Biblische Zeitschrift*
BZNW	Beihefte zur *Zeitschrift für die neutestamentliche Wissenschaft*
CBQ	*Catholic Biblical Quarterly*
CurTM	*Currents in Theology and Mission*
FRLANT	Forschungen zur Religion und Literatur des Alten und Neuen Testaments
GBS	Guides to Biblical Scholarship
GNS	Good News Studies
HeyJ	*Heythrop Journal*
HTKNT	Herders theologischer Kommentar zum Neuen Testament
HTR	*Harvard Theological Review*
IEJ	*Israel Exploration Journal*
Int	*Interpretation*
IRT	Issues in Religion and Theology

JAAR	*Journal of the American Academy of Religion*
JBL	*Journal of Biblical Literature*
JJS	*Journal of Jewish Studies*
JR	*Journal of Religion*
JSNT	*Journal for the Study of the New Testament*
JSNTSup	Journal for the Study of the New Testament Supplement Series
LTPM	Louvain Theological and Pastoral Monographs
NovT	*Novum Testamentum*
NTAbh	Neutestamentliche Abhandlungen
NTL	New Testament Library
NTS	*New Testament Studies*
NTTS	New Testament Tools and Studies
NVBS	New Voices in Biblical Studies
QD	Quaestiones disputatae
SBLDS	Society of Biblical Literature Dissertation Series
SBLMS	Society of Biblical Literature Monograph Series
SBLSBS	Society of Biblical Literature Sources for Biblical Study
SBLSP	Society of Biblical Literature Seminar Papers
SNTSMS	Studiorum Novi Testamenti Societas Monograph Series
TDNT	G. Kittel, ed. *Theological Dictionary of the New Testament.* Trans. G. W. Bromiley. Grand Rapids, Mich.: Eerdmans, 1964–76
TS	*Theological Studies*
WMANT	Wissenschaftliche Monographien zum Alten und Neuen Testament
WUNT	Wissenschaftliche Untersuchungen zum Neuen Testament
ZNW	*Zeitschrift für die neutestamentliche Wissenschaft*

Contributors

David R. Bauer is Professor of English Bible at Asbury Theological Seminary.

Mary Ann Beavis is a research associate at the Institute of Urban Studies, Winnipeg, Manitoba.

M. Eugene Boring is Professor of New Testament at Brite Divinity School, Texas Christian University.

Raymond F. Collins is Professor of New Testament at the Catholic University of America.

R. Alan Culpepper is Dean of Mercer School of Theology.

John P. Galvin is Associate Professor of Systematic Theology at the Catholic University of America.

Jack Dean Kingsbury is Professor of Biblical Theology at Union Theological Seminary in Virginia.

John P. Meier is Professor of New Testament at the Catholic University of America.

Halvor Moxnes is Professor of New Testament at the University of Oslo.

Gail R. O'Day is Associate Professor of Biblical Preaching at Candler School of Theology, Emory University.

Mark Allan Powell is Professor of New Testament at Trinity Lutheran Seminary.

David Rhoads is Professor of New Testament at the Lutheran School of Theology at Chicago.

John K. Riches is Professor of Divinity and Biblical Criticism at the University of Glasgow.

Richard L. Rohrbaugh is Professor of Religious Studies at Lewis and Clark College.

Fernando F. Segovia is Professor of New Testament and Early Christianity at the Divinity School, Vanderbilt University.

Klyne R. Snodgrass is Professor of New Testament Studies at North Park Theological Seminary.

Graham N. Stanton is Professor of New Testament Studies at King's College, University of London.

Robert C. Tannehill is Professor of New Testament at Methodist Theological School in Ohio.

Mary Ann Tolbert is Professor of New Testament at Vanderbilt University.

Urban C. von Wahlde is Professor of New Testament at Loyola University of Chicago.

Introduction

In the last two decades, research on the canonical Gospels has undergone profound change, and the quest of the historical Jesus has, for a third time in the last two centuries, captured the fancy of scholars. To chronicle these trends, *Interpretation: A Journal of Bible and Theology* did what it has shown it does best: As in its series on the Gospels in the 1970s and on the major prophets and Daniel in the 1980s, it has, in the 1990s, devoted five issues to the exploration of current research on the Gospels and Jesus. Because this series, like the two preceding it, enjoys widespread use among pastors and at colleges and seminaries, *Interpretation* is pleased to join with Harold Rast and Trinity Press International to make all five issues available in one volume.

The two most prominent new methodologies associated with gospel research are literary and sociological in nature. Sociologically, scholars are in search of new models and data that will enable them to understand better the social and cultural world in which the Gospels arose or Jesus of Nazareth was at home. Literarily, scholars devote the bulk of their attention to the study of the respective Gospels as narratives and the way readers, whether ancient or modern, may be said to respond to them.

As a discipline, therefore, narrative criticism is a branch of literary criticism that has as its object the study of the formal features of narrative texts. In narrative criticism, the text is construed as communicating the message that the (implied) author would convey to the (implied) reader. Still, the focus of attention is not, as in redaction criticism, on the author of the text or, as in social-historical and social-scientific study, on the Christian community that stands behind it. Instead, the focus is on the text itself. To say this, however, is not to imply that narrative critics are dismissive of historical studies. After all, the Gospels are texts written in the first century. Nevertheless, it is not historical reconstruction as such that interests narrative critics but, again, analysis of a text's formal features.

All four Gospels count as narrative texts, and these texts all tell, each in its own way, the story of Jesus of Nazareth. Whereas each story has its cast of characters, all four feature Jesus as the protagonist, the religious authorities as the antagonists, and the disciples, often with Peter as type or spokesperson, as a group-character. Part and parcel of each gospel story are also the settings that mark the time, place, or social circumstances in which characters act ("next day," "in a house," "at meal") and the many events that occur from beginning to end.

Of special interest is the way in which events are arranged. Arrangement may be in terms of time, place, or topic but will demonstrate cause and effect and aim to elicit from readers some desired response, like confessing Jesus to be the Son of God, or perceiving him to be the revelation of God, or doing the will of God as taught by him. It is in the arrangement of events, their causal force, and the persuasive power with which they are narrated that one discerns the plot and meaning of a story.

In all four Gospels, the axis on which the plot turns is that of conflict: Conflict between Jesus Son of God and Satan, between Jesus and religious authorities, and between Jesus and uncomprehending disciples. The point(s) in any gospel story at which major conflict comes to resolution signal(s) the culmination of the story. In the first three Gospels, the story culminates in the narration of Jesus' death on the cross and his resurrection (and, in Luke, ascension). In John's Gospel, Jesus' crucifixion marks the culmination of the story, but now crucifixion denotes glorification: Following the descent of the Word into the world and its incarnation in Jesus, Jesus completes the journey by returning to the Father, the first step of which is his being glorified through being lifted up on the cross.

Narrative critics explore not only the story of each Gospel but also how each story is told. Whereas all the Gospels were written in Greek, each exhibits a particular style or makes its own use, say, of rhetorical strategies or Old Testament quotations. Crucial to the telling of a story are its narrative voice and theological point of view, or perspective.

The narrative voice, or narrator, is the invisible speaker that tells the story. In the Gospels, narrators are to be thought of as reliable because the views they express are in accord with those ascribed to God or to Jesus, God's Son. Gospel narrators, therefore, are authoritative voices, and the reader is invited to regard them as imparting truth.

To understand a gospel story, the reader must understand the theological point of view, or perspective, that governs it. In all four Gospels, the authenticity and integrity of the respective theological viewpoints are rooted in the claim that these enjoy the sanction of God. But whereas God is seen as the inspiration for these viewpoints, it is principally Jesus or also the narrators who articulate them. As the Son of God, Jesus is the immediate and unique mouthpiece of God. As reliable voices, the narrators, too, speak the mind of God. And through canonization, the Patristic church affirmed on behalf of the church of every age that in all four Gospels the truth of God is proclaimed.

Whereas in all four Gospels God is made guarantor of the validity of their respective theologies, the unity of these theologies resides in a broader claim: that in fulfillment of Old Testament promise, God has acted decisively in Jesus Christ to save the world, Jews and gentiles, either by forgiving sins or by taking sin away through self-revelation. It is within the context of this fundamental christological unity that the theologies of the Gospels exhibit diversity. The early church was correct in understanding the four Gospels as announcing the one gospel of God's saving action in Jesus Christ.

To preach or teach a gospel story, acquaintance with both its plot and theological point of view is essential. To know the plot is to understand how a story begins and respective conflicts arise, develop, and are resolved. Familiarity with plot enables one to appreciate the positioning of each episode within the story and the literary role this episode plays within the story as a whole.

Similarly, knowledge of a Gospel's theological point of view enables one to get at the meaning of both the entire story and each episode within it. At bottom, the purpose of each gospel story is the same: to persuade the reader to appropriate the theological point of view it espouses. To discern this point of view, one must attend to both the overall rhetorical strategy of the author and how the author uses numerous rhetorical devices throughout the story to urge readers to see reality from his angle of vision. For example, the overall rhetorical strategy of Mark aims at eliciting confession and commitment: As the reader looks on, Mark guides him or her to approve or disapprove of characters in regard to whether or to what extent they, in seeing or hearing Jesus amid the events of the story, perceive his identity and destiny aright and respond by confessing him to be the Son of God in whose cross God proffers salvation and by becoming disciples who lead the cruciform life.

The two notions of consistency building and defamiliarization also explain how readers interact with gospel narratives. Consistency building addresses the fact that as the reader peruses a gospel narrative, he or she puts forth every effort to make sense of the narrative's story and to find in it specific meaning and significance. The alternative, which is inherently dissatisfying even when entertained, is for the reader to conclude that the narrative's story is too incoherent or inconclusive to permit definition of meaning or discernment of significance. To illustrate, the inconclusive manner in which Mark ends his Gospel has, from the beginning, left readers to wonder whether the women did or did not carry out the angel's command to convey the message of Easter to the disciples (Mark 16:6–8). Indeed, this question has so discomfited commentators and scholars that ancient Greek manuscripts attest to the existence of three different endings for Mark.

Defamiliarization takes note of the fact that when a reader experiences what is unfamiliar within the world of a narrative, he or she is led to view aspects of his or her own familiar world in new ways. To put it differently, the act of reading a Gospel requires that the reader take leave of his or her own daily world and enter for a time, through the power of imagination, into the narrative world of the Gospel. Upon leaving this narrative world and returning to his or her own daily world, the reader sees things in different perspective.

How do the Gospels effect defamiliarization? They do so through use of eschatology. In all four, the story of Jesus is cast in the light of the end-time: All four show what life is like when people receive Jesus either as the Messiah, the Son of God, or as the Son who reveals the Father, and lead life as disciples of Jesus in the sphere of either God's inbreaking rule or God's supreme self-manifestation.

We observed above that the final issue of *Interpretation*'s recent series deals with the quest of the historical Jesus. In reading the essays of this issue, one must not forget that the so-called "historical Jesus" is Jesus of Nazareth as scholars attempt to reconstruct his life in Palestine prior to Easter. To accomplish this, they sift through, or work behind, gospel texts, especially those of Mark, Matthew, and Luke. Begun in the 1770s, the quest of the historical Jesus bears witness to three stages and has achieved mixed results.

The first stage was the quest as conducted in the nineteenth century, which tended to depict the earthly Jesus as the ideal human being and teacher who purveyed the values of modern liberal Protestantism. This stage of the quest can be said to have come to grief on the recognition that eschatology is of crucial importance for understanding Jesus and his message. The second stage of the quest may be dated from the address Professor Ernst Käsemann delivered in 1953 in Germany on "The Problem of the Historical Jesus." During this stage, eschatology became the defining color of portraits of Jesus and the tendency was to picture him as an eschatological figure who proclaimed the imminent inbreaking of God's splendid rule. The beginning of the third stage is harder to pin down and no single portrait of Jesus can be said to be dominant. Thus, the Jesus Seminar began work in 1985 and, like the first stage of the quest, casts Jesus of Nazareth in noneschatological hues as, for example, an itinerant sage. Other scholars, however, insist that eschatology remains the key to a correct understanding of Jesus, namely, his sense that God's rule in splendor was imminent and qualifies life as led in the present. However the scholars who authored *Interpretation*'s essays on the historical Jesus nuance this view, it is the one they applaud most.

Apart from this final issue on the historical Jesus, the other issues on Matthew, Mark, Luke, and John all follow the same basic outline. In the first essay, the author touches on the recent history of narrative criticism or sketches how the latter "works" when applied to one of the Gospels. The second, third, and fourth essays deal with matters of plot, characterization, or some theological theme or topic that is prominent in one or the other gospel story (e.g., the "law" in Matthew). And the fifth essay rounds out the first four by treating aspects of the social and cultural world in which each Gospel arose. The idea is to showcase, for pastors and students, the potential that narrative criticism and sociological and historical inquiry hold for them as they discharge their duties of mounting pulpit or podium or of gaining new insight into the meaning and significance of the gospel stories, the circumstances in which they were first narrated, or the life of Jesus of Nazareth.

JACK DEAN KINGSBURY
Lent, 1997

The Gospel of MATTHEW

– 1 –

Toward a Narrative-Critical Understanding of Matthew

Mark Allan Powell

A scant decade ago, virtually anyone studying Matthew's Gospel approached it from the standpoint of redaction-critical method. Today, students of Matthew increasingly approach it from the standpoint of narrative-critical method. By observing how each method typically deals with the same topics, one can discern the considerable differences between them.

THE GOSPEL OF MATTHEW is a story about Jesus. Still, it has often been treated more as a resource for historical reconstruction than as a work of literature in its own right. By using such methods as source criticism, form criticism, and redaction criticism, scholars have been able to learn about the life and teaching of Jesus of Nazareth and to gain insight into the interests and concerns of the community that produced Matthew's Gospel. In the 1980s, however, the interests of scholarship expanded to include inquiry into the function of Matthew's Gospel as literature. For help in this inquiry, many scholars turned to the eclectic literary-critical methodology called "narrative criticism."[1]

Narrative criticism differs from traditional historical-critical approaches in significant ways. It views the text of Matthew's Gospel as a unified and coherent document rather than as a compilation of loosely related pericopes. It focuses on the finished form of the Gospel rather than on the compositional processes through which the text came into being. And it deals with the "poetic function" of the text to create meaning and affect readers rather than with its "referential function" to serve as a resource for historical knowledge. Thus, narrative criticism views Matthew's Gospel as a form of communication that cannot be understood without being "received" and experienced.

Traditional approaches to Matthew's Gospel have sought to answer historical and theological questions about the book. The questions that narrative criticism poses deal more explicitly with literary concerns. This does not mean, however, that narrative critics have abandoned interest in the historical or theological tasks. Instead, exploration of the literary dimension of Matthew's narrative is held to produce insights that are also relevant for understanding the historical and theological dimensions of the narrative.

To illustrate the "changes in thinking" that narrative criticism has brought to Matthean studies, we shall consider four matters that figure prominently in the historical-critical investigation of Matthew and indicate how differently narrative criticism views these same matters.

Redactor-Narrator

In recent years, historical-critical studies have thought of Matthew's Gospel as the product of a redactor, or editor. Matthew, the redactor, produced his Gospel by compiling and editing traditions about Jesus that had been handed down to him. Thus, scholars have argued that the person whom we call "Matthew" revised Mark's Gospel and other source materials to produce a work that would serve his own theological interests and meet the needs of his own community. In line with this, editorial activity has been scrutinized in order to define the particular concerns and perspective of his Gospel. The assumption has been that the meaning of a narrative is synonymous with the intentions of its historical author or redactor.

Narrative critics interpret Matthew's Gospel from the perspective of its narrator rather than from that of its redactor. Whereas the redactor was a historical person who once lived in the real world, the narrator is a voice that exists only within the world of Matthew's story. This voice guides us as we read the story, providing us with information and shaping our perceptions. Narrative criticism focuses on rhetorical features that reveal the perspective of the narrator rather than on editorial changes that reveal the perspective of the redactor.[2] Such features include the use of narrative patterns,[3] irony,[4] redundancy,[5] and intertextuality.[6]

The narrator, of course, is a "literary creation" of the Gospel's real author (or redactor) and may serve as an index of that historical person's thought.[7] But be this as it may, the perspective of the narrator also transcends the concerns of the Gospel's historical author in significant ways. For example, the narrator's perspective may be less tied to specific historical circumstances. To illustrate, redactional analysis of Matthew 15:1–20 usually relates the verses to first-century controversies concerning the relevance of Jewish purity laws for Christian communities. Such a connection, however, is not actually made by the narrator within the text of Matthew's Gospel. Because of this, narrative critics would be more likely to interpret these verses as a dramatic presentation of four different "points of view" (those of religious leaders, Jesus, the disciples, and the crowd). From this angle, Matthew 15:1–20 demonstrates the difference between divine perspective and human perspective with regard to one exemplary topic, namely, purity.

Community-Implied Reader

Historical-critical studies have attempted to discover the setting in which Matthew's Gospel was written and to describe the community in which it was first received. For example, some scholars have proposed that Matthew's Gospel was written for a mixed community of Jewish and gentile Christians who lived in a relatively prosperous urban environment during the latter part of the first century. Scholars who conduct such studies generally believe that the meaning of Matthew's Gospel should be defined in terms of the messages that it was intended to convey to its original audience.

Narrative critics realize that Matthew's Gospel has continued to be received as a meaningful narrative by audiences quite diverse from that for which it was originally intended. Rather than describing the historical community that constituted the book's original audience, they prefer to describe the work from the perspective of its "implied reader," an imaginary person who always responds to the story "with whatever emotion, understanding, or knowledge the text ideally calls for."[8] To describe the implied reader's perspective, one must concern oneself with two things: (1) definition of the reader's "repertoire," that is, the knowledge and values the reader is assumed to possess prior to any encounter with the narrative;[9] and (2) attention to the manner in which the reader is expected to be educated in the process of reading this narrative.[10]

Because the implied reader's perceptions and responses are presupposed by the text, they may serve as an index of the perceptions and responses that a work was intended to evoke in its original audience. But the effect of Matthew's Gospel on its implied reader may also transcend its original reception by a particular historical community in significant ways. Redaction criticism, for instance, tries to interpret Jesus' warning regarding "wolves in sheep's clothing" (7:15) from the perspective of Matthew's original readers and, thus, seeks to identify the particular characteristics of the false prophets who troubled Matthew's community. Narrative criticism is more apt to interpret this warning as a general description of false prophets whom the implied reader is expected to be able to identify within his or her own community.

In short, narrative criticism does not limit interpretation of Matthew's Gospel to discernment of the meaning that the book's author wanted his narrative to have for a specific community at a particular time and place. Rather, narrative criticism is interested in discerning the anticipated effects that this narrative may have on readers in any place or time who follow the guidance of the narrator.

Structure-Plot

Both redaction criticism and narrative criticism are interested in the structure of Matthew's Gospel. However, whereas redaction critics have focused on the book's *compositional structure*, narrative critics have focused on its *plot structure*.

Redaction criticism has typically understood structural analysis to mean discernment of the evangelist's strategy for organizing his source materials. An operating assumption has been that the changes an evangelist makes in the organization of source materials are especially significant for the determination of structure. Following this assumption, redaction critics have often noted that Matthew has added a large quantity of discourse material to what was taken over from Mark and has organized this material into five great blocks (5:1–7:29; 9:36–11:1; 13:1–53; 17:22–19:1; 23:1–26:2). Accordingly, many structural outlines for Matthew's Gospel favored by redaction critics have attempted to organize the Gospel around these five prominent blocks of discourse. The most famous such attempt was that of Benjamin Bacon, who claimed that Matthew deliberately organized his Gospel into five books modeled on the Pentateuch in order to present Jesus as the New Moses.[11]

Narrative criticism examines the structure of Matthew's Gospel without reference to any particular source theory. Narrative critics are interested in how the story that Matthew tells unfolds for the reader. They try to follow the flow of the narrative by describing features that preserve continuity between episodes.[12] They look for rhetorical patterns[13] and try to identify the causal links that provide the narrative with its particular logic.[14] They ask which of the several episodes mark key turning points in the unfolding drama.[15] They analyze the development and resolution of conflict within the narrative and trace the story lines of the most significant characters.[16] They attempt to delineate important thematic connections such as acceptance/rejection and promise/fulfillment.[17] By focusing on these and other literary aspects of Matthew's Gospel, narrative critics are able to describe the plot structure of the story that Matthew tells.[18] While they do not always agree as to how the major blocks of material should be defined,[19] they have been less inclined than redaction critics to grant primary structural significance to the five discourses.[20]

People-Characters

Matthew's Gospel tells us about a number of people, including Jesus and his disciples, certain political and religious leaders of Israel, and a variety of individuals who remain anonymous. Historical-critical studies have been interested in the accuracy with which Matthew describes these people and in his motivation for portraying them as he does. For example, historical critics have often observed that Matthew's depiction of the Pharisees is more negative than an objective account would warrant. The reason for this caricature, they surmise, is that Matthew's own church was engaged in competition with the Pharisees of Matthew's own day.

Narrative criticism recognizes that the people described in Matthew's Gospel are real people who once lived in history. Still, narrative critics claim that in describing these people, Matthew has created characters whose function must be understood within the world of the story that he tells.[21] For example, the Pharisees (as well as other religious leaders) appear to serve as a personification of evil.[22] They fill a stereotypical role as "the villains" or antagonists in the tale. As such, they become emblematic of the forces of evil that God is able to overcome through Christ. Narrative critics would not deny that the author of Matthew's Gospel may have had polemical purposes for casting the Pharisees in this role, but they also recognize that this characterization is a literary device that contributes to the overall meaning of the story. The point of Matthew's characterization is not that the Pharisees were bad people but that God, in Christ, has overcome the forces of evil that they symbolize.

Conclusion

The shift from an exclusively historical-critical approach to a predominantly literary-critical approach in Gospel studies has been felt in scholarly circles for at least a decade now. It already seems strange that, just recently, Matthew's Gospel was read as a catechism, a lectionary, an administrative manual, or an apologetic or polemical treatise but was not recognized to be what it most obviously is: a story. The implications of taking seriously this narrative character of the Gospel are profound. In the decade to come, the church is likely to gain a new understanding of what has been, historically, its favorite Gospel.

NOTES

1. On the development and methodology of narrative criticism, see Mark Allan Powell, *What Is Narrative Criticism?* GBS (Minneapolis: Fortress Press, 1990); on the use of other literary-critical approaches, including structuralism, reader-response criticism, rhetorical criticism, and poststructuralist deconstruction, see Mark Allan Powell, Cecile G. Gray, and Melissa C. Curtis, *The Bible and Modern Literary Criticism: A Critical Assessment and Annotated Bibliography* (Westport, Conn.: Greenwood Press, 1992).

2. On the narrator of Matthew, see David Howell, *Matthew's Inclusive Story,* JSNTSup 42 (Sheffield: Sheffield Academic Press, 1990), 93–248; Jack Dean Kingsbury, *Matthew as Story,* 2d ed. (Philadelphia: Fortress Press, 1988), 30–40.

3. David R. Bauer delineates fifteen "categories of compositional relationships" in *The Structure of Matthew's Gospel,* JSNTSup 31 (Sheffield: Almond Press, 1988). One of these, intercalation, is the key to John Paul Heil's *The Death and Resurrection of Jesus: A Narrative-Critical Reading of Matthew 26–28* (Minneapolis: Fortress Press, 1990). See also J. C. Fenton, "Inclusio and Chiasmus in Matthew," in *Studia Evangelica,* ed. Kurt Aland et al. (Berlin: Akademie Verlag, 1959), 174–79.

4. Harry Boonstra, "Satire in Matthew," *Christianity and Literature* 29, no. 4 (1980): 32–45. Three recent articles all interpret Matthew 27:25 as ironic: Timothy B. Cargall, " 'His Blood Be upon Us and upon Our Children': A Matthean Double Entendre?" *NTS* 37 (1991): 101–12; John Paul Heil, "The Blood of Jesus in Matthew," *Perspectives in Religious Studies* 18 (1991): 117–24; Robert H. Smith, "The Hardest Verse in Matthew's Gospel," *CurTM* 17 (1990): 421–28.

5. Janice Capel Anderson, "Double and Triple Stories: The Implied Reader and Redundancy in Matthew," *Semeia* 31 (1985): 71–89; Fred W. Burnett, "Prolegomenon to Reading Matthew's Eschatological Discourse," *Semeia* 31 (1985): 91–109.

6. Mark Allan Powell, "Expected and Unexpected Readings of Matthew: What the Reader Knows," *ATJ* 48 (1993): 41–51.

7. Narrative critics say that Matthew's narrator is a projection of the book's "implied author." See Powell, *What Is Narrative Criticism?* 5–6, 25–27.

8. Kingsbury, *Matthew as Story,* 38. See also Jack Dean Kingsbury, "Reflections on the 'Reader' of Matthew's Gospel," *NTS* 34 (1988): 442–60.

9. Powell, "Expected and Unexpected Readings."

10. Burnett, "Prolegomenon"; Richard Edwards, "Reading Matthew," *Listening* 24 (1989): 251–61; Howell, *Matthew's Inclusive Story,* 205–48; Terence J. Keegan, *Interpreting the Bible* (New York: Paulist Press, 1985), 110–30; Bernard Brandon Scott, "The Birth of the Reader," *Semeia* 52 (1990): 83–102.

11. Benjamin Bacon, *Studies in Matthew* (London: Constable, 1930).

12. Richard A. Edwards, *Matthew's Story of Jesus* (Philadelphia: Fortress Press, 1985).

13. Bauer, *Structure;* H. J. Bernard Combrink, "The Structure of the Gospel of Matthew as Narrative," *Tyndale Bulletin* 34 (1983): 61–90.

14. Frank J. Matera, "The Plot of Matthew's Gospel," *CBQ* 49 (1987): 233–53.

15. Ibid.

16. Kingsbury, *Matthew as Story.*

17. Howell, *Matthew's Inclusive Story.*

18. Mark Allan Powell, "The Plot and Subplots of Matthew's Gospel," *NTS* 38 (1992): 187–204.

19. Edwards: 1:1–4:2; 4:23–7:29; 8:1–11:1; 11:2–18:35; 19:1–25:46; 26:1–28:20. Howell: 1:1–4:16; 4:17–11:1; 11:2–16:20; 16:21–20:34; 21:1–25:46; 26:1–28:20. Kingsbury/Bauer: 1:1–4:16; 4:17–16:20; 16:21–28:20. Matera: 1:1–4:11; 4:12–11:1; 11:2–16:12; 16:13–20:34; 21:1–28:15; 28:16–20.

20. Dan O. Via suggests that the structure suggested by Kingsbury is "foregrounded," while the discourse-formula structure is "backgrounded"; see "Structure, Christology, and Ethics in Matthew," in *Orientation by Disorientation,* ed. Richard A. Spencer (Pittsburgh: Pickwick Press, 1980), 199–216.

21. On characters and characterization in Matthew, see esp. Kingsbury, *Matthew as Story,* 9–28; Howell, *Matthew's Inclusive Story,* 218–43.

22. Jack Dean Kingsbury, "The Developing Conflict between Jesus and the Jewish Leaders in Matthew's Gospel," *CBQ* 49 (1987): 57–73.

– 2 –

The Plot of Matthew's Story

Jack Dean Kingsbury

In Matthew's gospel story, Jesus becomes embroiled in mortal conflict with the religious authorities. In bringing Jesus to the cross, the authorities believe that the victory in the conflict is theirs. In raising Jesus from the dead, God shows that, ironically, the victory has gone to Jesus.

GENERICALLY, whatever else Matthew's Gospel may be, it is a narrative with a beginning, middle, and end.[1] This narrative tells the story of Jesus, from conception and birth to death and resurrection. The story of Jesus is one of conflict, so that its plot turns on conflict. At the human level, this conflict is between Jesus and Israel, and especially between Jesus and the religious authorities.[2] The fundamental resolution of this conflict comes at the end of the story, in the pericopes that tell of Jesus' death and resurrection. In point of fact, the "cross" is the place where Jesus' story reaches its culmination. The purpose of this essay is to trace the unfolding of the plot of Matthew's story of Jesus and, in so doing, to show how and to what effect Jesus' conflict with the authorities reaches its resolution in the cross and resurrection and its culmination in the cross.

I

In the beginning of his story (1:1–4:16), Matthew introduces the reader to both Jesus, the protagonist, and the religious authorities, Jesus' antagonists. In the pericopes that tell of Jesus' origin and baptism (1:18–25; 3:13–17), Matthew describes Jesus as the Messiah, the Son of God, whose God-given mission is to save his people from their sins. In describing Jesus as the Messiah, Matthew presents him as the Anointed One, Israel's long-awaited king. In describing Jesus as the Son of God, Matthew ascribes to him a unique filial relationship with God. By virtue of this relationship, Jesus is the wholly obedient, supreme agent of God, whom he designates as Father (4:1–11; 26:39), and God is the one who is authoritatively and decisively at work in Jesus to save (1:23; 3:17).

Without so much as permitting the religious authorities to come into contact with Jesus, Matthew also introduces them in the beginning of his story. Still, in the first pericope in which they appear — in the persons of the chief priests and the scribes of the people (2:1–6) — Matthew invites the reader to distance himself or herself from them by depicting them as standing in the service of wicked King Herod. Herod, eager to know where the Messiah is to be born, calls the chief priests and the scribes together and asks them. In ready reply, they inform Herod that Bethlehem is the place. By thus assisting Herod, the chief priests and the scribes make themselves complicit in Herod's plot to kill Jesus. In so doing, they signal the reader that, later in the story, they will prove themselves to be deadly opponents of Jesus.

It is, however, in the scene in which the religious authorities make their major debut that Matthew reveals unmistakably how he would have them understood in his story. This scene occurs in the pericope on the ministry of John the Baptist (3:7–10), and those representing the religious authorities are the Pharisees and Sadducees (3:7–10). Seeing the latter coming to him for baptism, John, the forerunner of Jesus, greets them with a scathing epithet: "Brood of vipers!" he calls them (3:7). What "brood of vipers" means becomes clear at a later point in Matthew's story. At 12:34 Jesus, addressing the Pharisees, exclaims, "Brood of vipers! How can you speak good when you are evil?" As Jesus' words indicate, John, in calling the Pharisees and Sadducees a "brood of vipers," describes them — and indeed the religious authorities as a whole[3] — as "evil." In Matthew's purview, "evil" is the "root trait" that characterizes the religious authorities; it is the trait from which such other traits as being "hypocritical,"[4] "spiritually blind,"[5] and "conspiratorial"[6] spring.[7]

It is apparent that Matthew, in introducing Jesus and the religious authorities to the reader, characterizes them in starkly contrasting terms. On the one hand, we have Jesus. Jesus stands forth as the Messiah, the Son of God, the one who enjoys a unique filial relationship with God and serves God in perfect obedience. Jesus, therefore, is "righteous." On the other hand, we have the religious authorities, who are Jesus' antagonists. Through the words of John the Baptist and Jesus, Matthew characterizes them as "evil." As such, they are like Satan, whom Matthew describes as the "Evil One" (13:38). As is obvious, therefore, Matthew works in stereotypes. For him, there is no middle ground: Whereas Jesus is "righteous," the religious authorities are "evil."

Despite this tendency on Matthew's part to stereotype characters, it is a mistake for modern readers to accuse him of being anti-Semitic. Because Matthew fervently believes that Jesus is Israel's Messiah and God's

Son, he necessarily equates the repudiation of Jesus with the repudiation of God himself. To Matthew's way of thinking, humans who repudiate God are "like Satan," that is to say, they are evil. Since in Matthew's eyes the religious authorities are those responsible for the ultimate repudiation of Jesus, namely, his death on the cross, Matthew portrays them as evil. By the same token, it is important to note that Matthew does not portray the crowds per se (i.e., the Jewish people) as evil. During his public ministry, Jesus remains open to them. Also, after he has been raised by God from the dead, Matthew presents Jesus atop the mountain in Galilee as commissioning the disciples to make of all nations his disciples. The expression "all nations" includes not only gentiles but also the Jews, both people and leaders.[8] Be that as it may, the crucial matter to recognize at this juncture is that Matthew, through his very characterization of Jesus and the religious authorities, leads the reader to anticipate that, sooner or later, Jesus and the authorities will become entangled in bitter conflict.

II

Jesus first clashes with the religious authorities in the middle section of Matthew's story. Still, to understand how the ongoing conflict between Jesus and the authorities evolves, we need to keep ourselves apprised of the movement of the story. Matthew divides the middle section (4:17–16:20) into two parts. In the first part (4:17–11:1), he tells of Jesus' proffering salvation to Israel through a ministry of teaching, preaching, and healing (4:23; 9:35; 11:1). In the second part (11:2–16:20), he tells of Israel's response to Jesus' ministry, which is that of repudiation. Because in the first part the motif of Jesus' proffering salvation to Israel is the leitmotif that governs the story, so in this part Matthew subordinates the motif of conflict to the motif of Jesus' proffering salvation. The upshot is that as conflict erupts between Jesus and the authorities in this first part of the middle of Matthew's story (4:17–11:1), such conflict is "preliminary" in nature and foreshadows the more intense conflict that will soon follow.

Chapter 9 is the point at which Jesus and the religious authorities first stand opposite one another. Virtually at once, conflict breaks out and persists through a cycle of four controversies (9:1–8, 9–13, 14–17, 32–34). As was just noted, however, this conflict is "preliminary" in nature, and Matthew signals this, albeit in retrospect, by avoiding all reference in chapter 9 to three features that generally distinguish Jesus' later conflict with the authorities.

The first feature to which Matthew does not refer in chapter 9 is the main one and has to do with the tone on which this cycle of four controversies ends. At the close of the final controversy (9:34), it is striking that Matthew says nary a word to the effect that the religious authorities conspire to destroy Jesus.[9] The absence of such a narrative remark reveals that Matthew, in chapter 9, has not yet invited the reader to look upon Jesus' conflict with the authorities as "to the death."

The second feature one does not find in chapter 9 is that none of the controversies proves to be "acutely confrontational" in nature; that is to say, in none of them is Jesus himself challenged because of something that he himself says or does. To illustrate this, consider these controversies. In 9:1–8, some men bring to Jesus a paralytic. Perceiving their faith, Jesus forgives the paralytic his sins. Witnessing this, some scribes standing there take umbrage at Jesus' act and charge him with committing blasphemy against God for having arrogated to himself the divine authority to forgive sins. In raising their charge, however, the scribes do not approach Jesus himself. Instead, they utter their charge "in their hearts," so that Jesus must read their thoughts in order to refute their charge.

In 9:9–13 Jesus, together with his disciples, reclines at table with many toll collectors and sinners. Observing this, the Pharisees take offense, for in having table fellowship with outcasts such as these, Jesus, in their view, defiles himself. Despite their enormous displeasure, however, the Pharisees do not assail Jesus himself for his behavior. Instead, they go to the disciples and take them to task: "Why does your teacher," they demand to know, "eat with toll collectors and sinners?"

In 9:14–17, the disciples of John, who on this occasion side with the Pharisees, insist on knowing why the disciples of Jesus do not fast, as custom dictates. In this instance, the disciples of John do indeed approach Jesus, and it is to him that they put their question. Regardless, the question they ask pertains not to Jesus but exclusively to the disciples: "Why . . . do your disciples not fast?"

Last, in 9:32–34 the Pharisees, having looked on as Jesus exorcises a demon, charge, either to the crowds[10] or, more likely, merely to themselves[11] that "by the prince of demons he [Jesus] casts out demons." Once again, therefore, Matthew pictures Jesus' opponents as attacking him, but not to his face.

The third feature that is conspicuous by its absence from chapter 9 is that none of the issues that provoke the authorities (or, in one instance, the disciples of John) to take exception to acts of Jesus touches on the Mosaic law as such, to wit: forgiving sins and then demonstrating through the performance of a miracle that God has given him authority to forgive (9:1–8); having table fellowship with toll collectors and sinners (9:11); temporarily suspending as far as the disciples are concerned the obligation to fast as dictated by prevailing piety (9:14); and exorcising a demon (9:32–34). Now it is true, of course, that not every matter, to be "utterly serious" within the world of Matthew's story, must have to do with the Mosaic law. After all, for forgiving sins and affirming that he is the Son of God, Jesus incurs the potentially capital charge of blasphemy (9:3; 26:63–66). But this notwithstanding, it is a mark of the enormous importance that Matthew attaches to the Mosaic law that he does not declare that the religious authorities are bent on killing Jesus until the conflict between Jesus and them has shifted to focus on a precept of the Mosaic law, as we shall see in a moment.

Accordingly, if one reviews the four controversies that Jesus has with the religious authorities in chapter 9, one discovers that they are not yet "to the death," that not one of them is "acutely confrontational" in nature, and that their focus is not on Mosaic law. In broader perspective, these insights corroborate the point we made at the outset of this discussion: In chapter 9, the conflict between Jesus and the religious authorities is yet "preliminary" to the more intense conflict still to take place.

III

This more intense conflict is not long in coming. Specifically, it occurs in the second part of the middle of Matthew's story (11:2–16:20). We recall that in the first part of the middle (4:17–11:1) the leitmotif that controls the action is that of Jesus' proffering salvation to Israel. In line with this, Matthew subordinated the motif of conflict to the leitmotif of Jesus' proffering salvation by depicting the conflict between Jesus and the religious authorities as "preliminary" in nature. Here in the second part of the middle, the leitmotif controlling the story focuses on Israel's response to Jesus' ministry; Israel, in fact, repudiates Jesus.[12] Because in this part the motif of conflict has now become part and parcel of the leitmotif of Israel's repudiating Jesus, Matthew as a matter of course shapes Jesus' conflict with the authorities so that it becomes noticeably more intense.

In chapter 12, Jesus once again clashes with the religious authorities. Unlike earlier conflict, the immediate issue that sparks debate is the Mosaic law itself: breaking the divine command to rest on the Sabbath (12:1–8, 9–14).[13] In the two controversies at hand, one discovers that there is clear progression as one moves from the first to the second in terms of how acutely confrontational each is. In the first controversy (12:1–8), the Pharisees confront Jesus, but the charge they make has to do not with him but with the disciples: "Behold, your disciples are doing what is not lawful to do on the Sabbath!" In the second controversy (12:9–14), the Pharisees again confront Jesus. This time, however — and, in fact, for the first time in Matthew's story — the accusation they make in the question they raise concerns an act that they anticipate Jesus himself is about to perform: If Jesus heals a man with a withered hand on the Sabbath who is not in danger of dying, he will have violated Moses' command that enjoins rest (12:10). In the case of both these controversies, Jesus rebuts the Pharisees by asserting that attending to human need in these instances is not only not unlawful but is necessitated by God's will that mercy be shown or that good be done (12:3–8, 11–12). In direct response to Jesus' setting himself against the law of Moses as they interpret it, the Pharisees now do what they hitherto have not done: They go out and take counsel against Jesus, how to destroy him (12:14). With this sharp turn of events, Matthew's story has arrived at that juncture where the conflict between Jesus and the religious authorities has intensified to the point where it has become "mortal." Indeed, it is a mark of Jesus' conflict with the authorities throughout the rest of Matthew's story that this conflict does remain mortal, and the observation that Jesus "withdraws" in the face of the conspiracy to destroy him (12:15) corroborates this.

Later in chapter 12, Jesus again confronts the religious authorities and again the note that his controversies with them sounds is shrill. In 12:22–37, Jesus exorcises a demon from a man who is blind and dumb so that the man sees and speaks. Whereas Jesus' miracle amazes the crowds and prompts them to wonder whether Jesus could perhaps be the Son of David, the Pharisees, on overhearing the crowds, reiterate their charge of 9:34: Muttering to themselves, they insist that Jesus casts out demons not on the authority of God but on the authority of Satan (12:24). Discerning their thoughts, Jesus minces no words in responding to them: He accuses the Pharisees of being agents of Satan (12:27); he contends that their vilification of him is tantamount to committing blasphemy against God (12:30–32); and he asserts that their charge springs from hearts that are evil (12:33–37).

In 12:38–45, the conflict is no less intense. In this controversy, some scribes and Pharisees accost Jesus and demand that he show them a sign. In demanding a sign, the scribes and Pharisees have in mind that Jesus should predict a miracle that God will subsequently perform and thus prove that he acts not on the authority of Satan but on the authority of God. Attacking the scribes and Pharisees, Jesus castigates them as an "evil and adulterous generation" (12:39), that is to say, as persons who are "like Satan" and "faithless to God."

Accordingly, as the second part of the middle of Matthew's story draws to a close (11:2–16:20), the reader is keenly aware that the conflict between Jesus and the religious authorities is beyond reconciliation. Each time Jesus and the authorities meet in controversy, the impression reinforces itself in the mind of the reader that their struggle is henceforth a struggle "to the death."

IV

From the middle of Matthew's story we turn to the end (16:21–28:20). Here Matthew tells of Jesus' journey to Jerusalem and of his suffering, death, and resurrection (16:21). So that the reader knows that the leitmotif guiding the narrative is indeed that of Jesus' journeying to Jerusalem and suffering, dying, and being raised, Matthew punctuates his story with three passion predictions (16:21; 17:22–23; 20:17–19); moreover, at the outset of the passion narrative Jesus reminds the disciples of these predictions (26:2). Because the motif of conflict is integral to the motif of going up to Jerusalem to suffer and die, the reader can be certain that Jesus' conflict with the authorities in Jerusalem will in no wise diminish in its ferocity.

On his way to Jerusalem, Jesus teaches the disciples. In fact, only once does he clash with religious authorities. In 19:3–12, Pharisees confront Jesus to put him to the test on the matter of divorce. In return, Jesus puts the Pharisees to shame, lecturing them on the attitude toward divorce taught by scripture. Yet, as Matthew reveals in the final verses of this controversy (19:10–12), the purpose the latter serves has relatively little to do with Jesus' larger conflict with the authorities. Instead, Jesus uses this controversy to instruct the disciples on divorce. The upshot is that it is not until after Jesus has arrived in Jerusalem that he has his last great confrontation with the authorities prior to his passion (21:12–22:46).

We recall that Matthew, in the middle of his story, depicted the conflict between Jesus and the religious authorities as gradually intensifying: In the first part of the middle (4:17–11:1), this conflict had a "preliminary" quality about it (chap. 9); in the second part of the middle (11:2–16:20), it intensified to the point where it became a struggle "to the death" (chap. 12). Here in the end of the story, Jesus has now entered Jerusalem (21:1–11). Although the conflict he has had with the authorities has already been "to the death," Matthew nonetheless makes use of some five literary devices to indicate that the conflict Jesus has in Jerusalem (21:12–22:46) is of still greater intensity.

The first such device Matthew uses is the setting in which he places all of Jesus' controversies in Jerusalem. This setting is the temple (21:12, 23), and the reason it heightens still more the intensity of Jesus' conflict with the authorities is that the temple is both the place of God's presence — God whom Jesus calls Father — and the seat of the authorities' power. It is from the temple that the authorities rule the land of the Jews. For Jesus to defeat the authorities in debate in the temple is for him to defeat them at the very center of their power and privilege.

The second device Matthew employs to show that Jesus' conflict in Jerusalem is of still greater intensity is the "acutely confrontational" tone with which he imbues each controversy. In each case, it is none but Jesus whom the authorities attack, and their constant aim is either to call him to account for something that he himself has said or done or simply to get the best of him in debate (21:15, 23; 22:16–17, 23–28, 35–36). In the final controversy, however, Matthew reverses the roles so that Jesus seizes the initiative and puts the Pharisees on the spot (22:41–46).

The third device Matthew uses to heighten still further the intensity of Jesus' conflict in Jerusalem is to arrange for all the controversies between him and the religious authorities to revolve around the critical question of "authority": the authority by which Jesus cleanses the temple (21:23), discharges his ministry (21:23), and interprets scripture and the law (22:17, 24, 36, 43–45). The importance of this issue of authority, of course, is that it underlies the whole of Jesus' conflict with the authorities and goes to the heart of whether Jesus is to be received as the supreme agent of God or repudiated as a fraud and agent of Satan (27:63).

The fourth device by which Matthew intensifies still further the conflict between Jesus and the religious authorities in Jerusalem is his depiction of all the groups that together make up the united front of the authorities as clashing with Jesus over a span of less than two days (21:12–17; 21:23–22:46): the chief priests, the scribes, the elders of the people, the disciples of the Pharisees, the Herodians, the Sadducees, a Pharisaic lawyer, and the Pharisees (21:15, 23; 22:16, 23, 34–35, 41). The effect that this parade of opponents over a short span of time has is that it not only enables the reader to look on as the respective groups or combinations of groups take their turn at trying to defeat Jesus in debate, but it also conveys the impression of "unceasing," and therefore highly intense, conflict.

Finally, the fifth device by which Matthew heightens still further the intensity of Jesus' conflict in Jerusalem is his characterization of the atmosphere in which this conflict takes place as being extremely hostile. To illustrate, Matthew reports, following Jesus' narration of the parable of the Vineyard (21:33–46), that the chief priests and the Pharisees become so incensed at hearing Jesus' parable that they want to arrest him immediately and hold back only for fear of the crowds (21:45–46). Short of the passion narrative, this is the one place in Matthew's story where the authorities are actually said to want to seize Jesus.

On what note does Matthew bring this last great confrontation between Jesus and the religious authorities in Jerusalem and prior to the passion to a close? Matthew states this pointedly at 22:46, where he declares: "And no one was able to answer him [Jesus] a word nor from that day did any one dare to ask him any more questions." Jesus reduces all of the authorities to silence. Reduced to silence, the authorities fade from the scene until Matthew has begun the passion narrative.

V

In the opening verses of the passion narrative, Matthew takes pains to inform the reader that, on the human level, it is the religious authorities who are squarely responsible for Jesus' death (26:3–4). At the palace of the high priest Caiaphas, the chief priests and the elders make their plans to have Jesus arrested and killed by deceit. This strategy on the part of the authorities to act with deceit shows that, during the passion, "being deceptive" is the character trait that they exhibit most.

For our purposes, the scene that is of greatest importance in Matthew's passion narrative is the last scene in which the religious authorities confront the earthly Jesus (27:41–43). In this scene, the members of the Sanhedrin look up at Jesus on the cross and mock him. They mock him because, in their eyes, he hangs helplessly and does not even possess the power to rescue himself from death. In other words, as the authorities look up at Jesus on the cross, they see him as a fraud[14] who is stripped of all authority, they see the cross as the sign of his destruction, and they see themselves as having won the victory in their conflict with him.

Ironically, however, what the religious authorities do not perceive is that God and Jesus, too, will the death of Jesus. Jesus wills his own death because he is the perfectly obedient Son of God. God wills Jesus' death because, through it, he will renew his covenant and proffer all humans everywhere the forgiveness of sins and salvation (1:23; 20:28; 26:28). To demonstrate that Jesus' death is in line with his saving purposes, God raises Jesus from the dead on the third day (28:5–6).[15] In raising Jesus, God both vindicates him and exalts him. The upshot is that this same Jesus whom the religious authorities see as stripped of all authority is, in fact, entrusted by God with all authority in heaven and on earth (28:18). In combination, therefore, the events of the cross and resurrection mark the places in Matthew's story where the principal conflict among humans in this story, that between Jesus and the religious authorities, comes to fundamental "resolution."

True as this is, the cross itself is nevertheless the place where Matthew's story reaches its "culmination." From the standpoint of the religious authorities, the cross attests to Jesus' destruction and their victory. From the standpoint of Matthew and of the reader, however, the cross stands as a sign of the victory Jesus has won. By the twist of irony, the cross attests, not to the destruction of Jesus, but to the salvation that God henceforth proffers through Jesus to all humankind.

VI

In retrospect, we have now seen how the plot of Matthew's story of Jesus unfolds. This plot is one of conflict, and this conflict, at the human level, is above all between Jesus and the religious authorities. As Matthew's story progresses, Jesus' conflict with the authorities becomes ever more intense until, at the last, it finds its fundamental "resolution" — in favor of Jesus — in his cross and resurrection. By the same token, it is in Jesus' cross that Matthew's story reaches its "culmination," for the cross becomes the place where God in Jesus accomplishes universal salvation. It is to announce this salvation that Matthew tells his story. In addition, Matthew is concerned to show that despite his conflict with Israel and especially the authorities, Jesus does not turn his back on them. At the close of the story, the risen Jesus commissions the disciples to go and make of all nations his disciples. To be sure, the expression "all nations" includes the gentiles; besides them, however, it also includes the people and the leaders of Israel.

Although during his earthly ministry the leaders were Jesus' inveterate enemies and Matthew himself seems doubtful that they will ever turn to Jesus, the risen Jesus would nonetheless also have them become his disciples. It is on this saving note that the reader exits from Matthew's story.

NOTES

1. For a discussion of the structure of Matthew's Gospel, see Jack Dean Kingsbury, *Matthew: Structure, Christology, Kingdom,* reprint (Minneapolis: Fortress Press, 1989), 1–39. For the most thorough exploration of this topic to date, see David R. Bauer, *The Structure of Matthew's Gospel: A Study in Literary Design,* Bible and Literature Series 15 (Sheffield: Almond Press, 1988).

2. For an approach to the overall plot of Matthew's gospel story that views the conflict between God and Satan as constituting the main plot and the conflict between Jesus and the religious authorities as a subplot, see Mark Allan Powell, "The Plot and Subplots of Matthew's Gospel," *NTS* 38 (1992): 198–202. For yet another approach to the plot of Matthew, see Frank J. Matera, "The Plot of Matthew's Gospel," *CBQ* 49 (1987): 233–53.

3. On treating the religious authorities as a single character, see Jack Dean Kingsbury, *Matthew as Story,* rev. and enl. ed. (Philadelphia: Fortress Press, 1988), 17–18.

4. See, e.g., Matt. 23:13, 15, 23, 25, 27, 29.

5. See, e.g., Matt. 15:14; 23:16–22, 24, 26.

6. See, e.g., Matt. 12:14; 26:3–4; 27:1.

7. Concerning the way in which Matthew characterizes such persons or groups of persons as Jesus, the disciples, the religious leaders, the crowds, and

minor characters, see Kingsbury, *Matthew as Story,* 9–28. For an insightful discussion of the religious leaders in all three synoptic Gospels, see Mark Allan Powell, *What Is Narrative Criticism?* GBS (Minneapolis: Fortress Press, 1990), 51–67.

8. For a careful study of the expression "all nations," see John P. Meier, "Nations or Gentiles in Matthew 28:19?" *CBQ* 39 (1977): 94–102.

9. How different this is in Mark's gospel story! At the end of Jesus' first cycle of controversies, Mark reports, "The Pharisees went out, and immediately held counsel with the Herodians against him, how to destroy him" (Mark 3:6).

10. See Matt. 9:33.

11. See Matt. 12:24–25a.

12. On this point, see Kingsbury, *Matthew as Story,* 72–74.

13. See Exod. 20:8–11; Deut. 5:12–15.

14. See Matt. 27:63.

15. See also Matt. 16:21; 17:23; 20:19.

– 3 –

The Major Characters of Matthew's Story

THEIR FUNCTION AND SIGNIFICANCE

David R. Bauer

Far from being insignificant, an analysis of the characters within Matthew's gospel story provides insight into Matthew's message, especially as it pertains to God, Jesus, and discipleship.

THE GOSPEL OF MATTHEW is a story about Jesus. This simple observation implies two highly significant things about Matthew's Gospel. First, the recognition that Matthew is a *story* suggests the importance of the persons, or characters, within it, for every story contains characters and every storyteller uses characters to communicate to the reader.[1] Second, the recognition that Matthew is a story *about Jesus* suggests both that Jesus is the central character in the Gospel and that the reader must understand all other characters in terms of their relationship to him. Thus, an analysis of the person of Jesus, and of other persons and groups of persons in their interaction with Jesus, will provide insights into the message of Matthew's Gospel, especially as this message pertains to God, Christ, and discipleship.

Jesus

The Gospel of Matthew falls into three main units, each one focusing upon a dimension of Matthew's presentation of Jesus.[2] The first main division, 1:1–4:16, involves the preparation of Jesus Messiah, Son of God, for the ministry he will undertake and the passion he will endure in 4:17–28:20. Here in 1:1–4:16, Matthew introduces Jesus to the reader through a string of reliable witnesses who give testimony about him.

Matthew begins with his own testimony: In 1:1 he declares that Jesus is the Christ, Son of David, and Son of Abraham, a threefold claim that Matthew supports and develops in the genealogy that follows (1:2–17). The structure of the genealogy indicates that Jesus is the Christ in the sense that he has been anointed by God to bring salvation history, which began with Abraham, to its climax (1:16). As such, persons can understand God's previous revelation in salvation history only in light of its *telos,* Jesus as the Christ, and conversely persons must understand Jesus in light of Old Testament revelation. As Son of David, Jesus is the Messiah-King in the line of David whom God has sent specifically to Israel in order to bring to Israel salvation and healing. Three times in the Gospel persons in need of healing cry out, "Have mercy upon me [us], Son of David" (9:27; 15:22; 20:31), and Jesus Son of David heals them. On two other occasions Jesus' healings induce persons to speak of him in terms of "Son of David" (12:23; 21:15). Jesus thus fulfills the messianic expectation that the Son of David would bring wholeness to the oppressed.[3] As Son of Abraham, Jesus fulfills the promise God made to Abraham regarding his descendants, that in his seed all the nations (*ethnoi*) of the earth would be blessed.[4] Jesus Son of Abraham is therefore God's agent for bringing gentiles to the worship of God and into the end-time community of God.

The witness of Matthew is followed by the infancy narrative, which contains the witness of the angel and of the wise men (1:18–2:23). The witness of the angel points especially to the mission of Jesus Son of David: to save his people from their sins (1:21). The primary work of Jesus is salvation, and everything he does in this Gospel must be understood in light of this. Jesus can function as savior because he has been conceived by the Holy Spirit (1:18, 20) and therefore has an absolutely unique, filial relationship with God (see 11:25–27) — and because God dwells with God's people in the person of Jesus, thereby giving them victory over sin (1:22–23).

The wise men bear witness that Jesus is "the king of the Jews" (2:2); Matthew takes advantage of this reference to Jesus to develop the meaning of the kingship of Jesus by contrasting it with the kingship of Herod. The kingship of Herod is characterized by self-serving attempts by Herod to maintain his own power, even to the point of taking the lives of his subjects for his own sake (2:1–18). By way of contrast, Matthew sets forth the essential character of Jesus' kingship in the scriptural quotation at 2:5–6: Jesus is the Davidic ruler who governs by "shepherding" the people of God. The broader context of the Gospel indicates just what this shepherding involves: Jesus rules as one who dies on behalf of his people in order to bring salvation to them (1:21; 20:28; 26:27–28).

The next witness to appear on the scene is John the Baptist (3:1–12), who declares that Jesus is "the coming one," that is, the Christ (see 11:2–3), who is mightier and more majestic than John (3:7–12). By emphasizing that Jesus is consummately superior to John, the last and greatest of the prophets (3:3; 11:7–15; 17:9–13), Matthew points to the transcendent significance of Jesus over against the prophetic agents of God in the preceding stages of salvation history.

One must not construe the person and ministry of Jesus as simply a continuation of the work of the prophets. God is doing something utterly new in Jesus. Jesus is more than a prophet, and to understand him primarily as a prophet is entirely inadequate (see 16:13–17).

Moreover, John asserts that Jesus is inescapable. John announces that Jesus, as the Christ, is about to bring eschatological salvation and judgment. As such, Jesus the Christ functions not only as the climax to salvation history, thereby giving meaning to the history of Israel (1:1–17), but also as the climax to world history and the history of every individual within the world. All history is moving inexorably toward its grand culmination in the judgment of Christ, and therefore history gains any meaning or significance it has only in relation to Jesus the Christ, its end or *telos*.

The final witness to Jesus in 1:1–4:16 comes from God. As Jesus emerges from the baptismal water, the heavenly voice declares, "This is my beloved Son, in whom I am well pleased" (3:17). This direct witness from God that Jesus is God's own Son brings to a climax all the previous testimony about Jesus; this climax indicates that Jesus is to be understood primarily as Son of God, and that this truth about Jesus' divine Sonship is known only to God and those to whom God reveals it (see 11:25–27; 16:13–17; 27:51–54). As Son of God, Jesus has been conceived by God and therefore experiences a relationship with God that is unique, intimate, and ultimately mysterious (1:18–25). Matthew presents this filial relationship primarily in terms of knowledge of and obedience to the will of God. As Son of God, Jesus knows and teaches the will of the Father (5:17–48; 7:28–29; 11:25–27) and perfectly obeys his Father (3:12; 4:1–11).[5]

At 4:17 the time of preparation is complete, and Jesus is ready to embark upon his public ministry. The second major division in the Gospel, 4:17–16:21, centers upon Jesus' proclamation of the kingdom to Israel (4:17). Here Jesus announces to Israel that the long-awaited rule of God has come in the ministry of Jesus (e.g., 12:28) and will eventually be manifested upon the earth in its full, consummated form (e.g., 5:20; cf. 25:34, 46).

Jesus announces the kingdom to Israel by means of three activities: teaching, preaching, and healing (4:23; 9:35; 11:1). "Preaching" involves the proclamation of the kingdom itself (4:17). "Teaching" entails primarily instruction to disciples regarding life within the kingdom and therefore has chief relevance for the disciples (e.g., 5:1–2);[6] but Matthew emphasizes that the people in general hear the teaching of Jesus and recognize its transcendent authority.[7] The teaching of Jesus, then, marked as it is by preeminent authority, itself proclaims to the people the presence of the kingdom. The healings of Jesus (and his other "mighty acts") also bear witness to the presence of the kingdom and thereby constitute a form of proclamation (11:2–6, 20–24).

In addition to describing the activities of Jesus' ministry, Matthew also sets forth the general characteristics of this ministry. For one thing, the ministry of Jesus is *authoritative*. Jesus teaches with an authority that surpasses both the scribes (7:29; cf. 5:20) and Moses (5:21–48; 19:3–9), because he possesses unique knowledge of the mind and will of God. Jesus also performs mighty works with authority (9:8; cf. 9:33); with just a word or a touch he calms the sea, casts out demons, heals the sick, and raises the dead (esp. chaps. 8–9). The story of the healing of the paralytic indicates that the authority to perform these mighty acts points to the authority of Jesus to forgive sins (9:1–8). The authority of Jesus is eschatological, for through the ministry of Jesus God is manifesting end-time rule; in his teaching Jesus reveals ("fulfills") the divine will that stands behind the letter of the law (5:17–48; 7:12; 22:34–40), and in his mighty acts he breaks the power of Satan (12:24–29).

This concern for authority leads to a second characteristic of the ministry of Jesus: It is *evocative*. Both the teaching and the mighty acts of Jesus evoke response: The crowds are astonished (e.g., 7:28; 9:8, 33); the Pharisees conclude that he is in league with the devil and deserves death (9:34; 12:14, 24); and the disciples confess that he is the Son of God (14:33; 16:16). Persons cannot remain neutral or unaffected in the presence of the authority of Jesus.

There are, finally, two ways in which the ministry of Jesus points to the essence of his character. Jesus is *self-sacrificial* in that he ministers as one who "has nowhere to lay his head" (8:20) and is bereft of even privacy and rest (8:14–17; 14:13–14, 34–36). Jesus is a *person of integrity* in that there is complete congruence between the behavior of Jesus as narrated in the Gospel and the kind of behavior Jesus commends in his teaching; what he commands he also does (e.g., 16:24; 20:28).

The ministry of Jesus in 4:17–16:20 prompts opposition and thus leads to the third major division of Matthew's Gospel, 16:21–28:20, which centers upon the passion and resurrection of Jesus. Prior to this point in the Gospel, Matthew has subtly alluded to Jesus' death (e.g., 10:4, 38; 12:39–40), but only at 16:21 does Jesus begin to speak explicitly about death in Jerusalem and subsequent resurrection. There are three main elements in this description of Jesus' passion and resurrection: condemnation, crucifixion, and resurrection. We shall examine each in turn.

Matthew describes the condemnation of Jesus in two court scenes that are generally parallel in structure. Here Jesus stands condemned before the two major power structures in the world of the Gospel: religious authority (26:57–75) and political authority (27:1–31). At the trial before the Sanhedrin, Jesus is convicted on the charge of blasphemy for claiming to be the Son of God (26:63–65). During this trial Jesus remains silent; he neither says nor does anything to defend himself (26:62; cf. 27:12). There are two reasons for Jesus' silence. For one thing, he shows utter disdain for the false charges leveled against him. Furthermore, Jesus here assumes the role of the poor, powerless one. Like the Suffering Servant of Isaiah, Jesus has cast aside all forms of power and violence (see 26:47–56) and every attempt to vindicate himself (see Isa. 53:7). He will not so much as speak in his own defense. The focus of the trial before Pilate is whether Jesus is the "king of the Jews." Jesus affirms that he is (27:11) and is consequently condemned to death (27:15–26).

In the crucifixion scene itself Matthew picks up the two charges that have been leveled against Jesus and interweaves them: Jesus is crucified both as king of the Jews [Israel] (27:29, 37, 42) and as Son of God (27:40, 43, 54).[8] The consideration that Jesus dies as king of the Jews indicates that he is not the kind of king who usurps thrones and grabs power for himself. As king, Jesus submits to suffering and death in order to give his life for his people (20:28), thereby saving them from their sins (1:21). The crown of Jesus is the wreath of thorns (27:28) and his throne is the cross (27:37).

The consideration that Jesus dies as Son of God indicates that Jesus remains perfectly obedient to the will of the Father. In 4:1–11 Jesus was tempted to manifest his divine Sonship through display of worldly power, and in 16:22 he was tempted to construe his divine Sonship in ways that did not involve suffering and death. These two temptations come together at the cross: Three times Jesus is tempted to manifest his divine Sonship by the spectacular sign of escaping from the cross, thereby saving himself (27:40, 42, 44). But Jesus refuses to yield to these temptations, and he dies as one who is obedient and righteous in the sense that he trusts in God alone for salvation (27:43).

The resurrection narrative demonstrates that such trust in God is well placed. God does save Jesus, not by delivering him from the cross, but by raising him from the dead (28:1–10). Indeed, in consequence of Jesus' faithful obedience God has given to him "all authority in heaven and on earth" (28:18): Because Jesus rejected all power and prerogative and depended entirely upon God for his vindication, God has now given to him all power and prerogative everywhere. And in this all-inclusive authority Jesus continues to be with his disciples, speaking to them, until the end of the age (28:20); in this way Matthew indicates that Jesus cannot ultimately be understood as a character but must be seen as a living presence in the midst of his church.

Disciples

One of the chief dimensions of the ministry of the Matthean Jesus is the calling and nurturing of the twelve disciples. There are a number of components in Matthew's presentation of the disciples and their relationship to Jesus. We shall explore just three of these components.

Matthew discusses, first of all, the nature and expectations of discipleship. The essential characteristics of discipleship appear already in the calling of the first disciples at 4:18–22: (1) Discipleship requires that it be initiated by Jesus, for persons cannot take it upon themselves to become disciples but must be called by Christ (see 9:9); (2) discipleship involves submission to the *authority of Jesus,* for Jesus appears unexpectedly on the scene, utters the radical demand, and the brothers respond "immediately" (4:20, 22); (3) discipleship entails *genuine cost,* in that Simon and Andrew were forced to abandon the security of vocation, and James and John left both property and family (see 8:18–22; 13:44–46; 19:16–29); (4) discipleship means embarking upon *mission,* in that Jesus links the call to discipleship with the promise to make them fishers of people (4:19; cf. 9:35–11:1; 28:16–20); (5) discipleship involves the creation of a *community* around the person of Jesus, in that Jesus calls two sets of brothers and throughout the Gospel there is constant attention to the demands of the Christian community (e.g., 5:17–26; 18:1–35; 23:1–11). Yet, above all else, 4:18–22 emphasizes that discipleship involves *following Jesus.* This notion of following Jesus suggests that the disciples are to be "with" Jesus (e.g., 9:15; 12:30; 26:38–40) as those who accompany him (e.g., 9:19), align themselves with him over against his opponents (e.g., 9:10–17; 12:1–8) and therefore experience persecution (e.g., 5:10–12; 10:24–25), learn from him (e.g., 5:1; 10:24; 13:36), model their lives after his example (e.g., 20:25–28), and come after him by assuming for themselves the journey of self-denial and cross-bearing (10:38–39; 16:24–28; cf. 16:21).

This portrait of discipleship serves as a backdrop for the second component of Matthew's presentation of the disciples: the actual performance of the twelve. Positively, the disciples forsake everything to follow Jesus (4:18–22; 19:27); do the will of the Father and are therefore "sons" of the Father (17:25–26; 23:9) and "brothers and sisters" of Jesus (12:49–50); humbly accept Jesus' announcement of the kingdom (11:25–27) and, as a reward, receive the ability to understand the mysteries of the kingdom (13:10–17, 51–52); rightly confess Jesus to be the Son of God (14:33; 16:13–20); worship Jesus (14:33; 28:17); and obey him (4:18–22; 9:9; 21:1–7; 26:17–19).

But the portrait of the disciples is quite mixed, for alongside these positive elements are negative characteristics. The two main difficulties in 4:17–16:20 are lack of understanding and weakness of faith. The disciples have basic understanding, and God has given to them the potential for full understanding, represented by the ability to discern the mysteries of the kingdom that comes through the parabolic speech of Jesus (13:10–17); but the disciples repeatedly fail to appropriate this potential and consequently misconstrue the meaning of Jesus' parables (15:15–16; 16:5–12). Likewise, the disciples have faith, but their faith is little or weak; they cower in the presence of obstacles or threats and thereby fail to appropriate the divine resources for strength and endurance that properly belong to them (8:26; 14:31). In both cases Jesus addresses their failure: By being with the disciples and speaking to them Jesus brings understanding to them (15:17–20; 16:11–12) and gives to them strength and courage to fulfill their mission in the face of grave opposition (28:16–20; cf. 28:11–15).

The problems intensify in 16:21–28:20, where the twelve fail to accept fully Jesus' teaching that both messiahship and discipleship involve self-sacrificial suffering and death. Peter censures Jesus for such an understanding of messiahship (16:22–23), the disciples reject the notion that greatness in the kingdom means servanthood and childlike submission rather than power and prestige (17:24; 18:35; 19:13–15; 20:20–28), and in the face of the cross the disciples, depending upon their own strength, forsake and deny Jesus (26:30–46, 56, 69–75). Yet Jesus again fills up that which is lacking in the disciples, for the crucified Jesus reconciles the disciples to himself and sends them out on their worldwide mission by appearing to them in his exalted state, promising to be with them (28:16–20; cf. 26:32).

This reference to 28:16–20 leads to the third component in Matthew's portrayal of the disciples: the future of the disciples in the period between the resurrection and the Parousia. This is a period of worldwide mission conducted in the face of continuing opposition (28:10–20; chaps. 24–25), carrying with it the constant threat of apostasy because of persecutions and concern for material well-being (10:16–39; 13:20–22). In this situation the disciple must remain faithful (24:45; 25:21–23) by watching (24:42; 25:13), remembering that only those who endure to the end will be saved (10:22; 24:13). Both endurance and aggressive mission are possible because God dwells with the church in the person of God's Son, Jesus (28:20; cf. 1:23).

The disciples, then, possess conflicting traits. The positive traits prompt the reader to identify with the disciples, while the negative features point to the struggle and challenges of discipleship. The consideration that Jesus refuses to abandon the disciples to their failure, but rather addresses their shortcomings, gives hope to readers that the exalted Christ will likewise assist them in their own struggles.

Israel

In Matthew's Gospel, Israel consists of two groups: the people as a whole ("the crowds") and the religious leaders. While these two groups play distinctive roles throughout the Gospel, both of them serve as foils for proper response to Jesus and for true discipleship.

Matthew portrays the crowds as recipients of the eschatological ministry of Jesus. Jesus has compassion upon the helpless and harassed crowds (9:35–38) and attends to their need to be delivered from the evil power that afflicts them (see 12:25–29): Jesus heals their diseases (e.g., 4:23–25; 9:35; 8:16–17), raises their dead (9:23–26; cf. 10:8), casts out their demons (8:16), proclaims to them the kingdom of God (4:17, 23; 9:35), and teaches them (4:23; 9:35; 11:1). Out of his compassion Jesus feeds the crowds, thereby indicating both his willingness and ability to meet their most profound needs (14:14–21; 15:32–39).

The crowds respond (1) by expressing amazement (7:28–29; 9:33; 12:23) or fear (9:8) at the authority of Jesus; (2) by glorifying God because of Jesus' mighty acts of deliverance (9:8; 15:31); and (3) by "following Jesus," not in the sense of becoming disciples but in the sense of accompanying him and thereby experiencing the benefits of his ministry.[9] Throughout most of Matthew's Gospel the crowds are positively inclined toward Jesus. In contrast to the violent opposition of the religious authorities, the crowds consider Jesus to be a prophet (16:14; 21:11, 46); and therefore they serve as a "buffer" between the religious authorities and Jesus, preventing the authorities from arresting and destroying Jesus (26:5).

Yet this response of the crowds is inadequate. It is inadequate, in the first place, because it falls short of accepting Jesus' announcement of the kingdom; the crowds do not embrace the proclamation that the kingdom has come in the ministry of Jesus, nor do they respond to this proclamation with repentance (4:17; 11:20–24). Indeed, Jesus brings judgment upon the crowds for this failure: He withdraws revelation from them (by speaking to them in parables that they cannot understand [13:10–17]), and he repeatedly withdraws himself from them (13:36; 14:13; 15:21; 16:4). This initial judgment points ahead to the final judgment that awaits the unbelieving crowds (11:20–24; 22:1–10). The response of the crowds is inadequate, secondly, because it falls short of recognizing and affirming the operative truth about Jesus: that he is Son of God (3:17; 27:54). It is insufficient to view Jesus as (merely) a prophet, for that understanding repudiates the true eschatological significance of Jesus and reflects the opinion of humans unaided by divine revelation (11:25–27; 16:13–17). Thirdly, the failure of the crowds to respond by accepting the message and confessing Jesus as Son of God leads them ultimately to side with the religious leaders in crucifying Jesus

(26:47, 56; 27:15–26). Those who are not "with" Jesus are against him (12:30). The point is clear: Those who fall short of affirming the eschatological significance and the divine Sonship of Jesus (no matter how positive their response otherwise seems to be) ultimately participate in his death.

If the crowds draw back from full acceptance of Jesus and finally cast their lot with the religious authorities, the religious authorities themselves stand solidly opposed to Jesus throughout the Gospel.[10] Matthew identifies two major factors that lie behind this opposition. First, the religious leaders are in collusion with Satan. Indeed, the leaders share the root characteristic of Satan: They are evil.[11] In his first direct encounter with the leaders, Jesus accuses them of thinking evil in their hearts (9:4), and Jesus later declares that the evil of their hearts necessarily comes to expression in their speech and actions. Because they are evil, they cannot speak good (12:34–35; 15:4; 22:18); and because their hearts are evil, all kinds of defiling practices necessarily spring forth (15:19): evil thoughts (see 9:4), murder (e.g., 21:35–39; 23:29–36; chaps. 26–27), adultery (see the metaphorical use in 12:39; 16:4), theft (see 21:13; 23:25), false witness (see 26:60–61), and slander (e.g., 11:18–19; 12:24; 28:13). But the most profound expression of evil on the part of the religious leaders is their demand for a sign (12:38–40; 16:1–4; cf. 27:42); this demand reflects an insistence to have the kingdom on their own terms, thus bringing the kingdom of God itself under their own power and control.

In the parable of the Weeds Jesus makes an explicit connection between the evil of the religious leaders and that of Satan. They are "sons of the evil one," who have their origin in Satan and fulfill the purpose for which Satan has sown them in the world (13:38–39). Like darnel, they not only fail to produce good fruit (13:8, 23; cf. 3:8–10; 12:33), but they also exercise a corrupting influence upon the rest of the world, and especially upon disciples (in the imagery of the parable, the wheat); they are "causes of sin," persons whom Jesus elsewhere describes as "blind guides" who lead others into the pit with them (15:14; 23:16, 24) and whose teaching must be avoided because of its leaven-like corruption (16:5–12; cf. 15:14).[12]

Second, Matthew describes these leaders as anthropocentric, or human-centered. In the final analysis, they have no real interest in the divine; they are concerned only with approval from humans and power or control over humans. This anthropocentricism takes several forms. It manifests itself, for example, in their hypocrisy. Matthew understands hypocrisy as a dichotomy between act and motive: The act suggests one motive, but the actual motivation is quite different. The religious leaders are hypocrites in that their actions and speech express devotion to God, while their real concern is to receive praise from humans (e.g.,

6:1–18; 23:1–36). This anthropocentricism comes to expression also in their constant grasping for power. Like Herod, they will stop at nothing, including murder, to maintain their own power and control (2:1–18). In fact, this issue of power lies at the heart of the conflict between these religious leaders and Jesus. The leaders are jealous of Jesus' popularity with the crowds, and they finally deliver him up to death, as Pilate rightly perceives, out of envy (27:18). Moreover, because these leaders are controlled by desire for human approval and power they have no real authority to serve as spiritual leaders of the people. As interpreters of the law they are ignorant (e.g., 9:13; 12:7; 22:29), as facilitators of righteousness they are themselves unclean (e.g., 15:17–20; 23:25–28), as teachers they are reduced to silence before the arguments of Jesus (22:15–46). They are so completely devoid of divine authority that they are unable to recognize true authority when it confronts them in the person of Jesus (e.g., 12:1–14; 21:23–27).

Matthew describes these leaders, finally, as condemned persons. Their failure to produce "good fruit" and especially their rejection of Jesus Son of God leads God to take the kingdom away from them and give it to more worthy stewards (21:43), to destroy their city (22:7), and finally to commit them to the fires of hell, which have been prepared for the devil and his angels (3:10; 13:41–42; 23:33).

This portrait of the religious leaders plays two roles in Matthew's Gospel. First, by presenting Jesus over against the religious authorities, Matthew is able to show with clarity and forcefulness the majesty, righteousness, and authority of Jesus. Furthermore, the religious leaders serve as a negative model for discipleship: The disciples are to be like Jesus by being *unlike* the religious authorities (e.g., 23:1–12; 16:5–12). Thus, the religious authorities, and indeed Israel as a whole, become representatives of disobedience and judgment. Believers must do everything they can to avoid the behavior and consequent tragic end of unrepentant Israel. For readers who see this spirit of Israel in themselves, the Matthean Jesus has a word: "Repent, for the kingdom of heaven is at hand" (4:17).

NOTES

1. Seymour Chatman, *Story and Discourse: Narrative Structure in Fiction and Film* (Ithaca, N.Y.: Cornell University Press, 1978), 107–38; E. M. Forster, *Aspects of the Novel* (New York: Harcourt, Brace, 1927), 69–125. For characterization in New Testament narrative criticism, see Mark Allan Powell, *What Is Narrative Criticism?* GBS (Minneapolis: Fortress Press, 1990), 51–67.

2. On the structure of the Gospel, see David R. Bauer, *The Structure of Matthew's Gospel: A Study in Literary Design,* JSNTSup 31, BLS 15 (Sheffield:

Almond Press, 1988); and Jack Dean Kingsbury, *Matthew: Structure, Christology, Kingdom* (Philadelphia: Fortress Press, and London: SPCK, 1975), 1–39.

3. For discussions of the Davidic Sonship of Jesus in Matthew, see J. M. Gibbs, "Purpose and Pattern in Matthew's Use of the Title 'Son of David,' " *NTS* 10 (1963–1964): 446–62; Jack Dean Kingsbury, "The Title 'Son of David' in Matthew's Gospel," *JBL* 95 (1976): 591–602; C. Burger, *Jesus als Davidssohn: Eine traditionsgeschichtliche Untersuchung* (Göttingen: Vandenhoeck & Ruprecht, 1970), 72–106.

4. Gen. 12:3; 17:16; 18:18; 22:17–18; cf. Matt. 3:7–10; 8:5–13.

5. This full and unqualified approval from God, the ultimate reality in the world of Matthew's story, indicates that Jesus is an entirely reliable character, i.e., a character who consistently represents the appropriate way of thinking and acting.

6. Note that the content of the five great discourses, or teaching blocks, in Matthew focuses on issues of post-Easter discipleship (chaps. 5–7; 10; 13; 18; 24–25).

7. 4:23; 5:1; 7:29; 9:35; 11:1; 13:54; 21:23; 22:16; 26:55.

8. Matthew emphasizes the interrelationship between these two titles by symmetrical arrangement: king-king-son-king-son-son. The fact that the crucifixion scene comes to a climax in the confession of 27:54 indicates that Jesus dies primarily as Son of God.

9. 8:1, 10; 12:15; 14:13; 19:2; 20:29; 21:9. Each of these passages makes a connection between following and healing. The description of the crowds in 11:7–24 and 13:10–17(18) rules out the possibility that the crowds are in any way disciples. See Jack Dean Kingsbury, "The Verb *Akoluthein* ('to follow') as an Index of Matthew's View of His Community," *JBL* 97 (1978): 56–73. For a different understanding of the crowds, see Paul S. Minear, "The Disciples and the Crowds in the Gospel of Matthew," *ATR* Sup. Ser. 3 (1974): 28–44.

10. Matthew emphasizes this total opposition on the part of the religious leaders by refusing to make material distinctions between the various groups or sects (e.g., Pharisees and Sadducees). On the contrary, Matthew presents them all in essentially the same way as a "unity of evil" against Jesus. See Rolf Walker, *Die Heilsgeschichte im ersten Evangelium* (Göttingen: Vandenhoeck & Ruprecht, 1967), 38–74; Reinhart Hummel, *Die Auseinandersetzung zwischen Kirche und Judentum im Matthäusevangelium* (Munich: Kaiser Verlag, 1963).

11. Jack Dean Kingsbury, *Matthew as Story,* rev. and enl. ed. (Minneapolis: Fortress Press, 1988), 116–18.

12. All of this points to the essential meaning of evil: the dynamic subversion of the redemptive work of God in the world.

– 4 –

Matthew's Understanding of the Law

Klyne R. Snodgrass

When interpreted by the prophetic focus on love and mercy, Matthew views the law as completely valid.

DESPITE THE ATTRACTION and power of the ethical teaching in Matthew, its statements on the law seem to defy understanding. In Matthew, Jesus asserts the continuing validity of the law down to its least part (5:17–19) and yet seems to set aside great chunks of the law (as 15:11). The reader is warned both to avoid the teaching of the Pharisees and Sadducees (16:11–12) and to do all that the Pharisees say, though not what they do (23:2–3).

If the truth be admitted, most Protestants wish that Matthew had written differently than he did about law and ethics. His position requires too much, sounds too much like works righteousness, and does not fit well with Paul's theology—to say nothing of Martin Luther's. We need to read Matthew, however, on his own terms. Recent lessons from literary criticism ought to warn us against reading Matthew through a Markan lens or on the basis of Pauline theology.

Matthew uses the term *nomos* ("law") eight times. Although his understanding of the law may seem simple, the issues these eight occurrences raise are complex and difficult. Making matters worse, scholars approach Matthew's understanding of the law with varied and unacceptable biases. The result is a virtual circus of views, some expressing the very opposite of Matthew's intention.[1]

Much of the discussion about the law in Matthew is tied to other questions. How was the law understood in Judaism? Had Matthew's community already separated from the synagogue? Had its members rejected temple practice and circumcision? Can one detect debates about the law in such passages as 5:17–20? Especially if Matthew were written in Syria, did the Matthean community know about the conflicts over the law in Antioch referred to by Paul in Galatians 2? Evidence does not exist to answer some of these questions.

Of course, the real question is, "What position on the law does Matthew ascribe to Jesus?" The following are the most popular views:

1. Matthew thought that the Old Testament law was no longer valid after the coming of Jesus. Statements stressing the validity of the law are traditions that Matthew has retained, but qualified by his own reflections. The Old Testament law was either set aside because Jesus as Messiah brought a new Torah[2] or because he fulfilled the law through his death and resurrection.[3]

2. The historical Jesus thought that the law was no longer valid, but Matthew rejudaized or "retorahized" the message of Jesus.[4]

3. For Matthew, the law was only partially valid. Relatively few scholars would say that Matthew distinguished the moral law from the ceremonial and civil laws, but many would argue that he presents Jesus as radicalizing or intensifying the law so that some commands are set aside. Commands frequently referred to in this connection are the "antitheses" on divorce, swearing, and the *lex talionis* (5:31–42) and the discussion of food (15:11–20).[5]

4. The law is completely valid as far as Matthew presents Jesus' teaching.[6]

5. The law reveals God's purpose when interpreted by a specific hermeneutical key.[7]

Both options four and five, it seems to me, express Matthew's understanding.

To Matthew's way of thinking, Jesus *neither* set aside any of the law *nor* interpreted it the way many of his contemporaries did. The proper understanding of the law cannot be found by merely studying it and focusing on individual commands. Rather, the proper understanding of the law is attained through a "prophetic" reading of it that sees love and mercy as its real focus. This position is in keeping with Marcus Borg's contention that Jesus substituted the mercy code for the holiness code that so occupied his contemporaries.[8] Borg's contention may be too stark, but Jesus' teaching did bring about a shift in paradigms. At least Jesus *disregarded* the holiness code, which forced separation from the impure, so as to focus on the mercy code, which promoted association with sinners. Matthew 8 and 9 are primary evidence of such a shift. In these chapters Jesus touches a leper, a hemorrhaging woman, and a girl believed to be dead and associates with a gentile and tax collectors and sinners.

This is not to drive a wedge between holiness and love, for in Matthew, true holiness, or "righteousness," is characterized by love. Indeed, the command to love one's neighbor has its origin in the holiness code of Leviticus. Love and mercy were the intent of the law itself, for the two greatest commands of the law (Deut. 6:5 and Lev. 19:18) both focus on love. (See the discussion in Matt. 22:34–40.)

The prophets, however, were those who most forcefully stressed love, mercy, and justice. This means that we must take seriously Matthew's references to the *prophets* in contexts in which he deals with law. All eight occurrences of *nomos* in Matthew are linked to the prophetic writings. Four of the eight occur in the expression "the law and the prophets" (5:17 with "or" instead of "and"; 7:12; 11:13 in reverse order; and 22:40). Two more are in the immediate contexts of these passages (5:18 and 22:36). The occurrence in 12:5 is followed in 12:7 with a quotation of Hosea 6:6, and the one in 23:23 is an allusion to Micah 6:8. In addition, the hypocrisy of refusing to honor one's parents by the use of the *korban* (property dedicated to the temple after death) is described with words from Isaiah 29:13 (see 15:3–9), and the cleansing of the temple is justified with words from Isaiah 56:7 and Jeremiah 7:11. Nor ought we forget that the Pharisees are upbraided for their hypocrisy and for being against everything the prophets stood for (23:29–36). In 5:17, therefore, the expression "or the prophets" is not out of place or unnecessary, as the *inclusio* ("inclusion") with 7:12 shows. This expression is Matthew's indication that all of the Hebrew scriptures must be read together. Law is not given pride of place, as it was in most of Judaism, and cannot be viewed by itself. In Matthew, one cannot understand the law apart from the prophets, and Jesus is described — whatever else we say about him — with prophetic terms as one who imparts the proper understanding of the law.[9]

That mercy and love are the focus of Matthew's understanding of the law is without question. Note the following:

5:43–48 The love command provides the climax of the "antitheses" and is the principle that undergirds both the antitheses and the call for a righteousness that "goes beyond." Note the *inclusio* that *perisseusē* ("exceed") in 5:20 forms with *perisson* ("extra") in 5:47.

7:12 The "golden rule" encapsulates the law and the prophets, and it is synonymous with the love command.

19:19 Unlike Mark and Luke, Matthew lists the love command along with the commands from the Decalogue that one must keep if one is to enter into life. Note that *teleios* ("perfect" or "complete") appears only in 5:48 and 19:21, both in close proximity to the love command.

22:34–40 All the law and the prophets are said to "hang on" the two love commands, apparently meaning that these determine how the other commands are to be applied.

24:12 Love and lawlessness are viewed as opposites.

25:31–46 Love is the criterion by which one will ultimately be judged at the consummation of the age.

Matthew's focus on mercy goes hand in hand with this focus on love. Twice Matthew uses Hosea 6:6 ("I desire mercy and not sacrifice") to explain the intent of the law (see 9:13 and 12:7). In 23:23 mercy, along with justice and faithfulness, is one of the weightier matters of the law. In passages like 5:7; 6:1–2; and 18:33 the importance of mercy is also apparent.

The real questions demanding answer are, "What is the law?" and "How is the law to be read?" "Does the law constitute commands, all of which have the same value, that aim at separation and order life and produce holiness?" Jesus' answer is no. Nor may one focus on the law to the neglect of the rest of scripture. The law is *not a uniform codex* but a legal code with statements in unresolved tension.[10] Some commands are more important, especially those focusing on justice and mercy. As 19:3–9 reveals, parts of the law, like Deuteronomy 24:1, are concessions, whereas other parts, like Genesis 2:24, point to God's intent. Most of all, however, the integrating center of the law is found in love and mercy. In Matthew, Jesus provides a scriptural hermeneutic for reading the law.

Numerous questions still remain about Matthew's understanding of the law. One of the most difficult is his attitude toward the cultic law. We might hypothesize about this were we certain that the Matthean community had broken with Judaism; as likely as this may seem, however, we cannot be certain. In the statement in 12:6–7 that something greater than the temple is present and in the quotation of Hosea 6:6 that says, "I desire mercy and not sacrifice," the rejection of the temple may be intimated. But by the same token, one must acknowledge that these verses seems only to deemphasize the temple, for the validity of the temple and its sacrifices are assumed in 5:23–24; 17:24–27; and 21:12–17. Still of greatest significance is 8:4, which reports that Jesus sent the cleansed leper to the priest for verification of healing and to offer the sacrifice Moses commanded. In the end, questions about cultic law seem to have been secondary at best for Matthew.[11] He seems unconcerned to impose a noncultic theology back on Jesus, and there is no way to know what decisions his community made about circumcision, no matter what our suspicions may be.

Matthew 5:17–20

The legitimacy of understanding Matthew as presenting a "prophetic" reading of the law can be validated only by an analysis of specific texts on the law. The difference between more recent literary and sociological approaches and earlier tradition-historical and redactional approaches is most obvious at this point. Tradition-historical and redactional approaches assume the principle of "transparency." They view the Gospel as a window through which one may see the Matthean community and its situation. Literary criticism endeavors to concentrate on the Gospel itself and is aware of limitations in determining the actual situation of the community.[12]

Some scholars, convinced that neither Matthew nor the historical Jesus could have said or meant all the statements in 5:17–20, have isolated certain segments as Matthean redaction set over against other segments that allegedly stem from a conservative Jewish Christianity, preserved but not accepted by Matthew. For example, Robert Guelich argues that 5:17–19 was a distortion of Jesus' ministry and that Matthew added "or the prophets" in 5:17 and "until all things come to pass" in 5:18 to point to Jesus' own teaching and ministry. Matthew included 5:19, even though he did not agree with it, and countered it with 5:20 and the antitheses, which show that keeping the legal commands of the law is inadequate for entering the kingdom.[13] Similarly, John Meier argues that Matthew added 5:18*d*, "until all things happen," as a reference to the death and resurrection of Jesus. On these interpretations, the law has lost its binding force.[14] In fact, Matthew is made to say the opposite of his intent.

Such interpretations have always been suspect. One can only sympathize with Matthew's readers if such interpretations were the conclusion they were to draw. Recent literary approaches, especially the commentary by Daniel Patte, have offered a more likely understanding. For one thing, Patte points out that explicit "oppositions" are the direct expression of an author's convictions, and in 5:17–19 three explicit oppositions occur.[15] For another thing, the importance of the statements in 5:17–20 is attested to by their placement. After the necessary introductory material, Matthew gives a brief summary of Jesus' ministry in 4:12–25. Thus, Matthew moves as quickly as possible to the most significant part of Jesus' teaching, namely, the proper understanding of God's law. As W. D. Davies points out, "... the penetrating demands of Jesus... were part of 'the bright light of the Gospel,' that is, they were revelatory."[16] Accordingly, the material in 5:17–20 is not garbled tradition but the introduction to Jesus' interpretation of the law, a law he came to "fulfill," not set aside. Clearly 5:17–20 is intended to protect against any reading of the "antitheses" or other sayings of Jesus that would suggest that the law has been set aside.

Here we can give only a summary statement on the numerous exegetical difficulties found in 5:17–20. "The law or the prophets" is a reference to the whole of the Hebrew scriptures. *Plerosai* ("fulfill") in 5:17 does not refer to the predictive function of scripture and must be antithetical to the idea of destroying or nullifying. That is to say, Jesus came to affirm and to bring the law and the prophets into reality by his teaching and life. The intent of "fulfill" must include the idea of doing or accomplishing. One should note that Paul speaks of "fulfilling the law" with just this connotation in Romans 13:8 and Galatians 5:14, both of which have to do with the love command (see also Rom. 8:4).

The two "until" clauses in 5:18 are difficult to interpret, but for practical purposes they are virtually equivalent. To say, "until heaven and earth pass away," could be the same as saying "never" or "at the end of time." If the latter is correct, then we should note the contrast with 24:34–35, which states that heaven and earth will pass away but not Jesus' words. The implicit contrast, then, would be between the eternal permanence of Jesus' teaching and the this-worldly permanence of the law. In any case, the reader can rest assured that as long as life exists on earth, the law is valid. The second "until" clause may be synonymous with the first or may mean "until all God's will is accomplished."

The expression "one iota or one hook" in 5:18 refers, respectively, to the smallest letter of the alphabet and to distinguishing marks on letters. The expression is metaphorical for the smallest part of the law. The words "the least commands" in 5:19 are parallel.

Matthew 5:19 is a restatement of 5:17 and 18, but underscores the importance of doing and teaching the law. Observe the parallel between *katalysai* ("destroy") in 5:17 and *lyse* ("set aside") in 5:19. To be called "least" or "great" in the kingdom is a way of speaking about what is pleasing or displeasing to God. All three verses affirm the complete validity and importance of the law.

In many ways, 5:20 is the most important verse in 5:17–20. It is not intended to drive people to despair at their inability to keep the law. This verse emphasizes that a literalistic or atomistic interpretation of the law is unacceptable. What is required for entrance into the kingdom is a righteousness that goes to the core of one's being. In Matthew, righteousness refers to ethical behavior and not, as in Paul, to either a gift from God or a status in the eyes of God.

Matthew 5:17 and 20 are easy enough to accept, but could Matthew or Jesus have meant 5:18–19? Could either have insisted that the law was *totally* valid? The answer to this question depends on how literalistically one chooses to read the text. The temptation account (4:1–11) is particularly instructive in warding off any literalistic reading. In dealing with all three temptations, Jesus refers to Deuteronomy. His life is presented as in full accord with God's word to Israel. Also, after Jesus tells the devil that a person lives from every word that proceeds from God's mouth (Deut. 8:3), the devil bases the second temptation *on a word from God.* Jesus subordinates that particular word to one that is still more important. In the temptation account, Matthew makes it eminently clear that individual texts cannot be interpreted legalistically. They must be placed within the larger framework of the whole of scripture.

As with all texts, the question must be, "What is the *function* of verses 18–19 in their context?" Both are *hyperbole* and are to be understood as stressing the permanence of the law and the importance of teaching and doing it. These verses verify that Jesus did not come to destroy the law or the prophets. One should be reminded that verses 18–19 are popular literature, not technical theological writing.

The "Antitheses"

To show what kind of "greater righteousness" is required, Matthew provides commentary on 5:20 in the so-called antitheses ("You have heard — I say to you" sayings) in 5:21–48. The point in every case is to go beyond a surface level to the intention of the will of God underlying the command. What is required is an integrity of being that is characterized by love, mercy, and truth.

Two crucial questions must be addressed. Is the Greek word *de* in the six "antitheses" a *connective* that means "and" or a *mild adversative* that means "but"? Is the intent, "You have heard, *and* I say," or is it, "You have heard, but I say"? Most people treat these verses as if *alla* (a strong adversative meaning "but") were used, but this is to overplay the contrast.[17] Secondly, if one opts for antithesis here, is Jesus' teaching set against scribal tradition or against the Word of God? The truth of the matter is that each of the six "antitheses" must be treated in its own right, for there are differences among them. Obviously, Matthew did not intend to contrast Jesus' teaching with the Word of God. If that were his intent, great chunks of his Gospel, especially 5:17–20, make no sense. On the other hand, one cannot say that Matthew's Jesus is merely opposing scribal tradition. The expression found in 5:21 and 33, "to the people long ago," must refer to the generation at Sinai. More is opposed than simply scribal tradition if Jesus is providing a hermeneutic for reading the scriptures.

The first two "antitheses" do not seem to be antithetical at all. Jesus' teaching is an interpretation of the intent and extent of the commands. Obedience includes the core of one's being and thinking, not merely external performance.

The other four "antitheses" are all adversative in varying degrees. Jesus' saying on divorce (5:31–32) opposes a concession of the law that seeks to prohibit a woman's remarriage to her first husband after being "defiled" by a second (Deut. 24:1–3). If, as 19:3–9 indicates, Jesus bases his teaching on the intent of the law (Gen. 2:24) rather than on a concession, he is not setting the law aside. The Essenes also prohibited divorce and certainly did not see themselves as violating the law (see 11Q Temple Scroll 57.17–19 and Cairo Damascus Document 4.12b–5.14a). As E. P. Sanders comments, it is not a violation of the law to be stricter than what the law requires.[18]

On the surface, the saying on oaths (5:33–37) explicitly prohibits what the law commands. This notwithstanding, the problem here is with scribal interpretation and the abuse of oaths, as 23:16–22 shows. The function of the Old Testament commands about oaths was to verify truth. Casuistry had led to oaths becoming a means to avoid the truth. By limiting people to the truth, Jesus cannot be viewed as setting aside the law.

The strongest contrast between Jesus' teaching and the law is in the saying about retaliation (5:38–42). This *lex talionis* had the positive purpose of limiting revenge and making sure that injustice was not ignored (see Deut. 19:19–21). Jesus' teaching *is a redirection* of the law to focus on the ultimate concern of the law, the love command. Whereas the *lex talionis* is concerned with legal rights, Jesus' teaching about the kingdom asks that people give up rights and legal satisfaction in favor of love and mercy. The question repeatedly is, "What is the law really about?" Matthew's answer is "love and mercy."

The last "antithesis" (5:43–47) is further evidence of this. The law did not say "hate your enemies," although this sentiment could be drawn from the Old Testament and is expressed in the Qumran scrolls. Jesus' interpretation of the law requires love even for enemies. As elsewhere, Jesus will not allow boundaries to be set defining the limits of one's responsibility or to whom that responsibility is due. The love command is to control all relationships. Verses 45–48 tell us why Jesus focused on the love command and mercy in interpreting the law. The character of God *requires* this.

Matthew 15:1–20

The saying in 15:11, "that which enters the mouth does not defile a person," is perhaps the best example one can cite in claiming that Jesus violates the law. Matthew, however, did not himself view this saying as a violation of the law. For us, this saying brings into question regulations about unclean foods, but to argue that Jesus sets aside the law in this passage is to read Mark 7:15 and 19 into Matthew. Mark's statements, "Nothing outside a person entering in is *able* to defile" (7:15) and "this he said making all foods clean" (7:19), are nowhere to be found in Matthew. Matthew depicts Jesus as drawing no conclusion from this discussion with the disciples other than the statement that "to eat with unwashed hands does not defile." Thus, eating with unwashed hands does not defile, but breaking God's law does. (Note that the sins listed in 5:19 are mostly violations of the Decalogue, and most are treated in the "antitheses.") Once again, the text of Matthew portrays Jesus as being in conformity with the law.

Is Matthew Legalistic?

Some texts, however, seem to go too far in stressing Jesus' conformity to the law. Matthew 23:2–3, 23 and 24:20 suggest a concentration on details of the law that is hard to imagine. But such texts cannot be read atomistically, and Matthew is not promoting legalism. The statement in 23:2–3, if it is taken out of context, actually expresses the opposite of what Matthew writes in 15:14 and 16:11. However, 23:2–3 is hyperbole and intentionally creates tension with the rest of the chapter.[19] These verses show that whereas neither the law nor the authority of its teachers is rejected, Jesus is nonetheless the one who determines what legitimate or illegitimate interpretation is. Matthew tolerates neither misguided interpretation nor hypocrisy. In 23:23 hyperbole is again present and urges that one concern oneself with those matters about the law that are really important: justice, mercy, and faithfulness. It also adds that one should not neglect tithing spices. Surely 23:23 constitutes a way of emphasizing what the law is about while saying at the same time that the less important areas of life dare not be neglected (see Luke 16:10). One cannot legitimately interpret 23:23 as promoting legalism.

A legalistic view of Sabbath-keeping could be derived from 24:20, but this, too, would run counter to Matthew's intent. The parallelism between praying that flight occurs neither during winter nor on a Sabbath points to hardship as the concern rather than sensitivities about the law. Probably the reference is to the difficulty of flight if shops and gates were closed on the Sabbath and assistance were unavailable.

Christology and Law

Discussions about Matthew's understanding of the law often suggest that christology is the hermeneutical key for getting at his intent. We are told repeatedly that texts dealing with the law are really dealing with christology. Implicit in such statements is a contrast between Christ and the law.[20] As enticing as such statements sound, they do not do justice to Matthew. The law of God and the Son of God are not antithetical. The Son of God appeals to the law for guidance and validation (4:1–11). Jesus is the authoritative interpreter of the law, but not merely an interpreter. Matthew does not suggest we are now merely to follow "Rabbi Jesus." As important and abiding as the law is, something new has arrived with the kingdom. The law is no longer the center of gravity; Jesus is. He is the one to whom the scriptures point, the one who lives in accord with the scriptures, and who shows their intent. Disciples gather in his name, not around the law (18:20). He is not merely a teacher; he is the one who mediates the presence of the Father to his disciples. Following Jesus and obeying God's law understood through the love command belong together, as 19:16–22 reveals.

Concluding Remarks

Matthew's teaching on the law is surprising. He uses absolute statements where we expect nuanced ones. He views Jesus as upholding the law fully. Through an equal focus on the prophets, however, he presents Jesus as having brought about a shift in paradigms so that the law is not organized around ideas of separation and purity but around love, mercy, and justice.

From our standpoint today, Matthew's understanding of the law is an unfinished agenda. But this is also the case with *every other understanding of the law in the New Testament*. Matthew's view of the law cannot be described as inferior to that of any other author. Matthew focuses as fully on God's presence in the life of the believer as anyone else (1:23; 18:20; 28:20), and he believes that, with this presence, disciples of the kingdom are to do the will of God as revealed in a law of love.

NOTES

1. For a summary of views held, see my more detailed treatment in "Matthew and the Law," SBLSP (1988), ed. David J. Lull, 536–54.

2. Richard S. McConnell, *Law and Prophecy in Matthew's Gospel* (Basel: Friedrich Reinhardt Kommissionsverlag, 1969), 90–94.

3. John P. Meier, *Law and History in Matthew's Gospel: A Redactional Study of Matthew 5:17–48* (Rome: Biblical Institute Press, 1976), 63–65.

4. On this option see Hans Hübner, *Das Gesetz in der synoptischen Tradition,* 2d ed. (Göttingen: Vandenhoeck & Ruprecht, 1973), esp. 237–39.

5. See, e.g., Gerhard Barth, "Matthew's Understanding of the Law," in Günther Bornkamm, Gerhard Barth, and Heinz Joachim Held, *Tradition and Interpretation in Matthew* (Philadelphia: Westminster Press, 1963), 94–104.

6. A. E. Harvey, *Jesus and the Constraints of History* (Philadelphia: Westminster Press, 1982), 53–54.

7. Alexander Sand, *Das Gesetz und die Propheten* (Regensburg: Verlag Friedrich Pustet, 1974), 44–45, 59–60, 187–89, and 208–16. See also Birger Gerhardsson, "The Hermeneutic Program in Matthew 22:37–40," *Jews, Greeks, Christians,* ed. R. Hamerton-Kelly and R. Scroggs (Leiden: E. J. Brill, 1976), 134, 140.

8. Marcus Borg, *Conflict, Holiness, and Politics in the Teaching of Jesus* (New York: Edwin Mellen Press, 1984), 123, 128.

9. See Sand, *Das Gesetz und die Propheten, passim.*

10. E.g., divorce is both mandated (Exod. 21:11 and Deut. 21:14) and prohibited (Deut. 22:19 and 29), in both cases to protect the wife. Deuteronomy prohibits seeking peace and good relations with Ammonites and Moabites (23:6), but commands love of the alien (10:16–19). Such examples could easily be multiplied.

11. See Harvey, *Jesus and the Constraints of History,* 64.

12. Note the critique given by Jack Dean Kingsbury ("Conclusion: Analysis of a Conversation," *Social History of the Matthean Community,* ed. David L. Balch [Minneapolis: Fortress Press, 1991], 259–69) of Alan Segal's easy acceptance of a transparency method in his "Matthew's Jewish Voice" (pp. 3–37 of the same volume).

13. Robert Guelich, *The Sermon on the Mount* (Waco, Tex.: Word Books, 1982), 134–74.

14. John Meier, *Law and History in Matthew's Gospel,* 38–40, 63–65.

15. Daniel Patte, *The Gospel according to Matthew* (Philadelphia: Fortress Press, 1987), 6–11, 70–75.

16. W. D. Davies, *The Setting of the Sermon on the Mount* (Cambridge: Cambridge University Press, 1966), 437.

17. See the discussion of W. D. Davies and Dale C. Allison, *The Gospel according to Saint Matthew* (Edinburgh: T. & T. Clark, 1988), 1:507.

18. E. P. Sanders, *Jesus and Judaism* (Philadelphia: Fortress Press, 1985), 256, 260. We should note that Judaism had altered numerous commands with no thought that the law had been violated. See Davies and Allison, *The Gospel according to Saint Matthew,* 1:492.

19. Patte, *The Gospel according to Matthew,* 319–21.

20. See, e.g., Robert Banks, *Jesus and the Law in the Synoptic Tradition* (Cambridge: Cambridge University Press, 1975).

– 5 –

The Communities of Matthew

Graham N. Stanton

With considerable literary, catechetical, and pastoral skill, Matthew composed a Gospel for a "new people." Specifically, this new people consisted of Christians of Jewish and gentile origin living in a cluster of communities. In view of their recent and painful separation from Judaism, Matthew penned for these communities a "foundation document" in which he told the story of Jesus and thereby addressed their needs.

WHY SHOULD WE TRY to reconstruct the main features of the communities for which Matthew wrote? Would it not be preferable to concentrate our attention on the text of the Gospel itself, on the evangelist's story of Jesus? These are fair questions that ought not be ducked.

Whenever a text is read or listened to, the recipients bring assumptions and expectations from their background. They may be surprised by the text, they may even find that their assumptions are overturned, but nonetheless their initial "horizons of expectation" are clearly important. So as soon as we inquire about the ways the original recipients would have appropriated the text of Matthew's Gospel, we find we must try to clarify their social and religious setting. Who were they? Where and when did they live? What political, cultural, and religious assumptions shaped the ways they understood the text? Were they Christians, both Jews and gentiles, who saw themselves as a sect or party within Judaism? Or were they conscious of a recent painful parting from local synagogues? Were their Christian communities racked with internal divisions? If so, what "heretical" views did Matthew oppose?

Such questions have nearly always been on the agenda of students of Matthew's Gospel.[1] Their place on the agenda, however, has varied. Redaction critics and scholars who advocate social-historical or sociological approaches place them near the top. Literary critics, on the other hand, give a higher priority to a sensitive reading of the text itself. But most Matthean literary critics have spurned the radical ahistorical or text-immanent approaches that were advocated by many literary theorists during the heyday of New Criticism in the 1950s and 1960s, views that are still having an afterlife in the work of some New Testament scholars.

"Text-immanent" perspectives that deliberately set aside the social context of the author and the original recipients of writings in order to concentrate attention solely on the text itself are now out of favor with literary theorists. The distinguished Cambridge literary critic Frank Kermode, for example, has recently noted that "more and more people are turning away from the idea that literary works should be treated as autonomous and without significant relation to the world in which they are produced and read."[2] I hope that these wise words will be heeded by Matthean scholars. If they are not, and if "reader-response criticism" ignores the horizons of expectation of the *first-century* recipients of Matthew, interpretation will be like a picnic—a picnic to which the evangelist brings his text, and we all bring our meanings.[3]

As soon as we establish that a quest for the original recipients of Matthew is imperative, we discover that it is much more perilous than we might have supposed. Unfortunately we do not know either when or where the Gospel was written.

Along with most scholars, I accept that Matthew's carefully revised and considerably extended edition of Mark must have been written some time after the traumatic events of 70 C.E., probably between 80 and 110, and within this period earlier rather than later.[4] But it is impossible to be more precise. This is a real frustration since both Judaism and Christianity were developing very rapidly in these years. It is obviously hazardous to link the origin and setting of the Gospel to any particular historical event within this broad period.

Although it has often been suggested that the Gospel was written in Antioch, there is no conclusive evidence, and the cumulative case is not compelling.[5] We know a good deal about earliest Christianity in Antioch[6] and a certain amount about the social makeup of the city itself.[7] If only we could be certain that Matthew's Gospel were written in Antioch, its social setting would be much clearer.

I do not even think we can assume that Matthew was written in an urban setting. This almost universally held view is based on two main points. As G. D. Kilpatrick noted, Mark uses "city" eight times in his Gospel, Matthew twenty-six times; Mark uses "village" seven times, only three of which were retained by Matthew. However, these statistics are no more than straws in the wind.[8]

More frequently, scholars claim that the rapid dissemination and the early popularity of Matthew suggest that it originated in a large thriving urban Christian community. But even this point is less secure than most have supposed. F. W. Norris has recently noted that church history will not sustain the presupposition that influential writings must come from large urban centers, since many often-copied writers in the patristic period did not live or work in major centers.[9]

Would that we knew as much about the communities for which Matthew wrote as we do about the recipients of the Pauline epistles. As Wayne Meeks and other social historians have shown, our knowledge of the social setting of the Pauline communities in the middle of the first century is immensely helpful. Of course, Matthean scholars can draw to good effect on our increasing knowledge of the Greco-Roman world, but our inability to date and locate Matthew's Gospel with any precision is a considerable handicap.

Specific evidence concerning the setting of the Gospel that comes from *outside* the text is sparse. We are forced to rely on inferences *in the text itself*. This raises immediately the specter of the hermeneutical circle: In order to read the text responsibly, we need to know about the circumstances that elicited it, but in our quest for its setting we have only the text of the Gospel itself. There is no way of avoiding this dilemma in the case of Matthew nor, indeed, in most forms of historical reconstruction. One can only read and reread the text with as much sensitivity and rigor as possible — and that includes openness to the possibility that one's preliminary judgments may have to be corrected.

Even when we rely on inferences from the text itself, the path of our quest for the social setting of the communities for which Matthew wrote is far from smooth and straight. There are two more obstacles to be negotiated. The first is a general point that has been overlooked surprisingly frequently. Whereas Paul wrote *letters* to specific Christian communities whose foibles he knew well, Matthew wrote a *Gospel*, a particular kind of Greco-Roman biography whose primary focus is on the story and significance of Jesus of Nazareth. Matthew's primary aim was to set out the story of Jesus. That he does so from a particular perspective is undeniable. What is less clear is the extent to which that perspective is *directly* related to the views and circumstances of the addressees.

Many redaction critics cheerfully ignore the genre of the Gospel and assume much too readily that every pericope provides an uninterrupted vista onto one or more facets of the community life of the original recipients. How do we know which parts of Matthew were intended to challenge or change the views of the readers or listeners? In the New Testament letters, it is difficult enough to make this distinction; the genre Matthew has chosen makes this doubly difficult.

Secondly, we need to note that in a quest for the social setting of a writing, the social historian's eye often alights on incidental details in the text. In the case of Matthew, however, it is often difficult to know whether such details reflect the community life of the recipients of the Gospel or that of an earlier period.

Take, for example, Matthew 5:23 and 24, verses in which Jesus insists that reconciliation with one's brother (or sister) should precede the offering of a sacrificial gift at the temple altar. Do these verses reflect the religious practices of Jesus and his followers in his own lifetime? Or do they put us in touch with the period immediately after Easter when, according to the early chapters of Acts, followers of Jesus continued to frequent the temple? Or do they suggest that at a still later time Matthew's readers continued to offer sacrifices at the temple? In the latter case, the Gospel must have been written before the destruction of the temple in 70 C.E., and since sour personal relationships can hardly have been a rarity, Matthew's readers must have lived within easy traveling distance of Jerusalem.

I much prefer an alternative explanation: Matthew knew full well that his readers would be able to appropriate the key point in Matthew 5:23–24 concerning reconciliation, even though it was impossible for them to offer sacrifices at the temple in Jerusalem since it had been in ruins for a decade or more. The corollary is that these verses reflect a social world that was very different from the context for which Matthew wrote; they tell us next to nothing about the social and religious world of Matthew's readers and listeners.

I

Now that we have read our map and noted the obstacles, it is time to set out on our quest for the "horizons of expectation" with which the first recipients of the Gospel responded to the text. Our guides? Redaction criticism, literary criticism, social history, and sociology are all friendly, and they should not squabble with one another. In fact, the quest is so hazardous that we would be wise to take the advice of at least two of them.

Our guides all point out that the conflict of Jesus and his followers with the Jewish leaders is a central theme of Matthew's Gospel. One of the most important horizons of expectation of the first recipients was their acute awareness that they had parted painfully from local Jewish synagogues. The evidence that points to this conclusion is cumulative and impressive.[10]

1. In Matthew, Jewish religious leaders and groups — and, in particular, scribes and Pharisees — are consistently placed in a negative light. The invective against the scribes and Pharisees in chapter 23 brings to a climax the hostility that pervades the Gospel, a hostility that is sharper and more sustained than in the other Gospels. Whereas Mark refers to

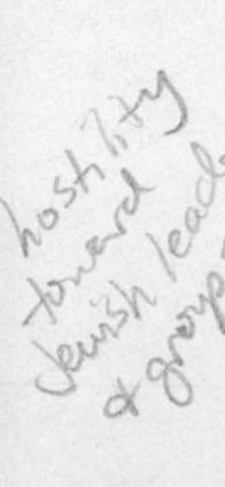

the Pharisees as hypocrites only once (7:6) and Luke not at all, Matthew has twelve such references, six of which are in chapter 23.

The bitterness is unrelieved by any suggestion that some individual scribes or Pharisees might be sympathetic to Jesus or his followers. There is no sign in Matthew of the friendly Pharisees who, according to Luke 7:36 and 14:1, invited Jesus to dine with them; nor is there a reference to Pharisees who (helpfully) warned Jesus that Herod wanted to kill him (Luke 13:31). Mark's sympathetic scribe (12:28) becomes a hostile Pharisee in Matthew (22:35). So it is no surprise to find that in his important summary statement at the end of the Sermon on the Mount (7:29), Matthew carefully distances Jesus from the scribes by adding "their" to the reference to "the scribes" at Mark 1:22.

Matthew 8:18–22 is all of a piece. The eager scribe who seeks to follow Jesus merely on his own initiative and without a prior "call" from Jesus is repudiated, but someone else, who is not a scribe, is portrayed as a disciple and reminded sharply of the radical nature of discipleship.[11] In typical Matthean fashion, the repudiated scribe addresses Jesus as "teacher," while the true disciple addresses Jesus as "Lord."

At 9:18–26 Matthew revises radically Mark's striking portrait of Jairus, whose daughter Jesus heals. Mark refers to Jairus four times as a "ruler of the synagogue" (5:22, 35, 36, 38). In Matthew he is still portrayed as a man of faith, but he loses his name and becomes merely an anonymous "official" (9:18, 23); there is not even a hint that he has any connection with a synagogue.[12] Matthew and Luke both include the Q tradition of the healing of the centurion's servant (Matt. 8:5–13= Luke 7:1–10), but there is no sign in Matthew of Luke's note that the centurion loves the Jewish nation and has built a synagogue (7:5).

In Matthew, Jewish leaders are always at odds with Jesus and his disciples (and later followers), so a "ruler of the synagogue" cannot be a "man of faith," and a scribe cannot be portrayed as a true disciple. The wide gulf between scribes and Pharisees on the one hand and Jesus and his disciples on the other reflects the circumstances of Matthew's day: "synagogue" and "church" had parted company.

2. Matthew explicitly associates scribes and Pharisees with synagogues (23:6, 34; cf. also 10:17). His sustained hostility to the former is echoed in his references to synagogues. At 4:23; 9:35; 10:17; 12:9; 13:54, all passages where Matthew's own hand is clear, he uses the phrase "their synagogue(s)"; at 23:34 he uses the redactional phrase "your synagogues." With these slight changes Matthew drives a wedge between Jesus and his disciples on the one hand and the synagogue on the other.

Matthew refers to "synagogue" in only three further passages, 6:2, 5; 23:6. In each case there is a strong negative connotation: Disciples of Jesus are not to follow the example of scribes and Pharisees in the synagogue.[13] These passages strongly suggest that for Matthew (but not for Mark) the "synagogue" had almost become an alien institution.

3. Over against *synagoge* stands the *ekklesia* founded by Jesus himself and promised divine protection (16:18). Matthew uses "church" three times (16:18 and twice in 18:17), but this term is not found in the other three Gospels. The church has its own entrance rite: baptism in the triadic name (28:19). Matthew's reshaping of Mark's account of the last supper (26:26–30) reflects liturgical usage and thus confirms that the church in Matthew's day had its own distinctive central act of worship.

In a series of striking passages, disciples of Jesus (and their later followers) are promised that Jesus will be present with them in their community life in ways analogous to the manner in which God was understood to be present in temple and synagogue (8:23–27; 14:22–33; 18:20; 28:20). At 23:21 Matthew confirms that many Jews continued to regard God's presence (his *shekhina*) in the temple as a central belief.[14] But Matthew emphasizes that whereas the Jerusalem temple is "forsaken and desolate" (23:38), with the coming of Jesus "something greater than the temple is here" (12:6).[15] Adolf Schlatter is one of the few who have appreciated the importance of this bold Matthean christological claim; he notes that "God is present in Jesus to a greater extent than in the temple."[16]

Whereas the reading of Torah and instruction in it were central in the synagogue, in the church the commands of Jesus took precedence. Although Matthew insists strongly on the continuing importance of the law (5:17–19), hearing and doing the authoritative words of Jesus are of paramount importance (7:24–27), for the words of Jesus are "commands" for the life of the church (28:20).

Matthew's communities seem to be developing structures that were quite independent of the synagogue. They exercised, with divine sanction and on the authority of Jesus, the right of inclusion into and of exclusion from the community (16:19; 18:19). Some groups within Christian communities were modeled on their Jewish counterparts: There seem to have been Christian prophets (10:41; 23:34); Christian scribes (13:52; 23:34); and Christian wise men (23:34). But in contrast to the synagogue, no individual or group within the life of the church was to be accorded special honors or titles (23:6–12).

The *ekklesia* founded by Jesus continued to have a firm commitment to Torah, but it had accepted gentiles and developed its own patterns of worship and of community life. Its self-understanding was quite distinct from that of the synagogue.

4. Further compelling support for the conclusion that in Matthew's day synagogue and church were going their separate ways is provided by passages that speak about the "transference" of the kingdom to a new people who will include gentiles. At 8:5–13 Matthew links two Q tradi-

tions (Luke 7:1–10 and 13:28–29) in order to state starkly that "those born to the kingdom" will be replaced by gentiles — including the Roman centurion whose faith is commended — who will sit with faithful Israel (Abraham, Isaac, and Jacob) at the banquet in the kingdom of heaven.

At 15:13 Matthew adds a strongly polemical saying to a Markan tradition. The Pharisees are no longer considered to be "a plant of the heavenly Father's planting." By implication their place will be taken by another people. This becomes explicit at 21:41 and 43 in Matthew's redaction of Mark's parable of the Wicked Husbandmen. The Jewish leaders will be rejected by God. The vineyard will be transferred to other tenants — a people who will yield the proper fruit.

5. At the climax of his story at 28:15 Matthew addresses his readers directly and refers explicitly to the relationship between synagogue and church in his own day. He tells them that a rival account of the resurrection of Jesus — his disciples stole his body from the tomb — "has been widely circulated among Jews to this very day." This comment brings out into the open what has been hinted at again and again throughout the Gospel: Jews who have not accepted Christian claims are set at a distance and referred to as an entity quite distinct from the new people. They have an alternative story that Matthew claims can be shown to be patently absurd.

6. Matthew's communities still felt seriously threatened by Jewish opposition at the time the Gospel was written: Alongside 5:10–12 we may set 10:17–23, and 23:34 and 37.[17] Immediately after the reference to opposition and persecution in 5:11, disciples are warned that the persecution endured by the prophets of old is experienced anew by Christian prophets in their own day. This point is made much more explicitly and vigorously in 23:34, where once again Matthew's own hand can be traced. These passages strongly suggest that the Christian communities to which Matthew wrote were coming to terms with the trauma of separation from Judaism and with the perceived continuing threat of hostility and persecution.

II

The communities for which Matthew wrote are clearly at odds with contemporary Judaism. From the text of the Gospel itself, we may infer that the evangelist and the recipients of his Gospel were also at odds with the *gentile* world.

In the Sermon on the Mount there are three derogatory references to the gentiles: 5:47; 6:7; and 6:32. The second reference was probably added by Matthew himself; the other two were taken over from Q. In the mission discourse in chapter 10, the disciples are told much more explicitly than in Mark 13 to expect hostility from gentiles as well as from Jews (10:18, 22).

In Matthew's fourth discourse, the Markan tradition that gives a warning not to cause one of the little ones to stumble is set in an eschatological context by an additional logion inserted by Matthew himself: "Woe *to the world* for temptations to sin. For it is necessary that temptations come, but woe to the man by whom the temptation comes" (18:7). This apocalyptic saying was taken from Q in order to introduce a woe on the entire world as a part of the prophecy of the eschatological terrors that were expected soon. Here, Matthew has heightened an apocalyptic theme — as he does elsewhere — and he indicates that his communities were alienated from a threatening world. Later in the same discourse, at 18:17, there is a further derogatory reference to gentiles; as at 5:46–47, they are linked with tax collectors in a general reference to society outside the Matthean communities, a society with which these communities had little to do. At 24:9 there is yet another reference to the hostility that Matthew's communities may expect from gentiles at the end-time; the specific reference to gentiles is Matthew's own addition to the Markan tradition.

The evangelist's firm commitment to a mission to the gentiles is well known. But there is a string of other references to gentiles and to the world in general that is often overlooked. In many of them Matthew's own hand can be discerned. They suggest that the Matthean communities, just like the Pauline and Johannine communities, had an ambivalent attitude toward society at large: They were committed to the task of evangelism "to all nations," but saw themselves as a group quite distinct from the "alien" world at large.

III

We have now seen that the Matthean communities perceived themselves to be under threat of persecution from the Jewish religious leaders, a somewhat beleaguered minority at odds with the parent body and, to a certain extent, with the gentile world. These are well-known features of sectarian groups, as are the very stringent moral requirements (5:20, 48; 18:8–9; 19:11–12) and the strong internal discipline of Christian communities (18:5–19), both of which Matthew emphasizes.[18]

Some readers of this essay will resist my suggestion that Matthew's Gospel betrays a sectarian outlook. Their own knowledge or even experience of inward-looking or bigoted modern sects will rule this out. But once we set Matthew's communities alongside minority first-century groups, the case for reading the text this way becomes strong.

The openness of Matthew's Gospel (especially to the gentiles in 28:18–20) and the breadth of his theological vision will seem to some to be far removed from the outlook of a sectarian. However, since sects need to recruit in order to survive, partly open community boundaries are typical. And the evidence suggesting a broad theological vision is counterbalanced by contrary evidence. For example, a similar juxtaposition of a broad theological vision and a sectarian outlook is found in John's Gospel. Since sects often change their character quickly, especially when they are successful, the rapid dissemination and wide acceptance of Matthew within early Christianity do not tell against its sectarian origins.

Sectarian communities, whether ancient or modern, are usually very concerned about their internal cohesion. Apostates who reject totally the worldview and values of the community can be ignored, but "heretics" who still share some of the values of the community, as well as erring or unfaithful members, are often roundly condemned. Several passages in Matthew's Gospel can be read from this perspective. In contrast to Luke's version of the parable of the Lost Sheep (15:1–7), where a sinner outside the community is in view, in Matthew 18:10–14 the "church" (18:15) is urged to search out the erring member of the community, the "little one" who has gone astray.

Several passages pronounce judgment on unfaithful members of the communities. In 7:19 those who do not bear good fruit will be cut down and thrown into the fire. In the pericope that follows, judgment is pronounced on those whose deeds are evil (7:23). In the explanation of the parable of the Weeds (13:36–43), a passage in which Matthew's own hand is evident, the "sons of the evil one" are evildoers who will be thrown into the furnace of fire at the close of the age. In 24:51 Matthew made a redactional change to the Q tradition he was using and stresses that unfaithful Christians will share judgment with "the hypocrites," that is, with the scribes and Pharisees on whom judgment is pronounced in chapter 23. In short, Matthew was as ferocious in his denunciation of his fellow Christians as he was of the Jewish religious leaders.

Is it possible to say more about the "heretical" views of some members of Matthew's communities? Many scholars have accepted Gerhard Barth's view that Matthew was "fighting on two fronts": He was opposing both the leaders of contemporary Judaism and Christian antinomian heretics.[19] Barth claims that Matthew's emphasis on the abiding validity of the law in 5:17–19; 7:15–20; and 24:11–13 was directed at antinomian opponents who can best be described as Hellenistic libertines; they were to be equated with the false prophets of 7:15 and 24:11.

While Matthew clearly levels harsh criticisms at his Christian readers, I am not persuaded that he was attacking one particular "heretical" group. In his composite picture of the opponents Barth appeals to several passages and themes. But Matthew may have had in mind several different groups, or he may have been addressing his readers in very general terms. Matthew uses "lawlessness" three times to refer to Christians (7:23; 13:41; 24:12); these are general references to disobedience to the "will of the Father" and are not to be limited to antinomians. Matthew's warnings about false prophecy do not go beyond the similarly indefinite comments about heresy that we find in passages such as 1 Timothy 6:3–5; Titus 1:16; and *Didache* 11:1–8.[20]

Use of the text of New Testament epistles to "mirror" opponents and their arguments is fraught with difficulties.[21] We do well to be even more cautious in our use of redactional passages in Matthew to identify groups who were being opposed. Hypotheses based on a possible interpretation of one verse, or even of a cluster of verses, are likely to be insecure. The only opponents who are in view from the beginning to the end of Matthew's Gospel (from 2:1 to 28:15) are the Jewish leaders. Many redaction critics have assumed that Matthew's relationship with his readers was rather like Paul's intimate relationship with the Christian communities to whom he wrote. That view needs to be reconsidered. I have already emphasized that Matthew wrote a Gospel and not a letter and that it is most unlikely that Matthew intended to counter the views of a particular group.

A further consideration suggests that the Pauline analogy is inappropriate. First-century Christians met in houses; it would have been difficult for many more than fifty or so people to crowd into even a quite substantial house. Is it likely that Matthew would have composed such an elaborate Gospel for one relatively small group? Is it not much more likely that Matthew, like Luke, envisaged that his Gospel would circulate widely? If, as I envisage, Matthew wrote for a cluster of small Christian communities, then it is no surprise to find that his criticisms of them are severe but imprecise. Matthew was well aware of the tensions and pressures his readers faced, but we must not read his Gospel as if it were Galatians, 1 or 2 Corinthians, or even Romans.

IV

Matthew wrote following a period of prolonged dispute and hostility with fellow Jews. He and his opponents were heirs to the same scriptures and shared many religious convictions, but differences ran deep. Mutual incomprehension led to mutual hostility and, eventually, to a clear parting of the ways.

With considerable literary, catechetical, and pastoral skill Matthew composed a Gospel for a "new people": fellow Christians (both Jews and gentiles) in a cluster of Christian communities. Although they were minority groups still living in the shadow of thriving local Jewish synagogues, they had grown rapidly: Shallow faith and dissension were much in evidence. For this reason Matthew encouraged community solidarity in the face of perceived hostility from external sources.

Matthew wrote with several strategies in mind. His primary intention was to set out the story and significance of Jesus as a "foundation document." But in many respects Matthew's Gospel is an apology, for it contains a whole series of "legitimating answers" for the new people.[22] It responds both directly and indirectly to polemic from the parent body,[23] and it defends vigorously its own distinctive convictions and self-understanding.

Matthew legitimated the recent painful separation of his communities from Judaism by providing divine sanction for the parting of the ways: As a result of the hostility of the Jewish leaders to Jesus and his followers, *God* initiated the rupture and transferred the kingdom to the new people (21:43; 8:12; cf. also 15:13–14). Matthew repeatedly reinforces Christian convictions concerning the significance of Jesus that shaped the community life of the new people. God disclosed to the new people that Jesus is the Son of God (3:17; 11:25–27; 16:17; 17:5). Jesus was sent on *God's initiative* (1:20; 10:40; 21:37). Through Jesus, *God is present with God's people* (1:23; 8:23–27; 14:22–33; 18:20; 28:20); these verses have deep roots in Old Testament references to the presence of God with his people: An old theme is transposed into a new key.

One of Matthew's "legitimating answers" is particularly prominent. He included as part of his story a sustained defense of open and full acceptance of gentiles. He carried this out with such literary skill that it is highly likely that it was a matter of continuing importance for the new people.[24] Even if the principle were largely accepted when Matthew wrote, it was still necessary to repeat the explanation of how this step had been taken, a step that ultimately proved to be crucial for the parting of the ways with Judaism.

Matthew's crowning achievement in his foundation document for the new people is undoubtedly his provision of five major and several shorter carefully arranged discourses. Matthew took great care over the composition of the discourses because he valued the sayings of Jesus highly. The sayings of Jesus were to be prominent in the missionary proclamation and catechetical instruction of the new people (28:18–20). The closing verses of the Sermon on the Mount emphasize strongly the importance of hearing and acting on the words of Jesus (7:24–27). For Matthew, "the will of the heavenly Father" was equated with carrying out the sayings of Jesus (7:21; cf. Luke 6:46).

In some respects, the sayings of Jesus (and Matthew's Gospel as a whole) must *in practice* (though not in theory) have taken priority over the law and the prophets in the community life of the new people. The Gospel provided the new people with a prayer of Jesus (6:9–13) which probably became central in their worship quite soon; this is strongly suggested by *Didache* 8:3, written just a generation or so after Matthew's Gospel and deeply dependent on it. With even more confidence we can affirm that the traditions in Matthew concerning baptism (28:19), the Eucharist (26:26–28, which reflects liturgical shaping of the Markan tradition), and community discipline (16:19; 18:16–18) were central in the life of Matthean communities. Above all, Matthew's Gospel provided the new people with a story that was new, even though it had deep roots in scripture.

NOTES

1. See esp. G. D. Kilpatrick's influential study *The Origins of the Gospel according to Saint Matthew* (Oxford: Clarendon Press, 1946), 2.

2. See Frank Kermode, *Poetry, Narrative, History* (Oxford: Oxford University Press, 1990), 49.

3. I have adapted the words of the literary critic Northrop Frye, as quoted by E. D. Hirsch, *The Validity of Interpretation* (New Haven: Yale University Press, 1967), 1.

4. A date well before 115 C.E. is probable because at about that time a redactional phrase from Matt. 3:15 was cited by Ignatius, the bishop of Antioch, in his letter to the Smyrneans. In his otherwise very illuminating essay in *The Social History of the Matthean Community,* ed. D. L. Balch (Minneapolis: Fortress Press, 1991), William R. Schoedel is too cautious on this point. In his response to Schoedel in the same symposium, John P. Meier shows that beyond reasonable doubt Matthew's Gospel was used by Ignatius.

5. For a fuller discussion see Graham N. Stanton, "The Origin and Purpose of Matthew's Gospel: Matthean Scholarship from 1945–1980," in *Aufstieg und Niedergang der römischen Welt,* II, 25.3 (Berlin: Walter de Gruyter, 1985), 1941–42. Ulrich Luz accepts that Antioch "is not the worst of the hypotheses," but leaves the question open: The Gospel originated in a large Syrian city whose *lingua franca* was Greek; see *Matthew 1–7: A Commentary,* Eng. trans. (Minneapolis: Fortress Press; Edinburgh: T. & T. Clark, 1991), 92. In the first volume of their International Critical Commentary (Edinburgh: T. & T. Clark, 1988), W. D. Davies and D. C. Allison are almost equally cautious: Antioch "remains no more than the best educated guess" (147). See also L. Michael White, "Crisis Management and Boundary Maintenance," in *Social History,* 213–15; and Rodney Stark, "Antioch as the Social Situation for Matthew's Gospel," also in *Social History,* 189–210.

6. See Raymond E. Brown and John P. Meier, *Antioch and Rome: New Testament Cradles of Catholic Christianity* (London: Geoffrey Chapman, 1983). In their preface (p. ix) the authors concede that their attempt to set Matthew within the history of earliest Christianity in Antioch is speculative.

7. See esp. G. Downey, *A History of Antioch in Syria from Seleucus to the Arab Conquest* (Princeton: Princeton University Press, 1961).

8. Kilpatrick, *Origins,* 124–25. Four of the additional references to "city" are redactional, but are less striking than Kilpatrick implies: Matt. 8:34; 9:35; 21:10, 18. More significant are the references in 10:23 and 23:34 to the flight of the disciples from city to city.

9. F. W. Norris, "Artifacts from Antioch," in *Social History,* 249–50.

10. For a fuller discussion, which includes critical appraisal of alternative explanations of the evidence, see Graham N. Stanton, *A Gospel for a New People: Studies in Matthew* (Edinburgh: T. & T. Clark, 1992), 113–45.

11. See Jack Dean Kingsbury, "On Following Jesus: The 'Eager' Scribe and the 'Reluctant' Disciple (Matthew 8:18–22)," *NTS* 34 (1988): 45–59. RSV and NRSV translate 8:21 as "another of the (his) disciples," thereby implying that both men are scribes and are accepted by Jesus as true disciples. NEB and REB correctly translate "another man, one of his disciples," thereby avoiding any suggestion that he is a scribe.

12. NEB incorrectly translates Matt. 9:18 as "a president of the synagogue"; the error was spotted by the REB translators, who have "an official."

13. At 6:2 and 6:5 "hypocrites" are referred to, but 5:20 informs the reader that they are none other than "the scribes and Pharisees."

14. See also Ps. 135:21; 11Q Temple 29:7–10; *m. Sukkah* 5:4. In *TDNT* VII, art. "*synagoge,*" Wolfgang Schrage lists a number of rabbinic traditions that emphasize that God's *shekhina* is present in the synagogue as well as in the temple (824). In their present form these traditions may be no earlier than c. 300 C.E., but since synagogue and temple were considered even in the first century to be equivalent in many respects, it seems probable that God's *shekhina* was associated with the synagogue.

15. Matthew has modeled 12:6 on the "greater than Jonah" and "greater than Solomon" Q logia he uses at 12:41 and 42.

16. Adolf Schlatter, *Der Evangelist Matthäus: Seine Sprache, seine Ziel, seine Selbständigkeit,* 6th ed. (Stuttgart: Calwer, 1963), 396. Although Schlatter assumes that 12:6 is an authentic Jesus logion, he would have agreed that it also represents Matthew's view. See also J. A. T. Robinson, *Redating the New Testament* (London: SCM Press, 1976), 104.

17. For a careful discussion of these passages, see D. R. A. Hare, *The Theme of Jewish Persecution of Christians in the Gospel according to St. Matthew,* SNTSMS 6 (Cambridge: Cambridge University Press, 1967), 80–120. However, I am not persuaded that by the time Matthew wrote these threats belonged to history. See Stanton, *A Gospel for a New People,* 159–60.

18. See, e.g., L. M. White, "Shifting Sectarian Boundaries in Early Christianity," *BJRL* 70 (1988): 7–24, esp. 7–9. B. R. Wilson's writings have been influential. See esp. *Religion in Sociological Perspective* (Oxford: Oxford University Press, 1982); *The Social Dimensions of Sectarianism: Sects and New Religious Movements in Contemporary Society* (Oxford: Clarendon Press, 1990).

19. Günther Bornkamm, Gerhard Barth, and Heinz Joachim Held, *Tradition and Interpretation in Matthew,* Eng. trans. (London: SCM Press, 1963), 62–76, 159–64.

20. See Georg Strecker, *Der Weg der Gerechtigkeit,* FRLANT 82 (Göttingen: Vandenhoeck & Ruprecht, 1962), 137, n. 4. See also J. E. Davison, "Anomia and the Question of an Antinomian Polemic in Matthew," *JBL* 104 (1985): 617–35.

21. See John Barclay's careful discussion, "Mirror Reading a Polemical Letter: Galatians as a Test Case," *JSNT* 31 (1987): 73–93.

22. In *The Social Construction of Reality: A Treatise in the Sociology of Knowledge* (Harmondsworth: Penguin Books, 1966), 31, Peter L. Berger and Thomas Luckmann note that "not only children but adults 'forget' the legitimating answers. They must ever again be 'reminded.' In other words, the legitimating formulas must be repeated."

23. See Stanton, *A Gospel for a New People,* 169–91 and 278–81.

24. Whispers gradually become a trumpet blast. In 1:1 and 3:9 references to Abraham allude to his role as the father of many nations. The four women in the genealogy (1:2–17) were considered at the time to be non-Jews. The magi come from right outside Judaism (2:1–12). In 4:15 and 8:18–21 scripture is cited as divine sanction for a mission to the gentiles. See also 5:13–14; 10:18; 24:14; 26:13.

The Gospel of MARK

– 6 –

Toward a Narrative-Critical Understanding of Mark

Mark Allan Powell

In narrative criticism, it is in the encounter between the text and the reader that "meaning" arises. Problems of interpretation, therefore, are construed primarily, though not exclusively, in literary terms. To observe how narrative-critical method can provide fresh answers to old problems associated with Mark, one may take note of the results it yields when applied to such major questions as that of the messianic secret, the portrayal of the disciples, and the abrupt ending of Mark.

Although narrative criticism has been used effectively in the study of all four Gospels, it was first applied to the Gospel of Mark. Much of the work that led to the development of narrative criticism[1] was originally undertaken in the Society of Biblical Literature's Seminar on the Gospel of Mark.[2] Two studies by seminar members that proved especially significant were Norman Petersen's "'Point of View' in Mark's Narrative" and David Rhoads's "Narrative Criticism and the Gospel of Mark."[3] Petersen discovered that the preshaped materials that have been incorporated into the Gospel of Mark are provided with rhetorical consistency through the imposition of a consonant point of view: the perspective of the seemingly omniscient narrator whose voice guides the reader's interpretation. Thus, "Mark has produced an integral system, and for this reason it is necessary to read his Gospel as a narrative, not as a redaction."[4] Petersen's study relied heavily on the work of such scholars as M. H. Abrams, Wayne Booth, Seymour Chatman, Norman Friedman, J. M. Lotman, Percy Lubbock, and Boris Uspensky. If these names are unfamiliar to students of the Bible, they are well known in academies devoted to the criticism of secular literature. The novelty of Petersen's study was that he applied to Mark's Gospel concepts usually reserved for the study of modern fiction.

Rhoads continued along this same line. His paper attempted to enter the world of Mark's story and to investigate such narrative features as plot, characters, settings, narrator, point of view, and so on. The shift away from purely historical concerns to literary ones was even more evident in Rhoads's subsequent book, *Mark as Story,* which brought narrative criticism to the attention of a much wider audience.[5]

Today, narrative criticism has all but replaced redaction criticism in many circles as the dominant methodology for study of Mark's Gospel. Numerous book-length studies have appeared on various aspects of Mark's narrative,[6] and some scholars have even begun to move beyond narrative criticism to approach Mark from other literary-critical perspectives.[7]

Narrative critics do not repudiate the work of historical-critical scholarship. They simply find that narrative criticism answers different kinds of questions than those posed by traditional modes of historical criticism, questions that up to now have been neglected in biblical scholarship. The result is that when narrative critics and historical critics look at the same texts or themes within Mark's Gospel, they frequently arrive at different explanations of what is going on. To illustrate this, we will look at three of the most significant issues in traditional Markan scholarship and indicate how a narrative critic might interpret the data differently than a historical critic.

The Secrecy Theme

In Mark's Gospel, Jesus is frequently portrayed as trying to maintain an element of secrecy with regard to his own person and work. He prevents demons from revealing his identity (1:25, 34; 3:12), commands silence from his disciples (8:30; 9:9) and persons he heals (1:43–45; 5:43; 7:36; 8:26), and speaks to the crowd in cryptic language (4:10–13).

Traditional critics have sought historical explanations for this literary motif. The classic hypothesis of Wilhelm Wrede, for instance, supposes that the secrecy motif allows Mark to present a messianic portrait of Jesus that is not historically accurate.[8] If anyone says, "I knew Jesus and I don't remember him as ever saying or doing the things that you report," Mark can respond, "He said and did these things in secret." Other historical critics have offered different explanations, but their theories always attempt to explain the motif in terms of the relationship between Mark's Gospel and the historical events that it claims to describe.[9]

Narrative critics take an altogether different tack. If the secrecy theme is a literary motif, then it ought to be understood in terms of its literary function. The motif exemplifies a common device in literature (ancient and modern) whereby the narrator reveals significant information to the reader that is not known to characters within the story. In Mark's Gospel, the narrator announces in the first verse that Jesus Christ is "the Son of God." But although the Gospel's readers know this, the people who interact with Jesus in Mark's story do not.

The effect of the device is twofold. First, the shared knowledge bonds the readers of the Gospel to the narrator, encouraging them to adopt the point of view from which this story is told. Second, the element of mystery draws the readers into the story as they wonder whether any of the characters in the drama will come to know the truth. As the story progresses, Mark's readers observe that neither Jesus' exorcisms (1:27) nor his authoritative pronouncements (2:7) nor his miracles (4:41) nor his teaching (6:2–3) are sufficient to lead anyone to recognize that he is the Son of God. The secret is not revealed until Jesus dies on the cross (15:39). Thus Mark uses this literary device to make a theological point. The reader is expected to realize that Jesus' identity as Son of God cannot be truly understood apart from his death on the cross.[10]

Portrayal of the Disciples

Scholars have often noted that Mark's Gospel presents the disciples of Jesus in an unflattering light. The disciples are typically unperceptive (4:41; 6:51–52; 8:14–21) and inordinately concerned with honor and glory (8:32; 9:32–34; 10:35–41). Ultimately they reject Jesus through betrayal (14:10–11), desertion (14:50), and denial (14:66–72). Moreover, this faithlessness is described without redress, for Mark does not report any post-Easter meeting of reconciliation between the disciples and Jesus.

Redaction critics have explained Mark's literary characterization of the disciples as indicative of the evangelist's historical concerns. Theodore Weeden, for example, believes that Mark wanted to polemicize against the original disciples of Jesus because they became the founders of a Jerusalem-based Christianity that was at odds with his own Galilean gentile church.[11] Werner Kelber thinks Mark wanted to minimize the contributions of these individuals in order to play down the significance of their loss for the continuance of the church after their deaths.[12] In either case, the assumption is that Mark's intent is to affect the way his readers will understand the role that the actual disciples played in the historical development of Christianity.

Narrative critics focus on the literary function that Mark's characterization of the disciples serves within the narrative. Most narrative critics agree that the disciples are the characters in this story with whom the Gospel's readers are most likely to empathize.[13] In Mark 13:14, the narrator actually interrupts a speech being given by Jesus to his disciples to speak directly to the reader. Such a practice assumes that the reader is empathizing with the disciples at this point and is applying Jesus' words to his or her own situation. What is the effect of inviting empathy with characters who are portrayed so harshly? First, such empathy may enable the narrative's readers to identify their own inadequacies. Second, Mark's readers are expected to notice that, no matter how faithless Jesus' disciples are to him, he always remains faithful to them. He chose these disciples in the first place (1:16–20; 2:13–14; 3:13) and continues to regard them as his family (3:34–35). He enlightens them with special teaching (4:33–34; 7:17–23), empowers them for the tasks they are given (3:14–15; 6:7–13), and invites reconciliation when they forsake him (14:26–28; 16:7). Once again, Mark uses the literary discourse of his narrative to score a theological point. Mark's characterization of the disciples demonstrates that true discipleship depends on the adequacy of Christ rather than on the adequacy of the disciples themselves.

The Abrupt Ending

In our best manuscripts, the Gospel of Mark ends suddenly at 16:8. Mark reports that the women who were commissioned at the empty tomb to take the news of the resurrection to the disciples "said nothing to anyone, for they were afraid." Such an ending leaves much unresolved. Did the disciples ever hear about the resurrection, and if so, how did they respond? Though Mark's narrative contains hints of a postresurrection mission involving these disciples (10:39; 13:9–11), the narrative itself ends with the disciples seemingly lost in apostasy.

Most historical critics believe that Mark's Gospel did originally end with 16:8.[14] Often, Mark's reluctance to report a reconciliation between Jesus and his disciples is related to the historical reasons discussed above for his wanting to cast those disciples in a negative light.

Narrative critics view the ending of Mark's Gospel as a classic example of unresolved conflict in literature.[15] Conflict that is left unresolved within a narrative tends to impinge directly upon the readers. Readers expect resolution of conflict and, so, are frustrated by loose ends. They may wonder what they would have done had the conflict affected them the way it did the characters in the story. They may try out various scenarios in their own minds as to how the conflict could be resolved.

Another famous example of unresolved conflict in biblical literature is Jesus' story of "the prodigal son" in Luke 15:11–32. The story ends without telling us whether or not the older son accepts his father's invitation to attend the banquet being given in his brother's honor. Accordingly, the reader is left to ask, "What would I do if I were he?" Narrative critics usually read the abrupt ending to Mark in an analogous way. At the end of the narrative the reader is left to imagine how Jesus' faithless disciples will receive the message that goes out from the empty tomb and how they will respond when they do receive it. This open-ended conclusion invites the readers' participation in the drama. Mark's readers are expected to put themselves in the place of the disciples and to consider whether they have truly heard the Easter message and whether they have responded appropriately to it.

Conclusion

For historical criticism, the "meaning" of Mark's Gospel is usually held to lie in the significance that the author attributes to the historical events and persons whom his work describes. For narrative criticism, the "meaning" of Mark's Gospel is more likely to be understood in terms of the effect that the story is expected to have on its readers. Narrative criticism is not an ahistorical discipline, but the concerns of narrative criticism often do transcend questions of historicity. Narrative critics focus on the literary dynamics through which Mark's story is told rather than on the historical processes that preceded or led to its production. The disciplines of narrative criticism and historical criticism are not mutually exclusive and work at times in a complementary fashion. Still, narrative criticism is bringing a fresh perspective to Mark's Gospel that often offers literary explanations for matters that scholars have traditionally interpreted from a purely historical perspective.

NOTES

1. For a survey of this development, see Stephen D. Moore, *Literary Criticism and the Gospels: The Theoretical Challenge* (New Haven: Yale University Press, 1989), 1–68. On narrative-critical method, see Mark Allan Powell, *What Is Narrative Criticism?* GBS (Minneapolis: Fortress Press, 1990).

2. This group met from 1970 to 1980 under the leadership of, first, Norman Perrin and, then, Werner Kelber.

3. Norman R. Petersen, "'Point of View' in Mark's Narrative," *Semeia* 12 (1978): 87–121; David Rhoads, "Narrative Criticism and the Gospel of Mark," *JAAR* 60 (1982): 411–34.

4. Petersen, "Point of View," 118.

5. David Rhoads and Donald Michie, *Mark as Story: An Introduction to the Narrative of a Gospel* (Philadelphia: Fortress Press, 1989).

6. See, e.g., Jerry Camery-Hoggatt, *Irony in Mark's Gospel*, SNTSMS 72 (Cambridge: Cambridge University Press, 1992); Joanna Dewey, *Markan Public Debate: Literary Technique, Concentric Structure, and Theology in Mark 2:1–3:6*, SBLDS 48 (Chico, Calif.: Scholars Press, 1980); Jack Dean Kingsbury, *The*

Christology of Mark's Gospel (Philadelphia: Fortress Press, 1982); idem, *Conflict in Mark: Jesus, Authorities, Disciples* (Minneapolis: Fortress Press, 1989); Elizabeth Struthers Malbon, *Narrative Space and Mythic Meaning in Mark,* NVBS (San Francisco: Harper & Row, 1986); Mary Ann Tolbert, *Sowing the Gospel: Mark's World in Literary-Historical Perspective* (Minneapolis: Fortress Press, 1989); Dan O. Via, Jr., *The Ethics of Mark's Gospel in the Middle of Time* (Philadelphia: Fortress Press, 1985).

7. For applications of not only narrative criticism but also reader-response, deconstructive, feminist, and social criticism, see *Mark and Method: New Approaches in Biblical Studies,* ed. Janice Capel Anderson and Stephen D. Moore (Minneapolis: Fortress Press, 1992). For an in-depth reader-response approach, see Robert M. Fowler, *Let the Reader Understand: Reader-Response Criticism and the Gospel of Mark* (Minneapolis: Fortress Press, 1991).

8. Wilhelm Wrede, *Das Messiasgeheimnis in den Evangelien,* 3d ed. (Göttingen: Vandenhoeck & Ruprecht, 1963).

9. *The Messianic Secret,* IRT 1, ed. Christopher Tuckett (Philadelphia: Fortress Press, 1983).

10. For an in-depth study, see Kingsbury, *Christology,* esp. chap. 3.

11. Theodore Weeden, *Mark: Traditions in Conflict* (Philadelphia: Fortress Press, 1971).

12. Werner Kelber, *The Kingdom in Mark* (Philadelphia: Fortress Press, 1974).

13. For narrative-critical studies of the disciples, see Kingsbury, *Conflict,* 8–14, 89–117; Elizabeth Struthers Malbon, "Fallible Followers: Women and Men in the Gospel of Mark," *Semeia* 28 (1983): 29–48; Rhoads and Michie, *Mark,* 122–29; Robert C. Tannehill, "The Disciples in Mark: The Function of a Narrative Role," *JR* 57 (1977): 386–405. For a literary study more compatible with the Weeden/Kelber hypotheses, see Fowler, *Let the Reader Understand,* esp. 256–60.

14. For an opposing, minority view, see Robert H. Gundry, *Mark: A Commentary on His Apology for the Cross* (Grand Rapids: Wm. B. Eerdmans, 1993).

15. See, for example, Norman R. Petersen, "When Is the End Not the End?" *Int* 34 (1980): 151–66.

– 7 –

How the Gospel of Mark Builds Character

Mary Ann Tolbert

The Gospel of Mark was written to do something, to persuade or move people to action. All the characters in the Gospel are fashioned to promote this goal, and all of them, regardless of their traditional or historical roots, are also subordinate to this goal.

FOR MOST OF THE LAST CENTURY, the group of characters in the Gospel of Mark drawing the most attention and causing the most problems has clearly been the twelve disciples. Their path through the Gospel begins with immediate decisions to follow Jesus (1:16–20), includes a commissioning to preach and cast out demons (3:13–19) on the one hand and examples of hardness of heart and lack of understanding (6:52; 8:14–21) on the other, and apparently ends with betrayal (14:10–11, 43–46), flight (14:50–52), and denial (14:66–72). From the arguments of William Wrede[1] at the turn of the century to recent redaction-critical or literary investigations,[2] the characterization, role, and fate of the twelve disciples have formed the centerpiece of historical reconstructions of the Markan community,[3] evaluations of Markan theology,[4] and hypotheses concerning the gospel genre.[5] Yet, with all of this modern study, little consensus exists about how these Markan characters are to be understood or their role and fate evaluated.

The continuing debate over the twelve disciples in Mark may well stand as a dramatic instance of a common problem plaguing all modern readings of the Bible, even those of some trained biblical critics: Our modern textual practices often appear to be a poor "fit" for ancient or culturally distant texts. The source of the problem lies in the fact that the way we in contemporary society have learned to read stories is quite different from the way ancient people wrote, read, or heard them. Since no one is born knowing how to read and write, literate societies must teach members these skills according to their own distinctive understandings, and these understandings vary remarkably from culture to culture and from age to age. Yet, biblical scholars are only beginning to chart the gulf between modern Western modes of reading on the one hand and the styles used by the Greek-speaking authors of the New Testament some two thousand years ago on the other and to speculate about the differences those styles might suggest for our interpretations of the Gospels.[6]

Nowhere is this gulf between modern and ancient conventions of reading and writing more crucial than in the function and evaluation of characters. By exploring how ancient Greek and Roman writers fashioned characters and how they viewed the relationship of characters to the plot and to the audience, it may be possible to understand in an entirely new light the nature and purpose of all the Markan characters, including those problematic disciples.

Ancient Character Building

The word "character" comes from the Greek *charassein,* which originally meant to mark on wood or to stamp an impression on a blank coin. It consistently bears that connotation from its entry into Greek literature in the plays of Aeschylus to its use in the rhetorical handbooks of the first century B.C.E. and later. Like individual coins engraved with common inscriptions, the stock "characters" of Greek drama and the "styles" adopted by the rhetoricians were typical strategies stamped on individual plots or circumstances. Moreover, in the *Poetics,* Aristotle discusses characters in tragedy under the rubric of *ethos,* meaning the custom or habitual pattern of a person's life. Both Greek terms underscore the typological nature of all character depiction in ancient writing.

Ancient characters existed as a "mouthpiece for the typical,"[7] and this usage was as true for biography as it was for drama. Ancient biographical writing was interested in the individual "as an exemplar of general, ethical qualities."[8] Thus, one might describe ancient characterization as the practice of particularizing the universal or individualizing the general. Furthermore, it is this intentional blending of the typical with the individual that distinguishes ancient characters from both the profoundly inward, psychological, realistic characters of modern writing and also the personified abstractions of later medieval allegorical writing.[9] The thirty character studies composed by Aristotle's student Theophrastus in 319 B.C.E., so popular with later rhetoricians and playwrights, provides a good illustration of the method. Each study presented the typical, recognizable actions and words of a social or moral category (the Coward, the Boor, the Flatterer, etc.), but each subject was portrayed as an individual person, located in a particular setting.

The effect on the audience of such characterization was intended to be quite different, as might be expected, from our modern preoccupation with being able to "identify" with the characters, a profoundly postromantic style of reading[10] and one that has figured prominently in debates over the Markan disciples. For writers of the Greco-Roman period, communicating their message effectively to the audience was the primary goal. Consequently, ancient characters, rather than being preeminent as they often are in modern narratives, were subordinate to the overall plot or action. Indeed, Aristotle's famous comment in the *Poetics* that tragedy could exist without characters but not without plot seems absurd to modern readers for whom character is everything. But for Aristotle, the communication of the universals of human life and fate could certainly be conceived without the particularized coloring provided by characterization. The action might require agents, but it did not necessarily need characters.[11] However, the use of individualized characters could make the communication more effective, if it, for example, clarified for the audience what universal verities might lie behind particular words and acts observed in daily life. The concern, then, was not whether the simple potter could "identify" with Oedipus the king but whether even the potter could recognize the ambiguity of fate and suffering in human life that Oedipus's story illustrates.

The ancients did not share our disdain of "mere rhetoric"; rather, language for them was a form of real power, a force acting upon and shaping the world. All ancient writing was rhetorical in the sense that it was an attempt to persuade or move people to action. The effective use of language was, indeed, the serious business of every writer, whether historian, playwright, popular novelist, biographer, or rhetorician. The author of the Gospel of Mark was no exception to this cultural rule. The Gospel was written to do something, to persuade or move people to action. All the characters in the Gospel are fashioned to promote that goal, and all of them, regardless of their traditional or historical roots, are also subordinated to that goal, for such an understanding of character building forms the horizon of writing, reading, and hearing in which the author and first audiences of the Gospel lived. But what is the overall goal or message that the Gospel of Mark communicates and all the characters strive to advance?

Mark's Good News

Mark's "good news" is announced in the very first lines of the narrative: As predicted in the writings of Isaiah the prophet, God has sent Jesus the Messiah, God's Son, as a messenger to proclaim to each person the way to God's coming kingdom.[12] Such introductory prologues alerted the ancient hearer to the main contours of the following story, a needed element since reading in the Greco-Roman world was done aloud for the benefit of the illiterate majority of society (and the majority of early Christians). The demands of the ear for repetition and summary were of paramount concern in all ancient writing and encouraged, in addition to prologues, other periodic summaries at crucial points within the narrative for the listener to use in orienting himself or herself to the ongoing plot.[13] For Mark, the two long parables of the Gospel, the Sower (4:3–9, 14–20) and the Tenants (12:1–12), perform this function admirably because they draw the listener's notice by their distinctive form and also prove easy to remember (the parable of the Sower is actually told twice to aid the hearer's memory) so that they can provide continuing orientation as the audience hears more of the story.

In the parable of the Tenants, Jesus tells the story of a lovingly created vineyard, whose owner has let it out to tenants and has gone off to a distant place. When the owner sends servants to ask for the produce that is rightfully his, the tenants refuse, mistreating and even killing the messengers. Finally, the owner sends the last messenger, his only son, expecting that the tenants will revere him and repent. Instead when the tenants recognize this messenger as the heir, they kill him, expecting that the vineyard will now belong to them. Jesus ends the story by asking what can the lord of the vineyard do except come and destroy the evil tenants and then give the vineyard to others. For an ancient audience (and even a modern one), this parable is easily recognizable as an allegory summarizing the position of Jesus, the beloved son (see 1:11; 9:7) and final messenger, in opposition to the present usurpers of God's creation, the Jerusalem religious authorities (12:12).

However, for the first hearers of the Gospel, who were attuned to the styles and conventions of ancient writing, the parable of the Tenants would have encompassed a much broader range of reference than just the relationship of Jesus to the Jerusalem leaders, for it also gives a brief summary of the history of God's dealing with humanity, the purpose of Jesus' mission, its failure, and its final outcome. While God lovingly created a good world, it now suffers in the grasp of evil authorities. God has sent many prophets through the centuries to demand the return of fruitful productivity but to no avail. Jesus' message is no different from that of those sent before him; his uniqueness lies in his identity as the heir and in his position as the last messenger to be sent. Mark's "good news" resides in the fact that, one way or another, the sending out of Jesus will bring the kingdom of God in full measure, as Jesus himself indicates by his very first words in the Gospel: "The time is fulfilled and the kingdom of God is at hand; repent and believe in the gospel" (1:15). If the people repent, God's kingdom will be restored, and if they do not, it will still be restored because God will have no choice but to destroy the present authorities and give the vineyard to the faithful.

Ultimately, Jesus' message is an apocalyptic one, as is the message of the Gospel of Mark as a whole. The world will be decimated because, instead of revering the Son, as God had hoped, it murdered him. With that act, the present generation proclaims its unshakable commitment to evil. If even God's own beloved child cannot convince most of humanity to repent, nothing and no one can. God's only choice, as Jesus confirms at the close of the parable, is to destroy this irredeemably corrupt world. The failure of Jesus' mission and his crucifixion becomes the final justification for the apocalyptic end of the age, an end that only the faithful elect who endure will survive (13:9–27).

But why is Jesus' mission, like those of the prophets before him, so unsuccessful? The major moral problem the Gospel of Mark faces and perhaps one troubling many early Christians is why so few people are willing to follow the way of Jesus. If Jesus is truly the Messiah, why are there not more who repent and believe? The story constructed by the author of Mark not only proclaims the good news of God's coming kingdom but also attempts to demonstrate why, because of the faithlessness and hard-heartedness of most of humanity, it must come by apocalyptic means. Mark summarizes, for the benefit of the listening audience, the problematic responses of humanity to the message of Jesus in the other long parable of the Gospel, the Sower (4:3–9, 14–20), and then dramatizes those responses through the characterization of all the groups and individuals around Jesus throughout the narrative. As in ancient characterization generally, each group is fashioned by blending social and historical particulars with the universal, typological patterns of response to the word that the parable of the Sower outlines.

The parable of the Sower (4:3–9) relates the failures and success of a sower sowing seed on four different types of earth, which Jesus explains allegorically (4:14–20) as the responses to hearing the word of four different types of people. Three of the four kinds of responses are unproductive, while only one of the four is productive, although impressively so. If three-quarters of those who hear the message of Jesus finally reject it and prove unfruitful, the failure of Jesus' mission — and those of the prophets before him — becomes more understandable. But what human traits and actions accompany these varying responses to the words of Jesus? The particular characterizations of the people and groups around Jesus in the narrative supply the author's answer to that question.

The Seed on the Path

In the parable of the Sower, the first ground on which the seed is sown is that of the path. There the earth is so hard that the seed stays on the surface and birds come and eat it (4:4); Jesus interprets this action as Satan's coming to take away the Word (4:15). In the Gospel of Mark, the group of characters who obviously exemplify this response to Jesus' word are his religious opponents, the scribes, Pharisees, chief priests, and other Jerusalem religious leaders. Mark makes little distinction among these historically diverse factions. He even coins a category called "the Herodians" (3:6, probably meaning those influenced by Herod), to which there is no other reference in antiquity, and speaks of the peculiar "scribes of the Pharisees" (2:16), which later textual emendators helpfully altered to "scribes *and* the Pharisees." The only special information the author presents about these groups is the somewhat confused discussion of purity practices in 7:3–4 and the Sadducees' disbelief in resurrection (12:18), both elements that the author evidently thought the listening audience would not know.

What is important to the author about these opponents, and thus what is stressed in their characterization, is their monolithically negative response to Jesus. The first appearance of any members of the group occurs in the episode of the healing of the paralytic in 2:1–12; there the scribes respond to Jesus' healing words to the paralytic with outrage and the charge of blasphemy: "Why does this man speak thus? It is blasphemy!" (2:7). By 3:6, the Pharisees and Herodians are plotting to kill Jesus, and the plot comes to fruition in 14:64 when the chief priest and the entire Jerusalem council condemn him as deserving death for his blasphemy. From first to last they reject Jesus' healing, forgiving word in favor of their own views and prerogatives and their own conceptions of God's laws (7:6–13; 12:38–40).

The Seed on Rocky Ground

The second type of ground upon which seed is sown is described as "rocky ground," where the seed springs up immediately; but because it has little root, it withers when the sun comes up (4:5–6). This complex response is interpreted by Jesus as those who accept the Word immediately with joy, but who stumble away when persecutions arise on account of the Word (4:16–17). In the Gospel of Mark, one group obviously illustrates this change-of-heart response: those troublesome twelve disciples. At the outset, the call stories for Simon, Andrew, James, and John (1:16–20) emphasize—by the repetition of one of Mark's favorite words, "immediately"—the haste with which the disciples follow Jesus.

Although there are a few early negative hints, the disciples as a group are characterized as basically positive figures through Jesus' healing mission (6:7–13).

The primary negative foreshadowings occur in chapter 3, when Jesus selects, from an evidently larger group of disciples, twelve specific ones to be with him, to preach, and to cast out demons. To three of those twelve, Simon, James, and John, he gives special "nicknames." Simon's new name, used exclusively for him from 3:16 to the end of the Gospel (except at 14:37, where Jesus tries to summon the faithful Simon once again) is Peter, in Greek *petros,* "rock." Although the author of the Gospel of Matthew will create a pun on Peter's name to indicate his authority among the disciples as the "rock" upon whom the church will be built (Matt. 16:18), Matthew may, in this case, have created that pun mainly as a defense against the pun Mark sets up. Mark calls Simon "rock" for the first time in 3:16 and then a short while later, in 4:5, introduces the "rocky ground" (*petrōdes*), in which the seed begins to grow and then fails during persecutions. Matthew's rock of the church is Mark's rocky ground, the hard-hearted disciple. Every time Peter's name is used throughout the Gospel of Mark, the listening audience is reminded of that shallow ground that cannot withstand trouble. One other blatant warning of the twelve's eventual failure is also sounded in the commissioning: the last named disciple, Judas Iscariot, is described as the one "who betrayed him" (3:19).

The earlier hints concerning the twelve's change of heart are realized dramatically following chapter 6 in their confrontations with Jesus and their inability to understand his words or emulate his actions. Their hearts are hardened (6:52); they lack understanding (8:21); they challenge Jesus' teachings (8:32–33); they cannot heal (9:18–19) but rebuke those who can (9:38–39); and they want glory where Jesus foretells suffering (10:33–45). In the passion narrative, when active persecution finally arrives, Mark epitomizes the type of reversal the disciples exemplify in two striking scenes: their flight (14:50–52) and Peter's denial (14:66–72). In 1:20, James and John are so eager to follow Jesus that they desert (*aphentes*) their father in the boat; then at Jesus' arrest, in a sharply ironic retreat, all the disciples desert (*aphentes*) Jesus and flee (14:50). Moreover, in 8:29, Peter is the first human character in the Gospel to confess Jesus as the Messiah (the listening audience has known this fact since 1:1, and the voice from heaven and various demons have confirmed it several times). Yet, it is this same Peter who, standing outside the chief priest's residence, denies with an oath that he knows who Jesus is — at the same moment that Jesus, inside, is proclaiming, "I am," to the chief priest's suggestion that he is the Messiah, "the Son of the Blessed" (14:61).

Mark's fashioning the twelve disciples as representatives of the rocky-ground type of response suggests that even those who appear faithful at first may not be so in the end. Along the same lines, chapter 13 of the Gospel suggests that some within the Christian community, in the author's opinion, are attempting to lead others astray (13:5–6, 21–22). That such a response to the Word forms one of the four general types lends a certain inevitability to defections among Christians and Christian leaders. Actually, in Mark's worldview, those aspiring to be leaders, whether among Jesus' followers or among his opponents, seem especially vulnerable to failing responses to the Word. Their desire for authority, fame, and glory makes Jesus' message of suffering, hatred by the world, and death particularly unappealing. "Fear" is the word most often contrasted to faith in the Gospel of Mark (4:40–41; 5:15, 36; 6:50), and given that faith in the Word Jesus proclaims leads to opposition, persecution, the cross, and death, fear for one's life or even for one's privileges and comfort would undoubtedly hinder accepting that Word. Moreover, both the disciples (4:41; 6:50; 10:32) and the Jerusalem leaders (11:18; 12:12) are firmly associated with fear.

Lastly, in a Gospel so full of human failure, it is appropriate, if profoundly disappointing, that fear has the final say. When the twelve male disciples have betrayed, fled, and denied Jesus, a previously unknown group is introduced, women followers from Galilee (15:40–41). They remain faithful to Jesus where the male disciples have failed; they watch the crucifixion and burial and go to the tomb with oils to anoint him (15:42–16:8). However, when they are commissioned — like the twelve before them — to go and tell the news of the resurrection, once again it is not faith but fear that determines the outcome: They "fled from the tomb; for trembling and astonishment had come upon them; and they said nothing to anyone, for they were afraid" (16:8).

The Seed among Thorns

In the parable of the Sower, the third type of ground upon which the seed falls is full of thorns, and although the seed begins to grow, the weeds finally choke it out (4:7); this almost productive response dies out because the cares of the world, joy in riches, and desire for other things overpower the Word (4:18–19). Mark does not present many examples of this type of response, which may suggest the scarcity of these particular temptations among the intended audience. However, three characters are molded to illustrate this reaction, the most noticeable being the rich man of 10:17–22. After learning that the man has kept all the commandments from his youth, Jesus responds to him in an extraordinary way: "And Jesus, looking upon him, loved him" (10:21). No disciple has drawn such an emotion from Jesus; surely this man is fertile ground.

However, when Jesus tells him to sell his goods and follow him, the man leaves sorrowfully; his joy in riches overwhelms the words of Jesus.

Two other characters with strong historical roots are similarly shaped by the author: Herod and Pilate. Mark depicts Herod favorably as holding John the Baptist in what might be described as protective custody to avert the murderous designs of Herodias (6:14–29). All goes well until Herod's birthday banquet, in which he promises Herodias's daughter anything she wishes because her dancing has pleased him. When the girl, at her mother's prompting, asks for the head of John, Herod is dismayed, but he does not want to go back on his word in front of his guests — the desire for other things chokes out the Word he was gladly hearing. Pilate is also initially portrayed positively (15:1–15), since he recognizes Jesus' innocence and the chief priests' envy and attempts to release Jesus. However, he, too, finally subordinates his better instincts to his desire to keep the crowds peaceful by ordering Jesus' crucifixion — the cares of the world crush out the truth.

The Seed on the Good Earth

The final ground upon which seeds fall in the parable of the Sower is good, and this brings forth an extraordinary yield (4:8); Jesus interprets this response as people who accept the Word and bear miraculous fruit (4:20). Those in the Gospel who react positively to the words of Jesus and bear the fruits of their faith for all to see are the ones who are healed. These supplicants for healing are not really a group but generally come as anonymous individuals from high (5:22–23) and low (10:46–52) stations in life, from among Jews (1:40–45) and gentiles (7:25–30), both men (8:22–26) and women (5:25–34). What they have in common is their faith that Jesus can change their lives (2:5; 5:34, 36; 10:52); it is a faith that drives away fear and empowers healing. Indeed, where Jesus finds no faith, he can do no healing (6:5–6). The fruits that they bear are not only a return to the created wholeness of their being but also the active and successful preaching of the Word to others (1:45; 2:12; 5:19–20), which Jesus designates as the primary human act needed to hasten the arrival of the kingdom (13:10).

Unlike either the twelve or the religious leaders, those healed do not desire honor, fame, power, or glory; instead, they mostly arise anonymously out of the crowds, often act unconventionally (5:27–28; 7:27–30; 10:47–48), and then go on their way, proclaiming the gospel to others. Just before the entry into Jerusalem, Mark epitomizes this productive response to the Word in the episode of blind Bartimaeus (10:46–52), the last person in the Gospel to be healed. Like other supplicants for healing, Bartimaeus initiates the action, crying out to the passing Jesus, and has this act of faith rewarded by the restoration of his sight. However, unlike the others who are healed but like the disciples, Bartimaeus is called by Jesus and then follows him on the way. So, for Mark, faith for healing becomes faith for discipleship.

The Sower and the Heir

Jesus is the central character of Mark's Gospel, actively appearing in every episode except the death of John the Baptist (6:14–29) and his own death and burial (15:40–16:8). But since Mark lacks the elaborate birth stories and resurrection appearance stories found in Matthew and Luke, it emphasizes the message of Jesus far more than the person of Jesus. For Mark, Jesus is the divine Son who is sent out by God to bring the message of the coming near of God's kingdom. The first ten chapters of the Gospel recount the spreading of this Word and the various reactions to it. Unlike his own disciples but like those healed, Jesus tries to avoid the fame of having his name and power made known (1:44; 3:12; 5:45) but without success; he refuses to lord it over those he leads (10:42–45); he spurns riches (10:25–27); and he rejects power (9:35–37). He exemplifies by his actions what he teaches with his words: The leader of all must be the servant of all.

While Jesus' message is similar to that of the prophets, Jesus himself is unique, for he is the heir of God's kingdom. In chapters 11–16 of the Gospel, it is this aspect of Jesus' identity that is paramount. In his controversies with the Jerusalem religious leaders, Jesus shows again and again that he is the true master of scripture (12:24–27, 35–37), the final arbiter of tradition (12:28–34), and the genuine assessor of religious ritual (12:38–44). He is the heir; they are merely usurpers. In his trial and crucifixion, Jesus not only provides the necessary condition for the apocalyptic end but also illustrates through his behavior how all of his followers must face persecution in this short but painful time before the coming of the kingdom in glory (13:9–13). He endures to the bitter end as Peter and the twelve cannot. However, God's promises do not fail as promises from human beings often do, and the bitter end turns out not to be an end at all but rather a resurrection of life and hope. The Gospel of Mark may fashion a human tragedy, but it just as deftly designs a divine comedy.

NOTES

1. William Wrede, *Das Messiasgeheimnis in den Evangelien* (Göttingen: Vandenhoeck & Ruprecht, 1901), Eng. trans., *The Messianic Secret,* trans. J. C. Greig (Greenwood, S.C.: Attic Press, 1971).

2. See, e.g., Robert Tannehill, "The Disciples in Mark: The Function of a Narrative Role," *JR* 57 (1977): 386–405; Elizabeth S. Malbon, "Fallible Followers: Women and Men in the Gospel of Mark," *Semeia* 28 (1983): 29–48; David Rhoads and Donald Michie, *Mark as Story: An Introduction to the Narrative of a Gospel* (Philadelphia: Fortress Press, 1982); and Ernest Best, *Mark: The Gospel as Story* (Edinburgh: T. & T. Clark, 1983).

3. See, e.g., Theodore J. Weeden, *Mark — Traditions in Conflict* (Philadelphia: Fortress Press, 1971), and Werner Kelber, *Mark's Story of Jesus* (Philadelphia: Fortress Press, 1979).

4. See, e.g., John R. Donahue, *The Theology and Setting of Discipleship in the Gospel of Mark* (Milwaukee: Marquette University Press, 1983), and Jack Dean Kingsbury, *The Christology of Mark's Gospel* (Philadelphia: Fortress Press, 1983).

5. See, e.g., Vernon Robbins, *Jesus the Teacher: A Socio-Rhetorical Interpretation of Mark* (Philadelphia: Fortress Press, 1984).

6. Recent attempts to chart this gulf in different ways may be found in John A. Darr, *On Character Building: The Reader and the Rhetoric Characterization in Luke-Acts* (Louisville: Westminster/John Knox Press, 1992); Werner Kelber, *The Oral and the Written Gospel: The Hermeneutics of Speaking and Writing in the Synoptic Tradition, Mark, Paul, and Q* (Philadelphia: Fortress Press, 1983); and Mary Ann Tolbert, *Sowing the Gospel: Mark's World in Literary-Historical Perspective* (Minneapolis: Fortress Press, 1989). For a recent, thorough exploration of how modern readers read Mark that recognizes this gulf but does not attempt to explore it, see Robert M. Fowler, *Let the Reader Understand: Reader-Response Criticism and the Gospel of Mark* (Minneapolis: Fortress Press, 1991), esp. 48–52.

7. Warren Ginsberg, *The Cast of Character: The Representation of Personality in Ancient and Medieval Literature* (Toronto: University of Toronto Press, 1983), 3. For more information on the typical nature of ancient characterization, see also Edward Burns, *Character: Acting and Being on the Pre-Modern Stage* (New York: St. Martin's Press, 1990), 18–38; Stephen Halliwell, "Traditional Greek Conceptions of Character" in *Characterization and Individuality in Greek Literature,* ed. C. Pelling (Oxford: Clarendon Press, 1990), 32–59; and Warren D. Anderson, *Theophrastus: The Character Sketches* (Kent, Ohio: Kent University Press, 1970), xi–xxxii.

8. Halliwell, "Traditional Greek Conceptions of Character," 56.

9. The blending of individual and general makes such terms as E. M. Forster's "flat" and "round" characters, drawn from the reading of English novels (as Forster plainly states in his introduction to *Aspects of the Novel* [New York: Harcourt, Brace & World, 1927], 18–21, 103–18), of very limited value in analyzing ancient characters, as some biblical critics unfortunately continue to do (see, e.g., Elizabeth S. Malbon, "Narrative Criticism: How Does the Story

Mean?" in *Mark and Method: New Approaches in Biblical Studies,* ed. J. C. Anderson and S. Moore [Minneapolis: Fortress Press, 1992], 29). Greek and Roman characters are neither flat nor round in Forster's sense; they manifest a totally different form of characterization.

10. See the discussion in Burns, *Character,* 6–15.

11. For further discussion of ancient rhetoric and characterization, see Tolbert, *Sowing the Gospel,* 41–79.

12. For Mark, the Isaiah quotation clearly refers to Jesus, since, among other things, Jesus is the only character introduced into the story before the quotation is given. Both Matthew and Luke alter the location of this quotation, so that it is made to refer to John the Baptist. For a full articulation of this argument, see Tolbert, *Sowing the Gospel,* 239–48.

13. For the structure of the Gospel and the importance of the prologue and later summary sections, see ibid., 90–126.

– 8 –

Losing Life for Others in the Face of Death

MARK'S STANDARDS OF JUDGMENT

David Rhoads

An examination of the standards of judgment in Mark's Gospel — those values and beliefs that implicitly govern the narrative world — reveals that Mark is a tightly woven narrative reflecting two contrasting ways of life: that of "saving one's life out of fear," and that of "losing one's life for others out of faith."

ONE WAY TO UNDERSTAND the purpose of the Gospel of Mark is to discern the standards of judgment for human behavior that govern the narrative.[1] The standards of judgment are the values and beliefs implicit in the narrative world by which readers are led to judge the characters and the events.[2] The narrator does not "tell" us what these standards are. Rather, the narrative "shows" us these standards in the depictions of characters and the description of events.

Thus, we infer the standards of judgment from features of Mark's narrative, such as evaluative comments by the narrator, the teachings of Jesus, the actions and fate of the characters, the words of God, quotations from scripture, and so on. From these, we can see the positive standards that the narrative promotes as well as the negative standards that the narrative condemns. Highlighting both positive and negative standards is illuminating. We see Mark's narrative condemning the standards opposite from those it approves. From the standards of judgment, we get a picture of the backbone and purpose of the Gospel.

The Two Ways: Saving One's Life Out of Fear or Losing One's Life for Others

A study of standards of judgment shows that the Gospel of Mark is a tightly woven narrative reflecting two contrasting ways of life. At one point in the narrative, Jesus rebukes Peter, saying: "Get behind me, Satan, because you are not thinking the things of God but the things of humans" (8:33). Here is a contrast between two sets of values, two orientations to life: what God wills for people and what people want for themselves.

The Markan Jesus states these contrasting standards at the beginning of the journey to Jerusalem (8:22–10:52). On the way there, Jesus elaborates these standards in teaching to his disciples. The disciples resist Jesus at every point, even though they eventually accept his teachings. So the journey becomes a clash of values between Jesus who teaches what God wills for people and the disciples who exemplify what people want for themselves. On the way, Jesus prophesies three times to the disciples about his impending persecution and death (8:31–9:1; 9:30–50; 10:32–45). After each prophecy, the disciples show that they do not understand or accept his teaching. After each of these reactions, Jesus explains to his disciples the values of the rule of God that underlie his words and actions.

The teachings that follow these three prophecies on the way to Jerusalem are the core standards of Mark's Gospel. After the first prophecy, Jesus says: "Those who want to save their lives will lose them, but whoever will lose their lives for me and the good news will save them" (8:35). After the second prophecy, Jesus teaches: "If anyone wants to be great among you, that person is to be least of all and everyone's servant" (9:35). After the third prophecy, Jesus says: "Whoever wants to be great among you will be your servant, and whoever wants to be most important is to be everyone's slave. For even the son of humanity came not to be served but to serve and to give his life a ransom for many" (10:43–45).

Each of these teachings involves a contrast between acquisition (saving) and relinquishment (losing).[3] People who follow the world's standards seek to acquire status and power for themselves. This way of life is motivated by fear. By contrast, people who follow Jesus' standards receive the blessings of the kingdom and are willing to relinquish life, status, and power in order to bring the good news of this kingdom to others. This way of life is made possible by faith. Thus, for Mark, the two ways of life are "saving one's life out of fear" or "losing one's life for others out of faith." The chart on the following page shows the characteristic Markan standards of these two ways.

Mark's narrative consistently promotes the one way and condemns the other.[4] For example, the characters in Mark's narrative embody one or the other of these two ways.[5] Jesus embodies "what God wills for people." He heals, drives out demons, pardons sins, and dies for this mission. Also, the minor characters who come to Jesus for healing often exemplify "the things of God." They have faith and are willing to serve

What People Want for Themselves	What God Wants for People
self-centered	other-centered
save one's own life	lose one's life for the good news
acquire the world	give up possessions
be great	be least
lord over others	be servant to all
be anxious	have faith
fear	courage
harming others	saving others
loyalty to self	loyalty to God for the world

and to be least. By contrast, the authorities embody "what people want" in order to aggrandize themselves at the expense of others. They are afraid and seek to save their honor and to maintain their positions of power.[6] Finally, the disciples vacillate between the two ways. They are torn between following Jesus in service to the good news and following Jesus in order to acquire status and power for themselves. In these characterizations, Mark promotes his values and beliefs by positive and by negative examples.

The Way of the World: The Fearful Saving of Self

The negative standards reflect Mark's view of human sinfulness, namely, that people are self-oriented and self-serving. People want to "save their lives" (8:35), to "acquire the world" (8:36), to "be great" (9:35), and to "exert authority over" or to "lord over" people (10:43–44).

As indicated, the authorities exemplify this way of life.[7] They have status, power, and security, and they are bent on maintaining them. They have taken control of the vineyard of Israel for themselves and do not bear the fruit on behalf of Israel's people, which God requires of them (12:1–12). They love their importance and abuse their power: They love to be greeted in the markets; they want the best seats in the synagogue and at the banquets; and they devour the houses of widows (12:38–40). At the crucifixion, they ridicule Jesus because he "cannot save himself" (15:31).

For Mark, the quest to maintain power and status is motivated by fear (11:18). The Jewish and gentile authorities are afraid. Herod fears John the Baptist (6:20). Pilate defers to the crowd (15:15). The Jewish authorities fear Jesus' popularity (15:10). They fear losing their position as a result of Jesus' activity (12:7), and they fear losing face with the crowds (6:26; 12:12). As we shall see, such fear is the opposite of faith, which brings courage in the face of threat and loss.

To protect their power and status, the authorities destroy others. Although Herod considers John the Baptist to be a righteous man, he nevertheless executes John because he does not want to break his oath to Herodias's daughter for fear of losing face before "the most important" and "the greatest" people of Galilee (6:26). Although Pilate knows that Jesus is innocent and that the high priests have handed him over out of envy, he nevertheless executes Jesus in order to "do the satisfactory thing" for the crowd (15:15). Also, the Jewish leaders seek to trap, discredit, and destroy Jesus. They bend the law, arrest Jesus surreptitiously (14:7), suborn witnesses (14:55), hold a kangaroo court (15:3), and stir up the crowd to release Barabbas (15:11) in order to maintain their status and their authority over the people.

The disciples often reflect the same values. Although the disciples leave all to follow Jesus, they desire status and power from following Jesus. Early on, the disciples are enamored of the crowds (1:37). On the journey to Jerusalem, they argue about who is greatest among them (9:33–34). James and John ask if they can sit on the right and left of Jesus in his glory in the age to come (10:35–40). When the other ten disciples find out about this, they become angry (10:41). The disciples have followed Jesus in the hope of acquiring glory and power.

So, too, are the disciples fearful. They are afraid in the storm on the lake (4:40). They are anxious about how to feed people in the desert (6:34–37; 8:4). They are afraid to ask Jesus about his death (9:34). They betray, flee, or deny Jesus, presumably in order to save themselves. Fear for themselves underlies their resistance to understanding, their lack of faith, and their failure to be faithful to the end.

The disciples harm others and generate dissension in their quest to acquire power and status. They argue with one another about who is greatest (9:33; 10:41); they stop an exorcist from driving out demons in Jesus' name (9:38); they rebuke the people who bring little children to Jesus for a blessing (10:13); and they vie for honors from Jesus (10:35–45). In response to Jesus' predictions of death, they seek to secure themselves. They become arrogant, exclusive, competitive, and domineering.

Mark's Gospel condemns the self-oriented quest for security, status, and power as contrary to what God wants for people. People who embrace these standards are destructive of others and ultimately of themselves. In Mark's view, the ultimate consequence of a destructive life is to incur God's judgment against them (9:42–48; 12:40; 14:62).

The Vision for Life: The Courage to Risk for Others

Characters who live the standards of the rule of God are willing to "lose their life for Jesus and the good news" (8:35), to "be least of all and everyone's servant" (9:35), and to "be everyone's slave" (10:43–45). These metaphors represent what God wills for people. While the Jewish leaders think that acquiring status and power over others makes them great, Jesus considers the truly great human being to be one who gives up the status and power that one has, or feels entitled to, on behalf of those with less power and status.

In Mark, Jesus lifts up particular metaphors as paradigms of these standards. The metaphor for being least is a child or a house servant (9:35–37). The metaphor for the use of power is a servant or slave (10:44). The role of "slave" exists to benefit others and offers no opportunity to use power over others for self-aggrandizement. These models of greatness are a contrast to the leaders of the gentile nations who lord over people (10:42–43). The world is turned upside down, so that the roles on the bottom become the moral paradigms for all human relations. Jesus does not give these models to the slaves or the women or the children (people forced to serve). Rather, Jesus gives these models of relinquishment to people who have status or power and want to maintain it (the authorities) and to people who do not have status or power but who want to acquire it for themselves (the disciples).

Minor characters embody these positive standards of judgment. Suppliants serve by bringing others for healing (2:3; 7:32; 8:22) or by coming on behalf of a relative (5:23; 7:26). The Syro-Phoenician woman is least by being willing to accept Jesus' designation of her as a little dog in order to get her daughter healed (7:28). The poor widow gives out of her need, "her whole living" (12:41–44). An unnamed woman uses expensive ointment to anoint Jesus ahead of time for his burial (14:3–9). Joseph of Arimathea takes courage and approaches Pilate for the right to bury Jesus (15:43). Women go to anoint Jesus' body at the grave (16:1–3).

The disciples sometimes exemplify these standards. They relinquish their homes, families, and occupations to follow Jesus in the service of the good news (1:14–20; 10:28–29). They serve Jesus in many ways: They protect him from the crowds (3:9), provide a boat for him (4:1), distribute food in the desert (6:34–44; 8:1–10), obtain a donkey (11:1–8), and prepare the passover meal (14:12–16). Also, as "fishers for people," they go from village to village without money, food, or extra clothes in order to drive out demons and anoint the sick for healing (6:7–13). They continue following Jesus until confronted with death.

Jesus is the primary example of the standards of the kingdom. He serves people in his healings and preaching without seeking acclamation for himself (e.g., 1:43; 5:34). He speaks the truth of God whether people favor him or reject him (12:14). He refuses to lord over others. As a result, he becomes a victim of those whom he condemns. In his execution, Jesus manifests the standards of the rule of God (15:1–37): He is least in the society as a human being ridiculed and rejected; he has relinquished power over anyone; and he loses his life in the service of bringing good news to the world. At Gethsemane, Jesus is afraid to die, but his prayer reveals the orientation of his life — "not what I want but what you want" (14:36). Jesus is the opposite of self-oriented. He is God-centered for others.

In Mark, God wills all the blessings of the kingdom for Jesus and his followers. Yet God also wills for people to suffer loss and persecution. This Markan view of suffering calls for clarification. First, Mark does not value suffering or loss for its own sake.[8] Rather, Jesus tells the disciples to pray that persecution not come (14:36). Second, in Mark's narrative, God does not will suffering due to illness, disability, demonic possession, and the destructive forces of nature. The extensive Markan healings, exorcisms, and nature miracles demonstrate this. Therefore, the suffering that comes from such nonhuman oppression is never "the cross" that Jesus calls people to bear.

Finally, God does not call people to suffer on behalf of people in a position of power over them. Jesus does not tell slaves that enforced service is among the standards of the rule of God. Hence, Jesus does not call for a wife to endure abuse to serve the needs of her husband, nor for a child to endure abuse to serve the needs of the parent. On the contrary, God wills to relieve all oppression by humans over other humans. In Mark, Jesus confronts and condemns such human oppression wherever he encounters it.

The suffering that God calls people to endure is the unavoidable loss and tragic persecution that comes to followers in the course of being or proclaiming the good news of God's realm of salvation. Proclaiming the good news often leads to active encounter with oppression. In Mark, God does not give agents of the kingdom the right to use force to stop those who oppress; otherwise, they would become like those whom they condemn. As a result, those who confront oppression may suffer at the hands of the oppressors they condemn, just as Jesus did. In Mark, this suffering by persecution in the course of proclaiming the good news is "the cross" that God calls people to bear for the sake of the world, a cross people take up because they have chosen the gospel.

Thus, the Markan Jesus calls disciples to lose their lives "for me and the good news." Those who have or exercise status and power at the expense of others are to relinquish it. Those who do not have power over others are not to seek it. And all are actively to oppose oppression in bringing good news. Because of the nature of the good news and because of the way the world is, people who bring or are good news to others will be risking their status, power, and life. Followers who are not prepared for such risks will shrink in fear and avoidance. Mark's narrative calls people to celebrate life and oppose oppression in spite of the risks. A contemporary parallel may help to clarify.

> In the late 1980s, a volunteer approached a leader of the Sanctuary Movement in the United States serving refugees from Central America, and she asked to join in the work of the movement.
>
> The leader said to her, "Before you say whether you really wish to join us, let me pose some questions: Are you ready to have your telephone tapped by the government? Are you prepared to have your neighbors shun you? Are you strong enough to have your children ridiculed and harassed at school? Are you ready to be arrested and tried, with full media coverage? If you are not prepared for these things, you may not be ready to join the movement. For when push comes to shove, if you fear these things, you will not be ready to do what needs to be done for the refugees."
>
> The woman decided to think it over.

Similarly, if followers of Jesus are not ready to give up their status and their power over others, then they will not be ready to proclaim the good news. Mark's Gospel leads people to confront their fear and to accept the persecution that may come in the course of following Jesus.

For Mark, living the standards of the kingdom is possible by faith.[9] The total response to the arrival of the kingdom, rightly understood, is to "put faith in the good news" (1:13). The arrival of the power of the kingdom in the person of Jesus makes such faith possible. In turn, faith is trust in the God for whom all is possible—the God who heals, drives out demons, calms storms, provides bread in the desert, and raises one to life and salvation in the new age. This faith gives courage. When one ultimately counts on God for life, one can dare to risk life for others (10:21). Thus, faith is the opposite of fear (4:40; 5:36; 6:50). In Mark, the faith that one's future salvation is in God's care gives one neither complacency nor passive security but the courage to risk even persecution, to live a life of abandon for the good news (10:29–30; 14:36).

The narrative calls followers of Jesus to have faith in God as Jesus had faith in God, the faith that enabled Jesus to live life for the kingdom in spite of the fact that it led to his execution (8:34). The ultimate consequence of living the standards of the kingdom is resurrection and eternal life in the age to come (10:30).

The Transition: Facing Death (Life, Sight, Empowerment)

How do self-oriented people become God-centered in service to others? How are people enabled to relinquish the values of the world and embrace the standards of the kingdom? For Mark, the first step is to receive the gift of God's rule with all its blessings, then to see in a new way, and finally to be empowered to live for the good news.

First, like the characters in the story, the readers of Mark are invited to receive the kingdom, for "unless you receive the rule of God as a little child [receives], you definitely will not enter into it" (10:15). The entire first half of the story is the offer of this kingdom that brings liberation from all forms of oppression. Jesus heals the sick, drives out demons, pardons sins, cleanses lepers, restores the disabled, delivers from the threats of nature, welcomes the outcast, challenges inhumane laws, calls the wealthy to give to the poor, confronts fraud, and calls the leaders of Israel to produce the fruits of the vineyard. Out of compassion, the Markan Jesus offers the power of the kingdom to restore people to physical and moral wholeness. Receiving and entering this realm of God is a matter of trusting that life, now and in the future, comes from God.

Second, Mark's narrative leads readers to experience a fundamental change of perception — to see and understand, in the face of all our human resistance, that God wants people to risk status, power, and even life to bring the liberating life of the kingdom to others. How does Jesus try to get the disciples to see and understand these standards? He teaches them, corrects their inappropriate behavior, tells them about his own death, and gives them models — children, slaves, servants — to show them what they are to be like. He tells them what they are not to be — kings who lord it over their subjects, the wealthy who refuse to give up their wealth, and those who want to acquire the world.

Yet in the end, Jesus' greatest witness to new sight is his own life. Can the disciples see this man as the Son of God?[10] He exercised the power of the kingdom on behalf of others, yet now he is rejected by society's leaders, is abandoned by the crowds, is betrayed by friends, is relinquishing his power over others, is misunderstood by all, and is dying as a result of opposing the oppressive authorities. If the disciples can see revealed in this executed man the embodiment of God's idea of true greatness (15:2, 18, 26), then they will have seen the world upside down. They will see that God wants people to bring life even when they end up being killed for doing it! Thus, at the crucifixion, God's full standards of judgment for humans are revealed. And the resurrection of

Jesus is God's affirmation that the way Jesus lived and died is the way for all humans to live.

Finally, Mark's narrative empowers readers to follow Jesus. As presented by Mark, Jesus' courage is more than example and revelation. Jesus' commitment in the face of execution empowers people to live for the good news in the face of rejection and loss. The narrative empowers readers by leading them to identify with Jesus.[11] The narrative distances readers from identification with the Jewish and the gentile leaders, because these leaders will kill others to save themselves. The narrative initially leads readers to identify with the disciples. However, when the disciples betray or abandon Jesus to save themselves, readers distance themselves from the disciples. In the end, readers identify with Jesus, because he is the one heroic figure left in the story. Jesus is afraid and does not want to die, yet he is willing to do what God wills, what God wants people to do (14:39). Readers identify with the courage of Jesus and come away from the story, saying, "I, too, want to be courageous in the face of death." Mark leads readers not so much to believe something about Jesus as to be like Jesus.

The narrative also empowers by purging readers of fear. Through identification with Jesus, readers face the experience of abandonment, rejection, mockery, physical suffering, and death. By going through Jesus' death vicariously in the experience of the narrative, they face with courage the fears that might otherwise paralyze them. When the Gospel ends with the women running away from the empty grave, terrified and telling no one (16:8), it is the readers who are left to tell this story. It is the readers who are led to say: "I will not be paralyzed into silence as the disciples and the women were. I will tell even if it means persecution and death." At the end, when all the characters in the story have failed to proclaim the good news about Jesus, the readers themselves will complete the Gospel by proclaiming with courage.

Thus, in Mark's portrayal Jesus does not die so that sins might be forgiven (Jesus offers forgiveness apart from his death); rather, his courage in the face of execution liberates from the grip of self-preservation in the face of persecution. Thus, Jesus' life, death, and resurrection liberate us from the self-oriented fear of death and empower us to live courageously for others. And even if the readers have themselves stumbled before in the face of persecution, they see new hope in the story. For Jesus remains loyal to his own stumbling disciples. Even after they have failed the ultimate test of discipleship, Jesus promises to go ahead of the disciples — including Peter — in order to begin the mission anew from Galilee (16:7). The narrative thus encourages readers to recommit themselves to proclaiming the good news, despite past failures and ongoing persecution.

The Purpose of Mark in Its Historical Context

The purpose of Mark's Gospel as inferred from a study of the standards of judgment fits well the generally accepted historical context of Mark's Gospel. The Gospel of Mark was probably written during, or just after, the Roman-Jewish War of 66–70 C.E.[12] In that war, the Jewish nation revolted against the Roman overlords. The Romans defeated the Jews, conquering Jerusalem, and destroying the temple. Mark wrote about Jesus to show that any attempt to dominate others by force — either by Rome or by Israel — was contrary to God's way of ruling over the world.[13]

Mark's Gospel announces that Jesus inaugurated God's rule, a realm that brings life rather than destruction, a realm that fosters service rather than domination. Jesus calls the disciples to announce this realm of God to the world. Mark also believed that Jesus' return and the final establishment of God's kingdom were imminent. Mark therefore enjoined urgency and alertness in the mission of spreading the news of God's kingdom to all the nations before the end came.

It is generally accepted that Mark wrote to followers who faced persecution in their mission to be or bring good news to the world. The time of the war was difficult for followers of Jesus. On the one hand, they were the target of persecution from other Jews, because they opposed the war. On the other hand, they were suspected by gentiles, because their leader had been executed as a revolutionary. They faced ridicule, rejection, ostracism from family and community, betrayal, arrests, trials, floggings, and death (13:5–23). It was a difficult time even to admit an association with Jesus, let alone proclaim the good news (14:66–72). Although followers of Jesus undoubtedly knew courage, they must often have failed to speak and act because of fear. Mark addressed this situation of persecution and fear. Mark's narrative led readers to face the fear of persecution and empowered them to spread the good news faithfully and courageously.[14]

Markan Trajectories

Down through history, the standards of the Gospel of Mark have been reflected in ordinary folk who have lived courageous lives of service for others. Markan Christians are represented by the orders of the church that called people to give up their livelihood and security to preach the gospel or care for the poor and the ill. Countless missionaries who have left home and country to bring the gospel to remote parts of the world belong in the Markan trajectory. In modern times, their numbers will include those who risked their lives to rescue Jews in Nazi Germany. And we might point to all who joined Martin Luther King in the struggle for civil rights. Most recently, we can point to the sanctuary movement in this country, the base communities in Latin America, and the struggle of blacks in South Africa. In all nations where people take courageous risks to bring life to others in the face of persecution, we find Markan Christians.

Lest we think that the glory and power Mark condemns is a caricature applying to other people, we should remember that these are the values that seem natural to our own culture. We want to live, to embrace opportunities for ourselves, to be of importance to other people and to receive recognition for it, to have power in life that would enable us to get things done, make things happen. We may think of our life as a journey moving toward greater and greater recognition—financial, social, and in terms of influence. These values are also reflected, sometimes crassly, in such slogans as "looking out for number one," "getting ahead," "climbing to the top," and so on.

We may also think that Mark's effort to get people to face death and persecution is not relevant to us because we do not face persecution and execution as Mark's first readers did. Yet any loss of status or wealth or power is a form of death. When we are embarrassed, we say, "I thought I'd die." When we are rejected, we say, "They treat me as if I'm nothing." When we encounter loss of job or financial security, we say, "I'm finished." These are death-like experiences of everyday life. In light of this pervasive threat of death, we might ask ourselves: How often do we avoid speaking up because we wish to avoid embarrassment? How many actions do we avoid taking because we wish to avoid rejection or loss? In what ways do we fail to give to the needy because we will not risk financial insecurity? In these ways, we are like the followers in Mark's story who do not proclaim or live the good news because they want to avoid threats to their security.[15]

Perhaps if we were committed to the Markan vision of what God wanted for the world—sharing our wealth, opposing oppression, reaching out to our outcasts, healing our sick, and so on — we might experience greater misunderstanding, rejection, loss, ridicule, persecution—and we might also gain true life! Instead, we tend to diminish our vision of life and function within the safe confines of actions that bring little threat to ourselves—and limited good for others! Mark seeks to shake readers from such fortresses of self-protection and lead them to face death and thereby to take risks in bringing or being good news to the world.

NOTES

1. See Thomas Boomershine, "Mark the Storyteller: A Rhetorical-Critical Investigation of Mark's Passion and Resurrection Narrative," Ph.D. diss., Union

Theological Seminary, 1974; Norman Petersen, "Point of View in Mark's Narrative," *Semeia* 12 (1978): 97–121; and Dan O. Via, *The Ethics of Mark's Gospel in the Middle of Time* (Philadelphia: Fortress Press, 1985).

2. See Wayne Booth, *The Rhetoric of Fiction,* 2d ed. (Chicago: University of Chicago Press, 1983).

3. On paradox and ambiguity in Mark's narrative, see Robert Fowler, *Let the Reader Understand: Reader-Response Criticism and the Gospel of Mark* (Minneapolis: Fortress Press, 1991).

4. On the complex integrity of Mark's narrative, see Joanna Dewey, "Mark as Interwoven Tapestry: Forecasts and Echoes for a Listening Audience," *CBQ* 53 (1991): 221–36.

5. On the characters in Mark, see David Rhoads and Donald Michie, *Mark as Story: An Introduction to the Narrative of a Gospel* (Philadelphia: Fortress Press, 1982).

6. It is inappropriate to see Mark's portrayal of the Jewish authorities as fostering anti-Semitism. The character-types in Mark are a rhetorical strategy that present caricatures of moral choices. Like the disciples, real people have good and bad traits. Also, the choice Mark offers to readers is not between Judaism and Christianity, for all the major characters in the narrative are Jewish.

7. See Jack Dean Kingsbury, *Conflict in Mark: Jesus, Authorities, Disciples* (Minneapolis: Fortress Press, 1989).

8. See Joanna Dewey, "The Gospel of Mark," in *Searching the Scriptures,* vol. 1: *A Feminist Introduction,* ed. Elisabeth Schüssler Fiorenza (New York: Crossroad Publishing, 1993).

9. See Christopher Marshall, *Faith as a Theme in Mark's Narrative* (New York: Cambridge University Press, 1989).

10. See Jack Dean Kingsbury, *The Christology of Mark's Gospel* (Philadelphia: Fortress Press, 1983).

11. Robert Tannehill, "The Disciples in Mark: The Functions of a Narrative Role," in *The Interpretation of Mark,* ed. William Telford (Philadelphia: Fortress Press, 1985).

12. For a recent treatment, see Joel Marcus, "The Jewish War and the *Sitz im Leben* of Mark," *JBL* 111 (1992): 441–62.

13. See Ched Myers, *Binding the Strong Man: A Political Reading of Mark's Story of Jesus* (Maryknoll, N.Y.: Orbis Books, 1988).

14. This essay is only one way to understand the purpose of Mark, based on the use of narrative criticism. For further discussion of variety in perspective and method, see *Mark and Method: New Approaches in Biblical Studies,* ed. Janice Capel Anderson and Stephen D. Moore (Minneapolis: Fortress Press, 1992). On narrative criticism, see Mark A. Powell, *What Is Narrative Criticism?* GBS (Minneapolis: Fortress Press, 1990).

15. For a contemporary psychological analysis of the human condition and of redemption that is similar to that of the Gospel of Mark, see Ernest Becker, *The Denial of Death* (New York: The Free Press, 1973); and *Escape from Evil* (New York: The Free Press, 1975).

– 9 –

The Significance of the Cross within Mark's Story

Jack Dean Kingsbury

The story of Mark culminates in the episode of Jesus on the cross. At the cross, Mark unveils the secret of Jesus' identity, describes the fundamental resolution of Jesus' conflict with the religious leaders, and calls attention to the salvation that God accomplishes in Jesus' death.

IN ALL FOUR CANONICAL GOSPELS, the scene of Jesus' death on the cross is climactic.[1] Still, Mark stands out in a special way as the Gospel of the cross. The reason is that two major motifs, which run the length of the story, reach their culmination in the scene of the cross. The one motif is that of the so-called "messianic secret," at the heart of which lies Jesus' identity as the Son of God: Not until after Jesus has died on the cross does any human being within Mark's story other than Jesus himself perceive that he is God's Son. The other motif focuses more directly on the ministry of Jesus: Throughout his ministry, Jesus becomes embroiled in fierce conflict with the religious leaders, and it is not until Jesus dies on the cross that this conflict comes to fundamental resolution. Once we see how the secret of Jesus' identity is gradually unveiled and his conflict with the religious leaders is fundamentally resolved, we shall attend to the pericope of Jesus on the cross itself. Here the analysis will concentrate on the salvation that God accomplishes through the death of Jesus, God's Son.

Mark's story of Jesus unfolds in three phases: In the beginning phase, Mark introduces the reader to Jesus (1:1–13); in the middle phase, Mark describes Jesus' public ministry to Israel (1:14–8:26); and in the end phase, Mark tells of Jesus' journey to Jerusalem and of his suffering, death, and rising (8:27–16:8). This broad sketch of the contours of Mark's story is the one we shall follow in tracing the development of the two motifs of Jesus' identity and his conflict with the religious leaders.

I

In the beginning phase of his story (1:1–13), Mark sets the stage for the drama that follows by presenting Jesus to the reader. Obliquely, Mark broaches the motif of the secret of Jesus' identity by informing the reader of how three key figures construe Jesus' identity: he himself, as the reliable narrator; John the Baptist, as the forerunner of Jesus; and God, whose understanding of Jesus' identity is normative for all the characters inhabiting the world of the story.

Mark apprises the reader of his own understanding of Jesus' identity in the epigraph he has placed at the head of his story: "The beginning of the gospel of Jesus Christ, Son of God" (1:1). Through use of the name "Jesus Christ," Mark raises the claim on behalf of Jesus that he is the Christ, Israel's "anointed" king, the long-awaited Messiah. And with the name "Son of God," Mark alludes to the unique filial relationship that Jesus has with God whereby Jesus knows God as "Father." Accordingly, here at the very outset of his story Mark privileges the reader by informing him or her of the identity of Jesus, the protagonist.

John the Baptist, whom God sends to fulfill the end-time expectations associated with Elijah by readying Israel for the one who will come after him (1:2–8; 9:11–13), thinks of this coming one as the "Mightier One." This Mightier One, asserts John, will baptize not merely with water but with the Holy Spirit, which is to say that he will mediate to people God's eschatological salvation. Since John is an agent of God (1:2–3), the reader knows that his understanding of the Mightier One is correct. Nevertheless, because John's witness to the Mightier One takes the form of prediction, it is only the reader, and not John himself or the Jewish public, who is in a position to apply this witness to Jesus.

In the climactic baptismal episode (1:9–11), the reader learns of God's understanding of Jesus' identity. As Jesus goes up from the water, he becomes the recipient of two revelatory events. In the first event, God sends the Spirit upon Jesus and thus empowers him for messianic ministry (1:10). In the second event, God addresses Jesus from heaven and declares him to be God's Son (1:11). As God's Son, Jesus obeys God perfectly, and God acts decisively in Jesus to save. Because Jesus is the sole recipient of the two revelatory events, Mark again privileges the reader so that it is the reader — but not human characters within the story besides Jesus — who knows that both Mark as narrator and God look upon Jesus as God's Son.

The temptation scene (1:12–13) rounds out the beginning phase of Mark's story. Its purpose is to show that Jesus Son of God is stronger than Satan, his cosmic antagonist, and that Jesus inaugurates the eschatological age of salvation.

In the middle phase of his story (1:14–8:26), Mark describes Jesus'

Galilean ministry. In so doing, he shows how beings, both human and supernatural, deal with the matter of Jesus' identity. As Jesus traverses Galilee preaching (1:14–15), calling disciples (1:16–20), teaching (1:21–22), healing (1:34), and exorcising demons (1:34), his fame spreads throughout Palestine and even beyond so that great crowds flock to him (e.g., 3:7–8). But despite Jesus' fame the reader soon learns that whereas supernatural beings such as God or demons know that Jesus is God's Son,[2] human beings do not. Indeed, even when demons shout aloud that Jesus is God's Son, Mark forecloses the notion that these shouts ever reach the ears of humans to dispel their ignorance of Jesus' identity by having Jesus immediately suppress them.[3] In point of fact, the only human ears for whom Mark intends the demonic shouts — so that he or she is continually reminded that Jesus is God's Son — are those of the reader.

To illustrate such human ignorance concerning Jesus' identity, the people in the synagogue at Capernaum, having watched Jesus perform an exorcism by mere command, both ask and assert in astonishment, "What is this? A new teaching — with authority!" (1:27*b–c*). As Mark tells it, these people, in asking about "what" Jesus has done, wonder in effect about "who" this Jesus is who possesses such authority as to perform so mighty an act (1:27*d*). Later Jesus, having forgiven a paralytic his sins, causes certain scribes to question within themselves who he might be: "Who [is this who dares to] forgive sins but God alone?" (2:7). Again, out on the water the disciples, awed by Jesus' power to calm wind and sea, query one another, "Who then is this, that even the wind and the sea obey him?" (4:41). And in the synagogue at Nazareth, the family, relatives, and acquaintances of Jesus, convinced that he presumes to be more than they judge him to be, ask themselves if they do not know who he is: "Is not this the carpenter, the son of Mary . . . ?" (6:3). As these episodes indicate, neither the Jewish crowd, nor their leaders, nor the disciples, nor the family, relatives, and acquaintances of Jesus have any inkling that he is God's Son.

At this juncture in his story, Mark anticipates the sharp change in direction he will soon take. For the first time, he describes humans, not as wondering about Jesus' identity, but as having reached a decision about it. Owing to Jesus' fame as a miracle-worker, the Jewish public has concluded that he must be some prophet of great repute: John the Baptist come back to life, Elijah, or a prophet like one of the great Old Testament prophets (6:14–15). As rumors of these views reach Herod Antipas, he believes that the first notion is correct: Jesus is John the Baptist come back to life (6:16). With this scene, Mark prepares the reader for the end phase of his story.

In the end phase (8:27–16:8), Mark tells of Jesus' journey to Jerusalem, where he suffers, dies, and rises (8:31; 9:31; 10:32–34). Hewing to his change in direction, Mark now describes humans as expressing various convictions about Jesus' identity. Indeed, Mark traces, in three stages, the gradual unveiling of the secret of Jesus' identity.

In the first stage (8:27–30), Mark takes up the view of the Jewish public, according to which Jesus is some prophet of great repute, and compares it with the disciples' understanding of Jesus' identity. In Mark's perspective, the Jewish public, in holding Jesus to be a prophet, is altogether mistaken in its understanding of him: Jesus cannot be John or Elijah or one of the ancient prophets, for neither he himself as narrator (1:1) nor God (1:11) regards Jesus as a prophet (1:1). By contrast, Mark judges the disciples' understanding of Jesus' identity as expressed by Peter — that Jesus is "the Messiah" (8:29) — to be correct. It is so because Mark himself, in the epigraph of his story, named Jesus "Messiah" (1:1). Still, correct as the disciples' understanding is, Mark also calls upon the reader to recognize that it is insufficient. It is so because, in the disciples' own conception of the Messiah, the latter is in no wise destined to suffer and die. This explains why, when Jesus teaches the disciples about his passion, they reject his teaching out of hand (e.g., 8:31–33).

In the second stage of the unveiling of the secret of Jesus' identity, Mark twice pictures Jesus as accepting the name Son of David. As blind Bartimaeus insistently appeals to Jesus as Son of David to restore his sight, Jesus does not refute Bartimaeus but graciously grants his request (10:46–52). Then, as Jesus is about to enter Jerusalem, he openly receives the shouts of the huge throng accompanying him that hail him as the bearer of "the coming kingdom of our father David" (11:8–10). The perception that Jesus is the Son of David is correct.

Despite this, Mark discloses that Son of David, too, is an insufficient acknowledgment of Jesus' identity (12:35–37). While addressing the people in the temple, Jesus asks how it is possible for the Messiah to be both "less" than David and "more" than David. The answer, which Mark expects the reader to supply, is that the Messiah, as the son of David, is less than David but that, as David's Lord and the Son of God, he is more than David.

The third stage in the unveiling of the secret of Jesus' identity is the climactic one. Notably, the reader has now arrived at that point in Mark's story where Jesus hangs upon the cross (15:25–39). After Jesus twice calls out and expires, Mark reports that the Roman centurion standing opposite him cries aloud, "Truly this man was the Son of God!" (15:39). The uniqueness of the centurion's declaration is apparent to the reader: For the first time in Mark's story, a human being other than Jesus himself both publicly and correctly understands Jesus' identity in the same way as both Mark as narrator and God: Jesus is the Son of God (1:1, 11; 9:7). In the declaration of the centurion, therefore, Mark dramatically lifts the secret of Jesus' identity.

Why is it that Mark waits until Jesus dies on the cross before permitting the full secret of his identity to surface? The reason is that it is only from beyond the cross that any human — and therefore also the reader — can understand what it means for Jesus to be the Davidic Messiah, the royal Son of God. What it means is that Jesus be commissioned to his ministry by God and anointed with the power and authority of the Spirit, that he summon Israel to enter the sphere of God's eschatological rule through his Galilean ministry of preaching the gospel of God, teaching the people, healing the sick, and exorcising demons, and that, above all, he travel to Jerusalem and there obediently suffer and die to the end that, by his death, God might accomplish salvation for all humankind. Although the reader has been privileged from the very beginning of Mark's story to know "that" Jesus is Messiah Son of God (1:1, 11), it is not until the end of the story, at the cross, that the reader can know "what" it means for Jesus to be Messiah Son of God. Hence, as far as the human characters inhabiting the story are concerned, only gradually does Mark lift the secret of Jesus' identity.

II

Besides the secret of Jesus' identity, the second motif we want to trace is the conflict that characterizes Mark's story of Jesus. It, too, leads straight to the cross. At the human level, this conflict is between Jesus and Israel and especially between Jesus and the religious leaders. The leaders, in turn, are made up of such groups as the Pharisees, Sadducees, Herodians, chief priests, scribes, and elders. With the exception of individuals perhaps (e.g., 15:43), Mark stereotypes these groups as the implacable enemies of Jesus who form a united front against him.

Not until the middle phase of Mark's story, after Jesus has embarked on his public ministry (1:14; 8:26), do the religious leaders make their debut. As Mark presents them, they see themselves as those appointed by God to govern Israel. To oppose them, therefore, is to oppose God, and to challenge their rule and teaching is to summon Israel to stray from God's rule and teaching. In the eyes of the leaders, Jesus poses the gravest sort of threat: Not only does he challenge their leadership but he also woos the people, undermines their teaching, and, toward the end of his ministry, violates the sanctity of the temple.

As early as the first summary passage devoted to Jesus' teaching (1:21–22), Mark raises the specter of conflict between Jesus and the religious leaders. As Jesus teaches in the synagogue at Capernaum, Mark reports that the people "were astounded at his teaching, for he taught them as one having authority, and not as the scribes" (1:22). With this comment, Mark informs the reader of two critical factors: First, that whereas Jesus discharges his ministry on the authority of God, the leaders act on their own human authority; and second, that the crucial issue around which the whole of Jesus' conflict with the leaders revolves is that of "authority" itself. At stake ultimately is the answer to the question, Whom has God truly appointed to rule his people? Whereas the reader knows that God's Appointed is Jesus Messiah, the Son of God, he or she does not know how Jesus' conflict with the leaders either unfolds or is resolved.

As Mark depicts the unfolding of this conflict, he takes pains to show that it intensifies until it reaches its culmination in the death of Jesus on the cross. Here in the course of Jesus' public ministry to Israel (1:14–8:26), this conflict intensifies in two noticeable ways. For one thing, after only the first cycle of controversies Mark asserts with an eye to Jesus, "The Pharisees went out and immediately conspired with the Herodians against him, how to destroy him" (3:6). From early on, Mark shows that Jesus' conflict with the leaders is a struggle to the death.

For another thing, Mark so arranges Jesus' controversies with the religious leaders in 1:14–8:26 that it is not until the final controversy in 8:11–13 that Jesus' conflict with the leaders becomes "acutely confrontational" in nature: Not until this final controversy do the leaders challenge Jesus himself on a matter that pertains specifically to him. Prior to 8:11–13, the leaders attack Jesus or the disciples only indirectly. They charge Jesus "in their hearts" (2:1–12), or take umbrage at him but address their complaint to the disciples (2:15–17), or approach him but in dismay about the disciples (2:23–28), or, when confronted by him, remain silent (3:1–6), or slander him but not to his face (3:22–30), or object to him about the disciples (7:1–13). At last, however, the Pharisees do confront Jesus in such fashion as that their controversy with him becomes acutely confrontational in nature: They directly challenge him to give them a sign from heaven that will prove that he acts on divine authority (8:11–13). With this turn of events, Mark intensifies further the conflict between Jesus and the leaders, for attacks cease to be indirect and are henceforth face-to-face.

In the end phase of his story (8:27–16:8), Mark heightens the intensity of Jesus' conflict with the religious leaders still more. As Jesus makes his way to Jerusalem, he twice debates with the leaders but both times uses the debate as a vehicle for instructing the disciples (9:14–29; 10:2–12). Not until Jesus enters Jerusalem, therefore, does he become entangled in a last great confrontation with the leaders prior to his passion (11:27–12:34).

To alert the reader to the heightened intensity of the conflict that attends this last great confrontation, Mark makes use of various rhetorical devices. To begin with, the setting for this conflict is the temple (11:11, 27), and this in itself adds intensity to the conflict: In challenging the leaders in the temple, Jesus attacks them at the very seat of their power and privilege. Again, the atmosphere in which these controversies take place is, except for Jesus' exchange with the "friendly scribe," one of unmitigated hostility: Repeatedly, the leaders want to seize Jesus or destroy him (11:18; 12:12). Third, these controversies are all acutely confrontational in tone: In each instance, Jesus is himself challenged by the leaders on matters relating strictly to him. Fourth, the questions Jesus and the leaders contest are all critical in nature, for they have to do, directly or indirectly, with the matter of authority (e.g., 11:15–18, 27–33). Fifth, uninterruptedly during a single day, all the groups that together make up the united front of the leaders approach Jesus so as to challenge him or to get the best of him in debate (11:27; 12:13, 18, 28). And last, the leaders, unable to defeat Jesus in debate and daring no longer to put any more questions to him (12:34*c*), finally resort to the one option they believe is still open to them: They withdraw from the temple to search actively for a way to have Jesus arrested and killed (14:1–2).

In Jesus' death on the cross, his conflict with the religious leaders intensifies to the breaking point and comes to fundamental resolution. For our purposes, the scene of greatest importance in Mark's passion narrative (chaps. 14–16) is the scene in which the leaders confront Jesus for the last time during his earthly life (15:31–32). In this scene, the leaders mock the crucified Jesus on two counts. They mock him because although he demonstrated such astonishing authority in the course of his public ministry to rescue, or save, others from disease or plight, here he is unable even to save himself (15:31). And they mock him as the Messiah, the king of Israel, because, as they see it, his messiahship is a fraud since he does not even possess the power to get himself down from the cross (15:32).

In other words, as the religious leaders look up at Jesus hanging on the cross, they see him as one who is stripped of all authority, they see his cross as the sign of his destruction, and they see themselves as having triumphed in their conflict with him. Ironically, however, what the leaders do not perceive is that God and Jesus, too, willed Jesus' death. Jesus willed his own death because he is God's perfectly obedient Son (14:36). God willed Jesus' death because, through it, God will reestablish the covenant and proffer salvation and the forgiveness of sins to all humankind (14:24). To show that Jesus' death serves God's saving purposes, God vindicates Jesus by raising him from the dead (16:6). Accordingly, as the reader looks upon Jesus, he or she rightly recognizes that the victory in Jesus' conflict with the leaders has not gone to the leaders but to Jesus, and that Jesus' cross, far from being the sign of his destruction, is in reality the sign of the salvation that God accomplishes through him. In the episode of Jesus' death on the cross, Jesus' conflict with the leaders comes to fundamental resolution: The one whom God has appointed to rule, whether in Israel or over the world, is in truth Jesus, Messiah-King, God's own Son.

III

Earlier, in tracing the motif of the secret of Jesus' identity, we were led to the cross, for here is where Jesus is, for the first time, perceived by another human to be the Son of God. Now, in tracing the motif of Jesus' conflict with the religious leaders, we have been led to both the cross and the resurrection; nevertheless, the cross is the place where this motif, too, reaches its climax, for it is here that this conflict comes to fundamental resolution, and it is in his death that Jesus accomplishes salvation. Because these two major motifs both culminate in the episode of the cross, they reveal that the cross is the culminating point of Mark's entire story of Jesus. This, then, is the significance of the cross within the story of Mark.

Should it be correct that the cross is the place where Mark unveils the secret of Jesus' identity as the Son of God and where Jesus, through his death, accomplishes salvation, then one can anticipate that Mark, in the episode of Jesus on the cross, will devote special attention to these two themes of "salvation" and of Jesus as "the Son of God." To show that this is in fact the case, we turn now to a brief investigation of this episode (15:27–39).

This episode may be divided into two parts, each with a setting and three scenes (15:27–32; 15:33–39). In the first part, the setting depicts Jesus as crucified between two revolutionaries (15:27); in the three scenes that follow, Jesus is mocked, respectively, by the passers-by (15:29–30), the religious leaders (15:31–32*a–b*), and the two revolutionaries (15:32*c*). In the second part, the setting describes darkness as enveloping the whole region or earth from the sixth to the ninth hours (15:33); in the three scenes that follow, Jesus twice cries out and expires (15:34–37), and Mark describes two responses to his death: In the first response, God causes the curtain of the temple to split in two from top to bottom (15:38); and in the second response, the centurion affirms that Jesus was truly the Son of God (15:39).

The theme of "salvation" stands out prominently in both parts of the episode. In the first scene of Part I, the passers-by blaspheme Jesus by challenging him to "save himself" by coming down from the cross (15:29–30). In the second scene, the religious leaders mock Jesus, and they, too, challenge him to "save himself" by coming down from the cross (15:31–32*a–b*). And in the third scene, the revolutionaries crucified with Jesus revile him; that is to say, they, like the others, challenge Jesus to save himself by coming down from the cross (15:32*c*). Three times, therefore, Jesus is challenged to come down from the cross and thus save himself.

Jesus, however, does not rise to these challenges. The reason is that he is the perfectly obedient Son who wills what the Father wills (14:36). In addition, he is a man of integrity who does not break the counsel he gives others. Previously in the story (8:35), Jesus said to the disciples, "For those who want to save their life will lose it. . . . " Jesus makes no attempt to save his life. Hence, the theological point Mark stresses here is that salvation is not of oneself, not even when that someone is Jesus.

In the second part of the episode, the motif of salvation again stands out (15:33–36). When Jesus suddenly shouts out, "Eloi, Eloi, lema sabachthani," Jewish bystanders, hearing him, suppose that he calls upon Elijah to come and "take him down" from the cross, that is, to save him. To see whether Elijah might hear Jesus' cry, one of the bystanders attempts to give Jesus a drink of wine-vinegar so as to refresh him and delay the approach of death. On two counts, however, the reader knows that to await salvation from Elijah is futile: First, Elijah cannot be expected to come for rescue, for John the Baptist is the one in Mark's story who fulfills the eschatological expectations associated with Elijah (9:11–13) and John is now dead (6:14–29); and second, why should anyone await Elijah's coming when Jesus, in his cry, did not even call upon Elijah? The conclusion is inescapable: If salvation is not of oneself, neither is it of a popular figure of deliverance such as Elijah.

Of whom, then, is salvation? Jesus himself answers this question in his call to God: "My God, my God, why have you forsaken me?" (15:34). Jesus' cry comes from Psalm 22, which is a lament. In a lament, there are two main points of emphasis: The first is the strong sense of abandonment that the suffering, righteous person experiences (Ps. 22:1–2); and the second is the element of complete trust in God that typifies the righteous person (Ps. 22:3–5, 19–24). In other words, the reader is to understand Jesus' cry from the cross along these lines: O my God, even though you abandon me into death, nevertheless will I continue to trust in you for salvation. Does God honor Jesus' trust? The reader knows that God does, in the resurrection. Theologically, therefore, one major truth Mark drives home in this episode of Jesus on the cross is that salvation is neither of oneself nor of any popular figure of deliverance such as Elijah; on the contrary, salvation is of God alone!

Besides the theme of "salvation," Mark also focuses on the theme of Jesus as "the Son of God." Note that the entire episode of Jesus on the cross culminates in the second response to Jesus' death, at which point the centurion declares, "Truly, this man was the Son of God!" (15:39). Why, the reader must ask, is Mark so concerned that Jesus should die exactly in his capacity as the Son of God?

The clue Mark provides to the answer can be found in the first response to the death of Jesus: God causes the curtain of the temple to be split in two from top to bottom (15:38). Which curtain is meant? Probably not the curtain before the holy place but the curtain before the holiest place. What would God's tearing of this curtain symbolize? I take it to symbolize the destruction of the temple and therefore of the cult through which God has heretofore mediated the forgiveness of sins and salvation. The theological point Mark intends to make, therefore, is this: No more is salvation from sins to be mediated through the cult of the temple because the perfectly obedient and trusting Son of God has shed his blood once for all for the forgiveness of sins. Is there any support for this view? Yes, in Jesus' words both at the last supper and to his disciples: At the last supper, Jesus said, "This is my blood of the covenant, which is poured out for many" (14:24); and in his words to the disciples, Jesus said, "For the Son of Man came not to be served but to serve, and to give his life a ransom for many" (10:45). As I see it, Mark understands the freedom that comes from being ransomed in terms of the freedom from sins that comes through the forgiveness that God grants by virtue of the death of Jesus, God's perfectly obedient Son, who is henceforth the "place" of salvation.

In summary, then, Mark, through this episode of Jesus on the cross, conveys central theological affirmations as regards the themes of "salvation" and Jesus as "the Son of God." Mark affirms that no human being, not even Jesus, can "save" himself or herself. Mark also affirms that humans ought not deceive themselves into looking for salvation to some popular figure of deliverance, even should this figure be such as Elijah. On the contrary, Mark affirms that salvation is of God alone, and that God, through the death of the perfectly obedient Son, has reestablished the covenant whereby God proffers to all humankind salvation and the forgiveness of sins. Accordingly, the investigation of this episode of Jesus on the cross corroborates what we earlier discovered by tracing the twin motifs of the secret of Jesus' identity and of Jesus' conflict with the religious leaders: The significance of the cross within the story of Mark is that the cross is the place where this story reaches its culmination.

NOTES

1. Because space is at a premium, I have tried not to rely on endnotes. For those who may wish to know, however, this essay is informed by the research I conducted in conjunction with the following publications: *The Christology of Mark's Gospel,* reprint (Philadelphia: Fortress Press, 1989); *Conflict in Mark: Jesus, Authorities, Disciples* (Minneapolis: Fortress Press, 1989); and "The Religious Authorities in the Gospel of Mark," *NTS* 36 (1990): 42–65. As regards the views of other scholars, see, e.g., the annotated bibliography in *Conflict in Mark,* 139–43.

2. See, e.g., Mark 1:23–24, 34; 3:11–12; 5:7.

3. See Mark 1:24–25; 1:34; 3:12. Note that in 5:7 Jesus is alone with the demoniac.

– 10 –

The Social Location of the Markan Audience

Richard L. Rohrbaugh

One way to probe for the audience of Mark is to analyze the element of social stratification that is so apparent in his gospel story. Whereas the "crowd" is an indicator of the social location of Mark's audience, the "disciples" point most directly to the audience itself. Overall, the social milieu in which Mark's audience lived was that of the peasant class of antiquity.

ATTEMPTS TO DESCRIBE the social location[1] of the Markan audience are faced with a formidable obstacle right from the start: Scholars have been unable to agree on its place of origin. In recent decades, the view of many scholars, perhaps a majority, has been that Mark's Gospel was written for people in Rome. If that is correct, and if Mark is thus to be understood as an urban Gospel, we must locate its audience among the nonelite of the preindustrial city.[2] But an increasing number of scholars locate Mark's readers or hearers in the rural areas of southern Syria, Transjordan, or upper Galilee.[3] Obviously, if this is the correct location, the Markan audience must then be located among largely nonliterate peasants in a village or small town context. Since we cannot address the debate over geographical locale, however, the presumption of this essay will be that Mark's Gospel was in fact written in a village or small town context in either southern Syria, Transjordan, or upper Galilee and at a date very close to the events of 70 C.E. Our task, then, is both to provide a map of the various social groups present in, or having an impact upon, village life and to specify a few ways in which the Gospel of Mark would have struck a familiar chord in that kind of setting. Before we begin, however, we need to discuss several preliminary matters.

Literacy and Schools

In any attempt to gauge the social level of Mark's audience, it is essential to consider the extent of reading and writing in the type of village in which Mark's Gospel may have originated. Just how widespread was literacy in rural Syria-Palestine? Are we to imagine the recipients of Mark as reading privately to themselves, just as any modern American might do? Should we picture Mark's community as being literate or even scholastic, one in which educated persons studied the scriptures? Or did one of the literate members of Mark's community read the Gospel aloud for the majority who could not read for themselves?[4] In answering these questions, we shall take a view that differs substantially from many recent studies of Mark.

Among both classicists and New Testament scholars, there has been a longstanding tendency to imagine widespread literacy during the Roman period. It has been claimed that schools were common and that at least elementary education was broadly available. Yet, recent studies suggest that both literacy and the scope of the Hellenistic school system have been sharply overestimated.[5] Probably no more that 2 to 4 percent of the population in an agrarian society could read, or read and write, and the vast majority of these people lived in the cities. Especially important for our understanding of Mark's audience is the lack of evidence that significant schooling existed at the village level.[6]

Literacy rates (of at least a minimal sort) among elite males were indeed high, even a distinguishing mark of such status. In addition, officials, bureaucrats, servants of the elite, and high-ranking military officers were mostly literate, as were many Italian legionnaires. But in spite of the fond wishes of scholars, the fact is that country people, artisans, slaves, and women were mostly nonliterate. Not only could very few village people read or write, but many could also not use numbers. The reason for this can be traced to the cost of written materials and their relative scarcity at the village level. It was also due to the degree to which writing played a role in the control of the nonliterate. Fear of writing and of those who could write was widespread among peasants, who often regarded letters as a tool of elitist deception. This was especially true where the literate group was small and the nonliterate group large, which was exactly the situation in rural Syria-Palestine in the first century.[7]

The Audience of Mark's Gospel

A number of recent studies have located the author of Mark among the educationally sophisticated, usually by comparing the Gospel's literary structure to the rhetorical models of the Hellenistic schools. The commonly held view is articulated by Mary Ann Beavis, who asserts that "since the evangelist was literate, we can assume that he was educated in a Graeco-Roman school. His reader/audience would thus have brought certain skills and interests to the composition and reading of the text which can be illumined by data on education in the Roman empire."[8] Beavis believes that Mark's audience was made up of "competent" first-century Markan readers "trained to make connections between parts of a narrative" and able to catch sophisticated literary allusions the author might have used. Because of the difficulty of catching such things during oral performances, however, she hypothesizes that Mark's was a scholastic community in which his rhetoric might have been studied closely and therefore properly appreciated.[9]

Perhaps Beavis is correct. But if Mark's Gospel originated in a Christian community that reflected in any significant measure the social profile of a typical peasant village, and if Mark nonetheless expected his village readers to appreciate such rhetorical matters as literary allusion, style, and structure, then one thing must be made clear: Mark had precious little company. In fact, if Mark's Gospel embodies the plot, structure, and novelistic and dramatic features that would have been "attractive and instructive to Graeco-Roman audiences," as Beavis and many others claim, we are in a literary world that would have been lost on 98 percent of the people in rural Syria.

For our purposes, however, it is enough to assert that it is not necessary that the social level of the audience match that of the author, especially since Mark's Gospel was almost certainly written to be read aloud or recited from memory. There is no doubt that a few literate people, such as Beavis envisages, were in Mark's audience; and it is likely that one of them read his Gospel aloud for nonliterates. In fact, given the widespread fear of writing among nonliterates, it is highly unlikely that a Gospel like Mark could have gained broad acceptance in a village without being read aloud with great frequency.[10] In what follows, therefore, we shall presume a mixed audience for Mark, more nearly like the profile of an ancient village, and see if the evidence in the Gospel supports such a view.

Social Stratification in Mark's Story

Given the fundamental importance of social stratification in agrarian societies, we must begin by describing key social groups that would have been present in, or had an impact upon, the life of the villages and small towns of upper Galilee, southern Syria, or Transjordan. To order our comments, we shall refer to the accompanying diagrammatic description of social relationships in the Herodian period that was typical of advanced agrarian societies.[11] We shall look at each group in turn and then specify its presence in the story-world of Mark.

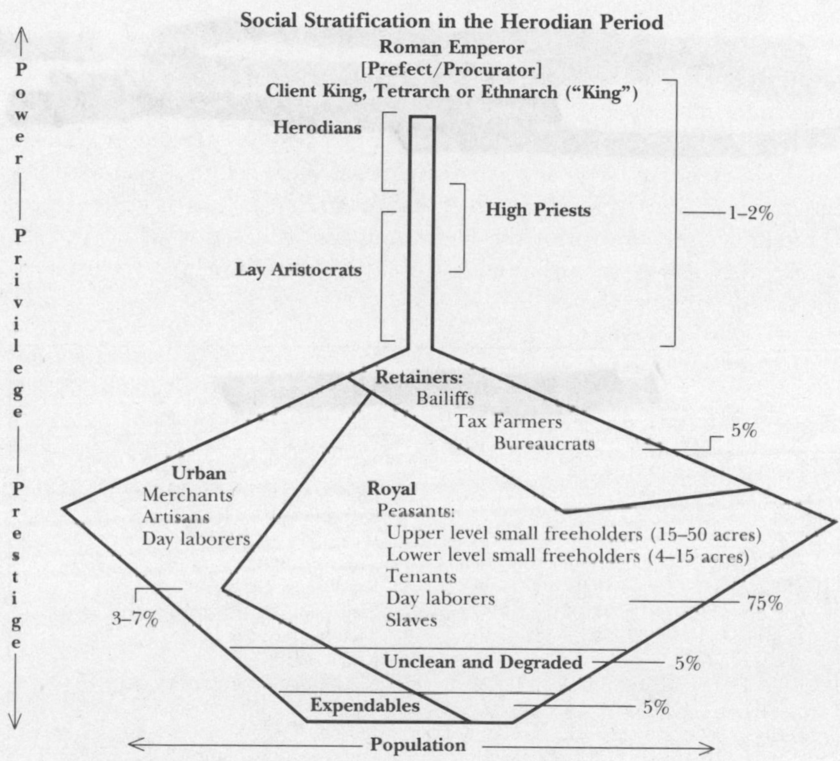

Urban Elite

As can be seen in the diagram, the urban elite made up about 2 percent of the total population. At its upper levels, this stratum included the highest-ranking military officers, ranking priestly families, the Herodians, and other ranking aristocratic families. These persons lived in the heavily fortified central areas of the cities, usually enclosed in separate walls, and hence were physically and socially isolated from the rest of the society. The literacy rate among this group was high, in some areas even among women. Together with their retainers, they controlled writing, coinage, taxation, and the military and judicial systems. Their control of politics and economics was legitimated by the religious and educational bureaucracy that had become the keepers of the so-called

"Great Tradition." Although birth rates were high in all segments of society, survival rates meant that large, extended families were characteristic only of this urban elite. Socially, culturally, and politically, they had little in common with the lower levels of society. Since they maintained their own etiquette, vocabulary, speech patterns, and dress, they could easily be recognized.

The wealth of the elite was primarily based on land ownership and taxation, which effectively drained the resources of the rural areas. In most agrarian societies, between 1 and 3 percent of the population owned the majority of the arable land, a fact readily attested in Galilee, southern Syria, and Transjordan at the time Mark wrote. Recent studies indicate significant loss of land by peasants in that region as large estates came under the control of the Herodians and other powerful families. Those members of the urban elite we can identify in Mark are listed in the accompanying chart.

Urban Elite Mentioned in Mark

Caesar, 12:14, 17
Pontius Pilate, 15:2, 8, 15
Rulers of the gentiles, 10:42
Herod, 6:14; 8:15
Herodias, 6:17
Herodias's daughter, 6:22
Philip, 6:17
Governors, 13:9; 15:16
High Priest, 2:26; 14:47, 53, 54, 60, 61, 63, 66
Chief Priests, 8:31; 10:33; 11:18, 27; 14:1, 10, 43, 53, 55; 15:1, 3, 10, 11, 31
Scribes, 1:22; 2:6, 16; 3:22; 7:1, 5; 8:31; 9:11, 14; 10:33; 11:18, 27; 12:28, 35, 38; 14:1, 43, 53; 15:1, 31
Strong man, 3:27
Those who have, 4:25
Elders, 8:31; 11:27; 14:43, 53; 15:1
Rich man, 10:22
Wealthy, 10:23, 25
Vineyard owner and son, 12:1, 6
Sadducees, 12:18
Family of seven brothers, 12:20
Rich people, 12:41
Kings, 13:9
Man going on a journey, 13:34
Owner of upper room, 14:14
Joseph of Arimathea, 15:43
Jairus and his family, 5:22, 23, 40

Because of the prominent role that conflict plays in Mark's story, it is not surprising that all of Jesus' opponents come from this group or its retainers. The fact that Jesus' opponents come from a single social stratum and act in solidarity with one another is sufficient to demonstrate that their conflict with Jesus is social as well as theological.

Prominent in the list above are the scribes. Urban scribes were often sages of considerable influence, though evidence from the Tebtunis papyri makes it clear that village scribes were more likely to be retainers beholden to the urban aristocracy for their appointments.[12] Mark's readers are warned to "beware of the scribes, who like to go about in long robes, and to have salutations in the market places and the best seats in the synagogues and the places of honor at feasts, who devour widows' houses and for a pretense make long prayers" (12:38–40). Together with the Pharisees, the scribes engage Jesus in controversy over ritual cleanliness (2:13–17; 7:1–23), which is why Mark explains that Pharisees and Judeans (usually incorrectly translated as "Jews") wash themselves and their eating vessels in keeping with the "tradition of the elders." The latter, of course, is the Great Tradition of the literate aristocracy that few peasants could afford to uphold. In Mark's story Jesus' disciples are clearly identified with this peasant inability (7:5), while the scribes show a typical aristocratic incomprehension of peasant attitudes or capabilities (Why do your disciples? . . .). In a retort to the scribes, Jesus not only defends the peasant attitude but also sharpens his criticism of the scribes and Pharisees (7:9–13) and thus distances himself from the practices of the elite ("your" tradition).

In Mark's passion narrative, Jesus' conflict with the elite intensifies as the scribes and Pharisees link up with the elders (nonpriests by birth) and chief priests. The latter are clearly the most powerful members of the Jewish aristocracy, and their struggle with Jesus is primarily one for political influence over the nonelite (11:18). Mark predicts that the chief priests will not only reject Jesus but also, in the end, destroy him (10:33). Pilate, another member of the (Roman) elite, clearly understands this struggle (15:10). So also do the Herodians and Sadducees whom Mark describes as joining the other elite groups in solid opposition to Jesus (12:13–17, 18–27; 3:1–6).

Three exceptions stand out in this list: the scribe who is "not far from the kingdom" (12:34), Joseph of Arimathea (15:43), and Jairus (5:21–43). The first two are clearly urbanites, though the third is probably part of village leadership. As Elizabeth Malbon has pointed out, these exceptions prevent us from excluding members of the elite from Jesus' community and may indicate that some such were part of the Markan community.[13]

Retainers

In a continuum from the lower echelons of the elite and ranging downward toward nonelite levels were those whom social scientists call retainers. These persons included lower-level military officers, officials and bureaucrats such as clerks and bailiffs, personal retainers, household servants, scholars, legal experts, and lower-level lay aristocracy. They worked primarily in the service of the elite by extending governmental and religious control to the lower strata and village areas. Still, they did not wield power independently but depended for their position on their relation to the urban elite.

In Mark's story such functionaries as these play key roles. Significantly, there are more people in this group who are followers of Jesus—

Retainers Mentioned in Mark

Pharisees, 2:16, 18, 24; 3:6; 7:1, 3, 5; 8:11, 15; 10:2; 12:13
People from Jairus's house, 5:35
Men arresting John the Baptist, 6:17
Soldier of the guard, 6:27
Levi, 2:14
Those selling in the temple, 11:15
Servant-girl of the High Priest, 14:66
Crowd sent from Chief Priests, scribes, and elders, 14:43
Physicians, 2:17; 5:26
Galilean priest, 1:44
Courtiers, officers, 6:21
Judas Iscariot, 14:11
Tax collectors, 2:15, 16
Moneychangers, 11:15
Doorkeeper, 13:34
Soldiers, 15:16
Centurion, 15:39
Slave/servant, 1:20; 9:35; 10:43, 44; 12:2, 4; 13:34; 14:47

the people from Jairus's house, Levi, tax collectors, and the centurion—than in the elite group. By the same token, the key actors are the Pharisees, and they are opponents of Jesus.

As Anthony Saldarini has shown, the Pharisees (of Mark's day) were a group of retainers competing with adherents of Jesus for influence among the nonelite. Although they possessed no independent wealth or power, they nonetheless could not have developed "their own interpretation of Judaism and propagated it among the people [had they been] full-time lower-class peasants."[14] Despite the fact that, in Mark's story, the Pharisees associate with the scribes (2:13–17; 7:1–23) and Herodians (3:1–6; 8:15; 12:13–17), they later prove not to be the chief opponents of Jesus. Most likely, they were literate local village leaders (in Mark, contra Josephus, the Pharisees are in Jerusalem only in 12:13) who depended on the elite for their livelihood and operated as brokers between the nonelite and the upper echelons of society. From that position they joined in with all of Jesus' elite opponents to form a united front.

Before leaving these various groups of retainers, we should take note of the great number of references to them in Mark's story. These numerous references do not appear because a large part of Mark's story takes place in an urban environment where these groups lived. It is rather because retainers extended elite control into the rural areas in a pervasive way (on the appointment of village scribes, see above). Conflict between these groups of retainers and the rural populations they sought to control was a constant reality in agrarian life.

Urban Nonelite

A third group playing a role in Mark's story is the nonelite of the cities. This group included merchants, artisans, day laborers, and service workers of various kinds that in most agrarian societies represented no more than 5 to 8 percent of the population. The economic situation of these persons could vary from extreme poverty among day laborers and certain artisan groups to considerable wealth among successful merchants. Yet even the rich among them exercised little social or cultural influence.

> **Urban Poor Mentioned in Mark**
>
> Those buying in the temple (likely includes peasants), 11:15
> Crowd/people, 1:5; 11:18, 32; 12:12, 37, 41; 14:2, 43; 15:8, 11, 15
> Widow, 12:42

Most of the urban poor lived in segregated areas at the outer edges of the cities, where neighborhood or craft associations were a common means of creating the social networks that enabled them to survive. Their health and nutrition were often worse than in the villages, and life expectancies were shorter. A child born in the lower social levels in the city of Rome during the first century had a life expectancy of only twenty years.

One should not be surprised that the urban poor play a very small role in Mark's Gospel because, aside from the passion narrative, so little of Mark's story takes place in an urban setting (the Jesus of Mark avoids all cities except Jerusalem). Where sentiments can be ascertained, the crowd is with Jesus until it is stirred against him by the authorities (15:11). The one person in this group who is clearly identified, the widow in 12:42, is pictured as unwittingly victimized by the redistributive economic system of the temple.

Degraded, Unclean, and Expendables

Outside the walls of every preindustrial city lived the degraded, unclean, and expendables: beggars, low-status prostitutes, the poorest day laborers, tanners (forced to live outside the cities because of their odor), and even some merchants. They were present in both cities and villages, though much more numerous in the former. All such persons were locked out of the cities at night but frequented them during the daytime to beg or find work. The poorest lived along the hedgerows of adjacent fields. While not a large portion of the population, the living conditions of these people were appalling, and their opportunities virtually nil.

Owing to the fact that these people constituted only about 10 percent of the population, the striking thing about them in Mark's story is their number and the frequency with which Jesus interacts with them (1:28, 32–34, 45; 3:7–10; 6:31–34, 54–56; 7:36–37). In fact, Mark wants us to know early on that Jesus' healing activity among these people is

Unclean, Degraded, and Expendables Mentioned in Mark

Man with an unclean spirit, 1:23
The sick and demon-possessed, 1:32–34, 39; 6:9, 13, 55; 9:38
Leper, 1:40
Paralytic, 2:3
Man with withered hand, 3:1
Those who have nothing, 4:25
Demoniac, 5:2
Hemorrhaging woman, 5:25
Syro-Phoenician woman and daughter, 7:25, 26
Deaf man with speech impediment, 7:32
Blind man, 8:22
Boy with an unclean spirit, 9:14
Blind Bartimaeus, 10:46
Simon the leper, 14:3
Swineherds, 5:14
Man carrying a jar, 14:13

a major reason for the reputation he develops (1:28). Note that two groups in the list above, swineherds and porters, are cited there because they are despised occupations. Another figure, the Syro-Phoenician woman, may originally have been a person of higher status, though with a daughter afflicted by an unclean spirit she would probably be understood by villagers as marginalized or ostracized.

Rural Peasants and Other Villagers

In agrarian societies such as that of the New Testament era, the cities dominated culturally, economically, and politically. Yet 90 percent of the population lived in the villages and rural areas, engaging in what social scientists call "primary" industries: farming and extracting raw materials. We want to look briefly at several of these rural groups who appear in Mark's story: freeholding peasants, tenant farmers, day laborers, slaves, and the various landless groups that included fishermen, artisans, and other craftsmen.

Freeholders. Although there is substantial debate over the percentage of land held by Galilean freeholders in the late first century C.E., nearly all scholars agree that if land held by the freeholders was the majority, it was not by much. Since land was the basis of most wealth and yields were both low and unstable, peasant debt leading to loss of land was epidemic. Determining standards of living for freeholding peasants has proved difficult, however, especially in view of the variability of soil and rainfall from area to area. Nonetheless, there is little doubt that peasants enjoyed minimal levels of survival. At the same time, the burden they bore of supporting the temple, priesthood, Herodian regime, and Roman needs for tribute (estimates for the total vary from 15 percent to as high as 35–50 percent) were crushing. Combined with other needs, this burden pushed peasant economic viability to the brink.

Isolated farms, on which peasant families lived separately from their neighbors, gradually disappeared prior to the New Testament period.

The majority of peasants came to live in villages or small towns, going out to the fields daily. Self-sufficiency was the ultimate goal for peasant families, who were the unit of both production and consumption. Barter sufficed for the majority of needs, and few peasants participated heavily in the slowly spreading monetarization of the economy. Evidence suggests that by New Testament times the extended families of an earlier period were being replaced by nuclear families living in close proximity around courtyards or clustered along narrow alleys.

Tenants, Day Laborers, and Slaves. Evidence for aristocratic control of major portions of arable land is most abundant for the period following the Jewish War, which broke out in 66 C.E. From these years, we get a clear picture of large estates employing tenant farmers, landless laborers, and slaves in producing crops for absentee landowners. Some tenants paid fixed rents in kind, others in money, and still others paid a percentage of the crop. Rents could go as high as two-thirds of a crop, though rabbinic sources more commonly mention figures ranging from one-fourth to one-half.

In addition to tenant farmers, there were both day laborers and slaves.[15] While day laborers were not necessarily landless people (freeholders often worked for others to supplement their farming income), those who were indeed without land were near the bottom of the social-economic scale. Commonly, they were either peasants who had lost land through indebtedness or the noninheriting sons of large families. Many such landless people drifted to the cities and towns that were in frequent need of new labor, not because of expanding economic opportunity, but because of extremely high death rates among the urban nonelite.

Other Rural Groups. Besides peasant farmers, most village and rural areas contained at least several other groups. Lower-level retainers and lay aristocrats often provided village leadership, and most villages of any size had a council to govern local affairs. Artisans, craftsmen, fishermen, and herders were also common, though few artisans or craftsmen could make a living in the smaller villages and thereby had to work in several locations. Since people who wandered about were considered socially deviant by villagers, itinerant workers were very low on the social scale. Shepherds were especially despised, being stereotyped as thieves without honor because their grazing sheep tended to wander into the fields of others.

As one might expect, these last groups, which were much the largest in ancient societies, are prominent throughout the story-world of Mark. An especially important group here is the crowd (Greek: *ochlos*, used thirty-eight times in Mark, translated variously in the RSV). Mark uses "crowd" both as a term for the poor (the equivalent of *'am ha'aretz*) and as an indicator of the social location of his own audience. The rabbis

Peasants or Villagers Mentioned in Mark

Jesus, *passim*
Those from the Judean countryside, 1:5
Peter, Andrew, 1:16
James, John, Zebedee, 1:19–20
Simon's mother-in-law, 1:30
Sower, 4:3
Seed scatterer, 4:26
Mary, 6:3
James, Joses, Judas, Simon, and Jesus' sisters, 6:3
Mary Magdalene, Mary the mother of James, Joses, Salome, 15:40
Little ones, 9:42
Children, 10:13
Bystanders in Bethphage, 11:5
Those buying in the temple (likely included urban poor as well), 11:15
Tenants, 12:1
Simon of Cyrene, 15:21
Crowd, 2:4, 13; 3:9, 20, 32; 4:1, 36; 5:21, 24, 27, 30, 31; 6:14, 17, 34, 39, 45; 7:14, 17, 33; 8:1, 2, 6, 34; 9:14, 15, 17, 25; 10:1, 46

taught that observant Jews should neither eat nor travel with the *'am ha 'aretz,* though the Jesus of Mark does both (e.g., 2:13–17; 8:1–8).

Another important group is the disciples. Mark tells us much about their fears, emotions, immaturity, stupidity, disloyalty, and eventual failure. While we cannot repeat here the many studies of the disciples as the prime indicators of Mark's audience, it is especially important to note that since failings were things talked about inside but not outside a Mediterranean family, we can only construe Mark's talk about the disciples' failures as "insider" or surrogate family talk. By taking the reader into his confidence on such matters, Mark indicates that he is writing for members of the Christian family.

Our primary interest is in Mark's social characterization of the disciples, though social information is readily available for only four of the twelve. Peter, Andrew, James, and John were fishermen, a despised occupation as Cicero sees it, since fishermen "cater to sensual pleasures."[16] Whereas James and John used a boat to fish (1:19), Peter and Andrew appear to have been net casters (1:16–18). Although Mark notes that James and John left their father with the hired hands (1:20), this does not automatically imply that the family was better off than most. Tax farmers often hired day laborers to work with contract fishermen. In any case, the four disciples that can be socially located are clearly members of the exploited nonelite. Socially and economically, they were below even peasant farmers and had less long-term security.

The persons from the Judean countryside (1:5), the sower (4:3), little ones (9:42), bystanders in Bethphage (11:5), tenants (12:1), and various other persons listed above were probably peasant farmers. Jesus and his family, however, were artisans. Though Mark does not mention the Bethlehem tradition, if Jesus' family was originally Judean, we can assume that a predecessor there had lost the land or they would not have moved to Galilee, where it would be difficult to make a living in a small village. (As the first chart shows, *village* artisans were even below peasants on the socioeconomic scale.)

The Social Level of Mark's Audience

Although there have been many attempts to characterize the Markan audience in recent years (e.g., Beavis, Malbon, Hengel, Tannehill), most have focused on various ethnic, geographical, or religious aspects of the group's identity. In contrast, it is our aim to locate the place of Mark's audience on the social spectrum we have heretofore described.

In looking over the five lists of characters in Mark cited above, we can safely say that the narrative world of Mark accurately re-creates the sharply stratified peasant society of his day. We can be sure that at some points this narrative world corresponds with the real world of Jesus, while at others it almost certainly does not. In the same way, Mark's narrative world and real world are probably not exact equivalents either, though the simple requirement of verisimilitude and relevance in literature designed to be persuasive makes substantial overlap between Mark's story-world and Mark's real world probable. The "truth" of Mark's text would be self-evident to a reader in large measure from the way it overlapped (or contravened) the real world. Trying to find contraventions or correspondences between the real world of social antagonisms described above and the story-world of Mark is thus the only real choice we have for finding the social location of Mark's audience. Basically, of course, it will come down to a question of how high or low on the social scale we might imagine it to be.

Group Boundaries and Self-Definition

We begin here with recent studies of the boundary language used by Mark so as to clarify the lines of demarcation between his own community and those outside.[17] As Jerome Neyrey has suggested, the pervasive conflict between Jesus and the temple authorities or their representatives belies a certain defensiveness on Mark's part about both Jesus and his own community. Mark reports that Jesus is affirmed as the "Holy One of God" (1:24), but this view is not shared by his elite opponents. The standards by which the latter define themselves as Israelites are disregarded by Jesus in every important respect. Jesus repeatedly violates the purity rules regarding persons (1:41; 2:13–14; 4:35–42; 5:24–28; 5:41; 7:24–30; 7:31) by coming in contact with the diseased, the dead, the malformed, and the demon-possessed. Jesus violates rules about the body (7:33; 8:23), meal practice (6:37–44; 8:1–10), times (2:24; 3:1–6), and places (11:15–16; 12:33). It is not surprising that in the controversy over the source of Jesus' power his opponents claim his rule-breaking has its origin in Satan (3:22–27).

Mark's defense of Jesus is a spirited one, however, and one that simultaneously functions as a form of self-definition for Mark's community. Mark asserts that, appearances notwithstanding, Jesus' purity is affirmed by God in both his baptism (1:10–11) and transfiguration (9:2–8). Mark claims that the scriptures offer justification (2:25–26; 7:6; 10:5; 11:17) for Jesus' actions even though others judge them to be violations of the rules of purity. As Mark sees it, Jesus legitimately promulgates new purity rules which imply that holiness is an internal matter of the heart rather than an external matter of protecting body surfaces and orifices (7:18–23). The key to acknowledging this lies in one's ability to confess Jesus to be the Christ (8:27–30). Moreover, as Neyrey reminds us, the membership criteria for belonging to the circle of Jesus' disciples in Mark are not the same as those of the synagogue, where blood and physical or genealogical concerns were paramount. Jesus' surrogate family is nonbiological and made up of believers: "Whoever does the will of God is my brother and sister and mother" (3:35). What makes one an outsider in Mark is objection to Jesus' teachings or practices (2:7; 7:1–4) or lack of belief in him (6:3–6).

The key point that Neyrey makes in all this, however, is that in constructing a defense for Jesus, Mark is also defending his own community. Mark's Jesus disregards the purity rules of the religiously correct and welcomes the unclean, the marginal, and gentiles. In telling the reader this, Mark is actually "re-drawing the boundaries of his own community."[18] He wishes to include all those unholy types with whom Jesus interacts in his story and who, in Mark's day, were to be defended as being part of the people of God in the same way that Mark's Jesus defends himself.

Focus on boundary definition is important in yet another respect. As Michael White shows in his study of Matthew, boundary definition is especially important for communities caught in conflict or crisis.[19] Such definition draws the lines between insiders and outsiders, loyalists and opponents. Similarly, Ched Myers argues that in the crisis of the impending Jewish-Roman war, groups in the border areas of upper Galilee and southern Syria were forced to define and declare themselves in terms of the emerging dispute. Myers's thesis that Mark 13 describes the situation just prior to the war, when Christians were in danger of being handed over to councils and beaten in synagogues in an attempt to force them to declare for one side or the other, is perhaps open to debate.[20] But he is surely correct when he claims that the community of Mark was caught in a crisis that required struggle on two fronts. On the one hand, the reconciliation of Jew with gentile was opposed by Pharisees for reasons of purity; on the other hand, it was encouraged by Romans on imperialistic grounds. Consequently Christians who reconciled themselves with Jews, but on pointedly nonimperialistic grounds, incurred the wrath of both sides. Thus, as Myers suggests, the dilemma that Jesus faces in 12:13–17 over the question of whether to pay taxes to Caesar may reflect the kind of crisis that faced the community for which Mark wrote. The choice seemed to be God or Caesar. To many Jews or Romans these were the only two alternatives.

Important as these studies of purity and boundaries are, they tend to overlook a critical factor in peasant life. The historical Jesus may have been seen as unholy and unwashed by the religious elite, and his behavior may have seemed iconoclastic or even perverse, but to a peasant it would not have seemed to be anything out of the ordinary. Very few peasants could have observed the Great Tradition even if they had wanted to. They came into constant contact with bodily secretions, dead animals, and unwashed foods. They could not always have afforded to keep Sabbaths and holy days: In dry-land farming with marginal or uneven rainfall, each day that passed between the first rains and plowing reduced the final yields. Nor could they always have afforded the prescribed sacrifices or guaranteed the cleanliness of meal companions. We must point out, therefore, that the very rules that the Markan Jesus breaks concerning dietary laws, washing, Sabbath observance, and temple sacrifice are precisely those that peasants had the most difficulty keeping. To the peasants of Mark's day Jesus' lifestyle would have been thoroughly familiar. At the same time, Jesus' defense of an internal purity that could be maintained without heavy expense or the disruption of necessary peasant farming practices would have come as a surprise to them. Jesus' lifestyle as such would not. Thus, if Mark's Jesus is also defending Mark's community, what Mark really asserts is that purity before God is possible within the limits of a peasant way of life.

The Character of the Folkloric Tradition

The social level of Mark's audience can be inferred in yet another way. To attempt to correlate Mark's audience with the social elite of his storyworld would make it extremely difficult to explain the characteristics of the folkloric tradition in the way Mark has perpetuated it. We may take it for granted that Mark was not simply a passive purveyor of what came down to him. He was a creative author. Nonetheless, as Vernon Robbins has shown, Mark's way of telling his story functioned to create social cohesion in the Markan community. It did so by articulating conflicts and antagonisms harbored by group members who still perceived themselves to be victims of the adversaries in the story.[21] By portraying the attitudes of the elite toward Jesus as being rejected and the responses of the degraded as being vindicated, Mark created a story that could be used to perpetuate identity, to educate children and new members, and to ensure conformity to the group's norms in contrast to those of their opponents.[22]

It could be objected, of course, that Mark holds up the negative examples of the elite in his story-world and the contrasting actions of Jesus to rescue the weak as a form of social criticism aimed at elite members of Mark's audience. This is certainly possible, though a narrative plotted to achieve this effect is much more evident in Luke's Gospel than in Mark's. Accordingly, it is best to conclude that Mark's particular way of telling his story implies a group of readers who celebrated the victories of the weak and the defeats of the strong and who found mirrored in the characters of the story and the events that engulf them the dramas of their own lives.

In any event, the latter plainly seems to be the case relative to the disciples. They are representative of Mark's audience.[23] As Mark's plotline returns again and again to the disturbing inability of the disciples to grasp what Jesus does and says, it invites the readers to question the clarity and meaning of their own responses to him. Within Mark's story, the disciples at the last abandon Jesus. The question this raises for the disciples or readers outside the story is whether they will do the same.

Perhaps they will. But the Gospel also celebrates the many victories of faith on the part of peasants, the degraded, the unclean, and expendables. So many are these people that they repeatedly crowd Jesus. They are key actors on Mark's stage. Moreover, as Mark often points out (e.g., 5:30; 6:2; 7:37; 12:34), two things frequently astonish them: Jesus' healing power, of which they are the beneficiaries, and his ability to defeat his elite adversaries at every turn. These elements in the social drama of Mark's narrative inevitably engender expectations and hopes in the life of its real readers or hearers. In fact, given the numbers of such low-level and degraded people who were presumably a part of Mark's real world, if high expectations and hopes for just these kinds of persons were not the essence of Mark's story, the latter could hardly have been termed "Good News."

NOTES

1. By this term we simply mean a position in a social system shared by a group of people.

2. This traditional location for Mark has been extensively argued on many occasions. Perhaps the best is Martin Hengel, "Entstehungszeit und Situation des Markusevangeliums," in *Markus-Philologie: Historische, literaturgeschichtliche und stilistische Untersuchungen zum zweiten Evangelium,* ed. H. Cancik, WUNT 33, 1–45. Donald Senior summarizes Hengel's case in "'With Swords

and Clubs . . . ' — The Setting of Mark's Community and His Critique of Abusive Power," *BTB* 17 (1987): 10–20.

3. The case for Syria may be found in Howard C. Kee, *Community of the New Age: Studies in Mark's Gospel* (Philadelphia: Westminster Press, 1977), 102–5; also see Ched Myers, *Binding the Strong Man* (Maryknoll, N.Y.: Orbis Books, 1988); and most recently Gerd Theissen, *The Gospels in Context: Social and Political History in the Synoptic Tradition,* trans. Linda M. Maloney (Minneapolis: Fortress Press, 1991), 238–39. A detailed review of the arguments for both locations that comes down on a Syrian, but not Galilean, provenance is Joel Marcus, "The Jewish War and the *Sitz im Leben* of Mark," *JBL* 111 (1992): 441–62.

4. William V. Harris argues that early Christianity did little to encourage ordinary believers to read for themselves and may, in fact, have contributed to a decline in literacy, *Ancient Literacy* (Cambridge: Harvard University Press, 1989), 305, 311, 319, 326.

5. Ibid., 241–44, 329, *passim.*

6. Contrary to the widely used comments of C. H. Roberts, "Books in the Graeco-Roman World and in the New Testament," *Cambridge History of the Bible,* I, ed. P. R. Ackroyd and C. F. Evans (Cambridge: Cambridge University Press, 1979). For a critique of Roberts, see Harris, who argues that the school system was in decline, at least in the eastern provinces, *Ancient Literacy,* 281.

7. Harris, *Ancient Literacy,* 333.

8. Mary Ann Beavis, *Mark's Audience: The Literary and Social Setting of Mark 4:11–12* (Sheffield: JSOT Press, 1989), 21.

9. Ibid., 42–44.

10. Frequent reading aloud was a key test of canonicity for Eusebius, *Ecclesiastical History* 3.3.6.

11. Dennis Duling, *The New Testament: An Introduction* (New York: Harcourt, Brace, Jovanovich, 1993), chap. 2, based on Gerhard and Jean Linski, *Human Societies: An Introduction to Macrosociology* (New York: McGraw-Hill, 1974), 207–62.

12. Loeb, *Select Papyri II: Non-Literary* (Public Documents), 9.339, 393.

13. Elizabeth Struthers Malbon, "The Jewish Leaders in the Gospel of Mark: A Literary Study of Marcan Characterization," *JBL* 108 (1989): 275–76.

14. Anthony Saldarini, "The Social Class of the Pharisees in Mark," in *The Social World of Formative Christianity and Judaism: Essays in Tribute to Howard Clark Kee,* ed. J. Neusner et al. (Philadelphia: Fortress Press, 1988), 71.

15. Sources indicate that they worked by the hour, day, month, year, three years, or seven years; see David Fiensy, *The Social History of Palestine in the Herodian Period: The Land Is Mine* (Lewiston, N.Y.: Edwin Mellen Press, 1991), 85.

16. Cicero, *De Officiis* 1.150–51.

17. This discussion of purity in Mark is summarized from Jerome Neyrey, "The Idea of Purity in Mark's Gospel," in *Social-Scientific Criticism of the New Testament and Its Social World,* ed. John H. Elliott, *Semeia* 35 (1986): 91–128. See also David Rhoads, "Social Criticism: Crossing Boundaries," in *New Ap-*

proaches in Biblical Studies, ed. J. C. Anderson and S. D. Moore (Minneapolis: Fortress Press, 1992), 135–61.

18. Neyrey, "The Idea of Purity in Mark's Gospel," 124.

19. Michael White, "Crisis Management and Boundary Maintenance: The Social Location of the Matthean Community," in David L. Balch, ed., *Social History of the Matthean Community* (Minneapolis: Fortress Press, 1991), 221–28.

20. Myers, *Binding the Strong Man,* 323–28. Marcus takes a similar view, "The Jewish War and the *Sitz im Leben* of Mark," 453.

21. Vernon Robbins, *Jesus the Teacher: A Socio-Rhetorical Interpretation of Mark* (Philadelphia: Fortress Press, 1984), 8.

22. Ibid.

23. Robert C. Tannehill, "The Disciples in Mark: The Function of a Narrative Role," *JR* 57 (1977): 386–405; Joanna Dewey, "Point of View and the Disciples in Mark," SBLSP (1982), ed. Kent H. Richards, 97–106; et al.

The Gospel of LUKE

– 11 –

Toward a Narrative-Critical Understanding of Luke

Mark Allan Powell

To ascertain the theology of the Gospels lies within the purview of both narrative and historical criticism, and narrative criticism also obligates the interpreter to deal with historical questions. To say this, however, is not to deny the distinctiveness of each method. Each method poses different questions, pursues different goals, and obtains different results. To observe this, one may note how each deals with such major questions as the purpose of Luke's Gospel, the role Luke's infancy narrative plays within his story, and the relationship of Luke's Gospel to Acts.

THE LITERARY QUALITY of the Gospel of Luke has long been appreciated. Excerpts from it, such as the account of the baby in the manger or the parable of the Good Samaritan, are regarded as masterpieces of ancient literature and continue to capture the popular imagination today. In the nineteenth century, the work as a whole was called "the most beautiful book in the world" by the French philosopher Renan.[1]

Such appreciation, however, usually reflects concern for the aesthetic value of Luke's Gospel rather than regard for its theological worth. The great contributions of historical-critical scholarship have helped to define the theological meaning of Luke's Gospel in terms of what it reveals about history, namely, what it teaches about the earthly Jesus or the early church or the evangelist himself. To do this requires only slight reference to the character of Luke's Gospel as a literary work of art.[2]

Narrative criticism challenges the dichotomy between literary or aesthetic appreciation and historical or theological understanding.[3] To assess the theological worth of Luke's Gospel, we ought to determine not only what the book reveals about history but also what effect it is intended to have on its readers. Thus, the insights of literary criticism may prove just as relevant for theological understanding as have those of historical analysis.

Narrative criticism and historical criticism are theoretically complementary but, in practice, quite distinct. Different questions are asked, different goals pursued, and different results obtained. To illustrate the respective contributions these approaches make to biblical scholarship, we will examine three key issues in Lukan studies and see how each is addressed by historical critics on the one hand and narrative critics on the other.

Purpose of the Gospel

Historical critics have suggested a number of reasons why Luke may have written this Gospel: to provide those who never knew Jesus with an accurate account of events concerning him; to present a theological scheme of salvation history that explains the delay of the Parousia; to combat the heresy of gnosticism; to further peaceful relations with the Roman Empire; to facilitate the incorporation of gentiles into the church; or to strengthen those experiencing tribulation, persecution, or doubt as a result of various developments in the latter third of the first century.[4] All of these suggestions relate the purpose of the work to its intended relevance for the historical period in which it was written.

Narrative critics recognize "transcendence of immediate context" to be an intrinsic quality of literature. (A "classic" is by definition a work that succeeds at being meaningful in a place and time other than when it was written.) Although knowledge of original context is essential for understanding certain aspects of Luke's Gospel, narrative critics refrain from identifying the purpose of the work with precise reference to the situation of its first readers. Instead, the purpose may be to preach to the reader[5] or to engage the reader's imagination[6] in ways that elicit faith, inspire worship, provoke repentance, or otherwise shape the perspective and conduct of those who encounter the work in a variety of life settings.

Josephine Ford

Role of Infancy Narrative

In historical-critical scholarship, the significance of the first two chapters of Luke's Gospel has been much debated in discussions of the book's theology. Hans Conzelmann regarded these chapters as of little importance because he suspected that they were written by someone other than the evangelist and attached to the Gospel as an afterthought.[7] Other redaction critics have disagreed, viewing Luke 1–2 as a prime expression of the evangelist's own perspective.[8]

Source-critical questions are generally irrelevant to consideration of the impact that a work of literature is expected to have on its readers. While Luke's readers might be expected to notice motifs or refrains drawn from the Old Testament, they are not expected to be familiar with the compositional history of the Gospel as a whole. Thus, narrative critics do not interpret Luke's Gospel by specifying what comes from Mark, Q, or L, for example; nor do they ascribe greater significance to those portions of the narrative that appear to have come directly from the evangelist's own hand. The assumption is that readers are expected to receive the work in the form in which it is presented and to make sense of it on its own terms. Accordingly, narrative critics may view the infancy stories with which the Gospel opens as an introduction to the main plot[9] or even as an overture that sounds major themes to be developed as the story progresses.[10] They read this portion of the narrative with attention to the rhetorical significance of "beginnings" in literature[11] and with an appreciation for such literary devices as foreshadowing[12] and intertextuality.[13] The concern is not to distinguish the theological perspective of the infancy narrative from what may be expressed elsewhere in the Gospel but to determine how this portion of the narrative contributes to the reader's experience of the work as a whole.

Relationship to Acts

With regard to the relationship of Luke's Gospel to the Book of Acts, narrative critics debate a matter that hardly evinces any discussion in historical-critical circles. For some time now, historical critics have accepted that the two volumes present a unified theological perspective. Most historical critics do not hesitate to interpret the theological intention of Luke's Gospel with reference to insights drawn from Acts (and vice versa). For example, Luke's mention in Acts of Pharisees who are Christians (15:5) or helpful to the Christian cause (5:34–39; 23:6–9) disposes some scholars to regard his attitude toward the Pharisees as more irenic than it might appear to be from references in the Gospel. The evangelist, they assume, inherits traditional material that presents the Pharisees negatively, but he believes the disputes between Pharisees and Christians can be transcended.[14]

For narrative critics, the question is not whether these two volumes come from the same author but whether they tell one story or two. In other words, is the Book of Acts a sequel to the Gospel, which is therefore complete in itself, or is it a continuation of the Gospel, which would be incomplete if read alone? Robert Tannehill has argued for the latter position, claiming that Luke-Acts has a unified plot because there is a unifying purpose of God behind the events which are narrated.[15] Mikeal Parsons suggests, however, that the Gospel comes to a fitting conclusion with its account of the ascension (Luke 24:50–53) and that Acts, which opens with a different account of the ascension, ought to be read as a separate, though related, story.[16]

Reading Luke and Acts as separate stories will obviously lead to different interpretations than those advanced by historical critics who view Luke-Acts as a single entity. But even narrative critics who consider the two volumes to be parts of a continuous work tend to read this work differently than historical critics. John Darr, for example, notes that historical critics do not attempt to make sense of the work sequentially, that is, with reference to how the reader experiences the work when it is read from beginning to end. Such a reading, favored by narrative critics, suggests an evaluation of the Pharisees that is the converse of what historical critics have found. Based on the negative portrayal of the Pharisees in the Gospel, Luke's reader will be suspicious of the "friendly Pharisees" in Acts and will tend to regard such friendliness as superficial or hypocritical.[17]

Conclusion

Historical critics begin their investigation of Luke's Gospel with a basic distinction between tradition and redaction. What is traditional derives from Luke's sources and from this we may learn about historical events and theological perspectives antecedent to the evangelist's own life setting. What is redactional derives from the evangelist himself and serves to inform us of Luke's own circumstances and ideas. From the perspective of the historical critic, then, Luke offers a superimposed photograph from which much can be learned if the images are properly distinguished.[18]

Narrative critics prefer to analyze Luke's Gospel with reference to story and discourse.[19] Whereas *story* refers to the content of the narrative, what it is about, *discourse* refers to its rhetoric, how the story is told. Narrative critics try to identify the basic storylines of the narrative[20] and consider such questions as how the narrator guides the reader,[21] how characters are constructed in the experience of reading,[22] how literary motifs[23] and patterns[24] are developed, and how the logic of the story is maintained.[25]

The distinctions between tradition and redaction on the one hand and story and discourse on the other are analogous but not parallel. Narrative critics recognize that the story Luke tells is mostly traditional and that distinctive Lukan theology is revealed primarily through the discourse, the way in which this story is presented. But no material separation can be made between story and discourse. The entire content of Luke's narrative constitutes the "story as discoursed." For narrative critics, Luke's Gospel might be compared to an impressionist painting. It is representational, but its meaning is better described in terms of the effect that the representation has on its audience rather than simply in terms of what is represented.

For historical critics, the theological value of Luke's work consists of its usefulness as a resource for historical reconstruction. It offers us photographs, albeit flawed ones, of the time of Jesus and of the early church. If only Luke had preserved his sources intact and written his own commentary on them separately, the task of historical criticism would be simpler. As it is, the goal of exegesis must be to undo what Luke has done, to separate tradition from redaction, so that we may see more clearly the images that Luke has superimposed.

Narrative criticism does not question the legitimacy of this enterprise or deny the effectiveness with which it is pursued. Most narrative critics regard historical knowledge as an essential basis for theological reflection and admit that historical criticism is well suited for obtaining such knowledge. Still, narrative critics do not limit the theological value of Luke's Gospel to its usefulness as a resource for historical reconstruction. The theological meaning of Luke's Gospel may also be defined in terms of the impact that it is expected to have on its readers. To arrive at such an understanding calls for exegesis that does not undo what Luke has done but appreciates it — that views the evangelist as a successful artist rather than as a failed photographer.

NOTES

1. Ernest Renan, *Les évangiles et la seconde génération chrétienne,* 2d ed. (Paris: Michel Lévy, 1877), 283. See also Geoffrey F. Nutall, *The Moment of Recognition: Luke as Storyteller* (London: Athlone Press, 1978).

2. See, for example, the discussion of Luke's literary style by Henry J. Cadbury in *The Making of Luke-Acts* (1927; reprint, London: SPCK, 1958). For Cadbury and the redaction critics who followed him, style became a means of determining what was Lukan rather than a feature of the Gospel that was itself judged to be theologically significant.

3. For a history of the development of narrative criticism, see Stephen D. Moore, *Literary Criticism and the Gospels: The Theoretical Challenge* (New Haven: Yale University Press, 1989), 1–68. For a description of narrative-critical method, see Mark Allan Powell, *What Is Narrative Criticism?* GBS (Minneapolis: Fortress Press, 1990).

4. For summaries of these and other views, see Mark Allan Powell, *What*

Are They Saying about Luke? (New York: Paulist Press, 1989); idem, *What Are They Saying about Acts?* (New York: Paulist Press, 1991), 13–19.

5. Picking up on terminology first advanced by Jack Dean Kingsbury, Robert J. Karris describes Luke as a "kerygmatic story" that is "meant to preach to the reader in narrative form and elicit from the reader an act of Christian faith"; see *Luke: Artist and Theologian. Luke's Passion Account as Literature* (New York: Paulist Press, 1985), 8.

6. Jack Dean Kingsbury describes how the reader or hearer "enters into the world of Luke's Gospel" through the use of imagination and thus "experiences Luke's gospel story and is shaped by it"; see *Conflict in Luke: Jesus, Authorities, Disciples* (Minneapolis: Fortress Press, 1991), 1.

7. Hans Conzelmann, *The Theology of St. Luke,* 2d ed. (1957; reprint, London: Faber and Faber, 1960).

8. Raymond E. Brown, *The Birth of the Messiah: A Commentary on the Infancy Narratives in Matthew and Luke* (Garden City, N.Y.: Doubleday, 1970).

9. Kingsbury, *Conflict in Luke,* 34.

10. Robert H. Tannehill says the infancy narrative "previews" the purposes of God to be realized in the story that follows. See *The Narrative Unity of Luke-Acts: A Literary Interpretation* (Philadelphia: Fortress Press, 1986), 1:15–44.

11. The best survey and bibliography of studies on narrative beginnings is found in a book that deals with the beginning of Acts. See Mikeal Parsons, *The Departure of Jesus in Luke-Acts: The Ascension Narratives in Context,* JSNTSup 21 (Sheffield: JSOT Press, 1987), 151–86.

12. See Tannehill on "previews," n. 10 above.

13. "Intertextuality" refers to citation or allusion to other texts—in this case, the writings of the Old Testament.

14. Robert L. Brawley, *Luke-Acts and the Jews: Conflict, Apology, and Conciliation,* SBLMS 33 (Atlanta: Scholars Press, 1987), 84–106.

15. Tannehill, *Narrative Unity,* 2.

16. Parsons, *Departure.* Cf. Mikeal C. Parsons and Richard I. Pervo, *Rethinking of Luke-Acts* (Minneapolis: Fortress Press, 1993).

17. John A. Darr, *On Character Building: The Reader and the Rhetoric of Characterization in Luke-Acts* (Louisville: Westminster/John Knox Press, 1992), 85–126. Cf. David B. Gowler, *Host, Guest, Enemy, and Friend: Portraits of the Pharisees in Luke and Acts* (New York: Peter Lang, 1991).

18. C. K. Barrett, *Luke the Historian in Recent Study* (London: Epworth Press, 1971), 24–25.

19. Seymour Chatman, *Story and Discourse: Narrative Structure in Fiction and Film* (Ithaca, N.Y.: Cornell University Press, 1978).

20. Kingsbury, *Conflict.*

21. William S. Kurz, *Reading Luke-Acts: Dynamics of Biblical Narrative* (Louisville: Westminster/John Knox Press, 1993); Steven M. Sheeley, *Narrative Asides in Luke-Acts,* JSNTSup 72 (Sheffield: JSOT Press, 1992). Cf. James M. Dawsey, *The Lukan Voice: Confusion and Irony in the Gospel of Luke* (Macon, Ga.: Mercer University Press, 1988).

22. Darr, *On Character Building.*

23. Karris treats three motifs ("faithfulness," "justice," and "food") in *Luke: Artist and Theologian.*

24. See Charles H. Talbert, *Literary Patterns, Theological Themes, and the Genre Acts* (Missoula, Mont.: Scholars Press, 1974), 1–61.

25. Robert L. Brawley, *Centering on God: Method and Message in Luke-Acts* (Louisville: Westminster/John Knox Press, 1990), esp. 58–85.

– 12 –

"Cornelius" and "Tabitha" Encounter Luke's Jesus

Robert C. Tannehill

Tabitha and Cornelius, imaginary persons based on characters in Acts, occupy two different places in the first-century Mediterranean world. In hearing Luke's gospel story, how would each construe the figure of Jesus? The social location of each would play a crucial role as each "builds" the character of Jesus in dialogue with Luke's story.

THIS ESSAY is influenced by two concerns: (1) the desire to recognize the value of reader-response criticism; and (2) the need to integrate literary approaches to the Gospels with traditional historical criticism and the new social-scientific criticism. The guiding question that enables me to bring these concerns together is this: How would two first-century persons, who differ in social location, understand the character Jesus as they follow the public reading of Luke's Gospel?[1] I am studying the characterization of Jesus in Luke's story, while recognizing, as reader-response criticism has done, that the text is only a schema that must be actualized by its audience, and also taking account of the fact, as reader-response criticism has not generally done, that members of an audience with different social locations will to some extent actualize the text differently.

Literary approaches to the Gospels have now established themselves sufficiently that we need not fear losing what we have gained if we endeavor to integrate our work with historical and social-scientific criticism. The need for this is clear even from a literary perspective. As John Darr has recently argued,[2] the text can be read with understanding only if the reader has access to the "extratext" — a complex body of knowledge consisting of language codes, literary conventions, social codes, some items of general historical knowledge, and some other texts (such as the Septuagint). The text is constructed so as to activate items from the extratext in communicating with the audience. The older historical criticism, the newer social-scientific criticism of ancient Mediterranean society, and studies in literary history can help us understand the extratext.

Darr has laid the foundation for a reader-response approach to characters in Luke-Acts. He argues that readers "build" characters during the reading process. Reader-response critics, in turn, must consciously "build" readers so that the critic can "read" the reader reading the text. Furthermore, "if our interpretive analyses are to be responsible, rigorous, and open to argument, then *we must identify the reader to whom we refer.*"[3] "To some degree," Darr admits, "*the* reader is always *my* reader, a projection of my own experience of reading the text," but the critic should nevertheless attempt to construct a first-century reader with the "cultural literacy" and "cultural scripts" appropriate to the text. This reconstructed reader enables us to imagine the reading process of the original readers.[4] Although Darr is content with a single first-century reader, the original recipients of Luke contained people of different social location (Jew and gentile, female and male, poor and relatively rich). There would be some significant differences in the way that two persons of different social location would process the presentation of Jesus in Luke. Thus I am attempting to go one step further than Darr in defining the reader, for reader-response critics need to be aware that there were different kinds of readers and multiple readings even in the first century.

For this experiment, I will adopt other features of Darr's method: I will assume that both text and reader must contribute to the actualization of a literary work. I, like Darr, will adopt the viewpoint of the first-time reader or hearer, who will have the full picture of the Lukan Jesus only when the end of the text is reached, but who will repeatedly form and revise pictures of Jesus as the text unrolls. I will try to suggest how expectations are aroused and then revised in the listening process, how the reader might try to build a consistent picture of Jesus from the material in the text and where this would be difficult, and how different hearers might identify with different characters as the reading proceeds.[5] Within the limited space of this essay, I can, of course, only begin this task.

Let me introduce my two "readers" or listeners. One I will call Cornelius. He is modeled after, but not identical with, the Cornelius who appears in Acts 10. The other I will call Tabitha. She is modeled after, but not identical with, the Tabitha who appears in Acts 9:36–43. The Gospel of Luke is unique in that it is followed by the story of Acts, which features characters who receive the message about Jesus. In the case of Cornelius, we have a scene in Acts in which Peter retells, in summary, the story of Jesus in its Lukan form (Acts 10:36–43).[6] Taking this scene of Cornelius's receiving Luke's story of Jesus as our clue, we will explore how two persons similar to those presented in Acts might respond to the Lukan story.

I will modify the figures of Cornelius and Tabitha in two ways that reflect about the likely time and place of the writing of Luke-Acts. I will assume that my two listeners encounter the Lukan story some time after 70 C.E. and that they live outside the Jewish homeland. Tabitha I will move from Joppa to the Jewish quarter of Syrian Antioch. I will locate Cornelius somewhere in the Roman east, but not at Caesarea.

In other respects I would like to retain the basic features of Cornelius and Tabitha. Cornelius is a centurion, either in a Roman legion or in the auxiliary forces. The legionary troops had higher status and pay, but the auxiliary forces also could be commanded by Roman officers. Cornelius is therefore a professional soldier serving Rome and a middle-rank officer. Even though higher officers were usually chosen from the nobility, a centurion, too, had opportunity for advancement because the centurions of a legion were ranked in a hierarchy. The first centurion of a legion held a position of considerable importance and status. Furthermore, a career as a centurion "was financially very advantageous," for "the pay was probably some sixteen times that of the basic legionary salary. In short, a centurion had both considerable military and social status and wealth."[7]

Cornelius has been strongly influenced by diaspora Judaism. Through contact with the local synagogue he learned some of the essentials of Jewish faith. For some time he has been praying to the God of the Jews. He has been a patron of the local Jewish community, contributing generously to the synagogue. Yet he remains a gentile. More recently, he has joined the community that proclaims Jesus as Messiah.

Tabitha was born of a Jewish family in the Jewish quarter of Antioch. She also has joined the local community that proclaims Jesus as Messiah. She was attracted to this community for two reasons: She experienced healing in the name of Jesus (we will not claim resurrection, as in Acts 9:36–43); and she also lost her husband some years ago and found that the followers of Jesus were offering support for widows in their community. She joined this group of widows and has become one of their leaders in providing clothing for other widows and poor people.

Any real person, of course, will have individual characteristics that cannot be predicted apart from actual acquaintance with this person. Our Cornelius and Tabitha, however, are not real persons. They are constructs that mark sociohistorical locations. We will imagine their responses in light of those sociohistorical locations, while ignoring the unpredictable features of actual individuals. Nevertheless, we will add this bit of realism to their definition: Although both participate in the local communities that honor Jesus, both have doubts and questions that will affect their hearing of Luke.

Now we will try to imagine how Cornelius and Tabitha might build a consistent picture of Jesus from the data supplied in the story, beginning at the point where Jesus is first mentioned (1:31). Gabriel's words to Mary about Jesus' future role could create problems for both Tabitha and Cornelius because of the heavy emphasis on Jesus' role as Davidic king. For Tabitha, of course, Gabriel is announcing the fulfillment of an ancient promise to her people, which should be a cause of joy, yet recent history does not support the belief that Jesus will restore the throne of David for the Jewish people. Jesus has come and gone. Rome has defeated the Jewish rebellion. Conflict between Jewish followers of Jesus and other Jews discourages the belief that Jesus will be welcomed by Jews as their king.

The problem is even more acute for Cornelius. Although he may admire the Jewish figures in the birth narrative, hearing that Jesus "will reign over the house of Jacob" does not fulfill his hopes, since he is not a member of the house of Jacob. Furthermore, as a professional soldier, sworn to serve the present government, he is likely to be disturbed by the emphasis on Jesus as the promised Jewish king. This emphasis makes it more difficult for Cornelius to reconcile his military profession and his faith. It leaves him open to the charge of disloyalty to Caesar brought against believers in Acts 17:7. ("All these people are acting against the decrees of Caesar, claiming that there is another king, Jesus.") Although Cornelius is attracted to Judaism, he is scarcely comfortable, as an officer in Caesar's army, with the messianic hope in Gabriel's announcement.

Nevertheless, Tabitha and Cornelius are being strongly encouraged to accept the proclamation of Jesus as messianic king. This description of Jesus is given by Gabriel, a messenger who speaks with divine authority. Furthermore, the narrative presents divine promises of wonderful births and then shows them coming to pass, illustrating the scriptural principle that "nothing will be impossible with God" (Luke 1:37; see Gen. 18:14). Mary is also praised in the narrative for believing "that there would be a fulfillment of what was spoken to her by the Lord" (Luke 1:45). Hearers of Luke's story are being encouraged to respond in a similar way to the promises in the birth narrative, including the promise that Jesus will sit on the throne of David and reign over the house of Jacob forever.[8]

Tabitha might identify with Mary, not only because she is a Jewish woman but also because Mary speaks in the Magnificat of her humble status. Attraction to Mary would encourage Tabitha to share in Mary's acceptance and then in her joy. It would also encourage her to believe that through Jesus the lowly will be exalted and the hungry fed (1:52–53). Cornelius would be more distant from the characters in the birth narrative. A Jewish priest and two Jewish women provide little opportunity for identification. Furthermore, Mary's Magnificat would create a problem for Cornelius. The message that God, in sending Jesus, "has brought down the powerful from their thrones" (1:52) puts a person of status, who is also a servant of the emperor, in a serious bind. The lowly in Israel can join Mary's song, but her joy is not easily shared by others.

Cornelius's problem becomes more acute with the Benedictus. Here the themes of the annunciation and the Magnificat return, but in sharper expression. Salvation for Israel through the Davidic Messiah is announced (1:69), and it is now defined as "salvation from our enemies and from the hand of all who hate us" (1:71; cf. 1:74). The Roman-Jewish war could not quickly be forgotten by a person like Cornelius, for it would represent his own conflicted loyalties. In this war the Roman army was the enemy of the Jewish people. Yet Jesus the Messiah is being presented as the rescuer of the Jewish people from such enemies. The reference to the "way of peace" at the end of the Benedictus does not solve the problem, if this refers to the peace that comes after the oppressive enemy is overthrown and justice is restored through bringing down "the powerful from their thrones" (1:52). For Tabitha, too, the Benedictus would be disturbing. It would be a reminder that although Jesus came to Israel and was proclaimed Messiah, he did not save Israel from the Roman enemy. Zechariah's words seem to be authoritative, for he speaks while filled with the Holy Spirit (1:67), but for both our hearers there would be a sharp conflict between his prophetic words and the actual course of events.[9]

The announcement to the shepherds does not relieve the difficulty, for the proclamation of the "Messiah Lord" born "in the city of David," who will bring "great joy" to "all the people" of Israel and be their "savior," summarizes the characterization of Jesus to this point without solving the problem created. The announcement of his birth to shepherds and the note that he is "lying in a manger" (2:12) may remind our hearers that he is coming for the lowly and hungry (1:52–53), but it is still not clear how Jesus can be the Davidic Messiah who frees his people from oppression.

The presentation of the infant Jesus in the temple carries the characterization of Jesus two steps further. (1) In 2:29–32 Simeon's prophetic hymn continues the theme of salvation and develops the theme of light introduced in 1:78–79, but Simeon also connects Jesus with Isaiah's expectation of the servant, who would be a "light of the nations" (Isa. 42:6; 49:6). The promised salvation represented by the infant Jesus, then, includes both the Jewish people and the gentiles. Cornelius's share in the promised salvation is here affirmed for the first time. Yet Jesus remains the "glory of [God's] people Israel." (2) The oracle of Simeon to Mary also adds to the portrait of Jesus. The reference to the fall and rising of many in Israel easily fits the picture of a new king who will put down previous rulers and exalt the oppressed (1:52), but when Jesus is described as a "sign provoking rejection" (2:34), the picture becomes more complex. Hearers can now anticipate that Jesus will encounter rejection. He will not easily mount his throne but must win it against strong opposition. In doing so, he will cause an upheaval in Jewish society.

The narrative, however, does not abandon its theme of salvation for Israel. After Simeon, Anna is introduced, a figure who would be attractive to Tabitha, for she is a devout Jewish woman and, like Tabitha, a widow. Anna speaks about Jesus to "all those awaiting the redemption of Jerusalem" (2:38). The reference to the redemption of Jerusalem is jarring in light of the conquest of the city in 70 C.E., but the birth narrative does not soften the theme of Israel's salvation from its enemies.

Very strong honor claims have been made for Jesus at his birth. He has been presented as a king whose rule will bless both Israel and the gentiles — an extreme claim for one born in a manger.[10] Cornelius and Tabitha might expect the narrative to provide further support for this claim, but this support is slow in coming.

The narrative tells that as the child grew, God's "favor" was manifest in his life, especially as precocious wisdom (2:40, 52), which is illustrated by the story of the youthful Jesus talking with the teachers in the temple (2:41–51). This story also emphasizes that Jesus has another father than Joseph and that he must act in obedience to that father, even when it causes pain to Mary and Joseph (recall the reference to the sword piercing Mary's soul in 2:35). The portrait of Jesus as the obedient Son of God will be developed further in the temptation story.

"All flesh shall see the salvation of God," according to Luke 3:6, a message that reinforces Simeon's words about light for the gentiles (for the benefit of Cornelius, among others). The accompanying imagery of bringing down mountains and filling up valleys, when connected with 1:52–53 and 2:34, reminds hearers of the social upheaval required. John's preaching also reminds hearers of the need for repentance. At this point, Tabitha and Cornelius have a chance, if they are alert, to understand how their lives may show repentance and anticipate the new society that Jesus is bringing. In 3:11 John the Baptist instructs those who have two tunics to share one. According to Acts 9:39 Tabitha was doing even better: She was making clothing so that she could share with those in need. Cornelius, too, is given a hint of a way he might participate now in the coming of God's salvation, as John gives instructions to the soldiers (Luke 3:14). Lives must change in anticipation of the "stronger one," who will come as judge and "baptize you in Holy Spirit and fire" (3:16–17). Insofar as Cornelius and Tabitha had experienced the power of the Holy Spirit in their religious communities (see Acts 10:44–48) and had seen changes in the followers of Jesus similar to those demanded by John, they would recognize Jesus as the "stronger one." Even though Jesus' kingship was acknowledged by few, his power would be apparent to Tabitha and Cornelius.

The Holy Spirit descends first upon Jesus (3:21–22). It is accompanied by the divine voice that designates Jesus as "my Son." This scene might remind our two listeners that the coming of the Holy Spirit upon Mary was associated with the designation of her child as "Son of God" (1:35). The divine voice also calls Jesus "the beloved," the one in whom God "has taken pleasure." The gift of the Spirit and the statement of the divine voice are strong affirmation of Jesus' special relation to God and his chosen role. God is presented as affirming the claims made for Jesus in the birth narrative. The exact meaning of Son of God is still somewhat unclear, however. In 1:32, 35, the title "Son of God" (or "Son of the Most High") both preceded and followed the description of Jesus as the Davidic king, suggesting that Son of God is a synonym for Messiah (see 2 Sam. 7:14). But the association of Son of God with the Holy Spirit could also suggest that Jesus is God's Son as a Spirit-bearer, a charismatic figure.[11] Our listeners will have to wait for further clarification. The genealogy in 3:23–38 shows that, even as human lineage would be counted, Jesus is a descendant of David and Son of God.

Since Jesus is presented as *growing* in wisdom and God's favor (2:52), his understanding of his role is not complete from the beginning. Therefore, the temptation scene can be understood as a real struggle by Jesus to clarify the meaning of the Spirit's descent and the divine voice. Jesus must reject a false understanding of his role as the Spirit-filled Son of God (proposed by the devil) and discover the true alternative (which he will announce in the Nazareth synagogue). The temptation scene might be of special interest to Tabitha if she is aware of accusations from fellow Jews that Jesus was a rebellious Israelite about whom his followers are making idolatrous claims. The devil addresses Jesus as Son of God and challenges him to exercise his power, but Jesus refuses to remove himself from the discipline and obedience required of all Israel in the wilderness. He is an obedient Son. The second temptation relates to the Messiah's role as ruler, for the devil offers a simple way to achieve world dominion. However, Jesus is unwilling to worship anyone except God. Thus, the question of how Jesus can be the messianic ruler, as promised in the birth narrative, remains open for our listeners. There must be some other way than the devil's.

The Spirit that descended on Jesus following his baptism continues to guide and empower him (4:1, 14). It leads him to a ministry of teaching in synagogues (4:15), which is not the expected role of one who is or will be king. Indeed, through much of his ministry Jesus will appear as a healing prophet, "a prophet mighty in work and word" (24:19), on the model of Elijah and Elisha. Our two listeners have a right to be puzzled at the course of the narrative. The one who was clearly announced as a king by authoritative voices appears through much of the story to be a healing prophet. How can he be the messianic king?[12]

Jesus' prophetic ministry is defined by the scene in the Nazareth synagogue. Alter rejecting the devil's false interpretation of his role as the Spirit-inspired Son of God, Jesus announces the true meaning of the descent of the Spirit upon him following his baptism. He uses the words of Isaiah 61:1–2 to declare that he was anointed with the Spirit for a particular purpose. Although the reference to anointing in this quotation (using the verb *chrio*) could suggest his role as the anointed ruler (*christos*), Jesus states here that he was anointed to proclaim a message. He does not present himself as a ruler.

Both Cornelius and Tabitha should be interested in the content of Jesus' message as announced in Nazareth, but it will affect the two differently. Tabitha, as one of the poor, would understand the importance of Jesus' "good news to the poor." Still, she might question privately whether Jesus' announcement is trustworthy. Is God really acting to rescue the poor from oppression? In her interpretation, the "captives" and the "broken" or "oppressed" might also refer to the poor within Israel or to the situation of the Jewish people after defeat by the Roman army. Cornelius must consider whether good news for the poor is bad news for him. The discomfort that the Magnificat caused would probably return at this point. Cornelius must wait to discover whether Jesus has a place in his community for those with wealth and power.

The way the Nazareth scene continues could create uncertainty for Tabitha, too. The people of Nazareth, initially, are favorably impressed by Jesus (4:22). They also ask, "Is this not Joseph's son?" and this question produces a negative response from Jesus. Those who emphasize that the ancient Mediterranean world was a culture of honor and shame may understand the question as a challenge to what some townspeople regarded as an excessive claim of honor by Jesus. He is not the anointed proclaimer of good news but only Joseph's son.[13] Jesus' response is more appropriate, however, if we bring a different sociological observation to bear on the scene. Strong in-group loyalties, typical of Mediterranean culture,[14] could explain the dialogue in the scene. Then the question "Is this not Joseph's son?" does not contrast with the preceding praise but indicates that those praising Jesus, quite happily, point out that Jesus is a member of a local family. Since he is part of their in-group, they expect to receive favors from him. Jesus, in response, reacts against the expectation that he owes Nazareth as much or more than Capernaum. Jesus, as a prophet led by the Spirit, is not bound by ordinary group loyalties. As soon as the Nazarenes discover that Jesus will not honor in-group loyalties but, like Elijah and Elisha, will give his benefits to outsiders, Jesus will not even be acceptable in Nazareth (4:24), and this quickly proves to be true.

Tabitha might wonder about the larger implications of this dialogue and conflict. She, as a widow, might be comforted by the reminder in 4:25–26 that Elijah helped a poor widow suffering from famine, but would it be comforting to be reminded that Elijah was sent to a widow in the territory of Sidon and not to the widows of Israel? Pairing the widow with Naaman the Syrian suggests that the contrast in 4:25–26 is not just geographical (land of Israel vs. diaspora) but ethnic (Jew vs. gentile). If so, Tabitha is being stretched to think beyond personal benefit to consider non-Jewish widows. Cornelius could easily associate himself with Naaman the Syrian, especially if he had sufficient knowledge of scripture to recognize that Naaman was an army officer. This association may be encouraging, but it does not relieve Cornelius's difficulty with Jesus' good news for the poor.

I must break off my consecutive reading of Luke's story of Jesus at this point owing to limits on space. I would like, however, to add the following remarks.

Since Tabitha has experienced healing through Jesus, the healing and exorcism stories that begin in Luke 4:31 are likely to loom large in her portrait of Jesus. The story in 7:11–17 of Jesus' compassion for a widow might be especially important to her. This story is preceded by a story that would challenge Cornelius. The centurion in 7:1–10 is an outstanding example of faith. The story speaks a soldier's language, for the centurion's faith is demonstrated when he attributes to Jesus an authority similar to that of an officer commanding his troops (7:7–8).

To trace the story of Jesus as Tabitha and Cornelius might have heard it reminds us that different readers of Luke's story will construct the character of Jesus in different ways. Constructing the character of Jesus requires the reader or hearer to assemble many elements of the story into a total picture. Even though different readers receive the same data from the text, they will assemble the elements differently, placing some of them in bright light and allowing some to recede into the background. There is a dialogical process between the reader and the text. On the one hand, the text has rhetorical devices that can influence the reader's work of assembly. Indeed, the rhetorical structure of the text suggests that the implied author anticipated the ways that various readers might respond, offering them various enticements and warnings. On the other hand, the reader's role is important. We should avoid thinking that the text *controls* the reader's responses. A narrative suggests rather than controls. This is clearest when we consider its significance for the reader. The narrative speaks directly about past events but indirectly (if at all) about the reader's present. Readers must decide for themselves what is prescriptive and what is simply descriptive, for a story will contain many elements not meant for duplication. This means that even for first-century recipients like Cornelius and Tabitha there are important interpretive moves that the narrative cannot completely control. Although a religious community may believe that the story has significance for the present, various people must decide *how* this story about the past is significant for the present. If control is exercised in determining that significance, the control may come from forces in the present rather than from the narrative.

NOTES

1. I am assuming that, in the first-century church, even an educated person would be more likely to encounter Luke's Gospel through an oral presentation to the community than through a private reading.

2. John A. Darr, *On Character Building: The Reader and the Rhetoric of Characterization in Luke-Acts* (Louisville: Westminster/John Knox Press, 1992), 21–22.

3. Ibid., 23. Italics in original.

4. Ibid., 25–27. Italics in original.

5. Ibid., 30–31.

6. On the close relation between Acts 10:36–43 and the Lukan form of the story of Jesus, see Robert C. Tannehill, *The Narrative Unity of Luke-Acts: A Literary Interpretation,* vol. 2, *The Acts of the Apostles* (Minneapolis: Fortress Press, 1990), 138–42.

7. David Kennedy, "Roman Army," *Anchor Bible Dictionary,* 5:790–91.

8. I was alerted to the importance of the theme of belief in God's promises in Luke through a paper presented by David Landry at the 1993 annual meeting of the Society of Biblical Literature.

9. I discuss this conflict further in "Israel in Luke-Acts: A Tragic Story," *JBL* 104 (1985): 69–85.

10. Recent discussion of the Mediterranean world as a culture of honor and shame leads me to assume that the first-century audience would be very sensitive to honor claims and initially skeptical of claims that seem unjustified by birth status. See Bruce J. Malina and Jerome H. Neyrey, "Honor and Shame in Luke-Acts," in *The Social World of Luke-Acts,* ed. Jerome H. Neyrey (Peabody, Mass.: Hendrickson Publishers, 1991), 25–65.

11. See Marcus J. Borg, *Jesus: A New Vision* (San Francisco: Harper & Row, 1987), 41.

12. However, the return of the theme of Jesus' kingship in 19:11–27, 38–40; 22:28–30; 23:37–38, 42 shows that the birth narrative was not misleading in suggesting that this is an important aspect of Luke's characterization of Jesus.

13. This is the view taken by Richard L. Rohrbaugh in a paper presented at the 1993 annual meeting of the Society of Biblical Literature. His reading of Luke 4:1–30 as an attempt to legitimate Jesus' honor claims is helpful, but I do not think his reading of 4:22*b* fits the immediate context.

14. See Bruce J. Malina, *Windows on the World of Jesus* (Louisville: Westminster/John Knox Press, 1993), 47–70.

– 13 –

"Expecting Nothing in Return"

LUKE'S PICTURE OF THE MARGINALIZED

Mary Ann Beavis

In the ears of his Greco-Roman audience, Luke's social teaching would have been heard with shock. In their world, the rich and the powerful despised the poor and the disadvantaged and took pains to preserve the gulf between them. Inspired by the prophetic denunciation of injustice, Luke criticized the rich and thus transgressed against Greco-Roman values. Still, Luke's enduring contribution to Christian social ethics is greater than this: Instead of merely condemning the rich, Luke forged a vision of community in which both rich and poor are spiritual equals and the social and economic inequities between them can be vigorously and conscientiously addressed.

IT HAS OFTEN BEEN OBSERVED that the author of Luke-Acts depicts socially disadvantaged individuals and groups in a sympathetic and compassionate way.[1] Robert Tannehill, for example, notes that in Luke's Gospel

> ...Jesus intervenes on the side of the oppressed and excluded, assuring them that they share in God's salvation and defending them against others who want to maintain their own superiority at the expense of such people....In his ministry Jesus helps the poor, sinners, tax collectors, women, Samaritans, and Gentiles.[2]

Not only does Luke use an abundance of material about what modern cultural critics would call "marginalized groups"[3] (e.g., the poor, the sick, the demon-possessed, women, sinners, and non-Jews), but he also concerns himself with the use and abuse of possessions.[4] Luke's writings would thus appear to be fertile theological ground for deriving a message of hope for the politically oppressed and economically dispossessed, a warning to privileged elites, and an important source of ethical and social teaching.[5]

While some biblical scholars wholeheartedly subscribe to the view that Luke preaches "good news for the poor" and "grim news for the rich,"[6] others argue that he evinces little interest in the social and economic injustices of his day; instead, the motif of "the rich and the poor" has literary, symbolic, and spiritual, as opposed to practical and ethical, significance.[7] Johnson, for example, has argued that Luke's material on possessions should be interpreted in a literary and symbolic sense, in that the various characters depicted in Luke-Acts illustrate their openness to God and his prophets through their use of possessions.[8] Johnson further observes that Luke contains at least five beliefs about possessions, some of which are mutually contradictory.[9] He argues that Luke's teachings on possessions should *not* be harmonized and that the social and economic inequities of his time were not of immediate concern to him; Luke-Acts, he concludes, does not contain a coherent social ethic either for Luke's church or for our day.[10]

From a biblical-theological standpoint, the question of whether Luke's message of "good news for the poor" (Luke 4:18) refers to literal release from social and economic oppression or to a "purely religious," or heavenly, deliverance from spiritual poverty and bondage to worldly things, is of great interest. (Of course, it is also possible that some interpreters have overdrawn the contrast between socioeconomic liberation and individual spiritual freedom.) To clarify the meaning of the portrayal of the socially marginalized in Luke-Acts, I shall address the following issues:

1. The extent and significance of the relevant material
2. Luke's views on "the marginalized" in relation to those of his non-Christian contemporaries
3. The reception of Luke's teaching on socioeconomic matters by his reader or audience
4. The scope of Luke's socioeconomic teaching
5. Luke's contribution to Christian social ethics

The Extent of the Material

Is there a coherent theme of "marginalized" groups in Luke-Acts, or does Luke's apparent sympathy for such persons as the poor, women, Samaritans, gentiles, and sinners simply arise from his use of a variety of traditional materials on disparate themes that only *appear* to be related to modern readers? In this section, we shall examine Luke's material on the groups usually identified by scholars as the "disadvantaged"[11] so as to determine whether "God's care for the marginalized" even exists as a theme in Luke-Acts. In addition, we shall survey the many Lukan references to the use of possessions.

The Poor

A striking aspect of Luke-Acts is that whereas references to the poor (*hoi ptōchoi*) and to poverty pervade the Gospel, they are virtually absent from Acts. To explain this phenomenon, some interpreters argue that it reflects the absence of destitution in Luke's idealized portrayal of the early Christian community.[12]

That the material on the poor and on poverty is important to Luke, and not simply the result of the mechanical incorporation of traditional material, is, as Esler notes, indicated by both the extent of this material and the fact that the references that "reveal an antipathy for the rich and sympathy for the poor" are drawn from Mark, Q, and Luke's special material.[13] Moreover, several of the early references to the poor or to poverty are programmatic, that is, they have a special significance within the plan of Luke's Gospel. Among the relevant passages scholars frequently identify as having a programmatic function are:

The Magnificat (1:46–55). Raymond Brown observes that Mary's canticle affirms that the "salvation that has come in Jesus of Nazareth is the definitive act by which God has kept His covenant with Israel, the ultimate manifestation of His mercy (covenant kindness) to His servant people.... The covenant mercy of God in Jesus will reach not only to all generations; it will reach to all peoples."[14] In the song, God's mercy to his people is expressed in terms of the exaltation of the lowly (1:52, 48), the feeding of the hungry, and God's rejection of the rich (1:53).

Jesus' inaugural sermon at Nazareth (4:18–19). Jesus announces the fulfillment in his ministry of Isaiah's prophecy of "good news to the poor," "release to the captives," "sight to the blind," and "liberty to those who are oppressed" (see 7:22).[15] Joseph Fitzmyer is typical of interpreters when he observes that this story "has a definite programmatic character. Jesus' teaching is a fulfillment of OT Scripture — this is his kerygmatic announcement.... Luke has deliberately put this story at the beginning of the public ministry to encapsulate the entire ministry of Jesus and the reaction to it."[16] For our purposes, it is important to note that in this prophetic passage, which was so carefully selected by Luke (see 7:22), "the poor" are mentioned together with other physically, socially, and economically disadvantaged groups: the blind, the captives, and the oppressed. This implies that the evangelist sees Jesus' message as of special relevance to a general group of "the marginalized" and not simply to the economically (or spiritually) impoverished.

Blessings and woes (6:20–26). Luke's version of the Beatitudes differs from Matthew's in its use of the second person ("blessed are *you* poor"), its inclusion of four, not nine, macarisms (cf. vv. 20–23 with Matt. 5:3–12), and the balance it strikes between macarisms and "woes to the rich" (6:24–26). Some scholars believe that the use of the second person suggests that the macarisms are addressed only to the disciples (see v. 20), who are thought of by Luke as those who have adopted a lifestyle of poverty in order to follow Jesus.[17] The fact that the woes to the rich are also framed in the second person mitigates this view. The addressees seem rather to include the crowd from Judea, Jerusalem, and Tyre and Sidon (the latter two being gentile areas), many of whom Jesus heals and exorcizes (vv. 17–18); again, the referent of the address to "the poor" seems to include more than just economic "outcasts."

As we noted earlier, whereas Matthew's version of the Beatitudes is spiritualizing (e.g., "Blessed are the poor *in spirit*"), Luke's version speaks of literal poverty and hunger. Moreover, whereas in Luke the section of the sermon that immediately follows the Beatitudes (6:27–38) is a compilation of ethical teaching from Q, which includes instructions on giving and lending, some of this material is not echoed until later in Matthew (5:39–48) and some of it is even found elsewhere (see Matt. 7:1–2).

Again, the programmatic character of the blessings and woes is noted by Fitzmyer: "[The Sermon on the Plain]...has...to be related to the mission of Jesus as presented thus far in the Gospel: he has come to preach to the poor, the prisoners, the blind, and the downtrodden of his day (in the words of Isaiah, quoted in 4:18)."[18]

Seccombe's suggestion that the Lukan motif of "the poor" is drawn from the Hebrew prophetic theme of Israel as suffering, oppressed, and in need of God's salvation and is therefore not to be construed in economic terms at all[19] is supported by such factors as the promises of the Magnificat (1:53–54), the portrayal of Jesus' parents as pious Jews, and the humble and poor circumstances of Jesus' birth. Perhaps the picture of the first (Jewish) disciples as being of lowly mien also echoes this idea (Acts 3:13). However, the juxtaposition of the message of good news (and blessings) to the poor to the promise of sight for the blind (4:18–19), together with miracles of healing (6:17–19) and instruction on whom to invite to a feast (the poor, maimed, lame, and blind [14:12–14]), all indicate that both physical and spiritual need are of concern to Luke.

In view of the many stories of healings and exorcisms found in Luke, it is surprising that the programmatic promises of relief for the poor are not obviously complemented by miracle stories, comparable to some of the tales found in the Elijah-Elisha cycle, in which Jesus provides for poor people. It may be that Luke's account of the feeding of the five thousand (9:12–17) is such a story (see 2 Kings 4:42–44).[20] Then, too,

Luke's is the only Gospel to refer to the story of Elijah and the widow of Zarephath (4:26), in which the prophet saves a gentile woman and her son from starvation (1 Kings 17:8–16).

The Rich

Corresponding antithetically to the programmatic promises of deliverance for the poor in Luke are condemnations of the rich (1:54; 6:24–26; 14:7–11, 12–14; 16:19–31). Although some of the traditions about the rich are also found in Mark and Matthew (e.g., 8:14; 12:33–34; 15:18–30; 20:45–47), much of the teaching is unique to Luke: the prophecy of the Magnificat (1:54); the woes on the rich (6:24–26); the warning against covetousness (12:5); the parable of the Rich Fool (12:16–21); the teaching on whom to invite to a banquet (14:12, 21); the notice that the Pharisees loved money (16:14–15); the parable of the Rich Man and Lazarus (16:19–31). As in the case of the theme of the blessedness of the poor, this theme of the culpability of the rich is virtually absent in Acts.

Possessions

Complementing, and sometimes overlapping, the teaching on the rich and the poor in Luke is the material on the use of possessions. Much of this material is also shared by Mark and Matthew, but again, some of it is unique to Luke (3:11–12; 10:4–8; 11:5–13; 16:1–13; 19:1–10; 21:34; 22:35–38; 23:3). Unlike the material on the rich and the poor, one finds frequent references in Acts to the use of possessions.

Since all the material on the use of possessions in Acts can be attributed to Luke's special source, it has particular relevance for uncovering Luke's viewpoint on such use. Clearly, running through this material is a theme regarding the use and abuse of possessions, which can be schematized as shown in the accompanying chart.

Observe in this scheme that whereas the support of missionaries, almsgiving, and placing one's property "at the apostles' feet" (4:35, 37) to meet the needs of the community are strongly commended, the use of ill-gotten gain (Judas's field) and dishonest dealings within the community (Ananias and Sapphira) are sternly prohibited.[21] If the earning of profit has unholy origins (e.g., the potentially lucrative proceeds from the sale of the magic books or of the Holy Spirit's power), it is firmly rejected. To epitomize the theme of the use and abuse of property, we find two vignettes of disciples' use of fields (Acts 1:18; 4:36–37). Judas, clearly identified as one who was "numbered among us" with "a share in this ministry," uses the proceeds of betrayal to buy a field, which, after he dies there, becomes a "field of blood" (1:19). In contrast to the "lie to the Holy Spirit" attempted by Ananias and Sapphira (Acts 5:3,

Good Use	*Abuse*
Barnabas sells a field and lays the proceeds at the disciples' feet (4:36–37).	Judas uses blood money to buy a field and dies a horrible death (1:18).
First believers hold all things in common (2:44–45; 4:32–35).	Ananias and Sapphira lie to the disciples about the disposition of their property (5:1–11).
	Hebrews accused by Hellenists of neglecting Hellenist widows in the daily distribution (6:1–6).
Christians burn valuable magic books (19:19)	Simon Magus tries to buy the Holy Spirit's power (8:14–24).
Tabitha, a charitable woman (9:30).	
Cornelius, an almsgiving centurion (10:1–8).	
Disciples send famine relief to Judean Christians (11:27–30; cf. 24:17).	
Paul's speech at Miletus (20:33–35).	

4, 9), Barnabas exemplifies the proper disposition of property when he sells a field and unreservedly donates the proceeds to the apostles. Later in Acts, Paul similarly cites as his motto the dominical teaching that "it is better to give than to receive" (Acts 20:33–35). Thus, the teaching of Acts on the use and abuse of property is coherent with the outlook of the uniquely Lukan Gospel material, to wit: the teaching of John the Baptist on sharing and honesty (3:11–12); the reference to the support of missionaries (10:7–8); the parables of the Rich Fool (12:16–21) and of the shrewd "Unjust" Steward (16:1–13); and the story of Zacchaeus (19:1–10). Both Luke and Acts regard one's life as "property" to be managed according to God's will, even to the point of martyrdom (Luke 23:46; Acts 20:24, 35).

Other Marginalized Groups

As we mentioned above, in some of Luke's programmatic assurances of deliverance, the sick, disabled, and possessed are classed together with the poor (Luke 4:18–19; 7:22; 14:13, 21).[22] Similarly, Jesus proclaims "tax collectors and sinners" as among the "sick" who are in need of a "physician" (5:31–32). The theme of Jesus' ministry to the economically, physically, and spiritually marginalized merges with the announcement of the offer of salvation to those who, from a first-century Jewish perspective, are ethnic and religious outcasts: first, Samaritans (Luke 9:52; 10:33; 17:16; Acts 1:8; 8:1, 5, 9, 14; 9:31; 15:3); and then gentiles (e.g., Luke 2:32; 4:26–27; 7:2–10; Acts 8:26–39; 10:1–44; 13:7–12). The Gospel theme of the reversal of sociocultural expectations (e.g., Luke 1:52–53; 6:20–36; 10:21–22; 14:11; 17:32; 18:14; 22:24–27) underlines the message of deliverance for marginalized people.

Women: A Marginalized Group or a Group Marginalized?

Both Luke and Acts contain a large body of tradition about women; much of the material in the Gospel is peculiarly Lukan.[23] However, the consensus of feminist scholarship is that Luke's portrayal of women promotes traditional, supportive female roles (prayer, almsgiving, and financial support of male missionaries) and deliberately downplays women's active participation in prophecy, mission, and leadership in the early church.[24] Nonetheless, Luke's message of hope to the oppressed is relevant to women insofar as "most of the poor in every age are women and the children who are dependent on them."[25]

Luke's Views on "the Marginalized" in Relation to Those of His Non-Christian Contemporaries

Social-scientific interpreters of Greco-Roman antiquity observe that ancient society was made up of two social classes: the elite (5–10 percent of the total population of the Roman Empire) and the nonelite (everyone else).[26] Both the elite and the nonelite are portrayed in Luke-Acts: Among the former are emperors (Augustus, Tiberius), the Herods, Roman prefects, centurions, the Jerusalem elite (chief priests, scribes, elders), and "the rich"; to the latter belong such people as shepherds, widows, the hungry and poor, debtors, and lepers.

Poverty, both rural and urban, was endemic in the Roman Empire,[27] but the idea of sympathy for the poor and outcast was alien to Greco-Roman ways of thinking, as was the notion of private or public assistance to the disadvantaged.[28] As Esler observes: "...in the ancient world gifts...were made from motives which were hardly disinterested. Those who gave to their social equals...did so in the hope of receiving benefits in return or to cement valuable friendships. Gifts to one's social inferiors...resulted in the donor gaining...honor or prestige."[29] Rather than attempting to reduce the socioeconomic distance between the classes, the elite (*honestiores*) regarded the nonelite (*humiliores*) with contempt and strove to parade their superiority "by their conspicuous consumption, their entourages in the cities, their dress and their titles, by offering their clients inferior food and wine at banquets, and even by the fact that the law discriminated positively in their favour."[30] The teaching of the Sermon on the Plain that one should lend, "expecting nothing in return" (Luke 6:35), would have been outlandish to a Greco-Roman audience.

Expressions of compassion for the poor, however, were not entirely absent from the ancient world. H. Bolkstein has traced the ethos of care for the poor (almsgiving) to the ancient Near East, including ancient Israel.[31] Some scholars see in Luke's portrait of the early church an attempt to synthesize the Greco-Roman ideology of reciprocity among equals ("friendship") with the Jewish-Christian ethic of almsgiving and assistance to the poor.[32]

Reception by Luke's Reader or Audience

The hypothesis that the Lukan community included both elite and nonelite members — a virtually unprecedented situation in antiquity — is well accepted.[33] Scholars differ as to whether the teaching on wealth, poverty, and possessions is addressed to "the rich" or to "the poor" in Luke's audience; Esler's argument that Luke has a message for both — "good news for the poor, grim news for the rich" — best fits this social situation.[34]

Luke's description of the Christian community's practice of sharing between elite and nonelite members would have been viewed by both audiences as extraordinary. As we noted above, the Greco-Roman upper classes despised their socioeconomic inferiors and took pains to preserve the gulf between them and the majority of the population. The *humiliores* were segregated both socially and spatially from the *honestiores;*[35] as Esler speculates, the poor, no doubt, alternated between deferential passivity and hatred of the elite.[36] Both rich and poor were accustomed to thinking in terms of limited good, that is, that goods exist in fixed amounts and that if one person gains, another loses.[37] In exchanges with strangers, the poor may have undertaken transactions conditioned by the value of *negative reciprocity,* "the attempt to acquire something of value for something of less or no value."[38] Whether Luke's portrait of rich and poor Christians as a community of friends in which need had been eliminated is purely utopian, or whether it reflects the values being practiced in the Lukan church, the ethic of sharing would have been difficult for Greco-Roman converts of any social status to assimilate and actualize.

The Scope of Luke's Teaching

Was Luke's teaching on the disadvantaged addressed solely to social relations among early Christians, or does Luke-Acts contain a broader mandate for Christians to alleviate poverty and oppression wherever they are found? Surprisingly, many scholars hold that the evangelist's concern was limited to the needy in his own circle.[39] Schottroff and Stegemann, however, argue that the term "almsgiving," *eleēmosynē* (found in the New Testament only in Luke-Acts), "has as its recipients the poor who are not members of the Christian community; for example, beggars, the blind, the lame, the crippled."[40] Pilgrim observes that although Luke's "good news to the poor" was an inner-Christian message, its full implications remain to be worked out in our time in theologies of liberation and hope and in the efforts of Christians to grapple with poverty and oppression wherever they are found.[41]

Luke's Contribution to Christian Social Ethics

Luke's introduction of the oriental tradition of care for the poor and outcast to Greco-Roman converts was ethically and culturally daring. Esler emphasizes the radical nature of Luke's teaching, suggesting that "the scheme of social welfare put forward indirectly in Luke-Acts may, in fact, have been a Christian invention."[42]

Luke advanced another aspect of Hebrew tradition foreign to Greco-Roman values: the critique of the rich. Esler adjudges the promises of eschatological rewards for the poor and punishment for the rich in Jewish apocalyptic (*1 Enoch* 92–105) as an inferior precursor to Luke's this-worldly social teaching.[43] However, a more immediate source of inspiration for Luke's social conscience was undoubtedly the Hebrew prophetic denunciation of the injustices perpetrated on the needy by the rich and powerful.[44] Perhaps Luke's most striking and innovative contribution to Christian social ethics is that he forges beyond the condemnation of the elite to a vision of a community of spiritual equals in which socioeconomic disparities are vigorously and conscientiously addressed.

NOTES

1. Throughout this essay, it is presupposed that Luke and Acts are two complementary volumes by the same author and that both must be examined for the fullest comprehension of the evangelist's thought.

2. Robert Tannehill, *The Narrative Unity of Luke-Acts* (Philadelphia: Fortress Press, 1986), 1:103.

3. Marcia Tucker calls marginalization "that complex and disputatious process by means of which certain people and ideas are privileged over others at any given time ... the process by which, through shifts in position, any given group

can be ignored, trivialized, rendered invisible and unheard, perceived as inconsequential, de-authorized, 'other,' or threatening, while others are valorized." See *Out There: Marginalization and Contemporary Cultures,* ed. R. Ferguson et al. (New York: New Museum of Contemporary Art; Cambridge, Mass.: MIT Press, 1991), 7. See also Russell Ferguson, "Introduction: Invisible Center," ibid., 9–14; and bell hooks, "marginality as a site of resistance" [*sic*], ibid., 341–44. For a social-scientific discussion of marginalization in contemporary urban society, see H. P. M. Winchester and P. E. White, "The Location of Marginalized Groups in the Inner City," *Environment and Planning D* 6 (1988): 37–54.

4. Luke T. Johnson, *The Literary Function of Possessions in Luke-Acts,* SBLDS 39 (Missoula, Mont.: Scholars Press, 1977).

5. E.g., W. E. Pilgrim, *Good News to the Poor* (Minneapolis: Augsburg Publishing House, 1981).

6. Philip Esler, *Community and Gospel in Luke-Acts,* SNTSMS 57 (Cambridge: Cambridge University Press, 1987), 187.

7. Johnson, *Literary Function;* idem, *Sharing Possessions: Mandate and Symbol of Faith* (Philadelphia: Fortress Press, 1981); E. Bammel, "*ptōchos,*" *TDNT* 6:906–7; R. Koch, "Die Wertung des Besitzes im Lukasevangelium," *Biblica* 38 (1957): 151–69; C. S. Hill, "The Sociology of the New Testament Church to A.D. 62: An Examination of the Early New Testament Church in Relation to Its Contemporary Social Setting," Ph.D. diss., University of Nottingham, 1972. W. Schmithals ("Lukas — Evangelist der Armen," *Theologia Viatorum* 12 [1975]: 153–67) argues that Luke's teaching on poverty and possessions arises out of a specific situation of persecution that should not be generalized (similarly, J. Dupont, *Les béatitudes,* vol. 3: *Les Évangelistes* [Paris: J. Gabalda, 1973]). David Seccombe (*Possessions and the Poor in Luke-Acts* [Linz: Studien zum Neuen Testament und seiner Umwelt, 1982]) argues that Luke construes the poor in terms of Israel's need for God. H. Degenhardt (*Lukas: Evangelist der Amen* [Stuttgart: Katholisches Bibelwerk, 1965]) sees Luke's message of renunciation of possessions directed primarily at office-holders in the Lukan church. Several scholars have noted that Luke-Acts seems to be directed more to the rich than to the poor (L. Schottroff and W. Stegemann, *Jesus and the Hope of the Poor* [Maryknoll, N.Y.: Orbis Books, 1986]; Robert Karris, "Poor and Rich: The Lukan *Sitz im Leben,*" *Perspectives on Luke-Acts,* ed. Charles H. Talbert [Danville, Calif.: Association of Baptist Professors in Religion, 1978], 112–25). Seccombe's assertion that "the dominant view" of biblical scholarship sees Luke as a message of hope to the poor and downtrodden (*Possessions and the Poor,* 13) finds very little support in the articles and monographs on this topic.

8. Johnson, *Literary Function;* idem, *Sharing Possessions.*

9. (a) The poor are privileged in the eyes of God, and the rich condemned, e.g., the Magnificat, the woes to the rich, the parable of the Rich Man and Lazarus. (b) Jesus demands complete renunciation of possessions for disciples, e.g., Luke 5:11, 28; 18:18–30. (c) Nevertheless, disciples of Jesus are to give alms to help the poor and to provide hospitality, e.g., 21:1–4; 19:1–10; 8:3. (d) Christian ministers are or (e) are not to travel and work without possessions, 9:3–5; 10:4–8; cf. 22:35–38 (Johnson, *Sharing Possessions,* 13–29). Johnson's

argument that these teachings on the use of possessions are inconsistent and even contradictory is overstated. The seeming contradiction between the instructions to disciples in 9:3–5 and 10:4–8 on the one hand and in 22:35–38 on the other has been interpreted as arising out of different missionary settings: peace (9:3–5; 10:4–8) vs. persecution (22:35–38); see Degenhardt, *Lukas,* 49. Note that Jesus' demand that the rich ruler sell all his possessions and give them to the poor occurs in the context of a *call to discipleship* (Luke 18:18–30; cf. Schottroff and Stegemann, *Hope of the Poor,* 75). The references in Acts 2:44–45 and 4:32–35 seem to refer, not to the literal practice of early Christians "holding all things in common," but to the willingness of the wealthier members of the community to make their goods available for disposition by the apostles in times of need, or to donate property as a sign of faith (see 19:1–10). The offense of Ananias and Sapphira in Acts 5:1–11 is not that they keep a portion of their proceeds for themselves but that they lie about it to the apostles. Providing hospitality and almsgiving (Luke 8:3) is a practice that *enabled* missionaries to travel unencumbered (Karris, "Lukan *Sitz im Leben,*" 119).

10. Johnson, *Sharing Possessions,* 25.

11. See Tannehill, *Narrative Unity,* 1:103; Seccombe, *Possessions and the Poor,* 23.

12. Schottroff and Stegemann, *Hope of the Poor,* 110. They further note that the Gospel's *characteristic* word for "poor" (*ptōchos*) does not occur in Acts, where the word "needy" (*endeēs*) is substituted (e.g., Acts 4:34).

13. See Esler, *Community and Gospel,* 165–69, who observes that Luke retains most of the Markan tradition on riches and poverty and tends to intensify the material from both Mark and Q. For example, in Luke the disciples "leave all" to follow Jesus (Luke 5:11 || Mark 1:18, 20; cf. Luke 5:28 || Mark 5:28; Luke 18:22 || Mark 10:21) and Luke's version of the Beatitudes refers to physical deprivation, as opposed to Matthew's spiritualized understanding of poverty, hunger, and thirst. Some examples of special Lukan material that deals with the theme of the rich and the poor are the Magnificat (1:46–55), the preaching of John the Baptist (3:10–14), and the parable of the Rich Man and Lazarus (16:19–31).

14. Raymond Brown, *The Birth of the Messiah* (Garden City, N.Y.: Doubleday, 1977), 364–65. Cf. Joseph A. Fitzmyer, *The Gospel according to Luke I–IX,* AB 28 (Garden City, N.Y.: Doubleday, 1981), 361.

15. Isa. 61:1–2; 58:6.

16. Fitzmyer, *Luke I–IX,* 529. Cf. Charles H. Talbert, *Reading Luke* (New York: Crossroad, 1989), 54; Tannehill, *Narrative Unity,* 1:62–68.

17. E.g., Schottroff and Stegemann, *Hope of the Poor,* 70; Fitzmyer, *Luke I–IX,* 629.

18. Fitzmyer, *Luke I–IX,* 629.

19. Seccombe, *Possessions and the Poor,* 38.

20. Tannehill, *Narrative Unity,* 1:217–18.

21. Seccombe's argument that the primary purpose of the cautionary tale in Acts 5:1–11 is to demonstrate the holiness of the primitive church does not rule out the issue of possessions (*Possessions and the Poor,* 210–15; see esp. 215).

22. Acts also has many stories of healings and exorcisms, but these are por-

trayed more as signs of the spread of the gospel than as release to the afflicted (see Howard Clark Kee, *Good News to the Ends of the Earth* [London: SCM Press; Philadelphia: Trinity Press International, 1990], 9–10).

23. For a survey of this material, see Jane Schaberg, "Luke," *The Women's Bible Commentary,* ed. Carol A. Newsom and Sharon H. Ringe (London: SPCK; Louisville: Westminster/John Knox Press, 1992), 275–92, and Gail R. O'Day's commentary on Acts in the same volume.

24. E.g., Schaberg, "Luke"; O'Day, "Acts"; Elizabeth Tetlow, *Women and Ministry in the New Testament* (New York: Paulist Press, 1980), chaps. 1–4; Elisabeth Schüssler Fiorenza, *In Memory of Her* (New York: Crossroad, 1984), 161–68; Mary Rose D'Angelo, "Women in Luke-Acts: A Redactional View," *JBL* 109 (1990): 441–61.

25. Schaberg, "Luke," 277. Widows are a group of women for whom Luke evinces special concern — and who were among the most socially and economically disadvantaged persons in antiquity (Luke 2:37; 4:25–26; 7:12; 18:3, 5; 20:47; 21:2–3; Acts 6:31; 9:39, 41). Bonnie Bowman Thurston argues that there was an early Christian order of widows that constituted one of the earliest ministries in the church (*The Widows* [Minneapolis: Fortress Press, 1989], 10–17); however, as O'Day notes, Luke describes a ministry *to* widows by men (Acts 6:1–6), not a ministry *by* widows ("Acts," 308).

26. See Douglas E. Oakman, "The Countryside in Luke-Acts," *The Social World of Luke-Acts: Models for Interpretation,* ed. Jerome Neyrey (Peabody, Mass.: Hendrickson Publishers, 1991), 162; Richard L. Rohrbaugh, "The Pre-Industrial City in Luke-Acts: Urban Social Relations," *Social World,* 133; Esler, *Community and Gospel,* 171–75.

27. See Rohrbaugh, "Pre-Industrial City"; Oakman, "Countryside."

28. See E. R. Hands, *Charities and Social Aid in Greece and Rome* (London: Thames & Hudson, 1968); M. Mayer, "Charity in the Western Empire," Ph.D. diss., Graduate School of Arts and Science, Washington University, 1973.

29. Esler, *Community and Gospel,* 176.

30. Ibid., 172–73.

31. H. Bolkstein, *Wohlhätigkeit und Armenflege im vorchristlichen Altertum* (Utrecht: A. Oosthoeck, 1939).

32. Karris, "Lukan *Sitz im Leben,*" 117; Schottroff and Stegemann, *Hope of the Poor,* 109–11, 118; Esler, *Community and Gospel,* 187–200.

33. Pilgrim, *Good News;* Karris, "Lukan *Sitz im Leben,*" 124; Esler, *Community and Gospel,* 197; Rohrbaugh, "Pre-Industrial City," 146–47.

34. Esler, *Community and Gospel,* 187. Pilgrim describes Luke's twofold message less dramatically as one of "good news" to the poor and "challenge" to the rich (*Good News,* 160–66).

35. See Rohrbaugh, "Pre-Industrial City."

36. Esler, *Community and Gospel,* 171.

37. Bruce J. Malina and Jerome H. Neyrey, "Honor and Shame in Luke-Acts: Pivotal Values of the Mediterranean World," *Social World,* 29.

38. Oakman, "Countryside," 156.

39. E.g., Pilgrim, *Good News,* 171–72; Karris, "Lukan *Sitz im Leben*"; Esler, *Community and Gospel,* 197–200.

40. Schottroff and Stegemann, *Hope of the Poor,* 111 (see Luke 11:41; 12:33; Acts 3:2, 3, 10; 9:36; 10:24, 31; 24:17).

41. Pilgrim, *Good News,* 171–72.

42. Esler, *Community and Gospel,* 198.

43. Ibid., 189–91.

44. Cf. Pilgrim, *Good News,* 24–28. The Hebrew tradition is very similar to other ancient Near Eastern material (see Thomas E. Schmidt, *Hostility to Wealth in the Synoptic Gospels,* JSNTSup 15 [Sheffield: JSOT Press, 1987], 41–60).

– 14 –

The Plot of Luke's Story of Jesus

Jack Dean Kingsbury

In the story of Luke's Gospel, the primary conflict at the human level is that between Jesus and the religious authorities. This conflict, which reaches its culmination in the death, resurrection, and ascension of Jesus, comes to its head in the episode of Jesus on the cross. Whereas the authorities believe that Jesus' death vindicates them as Israel's rulers, the reader knows that, ironically, the cross is the place where Jesus is at once publicly proclaimed as Israel's Messiah-King and anticipates the onset of his glorious reign of salvation.

THE GOSPEL OF LUKE is a narrative[1] that tells the story of Jesus. Like other narratives, it has a plot with a recognizable beginning, middle, and end.[2]

As with the other canonical Gospels, the plot of Luke revolves around conflict. At the human level, the primary conflict is between Jesus and Israel and especially between Jesus and the religious authorities. Within Luke's gospel story itself, the resolution of Jesus' conflict with the authorities comes at the end, in the events surrounding the death, resurrection, and ascension of Jesus.[3] The place where this conflict reaches its culmination, however, is in the episode of Jesus on the cross. In what follows, I should like to sketch the plot of Luke's gospel story so as to suggest how and with what result Jesus' conflict with the authorities reaches its resolution in the death, resurrection, and ascension of Jesus and its culmination in the cross.

I

In the beginning of his gospel story (1:5–2:52), Luke introduces the reader to John the Baptist and Jesus, the two protagonists whom he characterizes by comparing each with the other. Through inspired prophecy, the reader learns that whereas John will be the great prophet of God (1:15, 75), Jesus will be the Messiah-King from the line of David, the royal Son of God, who is Savior and Lord (1:31–35; 2:10–11).[4] In characterizing Jesus as Messiah, Son of God, and Savior, Luke portrays Jesus as an eschatological figure.[5] As Messiah, Jesus is Israel's long-awaited Davidic king whom God will "anoint" with the Spirit for his ministry of salvation (3:22; 4:18); as Son of God, Jesus enjoys a unique filial relationship with God by virtue of which he, in all righteousness, will fulfill God's purposes (3:22; 9:35); and as Savior, Jesus is the one through whom God will proffer salvation[6] to Israel first and then to the gentiles (2:30–32; Acts 13:46–47; 18:5–6).

At the human level, the antagonists of Jesus in Luke's gospel story are the religious authorities. The authorities function as a single character that encompasses a wide range of individuals and groups, such as the Pharisees, Sadducees, high priest, chief priests, elders, scribes (lawyers, teachers of the law), rulers of the people, and officers of the temple police. In characterizing the authorities,[7] Luke describes them both in terms of their attitude toward Jesus and in contrast to him. In terms of their attitude toward Jesus, Luke describes the authorities as the prime example of those in Israel who are spiritually blind and therefore refuse to recognize who Jesus is and to commit themselves to him.[8] In direct contrast to Jesus, Luke describes the authorities as persons who "reject the purposes of God" (7:30).[9] In Luke's view, those who reject the purposes of God are self-righteous[10] and live in a wrong relationship with both God and humans. The authorities live in a wrong relationship with God because they falsely believe that they are already righteous and hence have no need, for example, to submit to John's baptism of repentance.[11] The authorities live in a wrong relationship with humans because, instead of being leaders who serve Israel, they are hypocrites who strive for self-exaltation and the preservation of the status quo even while despising and taking advantage of others, especially the "poor."[12] Accordingly, in his characterization of Jesus and the authorities, Luke draws a sharp contrast: On the one hand, we have Jesus, the protagonist, who is righteous and serves the purposes of God; on the other hand, we have the authorities, the antagonists, who are self-righteous and reject for themselves the purposes of God.

Jesus' first encounter with religious authorities occurs in the beginning of Luke's gospel story (2:41–52). Though a twelve-year-old boy, Jesus is already aware that he is the Son and Servant of God.[13] Finding his way to the temple, Jesus engages in conversation with the teachers there (2:46). That the temple should be the setting for Jesus' first encounter with authorities is entirely fitting, for the temple is both the place of God's presence — God, whom Jesus calls "Father" (2:49) — and the seat of the authorities' power. In other words, the temple is the place where both Jesus and the authorities are "at home." In their conversation with the boy Jesus, the teachers are "astonished" (*existanōn*), or indeed "perplexed,"[14] by Jesus' understanding of the law. For the reader, such perplexity on the part of the teachers creates dramatic suspense: How, the reader wonders, will the authorities later receive Jesus when they encounter him, not as a pupil, but during his public ministry?

II

Jesus embarks on his public ministry in the middle of Luke's gospel story (chaps. 3–21) and soon confronts the religious authorities. The fact that this confrontation takes place precisely at that point in Luke's story at which the authorities make their major debut is a measure of the significance Luke attaches to it (5:17). Noteworthy is that virtually the moment Jesus and the authorities come together, conflict breaks out and persists through a cycle of five controversies (5:17–6:11). By examining this cycle, we can observe important features that typify Jesus' conflict with the authorities.

The first feature to observe is that, at one level, Jesus' conflict with the authorities has to do with the fundamental question of who rightfully rules Israel. Is it Jesus, Israel's Messiah-King, or the authorities?[15] In 5:17, the verse with which the cycle of five controversies begins,[16] Luke touches on this question by fashioning a setting for Jesus' first controversy that is itself striking because it characterizes Jesus' conflict with the authorities as a conflict between "leaders (figures) of authority."

Thus, Luke depicts Jesus as a figure of authority by stating both that he "teaches" and that the power of the Lord is present for him to "heal." Similarly, Luke depicts the Pharisees[17] and the teachers of the law (scribes) as figures of authority both by the names they bear and the physical position they assume. The very names "Pharisees" and "teachers of the law" convey authority, for those so designated are, within the world of Luke's story, among those who govern Israel. Hence, it is as a great assemblage of Israel's leaders that these Pharisees and teachers gather from "every village of Galilee and Judea and from Jerusalem," that is, from all Israel. Moreover, the physical position these Pharisees and teachers assume is that of "sitting." Specifically, the picture is that of Jesus debating his teaching before a huge, seated group of legal experts. In Luke's story-world, to "sit" in a setting like this is an act that in itself ascribes honor and authority to any so described. It is, then, as one leader facing other leaders that Jesus first confronts the authorities.

A second feature that typifies Jesus' conflict with the religious authorities in Luke's gospel story is that the issues that spark debate are all weighty in nature and go to the heart of what it means to rule God's people. By way of illustration, consider this cycle of five controversies

(5:17–6:11). In the first controversy (5:18–26), the point under dispute is that of possessing divine "authority": Does Jesus or does he not possess the divine authority to forgive sins? In the second and third controversies (5:27–32, 33–39), the topic of debate is that of "tradition": If Jesus' disciples eat with toll collectors and sinners, do they not thereby break the "laws of purity"? Also, with what right do Jesus' disciples not comply with the "custom of fasting"? And in the fourth and fifth controversies (6:1–5, 6–11), the matter being contested is that of "Mosaic law": In each instance, the question of concern pertains to proper observance of the Sabbath rest. One reason such issues as possessing divine authority and determining how tradition and Mosaic law are to be observed are of such weight in Luke's story is plain to see: To exercise authority in the name of God and to interpret law and tradition are the way in which either Jesus or the authorities will decide on what it means for Israel to live under God's rule and to be a righteous people serving God's purposes.

Yet another feature that typifies Jesus' conflict with the religious authorities in Luke's gospel story stands out in the first and second phases of Jesus' public ministry, as he reaches out to all Israel from Galilee and journeys to Jerusalem (4:14–9:50; 9:51–19:46). In these two phases, Luke carefully holds the intensity of Jesus' conflict with the authorities in check. This is apparent, for example, in Luke's tendency not to permit Jesus' controversies with the authorities to become "acutely confrontational" in nature: As Jesus clashes with the authorities in his outreach to Israel and on his way to Jerusalem, Luke only rarely depicts the authorities as challenging Jesus to his face because of something that he himself says or does.[18]

To illustrate this, consider again the cycle of five controversies in 5:17–6:11. When Jesus forgives the paralytic his sins, the scribes and the Pharisees, although they charge Jesus with speaking blasphemies, nevertheless utter their thoughts "in their hearts" (5:21–22); indeed, in order to dispute their charge, Jesus must "perceive" their thoughts (5:22). As Jesus and the disciples feast in Levi's house with toll collectors and sinners, the Pharisees and their scribes grumble about this but express their displeasure, not to Jesus, but to the disciples (5:29–30). Disturbed that the disciples do not honor the custom of fasting, the Pharisees and their scribes come to Jesus, but their complaint is about the disciples (5:33–35). Offended because the disciples, while walking with Jesus through fields of grain, have in their judgment broken the Sabbath rest by unlawfully working, some of the Pharisees say nothing to Jesus but take vigorous issue with the disciples (6:1–2). Although the scribes and the Pharisees watch Jesus to see if he will heal on the Sabbath and thus give them reason to charge him with breaking the Sabbath rest, they nevertheless do not confront him when he does heal but instead discuss among themselves what they might do to him (6:6–11). To reiterate, in Jesus' controversies with the authorities in the first two phases of his public ministry, Luke tempers the intensity of the conflict: As is the case in this cycle of five controversies, Luke tends not to permit this conflict to become acutely confrontational in nature.

The fourth feature that typifies Jesus' conflict with the religious authorities in Luke's gospel story goes hand in hand with the previous one: Until the third phase of Jesus' ministry in Jerusalem, the form this conflict takes is essentially that of a protracted, intermittent "conversation." To observe this, one may compare Luke's Gospel with that of Mark regarding the point in the plot of each story at which the conflict between Jesus and the authorities becomes "mortal" in nature and a struggle to the death. In Mark's Gospel, the plot of the story reaches this point at the close of only the first cycle of Jesus' controversies. As early as 3:6, Mark recounts: "The Pharisees went out and immediately conspired with the Herodians against him [Jesus], how to destroy him." In contrast to Mark, note the comment that Luke makes about the authorities in 6:11, the verse that parallels Mark 3:6 and closes the first cycle of Jesus' controversies in Luke's story: "But they [the scribes and the Pharisees] were filled with fury and discussed with one another what they might do to Jesus." The crucial difference between these two verses is that however furious at Jesus Luke says the authorities become, the latter are still said, not to conspire to destroy Jesus, but simply to discuss how they might handle him.

This raises the question, At what point in his story's plot does Luke finally inform the reader about the authorities' intention to destroy Jesus? The answer is that this does not occur until as late as 19:47–48, after Jesus has entered Jerusalem. Luke remarks: "Every day he was teaching in the temple; and the chief priests and the scribes and the leaders of the people began looking for a way to destroy him." Yet, as striking as it is that Luke should postpone this narrative comment until after Jesus has entered Jerusalem, such postponement does not occasion any great surprise for the reader of Luke. The reason is that, as early as 13:33, the Lukan Jesus has led the reader to anticipate this course of events: "Nevertheless," Jesus declared, "I must go on my way . . . ; for it cannot be that a prophet should perish [be destroyed] away from Jerusalem."[19] To sum up, therefore, whereas the "conversation" between Jesus and the authorities in Mark's story mutates into a struggle to the death as early as 3:6, this "conversation" continues in Luke's story until Jesus, in Jerusalem, begins the third phase of his ministry. Not until Jesus' last great confrontation with the authorities at the end of his public ministry does Luke show that his conflict with them becomes mortal.

Should Luke indeed construe Jesus' conflict with the religious authorities throughout the greater part of his public ministry as a protracted, intermittent "conversation"—acrid though the latter may be at times—then several episodes in Luke's story, which do not appear at all in the stories of Mark and of Matthew, become more readily comprehensible. Such episodes as the following come to mind. On one occasion, elders of the Jews earnestly plead with Jesus, on behalf of a Roman centurion, to come and heal the centurion's slave, which Jesus does (7:3–6). On three other occasions, Pharisees invite Jesus to dine in their homes, irrespective of the fact that Jesus each time excoriates both them and their guests (7:36; 11:37; 14:1). At another point, some Pharisees come to Jesus and warn him to leave that place because Herod is bent on killing him (13:31). And in two instances, the Pharisees or a ruler, although they do not benefit from Jesus' teaching, yet solicit it (17:20; 18:18). Still, the reader must make no mistake: Although Jesus' conflict with the authorities takes the form of an ongoing conversation throughout the first two phases of Jesus' public ministry (4:14–19:46), the authorities are nonetheless the inveterate antagonists of Jesus.

In summary of this lengthy discussion, we have seen from our investigation of Jesus' controversies in 5:17–6:11 that his conflict with the religious authorities exhibits four important features in Luke's gospel story. First, this conflict has to do with the crucial question of who rightfully rules God's people Israel: Is it Jesus, Israel's Messiah, or the authorities? Second, the issues that spark controversy in this conflict, which have to do with such matters as authority, tradition, and Mosaic law, are all weighty in nature and go to the heart of what it means to rule Israel. Third, in the first two phases of Jesus' public ministry, as he reaches out to all Israel from Galilee (3:21–9:50) and journeys to Jerusalem (9:51–19:46), the controversies Jesus has with the authorities tend not to be acutely confrontational in nature; that is to say, with few exceptions, Jesus is not challenged to his face for something that he himself says or does. And last, the form that Jesus' conflict with the authorities assumes during the first two phases of his public ministry is that of a protracted, intermittent conversation.

What events or episodes in Luke's gospel story signal the end of Jesus' "conversation" with the religious authorities? These episodes, which come at the very end of Jesus' journey to Jerusalem, are his entry into Jerusalem (19:28–44) and his cleansing of the temple (19:45–46). As Jesus draws near to Jerusalem, the whole multitude of his disciples begin to praise God by shouting aloud, "Blessed is the Coming One, the King, in the name of the Lord . . ." (19:38). In other words, Jesus is openly hailed here as Israel's Messiah-King.[20] Hearing this acclamation, however, some Pharisees at the scene strenuously object to it and call on Jesus to "rebuke" his disciples (19:39). With this gesture, these Pharisees publicly repudiate Jesus as Israel's Messiah-King.

The second episode that signals the end of Jesus' protracted conversation with the religious authorities follows almost immediately (19:45–46). Once in Jerusalem, Jesus' first act is to enter the temple. Earlier as a twelve-year-old, Jesus Son of God had entered the temple, the "house of his Father," and asserted his need to be there (2:49). Now Jesus, hailed by his disciples as Israel's Messiah-King, returns to the temple, cleanses it, and "takes possession" of it in preparation for his ministry there (19:47*a;* 20:1). In cleansing the temple, Jesus directly challenges the right of the authorities, for whom the temple is also their seat of power, to rule Israel in the name of God. Indeed, the authorities have turned the temple itself into a sign of their failed leadership,[21] for they have converted it from God's house of prayer into a den of thieves.

III

From the first and second phases of Jesus' public ministry, we move to the third (19:47–21:38), where Jesus discharges his ministry of teaching in the temple. Having cleansed the temple and taken possession of it, Jesus clashes with the religious authorities in unremitting controversy for the last time prior to his passion (20:1–40).

In this confrontation, Jesus' conflict with the religious authorities intensifies noticeably. To alert the reader to this, Luke makes use of various literary devices. Thus, Luke remarks for the first time, as we observed above, that the chief priests, the scribes, and the leaders of the people are out to "destroy" Jesus (19:47). From now until Jesus is hung on the cross, therefore, the conflict between him and the authorities is "to the death." Second, this conflict, situated as it is in the temple (19:47*a;* 20:1), takes place in a setting that in itself points to the intensification of ill will on the part of the authorities. The reason, as we noted, is that the temple is both the place of God's presence and the seat of the authorities' power. For Jesus to challenge the authorities in the temple on God's authority is for him to strike at the root of their status as Israel's leaders. Third, the controversies Jesus has with the authorities in the temple are all acutely confrontational in nature: In each one, Jesus is challenged to his face concerning matters that pertain directly to him (20:2, 20–22, 27–33). Fourth, the issues that incite controversy between Jesus and the authorities continue to be of critical significance and to press the question of what it is to rule Israel: the "authority" by which Jesus ministers in the temple (20:1–2) and the way in which he interprets Mosaic law relative to both social and religious questions (20:22, 27–33). And last, the atmosphere in which Jesus' controversies with the authorities in the temple take place becomes one of heightened hostility (20:19). This is apparent from Luke's comment that the authorities, having heard Jesus' narration of the parable of the Vineyard, want to "lay hands on him at that very hour" but fear the people (20:19).

What is the outcome of this last confrontation Jesus has with the religious authorities prior to his passion? Luke informs the reader of this at 20:40: "For they [the authorities] no longer dared to ask him anything." Having challenged Jesus in sustained debate and having lost at every turn, the authorities, intimidated by Jesus, acknowledge this by falling silent. Unable to defeat Jesus in debate, the authorities withdraw until they find in Judas the ally who will make it possible for them to arrest Jesus and bring him to trial (22:3–6; 23:48).

IV

With the onset of the passion account, Luke turns from the middle of his gospel story to the end (22:1–24:53). Because the three phases of Jesus' public ministry are now over — outreach to Israel from Galilee, journey to Jerusalem, ministry in Jerusalem — Luke sets the stage for Jesus' impending suffering, death, resurrection, and ascension.

In the opening scenes of the passion account (22:1–6), Luke depicts the gathering of the "coalition of darkness." Ominously, Luke relates that "Satan entered into Judas" and that Judas went and "conferred with the chief priests and officers of the temple police about how he might betray him [Jesus] to them." Later, as the religious authorities arrest him, Jesus himself declares, "But this is your hour, and the power of darkness" (22:53). In Luke's purview, those directly responsible for Jesus' death are Satan and the religious authorities, and these co-opt others, such as Judas, Pilate, and the Jewish people, as their pawns.

In the plot of Luke's gospel story of conflict, the scene in the passion account that interests us most is that in which the authorities confront the earthly Jesus one last time. This scene is found in 23:35, where the authorities ridicule Jesus as he hangs on the cross. In mockery, they refer to him as "the chosen Messiah of God" and assail him because, although he possessed such authority during his ministry as to save others through healing or rescue, here on the cross he cannot even save himself from death. In other words, the last time the authorities confront the earthly Jesus, they abjectly repudiate him as being Israel's Messiah-King, regard him as bereft of all authority, see him as doomed to destruction, and are utterly convinced that, in their conflict with him, they have gained the victory and been vindicated as the rightful leaders of Israel.

Ironically, what the religious authorities do not perceive is that Jesus has willingly submitted to death in accordance with God's plan of salvation.[22] In consequence of this, God raises Jesus to life and, in the ascension, exalts him to the right hand of Power (22:69; 24:5–7). The upshot is that the "end" of Jesus, unbeknownst to the authorities, proves itself to be the opposite of what they envisaged it to be: God vindicates Jesus as the Messiah-King of Israel, endows him with the authority to rule all, and grants to him, in his conflict with them, the victory. Early in Luke's gospel story, Mary burst forth in the Magnificat and praised God for "reversing the fortunes" of humans (1:46–55). By the close of this story, the reader recognizes that the one in whom God best demonstrates the truth of Mary's praise is none other than Jesus.

Accordingly, the resolution of Luke's gospel story of conflict between Jesus and the religious authorities is found in the events associated with Jesus' crucifixion, resurrection, and ascension. Nevertheless, it is in the episode of Jesus on the cross that this story reaches its culmination. In the eyes of the authorities, the Jesus who hangs on the cross is powerless and doomed and hence is himself a sign of both their triumph over him and their vindication as Israel's rightful leaders. In the eyes of Luke and the reader, however, the opposite is ironically the case: For one thing, it is as Jesus hangs on the cross that he is publicly proclaimed as Israel's Messiah-King;[23] for another thing, it is in anticipation of the time following his ascension that he already attests to his glorious reign of salvation by authoritatively receiving the repentant criminal "today" into the paradise of his kingdom (23:40–43).

V

In Acts, the story of Luke's Gospel has its sequel. There Luke will tell how the news of Jesus' reign of salvation is carried from Jerusalem to the ends of the earth (Acts 1:8). Moreover, Luke will also tell how the religious authorities, the chief antagonists of Jesus in the Gospel, will receive a "second chance" to repent of their "ignorance" and to receive Jesus, this time as Israel's resurrected and exalted Messiah (Acts 2:30–32, 36). But this story in Acts has its own plot, and to trace it is a task for another time.

NOTES

1. Increasingly, scholars seem inclined to agree that all four canonical Gospels belong to the genre of ancient Greco-Roman biography. See, e.g., Charles H. Talbert, "Once Again: Gospel Genre," *Semeia* 43 (1988): 54–62; David E. Aune, "Greco-Roman Biography," *Greco-Roman Literature and the New Testament,* SBLSBS 21 (Atlanta: Scholars Press, 1988), 122; Richard A. Burridge, *What Are the Gospels? A Comparison with Graeco-Roman Biography,* SNTSMS 70 (Cambridge: Cambridge University Press, 1992), 247, 254.

2. For a succinct but insightful discussion of "plot," see M. H. Abrams, *A Glossary of Literary Terms,* 4th ed. (New York: Holt, Rinehart and Winston, 1981), 137–40.

3. Notice carefully that the focus here is on Luke's Gospel. In Acts, Luke tells of further conflict with Jewish authorities, only now it is between them and the church.

4. Though Luke does not hesitate in his gospel story to align the ministry of Jesus with that of the prophets of old, he presents Jesus himself, not as "Prophet," but as "Messiah." On this, see Jack Dean Kingsbury, "Jesus as the 'Prophetic Messiah' in Luke's Gospel," *The Future of Christology,* ed. Abraham J. Malherbe and Wayne A. Meeks (Minneapolis: Fortress Press, 1993), 29–42.

5. As regards Luke's portrait of Jesus (and John) as an eschatological figure, see John T. Carroll, *Response to the End of History: Eschatology and Situation in Luke-Acts,* SBLDS 92 (Atlanta: Scholars Press, 1988), esp. 37–53.

6. With respect to Luke's interpretation of "salvation," see Frederick W. Danker, *Jesus and the New Age: A Commentary on St. Luke's Gospel* (Philadelphia: Fortress Press, 1988), 66–67.

7. In terms of Luke's characterization of the religious authorities, see Jack Dean Kingsbury, *Conflict in Luke: Jesus, Authorities, Disciples* (Minneapolis: Fortress Press, 1991), 21–28.

8. Concerning Luke's rhetoric of recognition and response, see John A. Darr, *On Character Building* (Louisville: Westminster/John Knox Press, 1992), esp. 53–58.

9. On Luke's notion of serving the "purposes either of God or of humans," see Kingsbury, *Conflict in Luke,* 11–13.

10. See Mark A. Powell, "The Religious Leaders in Luke: A Literary-Critical Study," *JBL* 109 (1990): 95.

11. See, e.g., Luke 5:32; 7:29–30; 16:13–14; 18:9.

12. See, e.g., Luke 5:29–32; 11:39, 42, 43, 46, 47, 52; 12:1; 14:7–11, 12–14; 15:1–7; 16:14–15; 18:9–14; 20:46–47.

13. Luke makes a point in 2:41–52 of designating Jesus as *pais* (2:43), which is a polyvalent term that can mean "boy," "son," or "servant." In this episode, Luke associates all three meanings with Jesus: Jesus is at once a youth (2:43) and the Son and Servant of God (2:49).

14. With regard to "amazement" as "perplexity," see, e.g., Acts 2:12; also Luke 24:22–24.

15. See, e.g., Luke 1:31–33; 23:2, 14*a,* 33, 35–43.

16. On the importance of Luke 5:17 for reading the whole of Luke's gospel story, see Robert C. Tannehill, *The Gospel according to Luke,* vol. 1 of *The Narrative Unity of Luke-Acts: A Literary Interpretation* (Philadelphia: Fortress Press, 1986), 172–73.

17. The role the Pharisees play in Luke-Acts is highly disputed; see, e.g., Jack Dean Kingsbury, "The Pharisees in Luke-Acts," in *The Four Gospels: 1992,* ed. F. Van Segbroeck et al. (Leuven: University Press, 1992), 2:1497–1512; also Darr, *On Character Building,* chap. 4.

18. The only three instances in which Luke seems inclined in this part of his story to permit the religious authorities to attack Jesus to his face because of his own actions are 10:25; 11:45, 53.

19. See n. 3.

20. See, e.g., Luke 3:15–16; 7:18–23.

21. See *Danker, Jesus and the New Age,* 315; also Charles H. Talbert, *Reading Luke: A Literary and Theological Commentary on the Third Gospel* (New York: Crossroad, 1982), 188.

22. See Luke 9:22; 17:25; 18:31–33; 22:42; 24:44–48.

23. See Luke 23:35, 37, 38, 39, and note again the irony.

– 15 –

The Social Context of Luke's Community

Halvor Moxnes

Apparently the social situation in which Luke's community lived was that of an urban setting in the Eastern Mediterranean. This situation was shaped by the honor and patronage culture of the Hellenistic city. At the heart of the Lukan community's ethos lay its common meals. The purpose of these meals was dual: On the one hand, they forged a common identity for a socially and ethnically diverse group of Christians; on the other hand, they functioned as a criticism of urban culture.

From Text to Context

HOW CAN WE MOVE from the text of Luke's Gospel to the social situation of his first readers? This problem in Gospel research has so far not been solved. Form criticism tried to find a *Sitz im Leben* for Gospel passages in typical situations in the life of the community, and redaction criticism attempted to go from the intentions of the author to the specific situations he addressed. More recently, an approach focusing upon the literary character of Luke's Gospel has emphasized the difficulties involved in drawing historical conclusions about Luke's community.[1] The Lukan text creates a narrative world, and it is this world we examine as we analyze the social relations, ethos, and symbolic universe of Luke. Still, this does not mean that we now have a "window" that opens directly onto the social situation of Luke's historical community.

Literary methods, however, can and do point toward new possibilities for locating Luke's community. Audience criticism has shifted away from a concentration on the intention of the author toward a study of the text itself and its communication with its readers. This approach finds its point of orientation in this very process of communication and in the "implied readers" to which the text refers. These readers are, so to speak, the "ideal readers" or the "ideal community" that the text would create through its "affective quality."[2]

Between the implied readers and the empirical audience we may presuppose some links. First of all, a text must communicate with an empirical audience. The social and cultural world of the text must give meaning to its readers and, in some way, be related to their world. Moreover, the Gospels also describe historically known characters, places, and events that require extratextual knowledge from their readers. Consequently, it is possible to draw a profile of the knowledge required of the readers and, on that basis, attempt to situate the empirical audience.[3]

In Lukan studies, most interest has been focused on the attempt to construct the situation of the community in terms of its religious background, that is, whether it was gentile Christian, Jewish Christian, or a mixture of both.[4] In this study, we are most interested in the social context of Luke's community. We are, therefore, primarily concerned with knowledge about social institutions, structures, and relations that are presupposed in the Gospel.

The narrative world of the text must be correlated with the social context of the Mediterranean world in antiquity. It is this combination of analysis of the social world of a text with its social and historical context, known from other sources, that makes it possible to suggest a profile of the social location of Luke's first readers.

"Community" or "Communities"?

It is widely accepted that the location of the author and the addressees is other than Palestine, which is the location of the narrative world of the Gospel. This hypothesis is based partly on specific information in the text. Luke's descriptions of houses appear to be informed by a landscape and culture different from that of a Palestinian village.[5] And Jesus' sayings, in Luke 12:11–12, about future persecution reflect a setting in the Hellenistic diaspora. The terminology used is that of a synagogue and of authorities of a Hellenistic city, not that of Roman rulers, vassal kings, and the Sanhedrin in Jerusalem.[6] It is plausible, therefore, that Luke's location is in an urban setting in the eastern parts of the Mediterranean.[7]

There is no consensus yet about any one city. Philip Esler has made a strong argument that Luke had a specific city in mind. His own suggestion is Ephesus, but Antioch has been seriously considered also.[8] Other scholars do not look so much for specific locations or historical events as for "typical situations" or a "general climate."[9] The difficulties in drawing specific historical conclusions from literary texts lead me to side with this approach. The main point in Esler's *Community and Gospel in Luke-Acts* is that there are "particular relationships" between Luke's theology and his social, political, and religious setting. These relationships required Christian congregations "of a certain type, all of them being characterized by a quite circumscribed set of tensions within their membership and with the world outside."[10] I think that these "tensions" are so general in character that they can be found in a number of Hellenistic cities in the eastern part of the Roman Empire.

Thus, instead of a specific setting, we shall look for "typical" aspects of urban life in a Greco-Roman city. Likewise, the attempt to locate Luke's audience is based, not on individual elements in the Lukan narrative, but on social structures and relations described by Luke. These are found not only in the Gospel but also in Acts, so we will draw on both parts of Luke's work.

An Urban Context: Urban Communities and Their Structures

How can we imagine what life in Hellenistic cities was like for Luke's readers? Some of the most relevant cities for early Christianity are now well known from excavations, in particular Ephesus, Pergamon, and Sardis in Asia Minor, Corinth in Greece, and Ostia and Pompeii in Italy. The best way to learn about ancient cities is, of course, through well-prepared site visits, but other sources of information are excavation reports, films, literature about ancient cities, good guidebooks, and museum exhibitions. These can help us move from literary descriptions to the visual imagination of ancient societies and their settings within a larger physical and social area. To structure and organize the information, we also need a clearer view of what a Greco-Roman city was like in terms of social and ethnic composition, political power, and socioeconomic relations.[11]

Spatial and Social Organization of the City

A city must be "interpreted" if we are to recognize the "meaning" of buildings of various types, market places, streets, gates, statues, and monuments.[12] The spatial organization reflects the social stratification of the city. The center contained temples and the central buildings for the city administration at the agora, or marketplace. Other buildings in the central area of a city were a theater, baths, and gymnasiums. In this area, we also find the residences of the elite; striking examples are the *slope hauses* in Ephesus. The elite made up only a small fraction of the population but controlled the land and its production as well as the political, social, and religious system. They combined wealth with offices as public officials and as priests in the major city cults. We must bear in mind that, in most cases, only the central areas of ancient cities of the elite residential areas have been excavated; therefore, the position of the nonelite population is underrepresented.[13]

The nonelite, that is, the great bulk of the population, comprised a large variety of groups. In addition to the servants and slaves of the elite, there were merchants, shopkeepers, and artisans organized into guilds, often grouped in special streets. Particularly in cities with a seaport, like Ephesus and Corinth, there were aliens, people from all over the area of the Mediterranean and Middle East. These people could ply their trade but could not become citizens and own property in the city. Among the lower groups were people with despised occupations (e.g., tanners, innkeepers, or prostitutes) and farther out, at the outskirts or beyond the city walls, were beggars and outcasts.

It is well known that Luke shows special interest in the relationships between rich and poor and between men and women. In Acts, relationships among Christians, Jews, and non-Jews play a prominent role. This places Luke's characters within the context of vital power relations within the Hellenistic city having to do with distinctions between elite and nonelite, men and women, and citizens and noncitizens.

Power and Social Relations in the Hellenistic City

The Roman emperor wielded his power and authority over the cities in the East through governors and other political and military representatives. However, most of the time Rome allowed the local elite to continue its rule.

What was the structure of power and social relationships that characterized life in these cities? First, there was the quest for honor that was an integral part of Greek culture, well known from Homeric society onward.[14] At first associated with warrior ideals, in a "softer" form it was central to the Hellenistic conception of the city as a community of citizens. Among the elite, this created a climate of constant competition to win honor. The costs involved were those of benefactions to the city in the form of public buildings, feasts, and plays, for example. These benefactions were rewarded by public office or other expressions of status, like statues, seats of honor, and city banquets.

Second, social relationships were governed by a system of patronage.[15] One's position was not based on universal human rights but on one's place in a personal hierarchy. Nonelite persons were dependent upon an elite patron for help, work, loans, and the like; and, in return, they had to give loyalty and public support.

Thirdly, social interaction was ruled by the requirements of balanced reciprocity. Studies of economic interaction in preindustrial societies speak of three forms of reciprocity: (1) generalized reciprocity (giving without specific demand for a return); (2) balanced reciprocity (giving with an expectation of quick recompensation); and (3) negative reciprocity (taking something, sometimes with force, without giving anything back).[16]

Luke's Community within the Hellenistic City

Meals as Centers of Sociability and of Conflicts

There is much material in Luke-Acts that pertains to Luke's evaluation of city culture, patronage, and the quest for honor. The best starting point may be a cluster of texts that focus on meals and hospitality. Meals represented a major expression of that social interaction among the city elite we outlined above. Among individuals, it served as a means of sociability as well as of competition and patronage. Hospitality represented a challenge that demanded a reply in the form of a quick return. City banquets were expressions of honor and status for the ruling elite. Festivals, with food offered to the public at large, served important community functions and were typical forms of benefactions.[17] Meals were also an integral part of temple worship and offerings, with special dining rooms or houses for groups of worshipers. Moreover, for associations, commensality was an important part of their common activity. Mithras or Dionysios cult members had special rooms built for eating meals. For Jews in the Diaspora, commensality served as an expression of their identity, circumscribed by strong rules concerning boundaries and purity.

Luke often portrays Jesus at meals, either as host or as guest (5:29–32; 7:36–50; 14:1–24; 19:5–10).[18] Several meal narratives are clearly written as "cult scenes," to be repeated in the life of the community (9:10–17; 22:14–30; 24:13–35, 36–42). In descriptions of life in the first community in Jerusalem, meals figure prominently as a typical element (Acts 2:46). Moreover, the acceptance of new members into the community took place at meals (Acts 10:17–29; 11:3). Thus, meals must have played an important part in the life of Luke's communities as well.

A common meal created a focus for a group that drew its members from various segments within the Hellenistic city, but it also fostered tensions in social relationships inside and outside that group. Luke's redaction of the meal narratives illustrates that "food dealings are a delicate barometer, a ritual statement as it were, of social relationships, and food is thus employed instrumentally as a starting, a sustaining, or a destroying mechanism of sociability."[19]

Godfearers as Patrons to the Community?

Esler has recently focused attention on the role of meal fellowships in the conflict over the mission to gentiles in early Christianity.[20] There were many Jews in the Hellenistic towns of Asia Minor and Syria, most of them in the nonelite sections of the cities. These Jews had established their own synagogues, and some were also well established in the city.[21] Therefore, it is very likely that some Jews were members of the Lukan communities. Whereas the earlier consensus was that Luke primarily addressed Hellenistic, non-Jewish Christians, there is now a growing number of scholars who argue that there must have been Jews among them.[22]

The result was that there were conflicts within the community with law-observant Christian Jews over Jewish purity laws that prevented Jews from having table fellowship with non-Jews. The most significant example of such conflict is the story in Acts 10–11 of how God's revelation made Peter break with purity rules and engage in table fellowship with the Roman centurion Cornelius. This story had a legitimating function in Luke's own communities on behalf of a praxis of commensality between Jewish and non-Jewish Christians.

Still, this commensality also had implications for the community and its social relationships in its Hellenistic environment. The description of Cornelius as a "Godfearer" with good reputation among the Jews (Acts 10:22; cf. 10:1–2) indicates that he was kindly disposed toward the Jewish synagogue and could act as its patron. In Luke's version of the story of the centurion's son (Luke 7:1–10), the aspect of patronage is again emphasized: The centurion donated a synagogue to the community (7:5).[23] The narratives of these two centurions may be significant in more than one way. They may indicate the social level of Romans who were interested in Christianity: They did not come from the very elite but were middle-level officers. Moreover, they signal an "ethnic mixture." Most importantly, they illustrate the need that groups, such as Jewish synagogues and the first Christians, had for patrons, who could provide not only material help in the form of houses and hospitality but also social protection.

Accordingly, the conflict with the synagogue was not just over purity rules but was also a competition to win the Godfearers, especially people of some standing. This competition may be reflected in narratives of how Jews try to make prominent members of the city turn against the Christian missionaries (Acts 13:50; 14:2; 18:12). Luke's writings in themselves may be a sign of the success of the Christian mission among Godfearers. Joseph Tyson has attempted to draw the profile of the implied reader of Luke-Acts. The result appears to correspond to the description of Godfearers in Luke-Acts. The implied reader

> would need to be a literate person, reasonably well informed about the history, geography, and political situation in the eastern Mediterranean world. . . . The most significant aspect of this profile is the claim that the implied reader is familiar with the Hebrew Scriptures and knowledgeable about some fundamental Jewish concepts but is probably not to be identified as Jewish.[24]

Tyson's profile does not identify these implied readers as belonging to the elite. The only empirical reader of Luke-Acts we know of is Theophilus (Luke 1:1–4; Acts 1:1), and we know nothing more about him than what the prescript tells us. But this may give us some information about the social location of Luke and thereby indirectly about Theophilus. Based on studies of his style and vocabulary, Loveday Alexander finds that, compared to other Hellenistic writers, Luke can best be described as a "technical writer."[25] This places his perspective closer to the artisan "class" than to the elite, a point that is also supported by his interest in artisans and their work. Moreover, Luke's address to Theophilus as "most excellent" is parallel to what subordinates use when they address Roman superiors. Hence, it is probable that Luke writes from a subordinate position, that is, as a client seeking a patron and not as an equal to Theophilus.

Women—On the Fringe of the Community?

Luke's portrayal of women in his Gospel and Acts is full of ambiguities that may reflect tensions within his communities.[26] Women are frequently associated with food, meals, and hospitality (4:38–39; 7:36–50; 10:38–42), but they are seldom explicitly mentioned as guests at meals with Jesus. Instead, women are described as "serving" Jesus and the apostles (4:38–39; 8:1–3). In some cases, this service actually means "to provide," as in the case of several prominent women who "served Jesus with their property" (8:1–3). These women were thus acting as patrons of Jesus. In Acts 16:14–15, we find Lydia, "a seller of purple goods," an economically independent nonelite woman. She serves as a hostess to Paul, but even if she acts as a patron, she is inferior to the apostle, who brings spiritual benefits.

Accordingly, women are portrayed as independent of their husbands, with means of their own, fulfilling an important role of providing for missionaries, acting as patrons. This may be somewhat unusual. In Greco-Roman society women could have a strong position in the household, but normally much less so in the public sphere of the city. That was equally true of elite women. Nonelite women could more easily make a career of their own, for example, through various crafts or as vendors and merchants. This oversimplified statement, however, must be adjusted for regional and individual differences. Paul Trebilco has shown that women held prominent positions in social and political life only in the western parts of Asia Minor.[27] In this region, there is also evidence that women served as synagogue leaders.

If we can locate Luke's communities in this area, it would provide a highly interesting background for the independent women in Luke's narrative. There seems to be a tension between the role of these women and Luke's characterization of them: Unlike male disciples, they did not claim honor or privilege, but exemplified Jesus' own model of the "patron who serves" (22:27). Moreover, in Luke's narrative they are never entrusted with the task of witnessing, healing, or proclaiming. As "ideal disciples" they remain confined to their domestic tasks and belong to the fringe of social power. Luke's narrative may not be so much a description as a prescription: It represents male ideals for women's behavior.

Tensions between Rich and Poor

From Paul's letters to the Corinthians we know that social tensions existed between the well-to-do and the poor at the celebration of the communal Eucharist.[28] Luke's interest in meals may imply that there were similar tensions in the communities that he addressed. Jesus' dinner at the house of a Pharisee in Luke 14:1–24 is one of several dinner scenes redacted by Luke. The conflict over Jesus' lack of Sabbath observance (14:1–6) was primarily relevant to a Jewish audience. But Jesus' address to the guests and host about proper behavior at meals and about whom to invite (14:7–14) is set in a Hellenistic context. When Jesus encourages the invitation of "the poor, the maimed, the lame, the blind" (14:13), his point is not that they should invite those who were impure according to Jewish purity laws. Instead, the prospective guests are described in terms of their social location, as unable to repay the invitation (14:14). Luke describes hospitality in the well-known terms of reciprocity, and he is the only New Testament author to use its technical vocabulary.

The guest list that Jesus criticizes is the typical inner circle: "Do not invite your friends or your brothers or your kinsmen or your rich neighbors, lest they also invite you in return, and you be repaid" (14:12). What is described here is the use of hospitality as a means to uphold and cultivate an elite group. It was exclusive by keeping strict boundaries toward outsiders. The term "friend" describes a social relationship different from patronage in that it was based on a comparable social standing but was similar in its foundation on the exchange of services. A failure to reciprocate in kind led to lack of honor and loss of standing as "friend."

To base one's hospitality on invitations to those who could not repay meant not only breaking with the elite system and all its values but also being exposed to social sanctions. Another example of a reversal of the reciprocal structure of social relationships is found in Jesus' farewell speech at the last supper, when he addressed the disciples who were discussing who was the greatest (22:24–27). Only in Luke's version of Jesus' rebuke is there an explicit reference to the benefactor system: "The kings of the Gentiles exercise lordship over them, and those in authority over them are called benefactors" (22:25). These examples are obviously intended as contrasts to the role that the disciples ought to play as "one who serves" (22:26).

Luke's redaction here tells us something about the social structure he envisages for his audience of Christian groups. He criticizes the system of reciprocity and the hierarchical structure of social relationships of benefactions. His alternative is a set of relationships based on "free" hospitality (generalized reciprocity), gift giving, and servanthood.

Are Luke's exhortations about almsgiving, or giving without a return, addressed to tensions existing between rich and poor within his community? We must be careful here about what we mean by "rich" in the context of a Greco-Roman city. Wealth and social position did not necessarily go together. To be designated "rich" did not in itself imply membership in the elite. Rich men could be outsiders and make their money in nonelite occupations (e.g., as toll collectors and merchants). Luke's criticisms of the "rich" (e.g., Luke 12:16–21; 16:19–31) portray them negatively, as members of the elite and not concerned with the poor. It is, therefore, more likely that they are portrayed as outsiders to the community.[29] The "ideal rich" in Luke, like the toll collector Zacchaeus (Luke 19:1–10), do not belong to the elite. It is a person on the fringe of society, showing compassion to others who are in a weak position, who serves as an ideal.

Community Ethos as Protest against City Ideals

We have now tried to outline the ethos of Luke's "ideal community" and to draw inferences to a plausible social setting for his empirical readers. Within the city culture of the Eastern Mediterranean, we can envisage Luke's community as a group of nonelite persons who are culturally and ethnically mixed but who also include among them some who come from the elite periphery.[30] Their life together centered on a meal that served as a means of integration, not just of Jews and non-Jews but also of members from various status groups and social positions. The ethos of the meal represented a break with the city ideals of patronage, benefactions, and the quest for honor. It is not unthinkable that such criticism of city ideals could also have been aimed at community members drawn from the "elite periphery." Similar criticism was also made by Stoic and Cynic groups at the time.[31] Thus, the goal of this ethos is best understood as that of creating a common identity for a mixed group of Christians.

NOTES

1. Luke T. Johnson, "On Finding the Lukan Community: A Cautious Cautionary Essay," SBLSP 16 (1979): 87–100.

2. Vernon Robbins, "The Social Location of the Implied Author of Luke-Acts," in *The Social World of Luke-Acts,* ed. Jerome H. Neyrey (Peabody, Mass.: Hendrickson Publishers, 1991), 312.

3. Joseph B. Tyson, *Images of Judaism in Luke-Acts* (Columbia: University of South Carolina Press, 1991), 22–23.

4. For recent reviews of this important discussion, see Philip F. Esler, *Community and Gospel in Luke-Acts,* SNTSMS 57 (Cambridge: Cambridge University Press, 1987), 24–33, and Jacob Jervell, "Retrospect and Prospect in Luke-Acts Interpretation," SBLSP 30 (1991): 383–404.

5. Cf. Luke 6:47–49 with Matt. 7:24–27; Luke 8:16 and 11:33 with Matt. 5:15. See the comments in Joseph A. Fitzmyer, *The Gospel according to Luke,* AB 28/1 (Garden City, N.Y.: Doubleday, 1979), 644, 719.

6. Cf. Luke's use of *archas* ("rulers") and *exousias* ("authorities") instead of *hegemonas* ("governors") and *basileis* ("kings") in Matt. 10:18. See Wolfgang Stegemann, *Zwischen Synagoge und Obrigkeit,* FRLANT 152 (Göttingen: Vandenhoeck & Ruprecht, 1991), 81–84.

7. Argued in the classic work by Henry J. Cadbury, *The Making of Luke-Acts* (New York: Macmillan, 1927), 245–49. More recently, see, e.g., Walter Radl, *Das Lukas-Evangelium* (Darmstadt: Wissenschaftliche Buchgesellschaft, 1988), 27; Robbins, "Social Location," 316–18.

8. Esler, *Community and Gospel in Luke-Acts,* 26. See also Peter Lampe, *Lokalisation der Lukas-Leser: Lk/Apg. als Quellen für das ephesische Christentum des ausgehenden 1.Jr.* (forthcoming from J. C. B. Mohr and Fortress Press).

9. Stegemann, *Zwischen Synagoge und Obrigkeit,* 10.

10. Esler, *Community and Gospel in Luke-Acts,* 26.

11. The literature on cities is so vast that only a few examples can be mentioned. On the development of city planning, see J. B. Ward-Perkins, *Cities of Ancient Greece and Italy: Planning in Classical Antiquity* (New York: Braziller, 1974). On cities in different regions, see G. M. A. Hanfman, *From Croesus to Constantine: The Cities of Western Asia Minor and Their Arts in Greek and Roman Times* (Ann Arbor: University of Michigan Press, 1975); Robin Osborne,

Classical Landscape with Figures: The Ancient Greek City and Its Countryside (Dobbs Ferry, N.Y.: Sheridan Press, 1987); Timothy W. Potter, *Roman Italy* (Berkeley: University of California Press, 1987). On economic and social relations, see Moses I. Finley, *The Ancient Economy* (London: Chatto & Windus, 1973), and Richard L. Rohrbaugh, "The Pre-Industrial City in Luke-Acts," in *Social World of Luke-Acts,* 125–49.

12. See William L. MacDonald, *The Architecture of the Roman Empire,* vol. 2: *An Urban Appraisal* (New Haven: Yale University Press, 1986).

13. A partial exception to this is Ostia, where we find some of the large apartment blocks (*insulae*) very well preserved.

14. A. W. H. Adkins, in *Merit and Responsibility* (Oxford: Clarendon Press, 1960), traces the development of the concept of "honor." For an overview of the structure of honor and its relevance for Luke, see Bruce J. Malina and Jerome H. Neyrey, "Honor and Shame in Luke-Acts: Pivotal Values in the Mediterranean World," in *Social World of Luke-Acts,* 25–65.

15. See Richard P. Saller, *Personal Patronage under the Early Empire* (Cambridge: Cambridge University Press, 1982).

16. See Marshall D. Sahlins, *Stone Age Economics* (Chicago: Aldine, 1972), 185–246.

17. See the magisterial survey by Paul Veyne, *Bread and Circuses* (London: Penguin Press, 1990).

18. This is studied, e.g., by David Moessner, *Lord of the Banquet: The Literary and Theological Significance of the Lukan Travel Narrative* (Philadelphia: Fortress Press, 1989) and David B. Gowler, *Host, Guest, Enemy, and Friend: Portraits of the Pharisees in Luke and Acts* (New York: Peter Lang Publishing, 1991).

19. Sahlins, *Stone Age Economics,* 215. For the complex character of meals in Luke-Acts, see Jerome H. Neyrey, "Ceremonies in Luke-Acts: The Case of Meals and Table-Fellowship," in *Social World of Luke-Acts,* 361–87.

20. Esler, *Community and Gospel in Luke-Acts,* 71–109.

21. Cf. Paul R. Trebilco, *Jewish Communities in Asia Minor* (Cambridge: Cambridge University Press, 1991).

22. See n. 4 above.

23. Halvor Moxnes, "Patron-Client Relations and the New Community in Luke-Acts," in *Social World of Luke-Acts,* 241–42, 252–53.

24. Tyson, *Images of Judaism in Luke-Acts,* 36.

25. Cf. Loveday Alexander, "Luke's Preface in the Context of Greek Preface-Writing," *NovT* 28 (1986): 60–61; Robbins, "Social Location," 319–23.

26. See T. Karlsen Seim, *The Double Message: Patterns of Gender in Luke-Acts* (Edinburgh: T. & T. Clark, 1994).

27. Trebilco, *Jewish Communities in Asia Minor,* 104–26.

28. See esp. Gerd Theissen, *The Social Setting of Pauline Christianity* (Philadelphia: Fortress Press, 1982).

29. Halvor Moxnes, *The Economy of the Kingdom* (Minneapolis: Fortress Press, 1988), 163–65.

30. This corresponds to Theissen's observation that Christianity drew members not from the "ruling elite" but rather from "fringe members" of the elite. See *Social Reality and the Early Christians: Theology, Ethics, and the World of the New Testament* (Minneapolis: Fortress Press, 1992), 270–71.

31. Dio Chrysostom (ca. 40–110 C.E.), from Prusa in Northwestern Asia Minor, is the most striking example from the time of Luke; see his *Or.* 44, 66.

The Gospel of JOHN

– 16 –

Toward a Narrative-Critical Study of John

Gail R. O'Day

The peculiar voice of the Fourth Gospel originated in the encounter of the Johannine community with the tradition it inherited. This suggests that the goal of interpretive methods must be to hold these two factors of community and tradition in creative tension.

The World of the Johannine Community as Interpretive Category

FOURTH GOSPEL SCHOLARSHIP in the early and middle decades of the twentieth century was shaped by categories and questions investigated by Rudolf Bultmann. The focus was on matters having to do with history-of-religions, literary history, and the history of ideas.[1] From Bultmann's existentialist perspective, the student of the Fourth Gospel is to understand the cultural and intellectual strands that determined the theological answers the Gospel gives to universal questions of human existence.[2] Of primary importance is the provenance of the *ideas* of the Gospel;[3] the search for origins is to be conducted in terms of both cultural and intellectual milieu and source documents. The sources are thought to be primarily written and intellectual in nature, and interpretation depends both upon identifying and isolating sources and a knowledge of the history of the Gospel's traditions.

In many ways C. H. Dodd stands as a transitional figure in Johannine scholarship. On the one hand, his first study, *The Interpretation of the Fourth Gospel,* is the classic example of an investigation of the history of ideas.[4] On the other hand, his second study ten years later, *Historical Tradition in the Fourth Gospel,* broke with scholarly consensus about written sources behind the Gospel and examines the role of oral tradition in the shaping of the Gospel.[5] Dodd's application of form-critical categories opened up new possibilities in Fourth Gospel research. His move from a strict focus on written sources to a consideration of oral tradition creates a place for the role of the community and its practices in the formation of the Gospel, a role overlooked or excluded by a concentration on written sources.[6]

The heuristic value of reclaiming the place of the community is dramatically illustrated in Raymond Brown's commentary on John.[7] Brown posits a detailed theory of composition and redaction that takes as its starting point not reconstructed written sources but the fund of oral traditions about Jesus circulating within the Johannine community. The stages of Brown's composition theory are well-known.[8] What is significant is that these literary stages are reflective of, and responsive to, stages in the historical life of the community. In Brown's work there is an intentional methodological intersection of the literature and the study of community, so that analysis no longer concentrates on the history of ideas but the history of the believing, struggling Christian community that shaped and consolidated the Gospel's traditions. This linking of community and tradition is a distinctly Roman Catholic insight. In Raymond Brown's commentary, the shift is away from establishing the history of the text and toward analyzing the formation of the text as part of the history of the community.

Perhaps the most important and thoroughgoing investigation of the Fourth Gospel that demonstrates this paradigmatic shift toward the life of the community is J. Louis Martyn's monograph *History and Theology in the Fourth Gospel.*[9] While others before Martyn had pursued the relationship of the Fourth Gospel to the synagogue, none had argued with such exegetical and methodological clarity. Nor had anyone so intentionally addressed the interaction between community and tradition in the formation of the Gospel. In the introduction to his book, Martyn reveals this plainly:

> Our first task . . . is to say something as specific as possible about the actual circumstances in which John wrote his gospel. How are we to picture daily life in John's church? Have elements of the peculiar daily experiences left their stamp on the gospel penned by one of its members? May one sense even in the exalted cadences the voice of a Christian theologian who writes *in response to contemporary events and issues* which concern, or should concern, all members of the Christian community in which he lives?[10]

To accomplish his task, Martyn combines exegetical and historical analysis to conclude that many of the Gospel's dialogues and narratives are to be understood on two levels: one, a witness to the time of Jesus; the other, a witness to the rearticulation of the tradition in response to events in the life of the Johannine community.[11] The decisive event for this second level is the conflict of the community with the synagogue, perhaps in conjunction with the Benediction against Heretics.[12]

The specifics and formality of Brown's stages are subjects for scholarly debate, as is the link Martyn forges between the dating of the Fourth Gospel and the dating of the Benediction against Heretics. Still, the contribution of the approaches of Brown and Martyn cannot be overestimated. Brown's commentary and Martyn's monograph signaled a significant change in the way the Fourth Gospel is conceptualized. In the intervening years, the term "Johannine community" has become commonplace in discussions of the Fourth Gospel.[13] One need only survey dissertations of the 1970s and 1980s to see the generative value of this paradigmatic shift toward community.[14] This is not to say that the lines drawn by Bultmannian research have disappeared;[15] it is to say that the work of Brown and Martyn has had discipline-shaping impact.

The World of the Gospel Text as Interpretive Category

What was gained in the paradigmatic shift away from the history of ideas in the text and toward the history and life of the community is a view of the Fourth Gospel that takes the needs, struggles, and crises of the Johannine community as generative theological categories. The Fourth Gospel is no longer treated simply as a historical artifact but as a witness to the life and faith of a developing, struggling community. Not coincidentally, the shift toward a focus on the community revealed by the text was accompanied by a parallel shift away from emphasis on a predominantly Gnostic provenance and milieu for the Fourth Gospel and toward a revitalized sense of Jewish provenance and milieu. In the preface to *History and Theology,* Martyn expresses his surprise that his research has led him away from prior convictions about links with Mandaean literature to the Jewish context he proposes.[16] When questions are asked about the everyday events with which the gospel community was confronted, the pivotal place of the relationship to Judaism reemerges. No longer is the Fourth Gospel read primarily as evidence to be dissected into traditions, strands, and sources in search of the earliest, and most authentic, formulations. Instead, the Gospel is read to see how the text reflects the history and needs of the generative community. Accordingly, the text is freed from its deterministic enslavement to its prehistory. The result is that the paradigmatic shift brought about by Brown and Martyn can also be described as a shift away from the world *behind* the text (so Bultmann) and toward the world *contemporaneous with* the text.

This one paradigmatic shift paved the way for another: the shift toward the world *in* the text. Once the Fourth Gospel was freed from the constraints of being read as a repository of earlier written sources, the way was open for the study of it as a literary text in its own right. Although this turn of events has its roots in the work of Brown and Martyn, it was nevertheless not until scholarship had moved beyond their categories that it could pursue such a literary reading of the Fourth Gospel.

To illustrate this turn toward a literary paradigm, we may consider the work of R. Alan Culpepper. His first study of John, *The Johannine School,* focused on the world of the particular community that created the text.[17] In his book *The Anatomy of the Fourth Gospel,* however, Culpepper directs attention almost exclusively to the literary characteristics of the Fourth Gospel, that is, to the world the text itself creates.[18]

Literary-critical analysis claims that the form and specific articulation of any given text must not be regarded as incidental or extraneous, but taken with utmost seriousness. Analyses of the structure, symbolism, irony, and imagery of John have enabled us to discern the distinctive voice of the Fourth Gospel and hence brought renewed vitality to our exegetical work.[19] Literary studies of the Fourth Gospel have essentially bracketed out the social-historical questions upon which Brown and Martyn concentrated and have focused instead on the story-world created by the text,[20] on the power of words to invoke and summon a new reality and to invite the reader to a new way of seeing the world.

The Worlds of Community and Text

Fourth Gospel scholarship may be doing itself and the text a disservice by employing a methodological bifurcation that investigates the world that created the text apart from the world created by the text. To comprehend the claims of the Fourth Gospel about God, Jesus, and life in a Christian community, social historians must work to read the texts more closely, and literary critics must work to read the text in conversation with the demands of its own world.

Because they are held together in the text itself, these two worlds, the social and the narrative, and the two methodologies appropriate to them must also be held together in our study of the Fourth Gospel. On the one hand, our most significant, if not exclusive, access to the Johannine community is through the text itself. The text cannot be defined only as the means to an end, because without the text there is no "end." We must reckon with the power of the text to summon its readers to a new world and a new social reality,[21] which is more, and other, than Brown and Martyn's community reconstructions can accomplish. On the other hand, whatever the originating point of the gospel traditions may be, the Fourth Gospel as we have received it is not a single-author text. It is a product of the ongoing life of the Johannine community. Unless we want to revert to a precritical literalism about authorship, we must factor into our literary study the communal formation of the text. Methods that rely exclusively on theories of authorship that have no place for the role of the community will come up short.[22] Neither social criticism nor literary criticism will have the maximum theological yield unless both take seriously *the community as creator of texts* and *the text as generative of new community.*

Literary-critical methodology, therefore, must operate in creative tension. Whereas literary criticism would have us read the text as we have it, we must remember that the text is the result of a community process.[23] Similarly, social criticism must operate in creative tension. Whereas social-historical criticism would have us read the text to capture the social and historical dimensions of the community, we must remember that the text cannot simply be used as a source, because it helped determine the shape of the community. This tension is inescapable. The text creates a world into which the Johannine community (and subsequent readers) is invited, but the world of the community also informed the shape of the invitation and the created world. The continuing life of the Fourth Gospel, both for its first readers and for ongoing generations of readers, depends on the world created by the text; still, the vitality of that world depends on its intersection with the social and political world of the originating community.[24]

The power of the Fourth Gospel's rhetoric depends in large measure upon its ability to create a linguistic, textual, imagistic world that addresses the needs and yearnings of a concrete religious community. It was in the encounter of tradition and community, story and theology that the Fourth Gospel first found its voice, and our methodology must strive to hold both sides of this encounter together. The Fourth Gospel speaks in a rich and distinctive voice that cannot be fully heard in one-sided studies of either social history or narratology. The Gospel itself challenges the interpreter to hold together social and narrative worlds in attempts to uncover its profound meaning.

NOTES

1. The two groundbreaking studies by Rudolf Bultmann are "Der religionsgeschichtliche Hintergrund des Prologs zum Johannesevangelium," in *Eucharisterion, Studies zur Literatur des Alten und Neuen Testaments* (Göttingen: Vandenhoeck & Ruprecht, 1920), 2:1–26; and "Die Bedeutung der neuer-

schlossen mandaïschen Quellen für das Verständnis des Johannesevangelium," *ZNW* 24 (1925): 100–46.

2. John Ashton, "Introduction: The Problem of John," in *The Interpretation of John,* ed. John Ashton (Philadelphia: Fortress, 1986), 6.

3. David Rensberger (*Johannine Faith and Liberating Community* [Philadelphia: Westminster, 1988], 17–19) provides a useful discussion of Johannine scholarship as a study of *ideas.*

4. C. H. Dodd, *The Interpretation of the Fourth Gospel* (Cambridge: Cambridge University Press, 1953).

5. C. H. Dodd, *Historical Tradition in the Fourth Gospel* (Cambridge: Cambridge University Press, 1963).

6. See Rensberger (*Johannine Faith,* 20–21) for helpful comments about Dodd.

7. Raymond E. Brown, *The Gospel according to John,* 2 vols., AB 29, 29A (Garden City, N.Y.: Doubleday, 1966, 1979).

8. Ibid., xxxiv–xxxix.

9. J. Louis Martyn, *History and Theology in the Fourth Gospel* (New York: Harper & Row, 1968; 2d ed., rev. and enl., Nashville: Abingdon, 1979). Page references are to the second edition.

10. Ibid., 18.

11. Ibid., 30.

12. Ibid., 50–62.

13. Ashton, "Introduction," 5.

14. E.g., Fernando Segovia, *Love Relationships in the Johannine Tradition: Agape/Agapan in 1 John and the Fourth Gospel,* SBLDS 58 (Chico, Calif.: Scholars Press, 1982); Bruce D. Woll, *Johannine Christianity in Conflict: Authority, Rank, and Succession in the First Farewell Discourse,* SBLDS 60 (Chico, Calif.: Scholars Press, 1981); G. I. Rennet, *The Life-World of the Johannine Community: An Investigation of the Social Dynamics Which Resulted in the Composition of the Fourth Gospel* (Ann Arbor: University Microfilms, 1982); Takashi Onuki, *Gemeinde und Welt in Johannesevangelium,* WMANT 56 (Neukirchen-Vluyn: Neukirchener Verlag, 1984).

15. In two recent review articles (Ashton, "Introduction," 1–2, and D. Moody Smith, "Johannine Studies," in *The New Testament and Its Modern Interpreters,* ed. Eldon Jay Epp and George W. MacRae, S.J. [Atlanta: Scholars Press, 1989], 272), the categories that shape the review of the discipline are determined by Bultmann's work. See also Ashton, *Understanding the Fourth Gospel* (Oxford: Clarendon, 1991). For continuing research in source criticism of the Fourth Gospel, see Robert Fortna, *The Fourth Gospel and Its Predecessor* (Philadelphia: Fortress, 1989).

16. Martyn, *History and Theology,* 11–12. See also Craig A. Evans, *Word and Glory: On the Exegetical and Theological Background of John's Prologue* (Sheffield: JSOT Press, 1993).

17. R. Alan Culpepper, *The Johannine School* (Missoula, Mont.: Scholars Press, 1975).

18. R. Alan Culpepper, *The Anatomy of the Fourth Gospel* (Philadelphia: Fortress, 1983).

19. E.g., Culpepper, *Anatomy;* Paul D. Duke, *Irony in the Fourth Gospel* (Atlanta: John Knox, 1985); Gail R. O'Day, *Revelation in the Fourth Gospel* (Philadelphia: Fortress, 1986); Jeff Staley, *The Print's First Kiss: A Rhetorical Investigation of the Implied Reader in the Fourth Gospel,* SBLDS 82 (Atlanta: Scholars Press, 1988); Mark W. G. Stibbe, *John's Gospel* (New York: Routledge, 1994).

20. Amos Wilder, "Story and Story-World," *Int* 37 (1983): 353–64.

21. The title of Norman K. Gottwald's introduction to the Old Testament, *The Hebrew Bible: A Socio-Literary Introduction* (Philadelphia: Fortress, 1985) suggests that the social and literary worlds are to be held together, but in fact Gottwald's work does not recognize the creative and creating power of the text.

22. See Gail R. O'Day, review of Culpepper, *Anatomy* (*JBL* 104 [1985]: 544–47), for a discussion of the limits of literary-critical categories.

23. For a discussion of the formation of the text from this perspective, see Walter Brueggemann, "The Social Nature of the Biblical Text for Preaching," in *Preaching as a Social Act,* ed. Arthur Van Seters (Nashville: Abingdon, 1988), 127–65.

24. The recent study by Norman Petersen, *The Gospel of John and the Sociology of Light* (Valley Forge, Pa.: Trinity Press International, 1993), incorporates both literary and sociological methods in its analysis of the Fourth Gospel. Takashi Onuki, *Gemeinde und Welt,* applies the literary hermeneutics of Gadamer to the Fourth Gospel in a creative blend of social and literary concerns. See also Rensberger, *Johannine Faith.*

– 17 –

The Plot of John's Story of Jesus

R. Alan Culpepper

The Gospel of John is an ancient biography in dramatic form. Based on the pattern of Wisdom's descent and return, it tells the story of Jesus as the Word incarnate who fulfills his commission to reveal the Father, take away the sin of the world, and empower the "children of God." The story unfolds in a series of recognition scenes, until at the end the question becomes whether the reader has recognized the eternal Word in Jesus.

ONE MEASURE of how recently literary approaches have entered gospel studies is the absence of any discussion of plot in the leading commentaries on the Fourth Gospel. Recognition of the existence of plot implies that the Gospels are "plotted" narratives arranged with attention to conflicts, progression, climax, and resolution. To summarize the plot of a narrative, one must be able to discern the basis for its integrity and unity. A collection of memories of various events would have no plot unless the artist or storyteller selected and arranged them so that there was logic and order to their sequence and progression. Such considerations entered the field of Johannine studies only recently.[1]

I

When I dealt with the topic in *Anatomy of the Fourth Gospel*, I found it necessary to argue that, as narratives, Gospels have plots.[2] Part of the difficulty now as then involves defining the term "plot." Plot is related to the genre, structure, and story-line of a narrative, but it is not synonymous with any of these. Definitions of "plot" offered by literary critics suggest the complexity of the term. The definition given by M. H. Abrams in a popular handbook for literary criticism blends several elements: "The plot in a dramatic or narrative work is the structure of its actions, as these are ordered and rendered toward achieving particular emotional and artistic effects."[3] On the basis of a survey of such definitions, I concluded that the plot of a narrative is that which explains its sequence, causality, unity, and affective power.[4]

Guided by this understanding of plot, I examined the relationship between the role of Jesus as the central character and the basic conflicts that propel the narrative. Jesus' mission is to reveal the Father, take away the sin of the world, and authorize the status of those who believe as "the children of God." The prologue announces the coming of the Revealer, and episode after episode replays and develops the story of the Revealer who is met by various responses of belief and unbelief. In short, "the plot of the gospel is propelled by conflict between belief and unbelief as responses to Jesus," and although the plot is episodic, it is "controlled by thematic development and a strategy for wooing readers" to accept the Gospel's interpretation of Jesus.[5] I am satisfied that this analysis of the plot of the Gospel exposed some of its vital features, namely, its relationship to Jesus' mission, its episodic quality, the conflict between belief and unbelief, and its relationship to the purpose of the Gospel (to lead the reader to accept the Gospel's affirmation of Jesus' identity).

Nevertheless, the discussion of plot in *Anatomy of the Fourth Gospel* does not adequately relate it to the issue of the genre of the Gospel or its structure. Subsequent discussions have suggested various ways in which John's plot may be related to genre and structure.

II

What are the canonical Gospels? The answer to such an ostensibly simple question has proved surprisingly elusive. Our understanding of the Gospels is shaped by assumptions regarding whether they are history, biography, drama, preaching, or theology. Once the Gospels were thought to be *sui generis,* a distinctive creation of the early church, resembling one another but distinctively different from any other form of literature. More recently, scholars have pointed to the flexibility of ancient genres and similarities between the Gospels and various forms of literature, renewing efforts to identify the genre of the Gospels. Still, literary genres evolve over time, with the result that modern expectations regarding history or biography differ from the ways these genres were understood in antiquity. Would an ancient reader have understood that John fit into one of the conventional literary genres and, if so, how does the genre of the Gospel affect our understanding of its plot? Or conversely, how does our reading of John's plot condition our judgments regarding its genre?

In recent discussions of its plot, the Gospel of John has been interpreted alternatively as biography and as drama. A brief review of the development of these two lines of interpretation may serve to clarify both the issue of the genre of the Gospel and the bearing its genre has on its plot.

F. R. M. Hitchcock observed that the Fourth Gospel "appears to be cast in dramatic form." Like a Greek drama, Hitchcock contended, the Gospel has five divisions: prologue (1:1–18); Act 1 (1:19–2:12); Act 2 (2:13–6:71); Act 3 (7:1–11:57), in which the raising of Lazarus is the center of the plot; Act 4 (12:1–19:42), in which the dénouement (*lysis*) begins with the scene in the garden, and the discovery (*anagnorisis*) is attempted by the soldiers and Pilate, but will not be achieved until Act 5 (20:1–31) with Mary and Thomas; and the epilogue (21:1–25). The reversal of fortunes (*peripeteia*) occurs with the crowd's rejection of Jesus in favor of Barabbas, and the dramatic element of *pathos* fills the crucifixion scene.[6]

Mark W. G. Stibbe adapted Hitchcock's analysis of the structure of the Gospel. Drawing parallels to Euripedes' story of Dionysus in the *Bacchae,* Stibbe argues that the basic story-type, or *mythos,* of the Fourth Gospel is tragedy. As in the *Bacchae,* the essential elements of tragedy are evident in John: purpose (commission), passion (*pathos*), and perception (*anagnorisis*). The analysis of the Gospel that follows will show that John has developed and extended the *anagnorisis* into a major plot element.[7]

In recent scholarship the earlier judgment that the Gospels are *sui generis,* conforming to no established genre, has yielded to evidence that the Gospels fit within the general category of ancient biography. Significant contributions toward establishing the Gospels as *bioi,*[8] which are also of particular relevance for the current discussion, include those made by Charles H. Talbert[9] and, most recently, Richard A. Burridge.[10]

Talbert identified as "constitutive of ancient biography that the subject be a distinguished or notorious figure," and that the aim be "to expose the essence of the person."[11] The issue has often been confused, Talbert contends, because the variability of the genre has not been recognized and elements accidental to it have been regarded as essential, thereby leading to the failure to recognize the Gospels as *bioi.* Talbert lists the following seven elements as "accidental" to ancient biography:

> First, it is incorrect to describe ancient biography as an account of the life of a man from birth to death.
>
> Second, the sort of person the hero is was assumed to appear not only in his deeds but also in insignificant gestures or passing utterance.
>
> Third, there is virtually no interest in tracing development.
>
> Fourth, some biographies have as their aim to affect behavior or opinions of their readers either positively or negatively.

Fifth, the "life" of a subject may be described in mythical terms or may be devoid of myth.

Sixth, the literary form in which "lives" are presented varies. The dominant form is a prose narrative similar to history except that it is anecdotal and unconcerned about cause and effect.

Seventh, ancient biographies perform a multiplicity of social functions.[12]

Given this variability, we are dealing with biographical traditions in antiquity any time we meet "the concern to depict the essence of a significant person."[13] This characteristic of ancient biography is particularly important for John, where other characters serve as foils for the reader's success or failure to discern and affirm Jesus' true identity.

Richard A. Burridge has undertaken to compare the Gospels with Greco-Roman biographies, noting especially the similarities in opening features, subject, external features, and internal features. As a genre, *bios* moves between the extremes of history on one side and encomium on the other.[14] The genre was flexible and developed over time, making it critical that the Gospels be compared with Greco-Roman biographies of their period. Burridge draws four conclusions for the study of ancient biographies:

1. Biography is a type of writing which occurs naturally among groups of people who have formed around a certain charismatic teacher or leader, seeking to follow after him.

2. A major purpose and function of *bioi* is in a context of didactic or philosophical polemic and conflict.

3. *Bios* is a genre capable of flexibility, adaptation, and growth.

4. Therefore it is eminently sensible to begin a search for the genre of the Gospels within the sphere of *bios,* but such an attempt to consider the Gospels as *bioi* must always take account of this wider picture of its flexible and developing nature.[15]

After establishing detailed observations regarding the external and internal features of the Greco-Roman *bioi,* Burridge draws the following conclusions regarding the Fourth Gospel's membership in this class. In terms of its allocation of space, John conforms well to the pattern of both the Synoptics and the *bioi.* Half of the Gospel is devoted to Jesus' ministry and signs, and a third of the total to the last week of the subject's life, which compares favorably with the allocation of space in the *Agricola, Agesilaus, Cato Minor,* and *Appolonius of Tyana.* Like the synoptic Gospels and the *bioi,* John's Gospel is a continuous narrative; it lacks such formal features of drama as poetic meters and choruses. In size the Gospel fits the length of a medium-range *bios*. John has 15,416 words, which places it midway between Mark on the one hand and Matthew and Luke on the other. John's structure of discourse and dialogue material inserted in a chronological outline and arranged topically is "typical of the structure found in many *bioi.*"[16] As in the *bioi,* the Gospel is narrowly focused on the subject, who is characterized by his "deeds and words, sayings and imputed motives."[17] The characteristic topics of the *bioi* are: ancestry; birth, boyhood, and education; great deeds; virtues; death and consequences. Despite some differences, John shares "a similar range of topics to that found in the Greco-Roman *bioi.*"[18] The Fourth Gospel has several purposes, evangelistic, didactic, apologetic, and polemical, and these are "some of the most common purposes of Greco-Roman *bioi,* particularly those originating within philosophical schools."[19]

On the basis of John's opening features, subject, and seven external and seven internal features, Burridge concludes that the Fourth Gospel is best understood as a *bios Iesou.* Not to be missed is his repeated observation that the Gospel fits particularly well among the *bioi* produced within philosophical schools, honoring the school's founder and offering a definitive interpretation of his teachings.[20]

The conclusion that John is biography has fueled several significant analyses of its plot. Fernando Segovia finds particularly significant the Gospel's use of the motif of the journey and the technique of patterns of repetition and recurrence. Following the generic conventions of biographical literature, Segovia identifies "an overall threefold division of the plot in terms of the Gospel as a biography of Jesus, the Word of God: a narrative of origins (1:1–18), a narrative of the public life or career of Jesus (1:19–17:26), and a narrative of death and lasting significance (18:1–21:25)."[21] The cosmic journey of the Word of God provides the framework for the plot of the Gospel, which unfolds in a series of geographical journeys marked by repetitive patterns.[22] Guided by these considerations, Segovia proposes that the narrative of the public life or career of Jesus (1:19–17:26) is structured around four journeys to Jerusalem and three return trips to Galilee:

A. First Galilee/Jerusalem Cycle (1:19–3:36)

B. Second Galilee/Jerusalem Cycle (4:1–5:47)

C. Third Galilee/Jerusalem Cycle (6:1–10:42)

D. Fourth and Final Journey to Jerusalem (11:1–17:26)[23]

The subunits of these sections need not concern us here. John 18:1–21:25 concludes the Gospel with an account of the preparatory events (18:1–19:16) and a narrative of death and lasting significance (19:17–21:25).

The strengths of Segovia's analysis are clear. It makes constructive use of external criteria and abandons redactional-diachronic concerns in favor of literary ones. Its focus on the career (i.e., "journey") of the Word of God lends coherence to the whole. The focus on the geographical journeys of Jesus is also an advance over analyses of the structure of the Gospel that are based on repetitive or chiastic features, since the journeys are related to the genre of the Gospel (a *bios),* its mode (narrative), and its *mythos* (the journey of the Word of God who descends and then returns to the Father). Moreover, it relates the plot of the Gospel to its structure without losing sight of considerations of either genre or plot. Its weakness is that it fails to develop either the underlying conflict in the Gospel (the conflict between belief and unbelief as responses to the revelation of the Word) or John's distinctive use of the *anagnorisis* (a motif drawn from Greek drama).

While not abandoning it, Mark W. G. Stibbe's recent work moves beyond his earlier concentration on John as tragedy. Using A. J. Greimas's actantial model, Stibbe produces a revealing structural analysis of John's plot. The Father is the *sender,* who sends Jesus (the *subject)* to complete the work of bringing eternal life to the children of God (the *object).* It appears that Jesus has no *helpers* and numerous *opponents* (the Jews, chief priests, Caiaphas, Judas, Annas, the world, the devil), but paradoxically the forces of evil overreach their purposes and "contribute towards God's eternal plan."[24] John actually has both a main plot, "Jesus' quest to do the work of the Father," and a counterplot, "the quest of the Jews to destroy Jesus."[25] The counterplot, moreover, is a satirical parody of the main plot: the sender is the devil, who sends the Jews to kill Jesus. Jesus is the devil's opponent, and Judas is the devil's helper.[26] Pressing the analysis further, Stibbe demonstrates that John draws upon "the archetypes of storytelling" and uses all four of Northrop Frye's plot types: it reverberates with "some of the deepest, archetypal patterns in romance, tragedy, satire and comedy."[27]

The strength of Stibbe's analysis of John's plot is that although he agrees with those who have shown that, in genre, the Gospels are biographies, he nonetheless recognizes the presence of elements drawn from drama and biography. Stibbe also makes constructive use of the actantial model and the inventory of archetypal story forms.

III

As the foregoing discussion has shown, John's plot derives from both internal factors (causality, and conflict between belief and unbelief as responses to Jesus, the Revealer from above) and external factors that are conditioned by its genre. The Gospel contains elements of drama (especially its use of recognition scenes) and biography (a depiction of the "essence" of the hero through a narrative of his origins, public work, and death), and the ministry of Jesus is structured around his journeys. As a biography, John draws upon both the form of Greek dramas and the content of the Moses stories and the Elijah-Elisha cycle. One of John's distinguishing features is its depiction of Jesus as the Revealer and the various responses to him in a narrative that draws the reader to affirm Jesus' identity through a series of episodes that describe attempted, failed, and occasionally successful *anagnorises* (recognition scenes).

Jesus' Origins, John 1

The prologue (John 1:1–18) establishes the identity of Jesus by describing the cosmic backdrop of his mission. The omniscient narrator reports the origins of Jesus as the preexistent Word. The prologue establishes the dynamics of the reading experience because it gives the reader privileged and authoritative information that the characters around Jesus do not have. In doing so, the prologue draws on the tradition of Wisdom personified and echoes the scriptures (especially Genesis 1). Verses 6–18 of the prologue summarize part of the story that is about to be told. Like Wisdom, the Word comes into the world, is characterized by light, reveals the nature of God, calls the chosen to faith, and gives them life. Jesus' coming will be announced by John, and he will be rejected by his own, but to those who receive him he will give the power to become "children of God." Through the Word become flesh, the community has "beheld his glory" (1:14), and through him they have received grace and truth. Most of the prologue, therefore, is devoted to the coming of the Word and the effects of his work. Nothing specific is said about his death or his return to the Father.

The narrative of Jesus' work as the Word incarnate systematically confirms the information given in the prologue. Jesus is announced by John, who adds further information regarding Jesus' mission in the first recognition scene: "Here is the Lamb of God who takes away the sin of the world!" (1:29, 36). The first disciples, who come seeking Jesus (1:38), add other titles. When Nathanael meets Jesus (the second recognition scene), he confesses, "Rabbi, you are the Son of God! You are the king of Israel!" (1:49).

Jesus' Public Ministry, John 2–12

The first journey cycle begins in John 1:43, when Jesus goes to Galilee. In Cana of Galilee Jesus does his first "sign," turning water to wine, and for the first time alludes to his "hour" (2:4; cf. 7:30; 8:20; 12:27; 13:1). This sign, like the others, "shows" the reader what the reader has been "told" in the prologue. Jesus does what only the creative Word could do. He continues the creative work of the Word, exercising sovereign power over the created order. The disciples respond with belief.

The first journey to Jerusalem is reported in John 2:13, at the time of the first Passover mentioned in the Gospel. Jesus drives the money-changers out of the temple, and "the Jews" question Jesus' authority. Although many believe because of the signs Jesus does, Jesus refuses to accept their faith. Nicodemus, perhaps representing those in Jerusalem whose belief Jesus did not accept, confesses, "Rabbi, we know that you are a teacher come from God" (3:2), but the ensuing dialogue demonstrates that this leader of the Jews is not (yet?) able to grasp who Jesus is. The scene is a failed *anagnorisis*. An interlude in Judea (3:22–36) completes John's testimony to Jesus and reinforces the prologue's initial exposition.

The second journey to Galilee serves as the occasion for Jesus' conversation with the Samaritan woman (4:1–42) and the second sign: the healing of the royal official's son (4:46–54). The first is clearly set up as a recognition scene by Jesus' challenge: "If you knew . . . who it is that is saying to you, 'Give me a drink,' you would have asked him, and he would have given you living water" (4:10). The woman comes by stages to see who Jesus is: "You, a Jew" (4:9); "Sir" (4:11); "Sir, I see that you are a prophet" (4:19). Then, after Jesus says, "I am he" (i.e., the Messiah who will proclaim all things), the woman returns to the city, saying, "Come and see a man who told me everything I have ever done! He cannot be the Messiah, can he?" (4:29), and many believe in Jesus because of her and say "We know that this is truly the Savior of the world" (4:42). The second sign underscores the link between believing and having life. The royal official believes Jesus, and his son lives.

Jesus' second journey to Jerusalem (John 5) is the setting for the first real opposition to Jesus. When Jesus heals the man at the pool, who would not even say that he wanted to be healed, the man reports Jesus to the authorities, who begin to persecute Jesus (5:15–16). The motive for the opposition is explained by the narrator: "For this reason the Jews were seeking to kill him, because he was not only breaking the Sabbath, but was also calling God his own Father, thereby making himself equal to God" (5:18). This sign fails to produce an *anagnorisis,* and instead mobilizes the opposition against Jesus. In a sense, the trial of Jesus occurs throughout his ministry. In John 5, Jesus calls as witnesses John, the works he does, the Father, the scriptures, and even Moses.

The third and final journey to Galilee occurs during the second Passover in the Gospel. At the beginning of John 6, the crowds follow Jesus because of the signs he does. At Passover, when many go to Jerusalem to commemorate the Exodus and Moses' feeding of the people in the wilderness, Jesus feeds the multitude in the wilderness in Galilee and then crosses the sea, walking on the water. The dialogue that follows further clarifies Jesus' identity as the prophet like Moses and the Bread of Life, but the people turn away from him. Just as their ancestors murmured against Moses in the wilderness, the people "murmur" against Jesus. At the end of the chapter Jesus is left with only the Twelve, and one of them will betray him. It is another failed *anagnorisis,* except that Peter, speaking for the Twelve, says, "You have the words of eternal life. We have come to believe and know that you are the Holy One of God" (6:69).

Although "the Jews" in Jerusalem are seeking to kill Jesus, he goes up again to Jerusalem in chapter 7 for the festival of Booths (the third journey to Jerusalem; 7:10, 14). The crowd is divided in their speculation about who Jesus is, but in John 8 the hostility results in a sharp exchange between Jesus and the Jews who oppose him. The identities of each are further revealed: The debate takes the form of claims and countercharges regarding the true paternity of each party. Jesus' opponents claim to be descendants of Abraham, but they are "children of the devil" (8:44), which is a charge confirmed by their desire to kill Jesus. On the other hand, they insinuate that Jesus is illegitimate (8:41), but he claims that God is his Father. Because they are not "of God" (8:47), they cannot grasp his identity. At the end of the debate his opponents take up stones against him, which constitutes another failed *anagnorisis* that has further clarified for the reader both Jesus' identity and the opposition to him.

While still in Jerusalem Jesus heals a man born blind. The man is characterized as a representative figure, for all are born blind and need to see the light. After Jesus sends the man to wash, the man, like the woman at the well in Samaria, comes step by step to recognize Jesus. By the end of the story, it is clear that the blind man has come to believe as well as to see, while the Pharisees, who could see, have had their blindness exposed. The story of the blind man and the Pharisees, therefore, interprets what is involved in an *anagnorisis* and why some fail to recognize Jesus.

In chapter 10, by means of the allegory of the shepherd and the sheep, Jesus further images his role and characterizes his opponents as hirelings, robbers, and wolves. In contrast, Jesus is the good shepherd who calls his sheep by name and lays down his life for them. "The Jews" are divided further; some oppose him, while others say that his works are not the works of one possessed by a demon.

John 11 and 12 are pivotal chapters that bring to a climax the mighty works of Jesus and set the stage for his death. At the request of Mary and Martha, Jesus returns to Judea, to Bethany, to raise Lazarus from the grave. The scene with weeping women and a stone sealing the grave foreshadows Jesus' own burial and resurrection. Just as the Word came into the world to give life to those who would receive him, so Jesus returns to Jerusalem to give life to his friend, knowing that it will cost him his own life. The scene turns once again into an *anagnorisis* when Jesus claims that he is the resurrection and the life, and Martha responds, "Yes, Lord, I believe that you are the Messiah, the Son of God, the one coming into the world" (11:27).

The giving of life, paradoxically and poignantly, becomes the impetus for Jesus' death. Caiaphas judges that it is better for Jesus to die than for the whole nation to perish, and the narrator comments that, as high priest, Caiaphas prophesied that Jesus "was about to die for the nation, and not for the nation only, but to gather into one the dispersed children of God" (11:54).

Jesus' Farewell Discourse, John 13–17

After eating with his disciples for the last time, Jesus lays aside his cloak and washes their feet as a sign of his death on their behalf and as a lesson that they ought to love one another as he loved them. Peter, however, fails to understand what Jesus is doing, and Judas goes out into the night to betray him. John 13–17 contains Jesus' farewell address to his followers, a type-scene found in both Jewish and Greco-Roman literature.[28]

Jesus' Death and Resurrection, John 18–21

The revelatory motif continues in John's account of the arrest, trial, and death of Jesus. At his arrest, Jesus says, "I am he" (repeated three times in 18:5–8), and the soldiers fall back powerless. Peter, in pathetic contrast, says, "I am not [his disciple]," and stands with the soldiers around a charcoal fire in the dark. The trial before Pilate unfolds in seven scenes (just as there are seven scenes in John 9). Jesus repeatedly challenges Pilate to confess him, but the cost is too great. Pilate condemns Jesus, forces the chief priests to say, "We have no king but Caesar" (19:15), and then writes the truth he would not affirm: "Jesus of Nazareth, the King of the Jews" (19:19). The trial and the inscription, therefore, represent yet another failed *anagnorisis* that once again depicts the true identity of Jesus for the reader.

The events that surround the death of Jesus continue to unfold and underscore his identity as the Word incarnate. His dying words are, "It is finished" (19:30); his mission is completed. John 20 and 21 report the discovery of the empty tomb and Jesus' appearances to his followers. At the tomb, Mary Magdalene does not recognize what has happened, but the Beloved Disciple "saw and believed" (20:8). Later, Jesus appears to Mary Magdalene, and she recognizes Jesus but seeks to hold him, failing to recognize that he must return to his Father (20:11–18). The narrative reaches a climactic *anagnorisis* with Thomas's confession, "My Lord and my God" (20:28). Analogously, the narrator comments that the Gospel was written so that its readers "may come to believe that Jesus is the Messiah, the Son of God," and that through believing they might have life in his name (20:30–31).

John 21 reports a further appearance by the Sea of Galilee. The tasks of the disciples are depicted as fishing (missions and evangelism), shepherding, and bearing witness. Characteristically, it is the Beloved Disciple who recognizes the risen Lord first: "It is the Lord!" (21:7). Peter is appointed as a shepherd who, like his master, will lay down his life (21:15–19), and the Beloved Disciple bears witness to the things written in the Gospel: "We know that his testimony is true" (21:24).

The Gospel of John, therefore, is an ancient biography in dramatic form. Based on the pattern of Wisdom's descent and return, it tells the story of Jesus as the Word incarnate who fulfills the Father's commission for him to reveal the Father, take away the sin of the world, and empower the "children of God." The authorities put Jesus to death, but paradoxically Jesus' death is the hour in which he fulfills his mission. The story unfolds in a series of recognition scenes, until at the end the question is whether or not the reader has recognized in Jesus the eternal Word.

NOTES

1. Especially helpful as a survey of the development of attention to the literary aspects of the Fourth Gospel is Mark W. G. Stibbe, ed., *The Gospel of John as Literature: An Anthology of Twentieth-Century Perspectives,* NTTS (Leiden: E. J. Brill, 1993). Even here, there is not one essay devoted to the plot of the Gospel.

2. R. Alan Culpepper, *Anatomy of the Fourth Gospel* (Philadelphia: Fortress, 1983), 77–98.

3. M. H. Abrams, *A Glossary of Literary Terms,* 3d ed. (New York: Rinehart and Winston, 1971), 127.

4. Culpepper, *Anatomy of the Fourth Gospel,* 80.

5. Ibid., 97–98.

6. F. R. M. Hitchcock, "Is the Fourth Gospel a Drama?" *Theology* 7 (1927): 307–17, reprinted in Stibbe, *John as Literature,* 15–24; see 15.

7. Mark W. G. Stibbe, *John's Gospel* (New York: Routledge, 1994), 35–36; see also his *John as Storyteller: Narrative Criticism and the Fourth Gospel,* SNTSMS 73 (Cambridge: Cambridge University Press, 1992), 1:21–47.

8. See C. W. Votaw, "The Gospels and Contemporary Biographies," *American Journal of Theology* 19 (1915): 45–73, 217–49; reprinted as *The Gospels and Contemporary Biographies in the Graeco-Roman World* (Philadelphia:

Fortress, 1970); Philip L. Shuler, *A Genre for the Gospels: The Biographical Character of Matthew* (Philadelphia: Fortress, 1982); and David E. Aune, *The New Testament in Its Literary Environment,* Library of Early Christianity (Philadelphia: Westminster, 1987), esp. 46–76.

9. Charles H. Talbert, *What Is a Gospel? The Genre of the Canonical Gospels* (Philadelphia: Fortress, 1977); and "Once Again: Gospel Genre," *Semeia* 43 (1988): 53–73.

10. Richard A. Burridge, *What Are the Gospels? A Comparison with Graeco-Roman Biography,* SNTSMS 70 (Cambridge: Cambridge University Press, 1992).

11. Talbert, "Once Again: Gospel Genre," 55.

12. Ibid., 56–57.

13. Ibid., 59.

14. Burridge, *What Are the Gospels?* 65.

15. Ibid., 80–81.

16. Ibid., 226.

17. Ibid., 230.

18. Ibid., 232.

19. Ibid., 237. While the view that John is biography has been well received, Margaret Davies has responded that it would have seemed to Greek readers to be "a strange and alien example of the genre" (*Rhetoric and Reference in the Fourth Gospel,* JSNTSup 69 [Sheffield: Sheffield Academic, 1992], 104).

20. Burridge, *What Are the Gospels?* 229, 237, 239; see also R. Alan Culpepper, *The Johannine School: An Evaluation of the Johannine-School Hypothesis Based on an Investigation of the Nature of Ancient Schools,* SBLDS 26 (Missoula, Mont.: Scholars Press, 1975).

21. Fernando F. Segovia, "The Journey(s) of the Word of God: A Reading of the Plot of the Fourth Gospel," *Semeia* 53 (1991): 23.

22. In his focus on the journeys of Jesus, Segovia builds on the work of Matthias Rissi, "Der Aufbau des vierten Evangeliums," *NTS* 29 (1983): 48–54; and Jeffrey L. Staley, *The Print's First Kiss: A Rhetorical Investigation of the Implied Reader in the Fourth Gospel,* SBLDS 82 (Atlanta: Scholars Press, 1988), esp. 50–73.

23. See Segovia, "The Journey(s) of the Word of God," 50–51.

24. Stibbe, *John's Gospel,* 45.

25. Ibid., 47.

26. Ibid., 48.

27. Ibid., 70; see also Northrop Frye, *Anatomy of Criticism* (Princeton: Princeton University Press, 1971), 163–242.

28. See Fernando F. Segovia, *The Farewell of the Word: The Johannine Call to Abide* (Minneapolis: Fortress, 1991), 5–20; and Charles H. Talbert, *Reading John: A Literary and Theological Commentary on the Fourth Gospel and the Johannine Epistles* (New York: Crossroad, 1992), 200–201.

– 18 –

From John to the Beloved Disciple

AN ESSAY ON JOHANNINE CHARACTERS

Raymond F. Collins

The Fourth Gospel is a dramatically unique story about Jesus, the Word become flesh. As the chief protagonist, Jesus is the one around whom the whole of the story revolves. Through interaction with him, characters can be seen to play roles of widely disparate importance: Whereas some are on stage only as bit-players, others are key to the unfolding of plot.

IN A GOOD STORY, is it characters who determine the plot or the plot that defines the characters? This is a Johannine question, for the Fourth Gospel is a story in which the literary identity of the chief protagonist, Jesus, is defined by his relationships with ever so many different characters. Groups of people, anonymous individuals, and named personalities appear in the evangelist's story. Whereas some characters participate in the unfolding of the plot, others are simply cited by Jesus or some other participant in the story.

In addition to Jesus himself, the named characters are John (1:6),[1] Andrew (1:40), Simon Peter (1:40), Philip (1:43), Nathanael (1:45), Nicodemus (3:1), Judas [son of Iscariot] (6:71), Lazarus (11:1), Mary (11:1), Martha (11:1), Thomas (11:16), Caiaphas (11:49), Judas [not Iscariot] (14:22), Malchus (18:10), Annas (18:13), Pilate (18:28), Mary [of Clopas] (19:25), Mary Magdalen (19:25), and Joseph of Arimathea (19:38). While some of these are incidental characters, many of them play major roles in the evangelist's story.

The same is true of the anonymous individuals who appear: God (1:1),[2] the mother of Jesus (2:1), the chief steward (2:8), the bridegroom (2:9), a Jew (3:25), the Samaritan woman (4:7), the royal official (4:46), the paralytic (5:5), a boy (6:9), the man blind from birth (9:2), the devil (13:2), the disciple whom Jesus loved (13:23), an officer (18:12), another disciple (18:15), the female doorkeeper (18:16), one of the police (18:22), a slave (18:26), and one of the soldiers (19:34).[3]

Similarly, groups of characters sometimes play a major role in the plot, while others have only bit-parts. Among these groups are Jesus' own people (1:11), the Jews (1:19), priests (1:19), Levites (1:19), Pharisees (1:24), two disciples [of John] (1:35),[4] disciples [of Jesus] (2:2), servants (2:5), the brothers of Jesus (2:12), people selling cattle, sheep, and doves (2:14), money changers (2:14), many who believe (2:23), the Samaritans of Sychar (4:39), Galileans (4:45), servants of the royal official (4:51), invalids (blind, lame, and paralyzed [5:3]), various crowds (5:13),[5] messengers (5:33), the twelve (6:67), people of Jerusalem (7:25), chief priests (7:32), parents of the blind man (9:2), neighbors and acquaintances of the blind man (9:8), the council (11:47), some Greeks (12:20), soldiers (18:3), the police (18:3), two others [who were crucified] (19:18), the sons of Zebedee (21:2), and two other disciples (21:2).

These allusive characters provide a horizon of reference for the Johannine narrative. As part of the evangelist's narrative world, they extend the time-line beyond the story and expand the readers' narrative horizon. Those cited by name include Moses (1:17), Elijah (1:21), Isaiah (1:23), the Spirit (1:32), Jacob (4:5), Joseph [the patriarch] (4:6), Joseph [father of Jesus] (6:42), David (7:42), Abraham (8:33), and Barabbas (18:40). The anonymous individuals are the Messiah (1:20), the prophet (1:21), a man who is not a husband of the Samaritan (4:18), the son of the royal official (4:46), the devil (8:44), the emperor (19:12), and someone else [who will lead Simon Peter where he does not wish to go] (21:18).[6]

Then there are the groups. These are often cited in the discourse of Jesus; occasionally, they are introduced into the discourse of an interlocutor or in the guise of a narrative aside. The allusive groups consist of prophets (1:45), angels (1:51), guests (2:10), all people (2:24), the world (3:17), Samaritans (4:9), those who drink (4:14),[7] ancestors (4:20),[8] five husbands (4:18), others who labor (4:38), the household of the royal official (4:53), the dead (5:21), the [generic] one who comes to Jesus (6:35), some who do not believe (6:64), the authorities (7:26), Greeks (7:35), sinners (9:31), thieves and bandits (10:8), other sheep (10:12), one flock (10:16), the Romans (11:48), the people (11:50), the poor (12:5), those who know Jesus' commandments and keep them (14:21), those who put the disciples out of the synagogues and kill them (16:2), those given to the Son by the Father (17:2), and those who have not seen and yet have come to believe (20:29).

Included in these lists thus far are neither the narrator nor those for whom Jesus serves as spokesperson. These, however, do indeed belong to the Fourth Gospel's cast of characters. For example, in many stories the narrator is one of the most important characters,[9] for he explicitly introduces not only his own persona into the story (21:25) but also points to the community on whose behalf he writes (1:16; 21:24). The narrator likewise refers to those on behalf of whom Jesus speaks (3:11).[10]

The impact this complex cast of characters has in the story is dramatically enhanced by the evangelist's use of what Tannehill calls "echo effects."[11] Thus, Nicodemus's second and third appearances (7:50; 19:39) evoke the memory of his first encounter with Jesus (3:1). Jesus' appearance before Caiaphas (18:13–14) is described so as to recall Caiaphas's speech to the council (11:50). And the slave who questions Peter about his presence in the garden (18:26) is identified as a relative of Malchus (18:10).

Many characters who appear in the Fourth Gospel have minor roles to play. These bit-players augment the dramatic quality of the narrative but have little interaction with Jesus or the major characters.[12] The latter play much larger roles. Whereas some are named, like John, others are left in telling anonymity, like the Beloved Disciple.[13] Often the evangelist's description of major characters is not fully developed. They are cast in a representative role and serve a typical function. Because they dramatize discourse and events, they help the reader to understand who Jesus really is.[14] Major characters are, for example, John, who serves as the witness par excellence to Jesus, and three pairs of individuals: Nicodemus and the Samaritan woman, the invalid and the man born blind, and Simon Peter and the Beloved Disciple. Observing these characters enhances our own appreciation of the evangelist's narrative art and his appreciation of Jesus.

The Johannine narrative begins its story when the first character is placed on stage by God: "There was a man sent by God whose name was John" (1:6). Nothing is said about John's lineage, nor is he identified by the sobriquet "the Baptist."[15] He is identified by his mission: "He came as a witness to testify to the light, so that all might believe through him" (1:7). John is a man with a mission: to be a witness, and nothing more, nothing less. To be a witness, to bear testimony, is to fulfill a forensic role. A courtroom atmosphere pervades the Fourth Gospel. This is especially evident in the initial presentation of John's testimony (1:19–28).[16] Asked to identify himself by hostile interrogators, John states that he is the voice of one crying out in the wilderness (1:23). This narrative comment, which is in substance found in all three Synoptics, is here placed on the lips of John himself. The evangelist's John proclaims that he is only a voice. The real issue is that of Messianic identity, and John has solemnly sworn that he is not the Messiah (1:20).[17]

The confrontation between John and the priests and Levites sent by the Pharisees (1:24) situates the priests and Levites opposite the one sent by God (1:6). The lines of conflict have been drawn, and they will continue throughout the narrative. In a courtroom setting, true testimony must be obtained. Initially, the evangelist tells the reader about the substance of John's testimony. Later, the reader will be told that John's testimony is true (5:32). In the meantime, the reader must be content with the knowledge that the testimony proffered by God's legate comes from God. On the day after his initial deposition, John testifies that Jesus is the Son of God before a favorably disposed audience (1:34).

The evangelist's stylized characterization of John as the incomparable witness to Jesus is enhanced by the subordination of John's other activities. In true life, the evangelist certainly knew that John baptized. In his narrative, however, the evangelist introduces John's baptismal activity only obliquely, as a subject of controversy (1:25). This occurs before John's baptismal activity has been described (1:28; 3:23; 4:1; 10:40) or John even acknowledges that he is sent to baptize (1:26, 31, 33). The delay in focusing on John as one who baptizes serves to highlight John's role as witness. Similarly, the evangelist has subordinated John's prophetic activity to his activity as witness (1:31). Acknowledged as a rabbi by his disciples (3:26), John is a prophet, who takes to himself the words of the prophet Isaiah (1:23) and speaks words of revelation (1:29, 36). Even John's imprisonment receives but passing mention (3:24).[18] Essentially, John does nothing but testify to Jesus.

That John is a witness to Jesus, and essentially nothing else, is highlighted by the use of foreshadowing (1:15, 30), repetition (1:29, 36), and the echo effect (4:26). After the initial presentation of John's testimony (1:19–35), to which 1:6–8, 15 serve as prelude, the evangelist reintroduces John at 3:25–30, 5:31–36, and 10:40–42. In each instance the evangelist reiterates that John is one who testifies to Jesus. His is effective testimony: Two of his own disciples become Jesus' disciples (1:35–37). Nonetheless, John continues to reiterate for the benefit of his disciples that Jesus is superior to him, even if the former came after him (3:26–30). Reduced in function to a witness, John acquires a consistency of character in the Fourth Gospel.[19] He only bears witness to Jesus; in effect, his is the voice not only of God but also of the implied author.[20]

Unlike John, Nicodemus is a character in the Johannine narrative who does not appear in the Synoptics.[21] Like John, Nicodemus is formally introduced, but no indication of his provenance is given (3:1). He is a Pharisee, a leader of the Jews. This twofold identification recalls the hostile interrogation of John, whose interlocutors were from the Jews (1:19) and from the Pharisees (1:24). It also identifies Nicodemus as one learned in the law. Thus, it prepares for the next appearance of Nicodemus (7:50–52), as a scribe who attempts to interpret the law for his fellow Pharisees but is accused by them of being a crypto-disciple of Jesus.

The evangelist's intricate presentation of Nicodemus as "a man (*an-*

thrōpos) of the Pharisees"[22] links the account of Jesus' meeting with Nicodemus to the pericope immediately preceding (2:23–25), which functions as an introduction to the episode.[23] By implication, Nicodemus is one of those people who believe in Jesus' name because of the signs they have seen (2:23; 3:2). He is someone to whom Jesus would not entrust himself, someone whose testimony Jesus does not need (see 3:11); yet he is someone who is truly known by Jesus.

Nicodemus came to Jesus by night, a not incidental reference. It characterizes Nicodemus not as a person of the light but as a nocturnal figure.[24] The signs Jesus has performed merit Nicodemus's acknowledgment that Jesus is a teacher come from God, someone who is appropriately called "Rabbi." The ensuing dialogue presents Jesus and Nicodemus in a remarkable reversal of roles. While Nicodemus acknowledges Jesus to be a teacher come from God, Jesus calls Nicodemus "a teacher of Israel" (3:10). Jesus speaks on behalf of those who know whereof they speak (3:11), but Nicodemus is a teacher who does not understand (3:10), not even, apparently, the scriptures (3:14). As a representative of institutionalized Judaism, Nicodemus is a person for whom the acknowledgment of Jesus' signs is the end as well as the beginning of his acknowledgment of Jesus.

The nighttime visit of Nicodemus to Jesus is so significant that the evangelist harks back to it when he reintroduces Nicodemus as a man of the Pharisees in 7:50 and 19:39. Nicodemus is attentive to the demands of the law (7:50), even confronting his fellow Pharisees (7:50–52). He observes pious rituals and, in this regard, is a companion of Joseph of Arimathea (19:39).[25] Still, he never comes to belief in Jesus.[26] The contrast between Joseph, the disciple of Jesus, and Nicodemus, who came to Jesus by night, is striking. Nicodemus is a faithful Jew, open to Jesus, but one who is convinced that the end of Jesus' story is the proper burial of a teacher come from God.

The story of Jesus' encounter with the woman of Samaria (4:1–42) creates a diptych with the story of Jesus' meeting with Nicodemus, the panels of which, notes Herman Servotte, depict the same theme in different tonality.[27] Biblical themes provide the background for these two panels. Each features an extended dialogue, in which water is a topic and misunderstanding plays a major role. These similarities invite the reader, as the contrasts become striking, to compare the two panels with one another. Nicodemus is a man of the Pharisees and a leader of the Jews; the Samaritan is a woman. That Jesus converses with a female from Samaria is doubly shocking: Jews had no dealings with Samaritans (4:9); and she is a woman at that. Rabbis were enjoined not to spend their time with women, and Jesus' disciples are amazed that he speaks with a woman (4:27). The circumstances of the two meetings are also quite different. One meeting takes place at night (3:2), the other at high noon (4:6). Nicodemus initiates the dialogue with Jesus; Jesus initiates the dialogue with the Samaritan.

Whereas Nicodemus's conversation with Jesus leads him to the tomb, Jesus' conversation with the Samaritan leads her to bear witness to Jesus. Because of her testimony, the Samaritans of Sychar go to Jesus and confess that Jesus is the Savior of the world. As Andrew and Philip before her encountered Jesus and brought Simon Peter and Nathanael to him, the Samaritan fulfills the role of the disciple. Her initial misunderstanding gives way to a request for the gift that Jesus alone can give. She comes to see who Jesus is (4:19). He invites her to believe in him (4:21). She knows that the Messiah is to come (4:25). Jesus reveals himself to her as the supreme Revealer: "I am [*egō eimi*] the one who is speaking" (4:26). This is the first time that the reader of the Fourth Gospel encounters this solemn formula of self-revelation. It is addressed to one who has sight and knowledge, hallmarks of the true believer in Johannine thought. The woman's reckless abandonment of the water jar (4:28) attests to her belief, which becomes complete in the testimony she bears. As a Christian witness, this unlikely heroine stands in stark contrast to Nicodemus, the teacher of Israel whose radical misunderstanding is confirmed by his failure to know.

Other characters who appear in the Fourth Gospel are two anonymous individuals who suffer from a long-term disability but are healed by Jesus: the man who has been an invalid for thirty-eight years, and the man who has been blind from birth. Together, the stories of Jesus' encounter with these long-suffering individuals frame a long unit of narrative (5:1–9:41). The accounts are similar in many respects.[28] Among the similarities are the anonymity of the characters, their long illnesses (5:5; 9:1), and the setting of the scene in Jerusalem near a pool (5:2; 9:7). In each instance, a miracle story is loosely linked with a discourse by means of a Sabbath observation (5:9; 9:14) that provides the occasion for the discourse. The topics under discussion are similar: sin, works, and the identity of Jesus. In each case, Jesus makes a follow-up visit to the still nameless individual whom he has healed (5:14; 9:35), and in each case there is a two-part dialogue between the one healed and the Jews.

The anonymity of the two disabled persons highlights the fact that it is their relationship with Jesus that merits their introduction into the story. The story of Jesus' encounter with the paralyzed man has the form of the classic miracle story, with its setting of the scene, the presentation of the problem, the authoritative intervention by the thaumaturge, and the affirmation that the intervention has been successful. The dialogue that ensues is revelatory. Ultimately, what is involved is Jesus' filial relationship with God. When asked who healed him, the once-lame man at first can only admit his ignorance of Jesus' identity. Only after Jesus searches him out a second time does the man come to know that it was he. Their conversation focuses on sin. Jesus' exhortation that the formerly paralyzed man should sin no more suggests that the disability is considered to be the result of sin. Forgiven of his sin and cured of his disability, the once-lame man proves to be an ingrate. Rather than giving thanks, rather than querying Jesus further, rather than seeking to understand fully who Jesus is, rather than testifying to Jesus — he goes off to the Jews and tells on Jesus. Ironically, he whom Jesus has told to sin no more continues in the sin of disbelief. Having experienced, indeed benefited personally from one of Jesus' signs, he nonetheless continues to be a disbeliever among the Jews.[29]

Sin and blindness provide the leitmotifs for the lengthy scene featuring the man born blind (chap. 9) and culminating in Jesus' retort to the Pharisees (9:41). The man is responsive to Jesus. Told to wash in the pool of Siloam, he goes and washes (9:7). When queried by his neighbors and former acquaintances, he responds that he was told to wash and did so (9:11). Unlike the healed paralytic, he openly acknowledges that it is Jesus who has effected his healing, admitting only that he does not know where Jesus is (9:12).

The narrator describes the healing of the man born blind as a work of God (9:3) and a sign performed by Jesus (9:16). It is clear that the reader is invited to take the narrative as a symbolic account. The narrator interprets the enigmatic name of the pool of Siloam (9:7) and comments on the blindness of the Pharisees (9:40–41). This sign is one in which Jesus reveals himself as the light of the world (9:5). The sign of the healing of the man born blind gives dramatic expression to Jesus' affirmation of this (8:12).

Twice interrogated by Pharisees and Jews,[30] the man who has been given his sight confesses Jesus to be a prophet.[31] In this regard he is like the Samaritan who, having once begun to perceive the depth of Jesus' insight, confesses him to be a prophet (6:14). After the hostile interrogators' mission to his parents, the once-blind man is asked to replay the events one more time. This he refuses to do, meriting from the interrogators a scornful accusation that he is a disciple of Jesus (9:28). Rather than denying that this is indeed the case, the healed man confesses Jesus to be from God (9:33).

Steadfast in his faith in Jesus, the once-blind man is again found by Jesus. Jesus asks him about his belief in the Son of Man. He responds with eager openness, "Who is he? Tell me." Once submissive, now open, the formerly blind man has already seen the Son of Man (9:37). Seeing is believing, and the blind man has now seen. Then, in a self-revelation remarkable for its use of the third person, Jesus announces that the one speaking to him is the Son of Man (9:37). Jesus' formula of self-revelation is akin to the Revealer's "I am [*egō eimi*] the one who is speaking," addressed to the Samaritan after her hesitant confession that he is the Christ (4:26). The once-blind man who now can see can only express his belief and acknowledge Jesus as Lord.[32] Anonymous to the end of the narrative and no more to appear, this man is a foil for Jesus, who reveals himself as the light of the world. In this respect the man contrasts with the Pharisees, who claim Jesus to be a sinner. A solitary anonymous figure, he also stands in contrast to the once-paralyzed man who, put in a critical situation, confesses ignorance of who Jesus is.

Of all the characters in the Fourth Gospel, only Simon Peter appears as a man of contradictions and ambivalence. While the other characters in the drama are cast in typed roles as representative figures, Peter alone appears as a complex individual. He is the only "round" character in the entire narrative, and even then he is not a fully developed character.[33] In his initial appearance, he is depicted neither as fisherman nor as married, but simply as the brother of Andrew (1:40).[34] Found by Andrew, who confesses Jesus to be the Messiah, Simon Peter is brought to Jesus, who identifies him as the son of John and gives him the nickname Cephas (1:42). The evangelist never again uses this Aramaic version of Simon's nickname, nor does he tell us why Jesus gave Simon a new name; instead, he identifies Simon throughout the story as "Simon Peter." This compound name serves to highlight the relationship between Simon and Jesus, who calls him Cephas/Peter. Peter intersects with the story of Jesus at several points in the narrative. Following his initial appearance, he first plays a significant role in 6:66–71. Here he functions as a spokesman for "the twelve," an anonymous group hitherto unknown to the readers of the Fourth Gospel. Using Johannine idiom, Peter proclaims Jesus as one who speaks the words of eternal life, the Holy One of God.

Thereafter, Simon Peter appears only in the final days of Jesus' life. He is with Jesus at table just before the festival of Passover, when he takes umbrage at Jesus' washing of his feet. Later, Peter responds to Jesus' act spontaneously and with exaggeration, which results in a critical comment by Jesus (13:1–11). In this scene, as in the discourse of chapter 6, the evangelist subtly contrasts Simon Peter with Judas who is, nonetheless, one of the twelve (6:71). In a second table scene (13:21–30), Peter is again played off against Judas, but a new character is also introduced into the narrative: the Beloved Disciple, who leans on Jesus' breast (13:23). At this point, the reader meets the third member of the triumvirate, whose interaction with Jesus will help elucidate the significance of his death.

In the third scene at table (13:36–38), the impetuous Peter proclaims his willingness to follow Jesus to death, only to hear a rebuke from Jesus and to learn that he will thrice deny him. In conversations with the gatekeeper at the house of the high priest, Peter does deny Jesus, as he does in the presence of a group of slaves and police, and talking with a slave who was a relative of Malchus — whose ear had been lopped off by Peter when he was with Jesus in the garden (18:1–18, 25–27; cf. 18:10–11). Simon Peter has not understood that Jesus' kingdom is not of this world. Throughout these events, the bumbling and impetuous Peter shows himself to be a disciple who really does not comprehend what Jesus is about. On each of the three occasions, he suffers a rebuke from Jesus. After Jesus' death and Mary Magdalen's announcement that the Lord is no longer in the tomb, Peter runs to the tomb in the company of the Beloved Disciple (20:2–10). There he sees the tokens of Jesus' resurrection (20:5–6; cf. 11:44). Still, he does not see and believe, for he has not yet grasped the scripture.[35]

In another trilogy of scenes in the epilogue to the narrative, Simon Peter is rehabilitated when Jesus shows himself to his disciples and Simon Peter is cited as first among them. Ever impetuous, though remembering to put on his clothes, Peter dashes into the sea to get to Jesus (21:1–14). For the first time the reader of the Fourth Gospel learns that Peter is a fisherman. Then, in a three-part dialogue, Jesus harks back to Peter's triple denial, charges him with the mission to feed the sheep, and challenges him to be a disciple (21:1–19). In a final scene, which is reminiscent of the supper, Peter manifests concern about the Beloved Disciple, only to be reminded again that he himself is called to discipleship, that is, to follow Jesus in a way he has previously not done (21:20–23; cf. 13:37).

The presence of the Beloved Disciple in these final scenes (21:7, 20–23) spotlights the contrast between him and Peter,[36] which permeates the close of the evangelist's Gospel. In different ways, the Beloved Disciple provides an entrée for Peter. For example, formally introduced in 13:23 as the one whom Jesus loves and consistently identified as a disciple,[37] the Beloved conveys Peter's request to Jesus (13:23–25). Next, the Beloved provides Peter with access to the courtyard of the high priest (18:15–18).[38] Third, the Beloved runs with Peter to the tomb, but allows Peter to enter (20:2–20). And last, the Beloved identifies the risen Jesus as the Lord (21:7).

In many ways, the enigmatic Beloved Disciple plays only a minor role in the Fourth Gospel. Never does he appear alone. Mentions of him are limited to a verse or two. Even the scene of the Beloved with the mother of Jesus near the cross encompasses only two verses (19:26–27). Nonetheless, the Beloved looms large in the narrative, appearing just as the drama is about to reach its climax. In many respects, he is a figure intended to contrast with Peter. In his anonymity and stylization, the Beloved is the epitome of discipleship; he is the disciple par excellence.

The Beloved Disciple is present at the supper, the crucifixion, the empty tomb, and the appearance of the risen Lord. Unlike Peter, he is one who sees and believes (20:8). In the presence of Peter he proclaims, "It is the Lord" (21:7). Identified as one loved by Jesus, his relationship with Jesus mimics Jesus' own relationship with the Father. Just as Jesus has been loved by the Father (15:9), so the Beloved has been loved by Jesus. Just as Jesus is close to the Father's heart, so the Beloved is close to the heart of Jesus (1:18; 13:23; 21:18).[39] Just as Jesus is qualified to make the Father known (1:18), so the Beloved bears witness to Jesus. Moreover, we, the readers, know that the testimony of the Beloved is true (21:24; cf. 19:35). In this respect the Beloved supersedes John, the witness. Without need of human testimony, the Beloved believes unhesitatingly that Jesus is Lord. Virtually reduced to a single trait, the Beloved is the consummate disciple and authentic witness to the rest of the story.

NOTES

1. The characters are listed in the order of their appearance in the Johannine drama. The references cited are to the first appearance of the character in this drama.

2. After 5:19, God appears as "the Father" or "my Father." On the absence of God's name from the Fourth Gospel, see Marianne Meye Thompson, " 'God's Voice You Have Never Heard, God's Form You Have Never Seen': The Characterization of God in the Gospel of John," *Semeia* 63 (1993): 188–89.

3. Were 7:53–8:11, the episode of the woman caught in the act of adultery, to be considered as part of the Johannine story, this woman could be added to this list, as could the scribes of 8:3 and the elders of 8:9.

4. See, further, the oblique reference in 4:1.

5. The crowds that appear in chapters 6, 7, and 12 are hardly incidental to the Johannine drama. Taking a cue from the playbill, I refer only to "the crowds." See 5:13; 6:2, 5, 22, 24; 7:12, 20, 31, 32, 40, 43, 49; 11:42; 12:9, 12, 17, 18, 29, 34.

6. To the list may be added the elusive "anyone who knew where Jesus was" (11:57).

7. The Johannine Jesus' references to those who accept him is often couched in metaphorical language. The evangelist's use of metaphor makes it difficult to determine the relationship among those groups. In this listing of the *dramatis personae,* I cite those allusive groups of believers as identified by distinctive descriptive language. Usually these are mentioned in contrast to similarly allusive groups who do not believe.

8. Literally, "the fathers" (*hoi pateres*). See also the use of this term in reference to the Exodus generation (6:31, 49, 58) and the patriarchs (7:22) as well as its use in the singular in reference to Jacob (4:12) and Abraham (8:39, 53, 56).

9. See John A. Darr, "Narrator as Character: Mapping a Reader-Orientation Approach to Narration in Luke-Acts," *Semeia* 63 (1993): 43–60, esp. 43.

10. The emphatic *hēmeis* ("we"), found in 4:22 and 1:16, underscores the

role of both the Johannine Jesus and the Johannine narrator as spokespersons for a community.

11. Robert C. Tannehill, "The Composition of Acts 3–5: Narrative Development and Echo Effect," in SBLSP (1984): 217–40.

12. Chatman calls them "walk-ons," as distinct from characters, while Reinhartz calls them "incidental characters." See Seymour Chatman, *Story and Discourse: Narrative Structure in Fiction and Film* (Ithaca, N.Y.: Cornell University Press, 1980), 139; Adele Reinhartz, "Anonymity and Character in the Books of Samuel," *Semeia* 63 (1993): 128.

13. Perhaps the author received these names from the traditions about Jesus. See M. Davies, *Rhetoric and Reference in the Fourth Gospel,* JSNTSup 69 (Sheffield: JSOT Press, 1992), 338.

14. See Mark W. G. Stibbe, *John as Storyteller: Narrative Criticism and the Fourth Gospel,* SNTSMS 73 (Cambridge: Cambridge University Press, 1992), 25, who comments: "Throughout the fourth gospel, and particularly in the passion narrative, characters act as foils: that is to say, they speak and behave in such a way that our understanding of who Jesus really is is enhanced." Cf. Davies, *Rhetoric and Reference,* 338.

15. Cf. Matt. 3:1; 11:11, 12; 14:2, 8; 16:14; 17:13; Mark 6:25; 8:28; ("the baptizer" in 1:4; 6:14); Luke 7:20, 33; 9:19.

16. See Raymond F. Collins, *John and His Witness,* Zacchaeus Studies, New Testament (Collegeville, Minn.: Liturgical Press, 1991), 14–18.

17. Cf. 3:28; also 1:8, 3:29, and 5:35 (John is described as a lamp but not the light).

18. See Mark 6:14–29, par.; Josephus, *Jewish Antiquities* 19.5.2.

19. According to Aristotle, consistency is one of the qualities an author should try to achieve in the portrayal of a character (*Poetics,* 1454a). The evangelist has done that. His portrayal of John is that of a flat character, to use the terminology of E. M. Forster (*Aspects of the Novel* [New York: Penguin, 1962], esp. 73, 81).

20. See Davies, *Rhetoric and Reference,* 318; and Collins, *John and His Witness,* 98–99.

21. See Raymond F. Collins, *These Things Have Been Written,* LTPM 2 (Grand Rapids: Eerdmans, 1991), 60–64; and Davies, *Rhetoric and Reference,* 337–38.

22. Cf. 7:50, "one of them," that is, the Pharisees.

23. "Person" (*anthrōpos*) is twice used in 2:25, which immediately precedes 3:1.

24. Cf. 11:10.

25. The evangelist's phraseology could almost be rendered "Nicodemus, who earlier had come to Jesus by night, came along, too."

26. At most, one could suggest that Nicodemus is a believer who, because he feared the Pharisees, did not confess his belief (12:42–43). See Collins, *These Things Have Been Written,* 15–16, 66–67; and Davies, who declares Nicodemus to be an "outsider" (*Rhetoric and Reference,* 337).

27. See Herman Servotte, *According to John: A Literary Reading of the Fourth Gospel* (London: Darton, Longman & Todd, 1994), 22; cf. Margaret Mary Pazdan, "Nicodemus and the Samaritan Woman: Contrasting Models

of Discipleship," *BTB* 17 (1987): 145–48; Collins, *These Things Have Been Written,* 16–19.

28. See R. Alan Culpepper, *Anatomy of the Fourth Gospel: A Study in Literary Design* (Philadelphia: Fortress, 1983), 139–40; J. L. Staley, "Stumbling in the Dark, Reaching for the Light: Reading Character in John 5 and 9," *Semeia* 53 (1991): 55–80, esp. 58. Culpepper highlights eleven similarities. Jeffrey Staley correctly observes, however, that the two accounts are not parallel in all respects.

29. Cf. 2:23–3:2. Nicodemus and the invalid are the only two characters formally introduced into the Johannine drama with a formulaic "there was a man" (*ēn de anthrōpos;* 3:1; 5:5).

30. Compare with the double interrogation of John (1:19–28) and the use of both "Pharisees" and "Jews" (1:19, 24; 3:1).

31. Cf. 1:21; 4:19; 6:14; 7:14.

32. Typically, it is Simon Peter who addresses Jesus in this fashion. See 6:68; 13:6, 9, 13–14, 25; 21:15, 16, 17, 21; cf. 20:28.

33. Using Chatman's criteria, Burnett opines that Peter "approaches characterhood and even 'personality.'" Apropos of Peter's dialogue with Jesus in John 21, Davies opines, "This is the only instance in the Gospel of character development, *if it can be called that*" (italics added). See Fred W. Burnett, "Characterization and Reader Construction of Characters in the Gospels," *Semeia* 63 (1993): 3–28, esp. 22–23; Davies, *Rhetoric and Reference,* 325 (cf. 332); also Forster, *Aspects of the Novel,* 73, 81.

34. See 6:8.

35. The evangelist's affirmation that the Beloved Disciple "saw and believed" (20:8) implies that Peter did not see and believe. Although neither of them understood the scripture that he must rise from the dead, the Beloved believed nonetheless.

36. For Pheme Perkins (*Peter: Apostle for the Whole Church,* Studies on Personalities of the New Testament [Columbia: University of South Carolina Press, 1994], 96), "the contrast between Peter and the Beloved Disciple highlights the irony with which the Fourth Evangelist treats Jesus' disciples."

37. This characterization is the epitome of what Shlomith Rimmon-Kenan calls "direct definition," which is distinguished from "indirect presentation" (*Narrative Fiction: Contemporary Poetics* [New York: Methuen, 1983], 59). To be beloved by Jesus is, in fact, the disciple's sole trait. He is the epitome of what Forster would call a "flat character" (Forster, *Aspects of the Novel,* 73, 81).

38. Neirynck forcefully argues for the identity of the "other disciple" and the disciple whom Jesus loved. See Frans Neirynck, "The 'Other Disciple' in Jn 18, 15–16," in *Evangelica: Gospel Studies — Études d'Évangile,* BETL 60 (Leuven: University Press, 1982), 335–64.

39. "Close to the Father's heart" (*eis ton kolpon tou patros,* 1:18); "reclining next to him" (*en tō kolpō tou Iēsou,* 13:23); "reclined next to him" (*epi to stēthos autou,* 21:20).

– 19 –

The Significance of Social Location in Reading John's Story

Fernando F. Segovia

In light of a pronounced emphasis on scientific methodology, the determinate meanings of texts, and the notion of scholars as objective, the question of how to relate the interpretation of biblical texts to real-life readers is one that biblical criticism has largely ignored. In cultural studies, however, a model of reading and interpreting is used that relates the significance of ancient texts to real-life readers. If one pursues Johannine research using this model instead of those typically associated with biblical criticism, the results one obtains are profoundly different.

IN THE LAST TWENTY years the discipline of biblical criticism has witnessed a profound shift that, in the mid-1990s, is still under way. This shift has to do with a change of critical paradigms or of umbrella models of interpretation, that is, with broad ways of approaching texts of Jewish and Christian antiquity, involving a certain sharing of values and practices, theory, and criticism.[1] Moreover, the effects of this shift can already be seen to be radical and far-reaching, and they impinge upon every dimension of biblical criticism. In this regard, Johannine studies are no exception.

To illustrate this, consider this issue of *Interpretation* ("The Gospel of John," October 1995). Clearly, it has been planned to highlight developments associated with the shift in paradigms. The rationale the editor provided went straight to the point: Whereas "a scant decade ago" most Gospel scholars were still engaged in the practice of redaction criticism, since then narrative criticism and social-historical criticism have come to the fore. The intent of this issue was therefore to focus on the Fourth Gospel from the standpoint of these newer methods. The proposed table of contents reflected this intent: Whereas the first three essays were to deal with questions of narrative criticism — a lead-in overview of its parameters followed by two essays on specific formalist features of the narrative of the Fourth Gospel (plot and characterization) — the other two essays were to address issues of social-historical criticism, namely, the role of the reader and the shape of the community behind the Gospel. The end product, I would argue, reflects very well indeed the main directions of the disciplinary shift I have in mind.

Three stages can be detected in this shift. The beginning stage was lengthy and characterized by the belief that historical criticism was firmly in place as a "scientific discipline." This stage extended from the 1850s through the 1970s, from the mid-nineteenth century and the aftermath of the French Revolution to the breakdown of the modernist consensus in the 1970s in the aftermath of the social and academic tumult of the 1960s. In the second stage, historical criticism was relentlessly displaced by two other paradigms, namely, literary criticism and cultural criticism. These emerged in the mid-1970s, solidified in the 1980s, and are presently entrenched as sophisticated methods. And the third stage, which is as yet nascent, has as its center still another paradigm, which is cultural studies. Cultural studies emerged in the late 1980s and, in the 1990s, has rapidly gained in prominence. Hence, as the twentieth century comes to a close, instead of a controlling paradigm (historical criticism) and a radical opposition (fundamentalism) — which was the case at the end of the nineteenth century — one discovers that biblical criticism encompasses four major paradigms: historical criticism, literary criticism, cultural criticism, and cultural studies. Of course each of these four paradigms has its own distinctive mode of discourse and broad critical spectrum. From the point of view of this issue of *Interpretation,* observe that whereas the first three essays may readily be classified under the paradigm of literary criticism and the last one under cultural criticism, my own essay is at home in the area of cultural studies.

In light of the preceding, the task I shall undertake is to address the question of social location, including its significance and consequences, in the reading and interpreting of the Fourth Gospel. The reason this question belongs to the field of cultural studies is that it has to do with real, or flesh-and-blood, readers, that is, with readers of the Fourth Gospel as sociohistorically situated and socioculturally conditioned. To pose this question of social location is, within the field of biblical criticism, radical, whether it be from the standpoint of history, theory, or method. To clarify this, I shall begin by examining how, in Johannine research, the reader and the process of reading are construed in the three paradigms of historical, narrative, and cultural criticism.

Reader-Constructs in Biblical Criticism

Constructing the Reader in Historical Criticism

As with all disciplines that emerged in the nineteenth century, biblical criticism subscribed wholeheartedly to the program and values of the Enlightenment. In fact, biblical criticism closely allied itself with historiography, giving rise to the historical-critical method of interpretation, which ultimately controlled biblical-critical discourse and practice for well over a hundred years.[2] The ideals and presuppositions of the historical-critical method were effectively the same as those of the Enlightenment in general: knowledge is rooted in science; the scientific method is applicable to all areas of inquiry; nature or facts are neutral and knowable; research is a quest for truth grounded in value-free observation and recovery of the facts; and the researcher is a titan of reason who surveys the facts with disinterested eyes. For historical criticism, which encompasses such subdisciplines as textual, source, history-of-religions, tradition, form, redaction, and composition criticism, the emphasis is on the text as evidence for the time of composition: a means by which to arrive at the world in which it was composed (the historical context), the author who composed it (authorial intention), or both. True to its nature, historical criticism exhibits a strong positivistic or empiricist foundation.[3]

Thus, historical criticism is imbued with a strong sense of the "otherness" of the text, of the text "out there," which is the text-in-itself, or the text as historical repository. At the same time, the meaning of the text is regarded as objective and univocal, or determinate, and hence retrievable, provided that the proper scientific methodology is rigorously applied. Further, because the text presupposes, reflects, and addresses a specific historical situation, the course of history itself, which is similarly thought to be objective and univocal, or determinate, can likewise be scientifically reconstructed. This notwithstanding, scholarly disagreements over all such retrievals of meaning and reconstructions of history have been both sharp and commonplace. What has resulted is a contradictory view of scholarship: In principle, scholarship is held to be progressive and evolutionary (it moves toward *the* meaning of the text); yet, it is known to be subject to errors in practice. Necessarily, such a view of scholarship ultimately leads both to the typical exposé of all previous scholarly work as somehow lacking and defective and to a presentation of one's own work as climactic.

Correspondingly, the reader in historical criticism is construed as a recorder of facts, that is, as a kind of *tabula rasa,* a removed and impartial observer. The notion is that a real reader, through the acquisition of the proper scientific know-how, can become an informed and universal reader who attains to a position of neutrality vis-à-vis the text and, in the process of interpretation, leaves behind his or her social location so that he or she may examine the text as a historical and theological object. Hence, if there is ever to be a proper retrieval of the meaning of a text, it is essential that there exist such a thing as an objective reader, which only science, via historical criticism, can create.

Johannine studies abound with scholarship of this nature, and it has typically focused on subject matter such as the following: the fissiparous nature of the text as it stands, its many and deep ruptures; the process of composition of the Fourth Gospel, from its earliest traditions and layers to the final redaction; the search for the historical contexts reflected in and through such layers of tradition; the theological messages of the various layers and authors; and the relationship of the Fourth Gospel to the wider religious world of the ancient Mediterranean world. In analyses such as these, the aim is to engage in a radical contextualization of the Gospel, while striving for a radical decontextualization of its real readers, who are its contemporary readers and interpreters.[4]

Constructing the Reader in Literary Criticism

Around the mid-1970s, a number of biblical critics, frustrated with certain methodological limitations of historical criticism, began to look to the study of literature rather than history for inspiration and dialogue. With the onset of literary criticism, which comprises such critical practices as narrative, structuralist, rhetorical, psychological, reader-response, and deconstructive criticism, the focus shifted to the text as a message from author to reader: the text is seen as a medium whose formal features, whether poetic (textual) or affective (audience), are worth analyzing in their own right. Since its inception, literary criticism has ranged from a text-dominant impulse, which was quite popular early on with its focus on the text as text, to a reader-dominant impulse, which came into vogue later and analyzes the reading process as such. Still, much of literary criticism retains the strong positivistic orientation of historical criticism.

By and large, the meaning of the text is still regarded as objective and univocal, or determinate. Such meaning is retrieved by means of the proper scientific wherewithal, which is now anchored in literary or rhetorical theory. For example, the formalist features of any given text, whether artistic or persuasive, are seen as present in the text and subject to recovery via the use of proper methods.[5] As in the past, scholarly disagreements concerning the properties of texts are sharp and commonplace, and these disagreements result not only in a conflictive view of scholarship (progressive and evolutionary, though subject to aberrations) but also in the use of the methodological exposé with regard to the scholarship of others as well as a climactic view of one's own work. By and large, the reader of the text is held to be universal and informed: The real reader is one who, through the mastery of a certain body of theory, can transcend his or her own social location and achieve a position of objectivity vis-à-vis the text. From this exalted position, the reader proceeds to engage in a correct analysis of the text as an aesthetic or rhetorical object or can focus on the reading process itself, paying due attention to reading strategies and their corresponding reader-constructs.[6]

Literary criticism has had a major impact on Johannine studies, involving such key areas of interest as the following: generic conventions of the Fourth Gospel as a whole or of its various episodes and sections; questions of plot, levels of narration, point of view, characterization, and so forth; analysis of implied author and implied or ideal readers of the Gospel; application of different reading strategies in approaching the narrative; analysis of rhetorical concerns and strategies of the Gospel; and demonstrations of ultimate collapse in the ideological message of the narrative. The aim of all such scholarship is that of contextualizing the Fourth Gospel, now largely in terms of literary history and conventions, with a continuing disregard for the contextualization of the real readers, that is, the contemporary readers and interpreters of the Gospel. The upshot is that even when the process of reading itself is foregrounded, the focus remains on formalist reader-constructs.[7]

Constructing the Reader in Cultural Criticism

Also in the mid-1970s, a number of other biblical critics, likewise stymied by particular methodological restrictions of historical criticism, began to look to the social sciences for dialogue and inspiration. With cultural criticism, which is concerned with critical practices grounded in sociological theory (e.g., millenarian or sectarian theory; the sociology of knowledge), neo-Marxist theory (class and ideological analysis), and anthropological theory (e.g., Mediterranean studies; grid-and-group systemic studies), the focus shifted to the text as a message from author to reader within a given sociocultural context: The text is regarded not only as a medium whose formal features, whether social, economic, or cultural, are worth examining in and of themselves but also as a means by which to approach the work within which the text was produced. In the twenty years of its existence, cultural criticism has ranged from the more universalistic models produced by sociology and neo-Marxism, which were prominent at first, to the more cross-cultural models of anthropology, which later became prominent. As in the case of literary criticism, however, much of cultural criticism also follows the strong empiricist orientation of historical criticism.[8]

For the most part, the meaning of the text is still viewed as objective and univocal, or determinate. As such, it is retrievable by way of proper scientific procedures, which are now grounded in the social sciences. In addition, since the text derives its meaning from the sociocultural world behind it, such a world, which is likewise objective and univocal, or determinate, can also be scientifically reconstructed. In effect, the formalist features of any given text are seen as reflecting the world behind the text, as present in the text, and as subject to decoding via the use of proper methods. Once again, however, there are, because of the cross-cultural nature of the inquiry, many and sharp disagreements concerning which methods are to be used, which features of the text demand attention, and how to reconstruct the world in and behind the text. Consequently, a contradictory view of scholarship still prevails (evolutionary and progressive, but subject to deviations) and is accompanied by the methodological exposé of the work of others and the exaltation of one's own work as climactic. In other respects, the reader of the text remains informed and universal: a real reader is one who, through the deployment of strict scientific methodology, can move beyond his or her own social location to adopt a position of neutrality vis-à-vis the text. From such a vantage point, the researcher can engage in an analysis of the text as a social or cultural object as well as a remnant of a period of the past.[9]

Like literary criticism, though perhaps not to the same extent, cultural criticism has had a major impact on Johannine studies. Characteristic subjects of inquiry are the following: the sectarian nature of the Johannine message and community; sociolinguistic analysis of the Gospel's language; analysis in terms of the categories of "pure" and "impure" and of "group" and "grid"; analysis based on the Mediterranean categories of "honor" and "shame"; and concern with the ideological message of the Gospel. As with the other paradigms, the aim of such inquiry is still directed toward a radical contextualization of the text, with a range of options regarding the contextualization of the real readers (i.e., contemporary readers and interpreters): from the specific and inevitable (neo-Marxist approaches) through the broad and surpassable (anthropological approaches) to the nonexistent (sociological approaches).[10]

Concluding Comments

In all three of the preceding paradigms, flesh-and-blood readers receive minimal attention, even when the question of readers and reading is at issue. In literary criticism, the focus throughout is on formalist reader-constructs, whether along the lines of intratextual readers, such as implied readers, or extratextual readers, such as first-time, naive readers. In cultural criticism, the focus lies either on readers engaged in self-conscious contextualization for the purpose of technical decontextualization or on readers caught in the binary socioeconomic and ideological positions of class struggle. As such, the question concerning the relationship between social location and interpretation is either completely bypassed or severely circumscribed.

Cultural Studies and Biblical Criticism

In cultural studies, it is precisely the question of social location that stands front and center. In the last decade, a number of biblical critics, dissatisfied with the largely faceless reader-constructs of the various paradigms at work in biblical criticism, have begun to emphasize the need to take real readers into serious consideration in the task of criticism and interpretation. As a result, they have turned to postmodernist theory and cultural studies for guidance and dialogue.[11] Suffice it to say that with cultural studies the age of empiricism, or positivism, draws to an end. Major tenets of cultural studies are the following: (1) Real readers lie behind all models of interpretation, reading strategies, re-creations of meaning from texts, and reconstructions of history. (2) All such models, strategies, re-creations, and reconstructions are constructs on the part of real readers. And (3) all real readers are variously positioned and active in their own respective social locations. Consequently, a critical analysis of real readers and their readings (their *representations* of ancient texts and the ancient world) becomes as important in cultural studies as is a critical analysis of the ancient texts themselves (the *remains* of the ancient world). The reason is apparent: The two foci are seen as interdependent and interrelated. In short, all re-creations of meaning and reconstructions of history are in the end regarded as constructs or *re-presentations:* They are *re-creations* and *re-constructions.*

In cultural studies, the meaning of a text arises in the encounter between a socially and historically conditioned text and a socially and historically conditioned reader. Because of this, the text is looked upon not as an autonomous and unchanging object "out there," with a determinate meaning that precedes and guides or controls interpretation, but as a "text," as something that is always read and interpreted by real readers. Thus, any reading and interpretation of a text constitutes a construction or re-presentation on the part of real readers: Such reading and interpreting constitute a re-creation of the text's meaning and a re-construction of its context by flesh-and-blood readers who read and interpret within specific social locations and with specific interests in mind. Consequently, a different view of biblical scholarship emerges: It is highly multidirectional and multilingual because it results from the application of multiple methods and theoretical orientations; and it is less competitive, since the concern is no longer with the final and definitive re-creation of meaning or reconstruction of history, and less "climactic," since it calls for critical analysis and engagement in a spirit of critical dialogue.

In this construal, the reader is never faceless but always a real reader: a reader who is always positioned and interested and worth analyzing in terms of the various factors that constitute human identity such as gender, socioeconomic class, race or ethnic origins, socioeducational standing, sociopolitical status, intellectual moorings, and socioreligious affiliation. Such a reader is viewed as actively and inevitably involved in the production of meaning, of "texts" and "history"; as keenly aware of the nature of all readings as "texts," whether academic or popular; and as profoundly interested in the social location and agenda of all readers and readings, including of course his or her own.

Cultural Studies and the Fourth Gospel

Without a doubt, cultural studies will also make its impact on Johannine studies. Although still in its infancy, its main concerns and parameters can be readily delineated: keen interest in the multiplicity of interpretations, both past and present; analysis of the constructed nature of all such readings or "texts" in terms of poetics, rhetoric, and ideology; analysis of the real readers behind all such "texts" or constructions, including their own constructions of themselves; explicit comparison of one's own "text" with those of other readers; and self-conscious description of one's own construction as a reader.[12]

To be sure, one should not forget in this regard that a primary source of human identity is socioreligious affiliation and the corresponding religions and theological stances that attend it. Thus, from the point of view of cultural studies, pastors and ministers who preach from the Fourth Gospel are called upon to engage such topics as these: the nature and background of the "gospel," the "text" they actually preach and with which they work; the contrast of this text with, and its selection over, other "texts" or meanings of the Fourth Gospel; and the rationale behind the choice of such a "text" and the ramifications of such a choice for the pastor, the congregation, the church in question, and society at large. In cultural studies, there is no meaning "back then" to be recovered and applied universally to the "here and now," no original and objective boundaries for the guidance and conduct of the Christian life at all times and in all places. All meaning is always also "here and now," thus calling for engagement and struggle with both past and present in the creation of the Christian life at all times and in all places. In the end, the world of cultural studies is a fascinating world but also a most challenging and demanding one, which is the case with any world that admits and values diversity and multiplicity at its very core. Such, I would propose, is the future of biblical criticism and hence of Johannine studies as well.

NOTES

1. For a full exposition of the shift, see Fernando F. Segovia, "'And They Began to Speak in Other Tongues': Competing Modes of Discourse in Contemporary Biblical Criticism," in *Reading from This Place,* vol. 1: *Social Location and Biblical Interpretation in the United States,* ed. Fernando F. Segovia and Mary Ann Tolbert (Minneapolis: Fortress, 1994), 1–32; also D. J. A. Clines, "Possibilities and Priorities of Biblical Interpretation in an International Perspective," *Biblical Interpretation* 1 (1993): 67–87.

2. On the rise of history as a discipline, see Joyce Appleby, Lynn Hunt, and Margaret Jacob, *Telling the Truth about History* (New York: Norton, 1994); Peter Novick, *That Noble Dream: The "Objectivity Question" and the American Historical Profession* (Cambridge: Cambridge University Press, 1988).

3. For historical criticism, see Joseph A. Fitzmyer, "Historical Criticism: Its Role in Biblical Interpretation and Church Life," *TS* 50 (1989): 244–59; Monika Fander, "Historical Critical Methods," in *Searching the Scriptures,* vol. 1: *A Feminist Introduction,* ed. Elisabeth Schüssler Fiorenza (New York: Crossroad, 1993), 205–24.

4. For recent examples of this approach, see John Ashton, *Understanding the Fourth Gospel* (Oxford: Clarendon, 1993); Martin Hengel, *The Johannine Question* (Philadelphia: Trinity Press International, 1989); D. A. Carson, *The Gospel according to John* (Leicester: InterVarsity, 1991).

5. With time such objectivism began to yield to a concept of multiple interpretations based on a greater awareness of the polysemic character of texts, but invariably with a corresponding emphasis on textual constraints. For literary criticism, see Elizabeth Struthers Malbon and Janice Capel Anderson, "Literary-Critical Methods," in Fiorenza, *Searching the Scriptures,* 241–54; Stephen D. Moore, *Literary Criticism and the Gospels: The Theoretical Challenge* (New Haven: Yale University Press, 1989). For narrative criticism in particular, see Elizabeth S. Malbon, "Narrative Criticism: How Does the Story Work?" in *Mark and Method: New Approaches in Biblical Studies,* ed. Janice Capel Anderson and Stephen D. Moore (Minneapolis: Fortress, 1992), 23–49; Mark Allan Powell, *What Is Narrative Criticism?* GBS (Minneapolis: Fortress, 1990).

6. With time such objectivism also began to yield to a concept of a plurality of interpretations based on the presence of narrative gaps and their completion in different ways by different readers, but again with a strong emphasis on textual constraints. For reader-response criticism, see Robert M. Fowler, "Reader Response Criticism: Figuring Mark's Reader," in Anderson and Moore, *Mark and Method,* 50–83; Edgar V. McKnight, "Reader Response Criticism,"

in Stephen R. Haynes and Steven H. McKenzie, eds., *To Each Its Own Meaning: An Introduction to Biblical Criticisms and Their Application* (Louisville: Westminster/John Knox, 1993), 197–220.

7. For recent examples of this approach, see *Semeia* 53 (1991); Mark W. G. Stibbe, *John, Readings: A New Biblical Commentary* (Sheffield: JSOT Press, 1993); Francis J. Moloney, *Belief in the Word: Reading John 1–4* (Minneapolis: Fortress, 1993).

8. For cultural criticism, see Dale B. Martin, "Social-Scientific Criticism," in Haynes and McKenzie, *To Each Its Own Meaning,* 103–19; Mary Ann Tolbert, "Social, Sociological, and Anthropological Methods," in Fiorenza, *Searching the Scriptures,* 255–71; David Rhoads, "Social Criticism: Crossing Boundaries," in Anderson and Moore, *Mark and Method,* 135–61.

9. It is only in the neo-Marxist approach that the reader is not expected to become universal but remains partial or interested. Thus, both texts and readers are considered ideological products and hence sites of struggle in the class conflict; consequently, only an informed and committed critic is able to perceive the ideological dimension of the text and take a position in the class struggle. For an excellent example of such criticism, see Itumeleng Mosala, *Biblical Hermeneutics and Black Theology in South Africa* (Grand Rapids: Eerdmans, 1989).

10. For examples of this approach, see Bruce J. Malina, *The Gospel of John in Sociolinguistic Perspective* (Berkeley: Center for Hermeneutical Studies in Hellenistic and Modern Culture, 1985); Jerome H. Neyrey, *An Ideology of Revolt: John's Christology in Social-Science Perspective* (Minneapolis: Fortress, 1988); David Rensberger, *Johannine Faith and the Liberating Community* (Philadelphia: Westminster, 1988).

11. For a full exposition of this model, see Fernando F. Segovia, "Cultural Studies and Contemporary Biblical Criticism: Ideological Criticism as Mode of Discourse," in *Reading from This Place,* vol. 2: *Social Location and Biblical Interpretation in Global Perspective,* ed. Fernando F. Segovia and Mary Ann Tolbert (Minneapolis: Fortress, 1995). For postmodernism, see Linda Hutcheon, *The Politics of Postmodernism* (New York: Routledge, 1989); for cultural studies, see Fred Inglis, *Cultural Studies* (Cambridge, Mass.: Blackwell, 1993).

12. For a beginning exercise in this regard, see Fernando F. Segovia, "The Tradition History of the Fourth Gospel," in *Studies in Honor of D. Moody Smith* (Louisville: Westminster/John Knox Press, forthcoming).

– 20 –

Community in Conflict

THE HISTORY AND SOCIAL CONTEXT OF THE JOHANNINE COMMUNITY

Urban C. von Wahlde

The theology of the Johannine tradition is one of the most developed and internally coherent in the New Testament. In contrast, the community in which this tradition arose is one of the most complex, turbulent, and anguished.

WE HAVE RICHER SOURCES of knowledge about the community that produced the Gospel of John than about any of the other communities responsible for our canonical Gospels. The reason is that our sources consist not only of John itself but of the three Johannine letters. Nevertheless, as rich as these resources are, to unlock the history and social situation behind the Johannine community is more difficult than in the case of other gospel communities. Why is this? Because the Gospel of John is a heterogeneous document, consisting of three stages of composition. Fortunately, each of these stages is remarkably transparent to the historical and theological issues of the moment in the Johannine community. As a result, when we speak of the Johannine community, we are able to provide not only a *description* of the community, but a *history* of it.[1]

Nor is this all. Once these three pictures lie before us, we are able, by looking to cultural anthropology for assistance, to gain some insight into the deeper interaction between the theology and social situation of the Johannine community. What results, finally, is a portrait, remarkable because of its richness of detail, of a community engaged in continual turmoil as it struggles to define its faith within a variety of social contexts during the last quarter of the first Christian century.

The Earliest Version of the Gospel

The earliest version of the Johannine community's written tradition was almost certainly a complete Gospel rather than simply a collection of miracles, as was once maintained. Indications are that this earliest version of the Gospel extended from the scene of the Baptist's meeting with Jesus to the scene of Jesus' resurrection.[2]

Although the whole of this earliest version is not extant, one can nonetheless say that its theology appears relatively simple and straightforward. For example, the christology is "low," the word "signs" denotes "miracles," and the religious authorities are identified by the characteristic terms "Pharisees, chief priests, and rulers." It is primarily through the signs of Jesus that persons come to believe in him. Such belief is "easy" in the sense that many share it, and it is expressed in stereotyped formulas. As Jesus performs ever more signs in various geographical areas and social situations and ever more persons come to faith in him, hostility on the part of the authorities increases and they ultimately convene the Sanhedrin and condemn Jesus to death to prevent the Romans from taking action and destroying the temple and nation. Jesus dies by crucifixion, is buried, but on the third day is seen as risen.

The Community as Reflected in the Earliest Version of the Gospel

The Johannine community in its earliest days was probably located in Palestine and most probably in Judea, given the Gospel's focus on this area.[3] The community was certainly Jewish Christian, as is evident from the use of numerous Hebrew and Aramaic terms, Moses typology, and traditional Jewish christological categories. Apparently, the Johannine community either contained former members of John's baptist movement or at least faced pressures from John's later followers. Many scholars conclude this because the first followers of Jesus are said to have been followers of John, and John is mentioned so frequently in the Gospel. The inclusion of Jesus' Samaritan miracle and the report of widespread Samaritan belief leads some scholars to think that, at an early period, the Johannine community also included Samaritans.

Was the Johannine community urban? The extant material from the first version of John is insufficient to make a definitive judgment. If we decide this matter on the basis of this version's focus on Jerusalem and the relative absence of agricultural motifs, we might suppose it was located there. But to argue from silence would be risky.

The impression created by this first version of John is that the response to Jesus on the part of wide sectors of society was positive and that it was only a relative minority of religious authorities that was responsible for his death. There is no indication at this stage that the Johannine community was beleaguered as there is at later stages.

We cannot be certain of the date of this version, but the general remark about the destruction of the temple (2:19) suggests that the latter had already taken place. If the second version of John can be dated at about 90 C.E. (see below), we may be justified in locating this first version at about 80 C.E.

The Second Version of the Gospel

In the second version of John's Gospel, the author preserved much of the narrative framework of the first. At the same time, he changed the character of the first version by adding discourse and dialogue material that focused in a new way on the identity of Jesus and the purpose of his ministry.

Literarily, among the distinguishing features of the second version[4] are references to the religious authorities as "the Jews" (although this term does not have the same meaning in all instances in the Gospel) and the naming of Jesus' miracles as "works." Belief is no longer based merely on miracles, nor is it depicted as an easy matter.

Eternal life becomes the focus of the community's hope. This life will come by means of rebirth from the Holy Spirit, sent by Jesus after he returns to the Father through his death. Possession of the Spirit is deemed so important that it renders the realm of the physical and material insignificant. This results in a dualism between Spirit and "flesh." Believers who have received the Spirit have received eternal life; hence, they experience the eschatological blessing in the present age and do not undergo judgment. The christology of the second version of John is the highest in the New Testament. Jesus is presented as Son of God in the fullest sense of the word, as *egō eimi* (I AM). He is therefore accused by the Jews of blaspheming God, of claiming God as his own Father, and of claiming equality with God. Jesus, in turn, speaks of his "glory," of his "hour," and of "witnesses" to him.

The most distinctive structural change of Jesus' public ministry in this second version is the addition of major discourses found in chapters 5, 6, 8, and 10. Beyond this, there is theological elaboration on events that range from the first appearance of John the Baptist to the end of his ministry. Much of the Last Discourse also first appears in this version, as does material relating to the passion and resurrection.

The Community as Reflected in the Second Version of the Gospel

At the second stage, the Johannine community continues to be primarily Jewish, understanding the eschatological outpouring of the Spirit exclusively in Jewish terms. Because of the escalating claims made for Jesus and for themselves, however, tension with the parent Jewish body increases to the breaking point.

The parent body expels those believing in Jesus from the synagogue (9:22; 12:42; 16:2). There are also predictions that the disciples will be killed, and it is said that those doing this will think they are thereby giving glory to God (16:2–4).

It is plain from expressions in this second version — such as "your" fathers (6:49) and "your" law (8:17) — that Jewish tradition was still dominant in the Johannine community and that the community itself was as yet Jewish in character. Regardless, the alienation of the community from its parent body can be seen in disparaging references to the authorities as "the Jews." The latter strongly suggests that the Johannine community had now become a minority persecuted by a "Jewish" majority. Members of the Jewish majority were thought of as representatives of the "world," and the Johannine community regarded itself as "in" the world but not "of" the world (15:18–19; 17:6, 14–16). In addition, the Johannine community may have been faced with the problem of "crypto-disciples," as the reference to Joseph of Arimathea ("a disciple of Jesus, but in secret for fear of the Jews"; 19:38) may indicate. Part of the purpose of the second version of John's Gospel may have been to encourage these crypto-disciples to make open confession of Jesus. The situation of the Johannine community was definitely one of persecution, estrangement, and alienation.[5]

The Third Version of the Gospel

After the material of the first and second versions has been identified, there remains material that shows that the Gospel underwent another revision.[6] This material includes features of apocalyptic dualism, such as: the symbolism of light and darkness and the description of believers as "sons of light," the figure of "the Son of Man," and an emphasis that is no longer on realized but on future eschatology (Final Judgment, resurrection of the body). In this third version, the dualism is not one created by whether one has the Spirit or not, but one which asks *which* Spirit one has: the Spirit of Truth (14:17; 15:26; 16:13) or the Spirit of Deception (as becomes explicit in 1 John 4:1–3, 6).

A new and final structure is imposed on the previous ones. The image of light becomes the symbol of Jesus' public ministry (e.g., 1:4–5, 9; 3:19–21), and such light constitutes a day of twelve hours during which Jesus will not be arrested (9:4–5). When darkness or night comes, however, he will be put to death. Beginning with chapter 13, the theme of love becomes dominant. Love motivates Jesus during his passion and is to motivate the disciples in their relationships to one another (13:34–35; 15:12–13).

The third version of John's Gospel likewise places emphasis on the role and permanent validity of the words of Jesus and, as the love commandment declares, on the importance of ethical behavior. In this same vein, several passages occur that tell of the "disciple whom Jesus loved" and compare him implicitly or explicitly with Peter. As we shall see, these passages give hint of the relationship in which the Johannine community stands to the Great Church.

The theological accents characteristic of the third version tell little directly about the situation of the community (with the exception of the Beloved Disciple passages). Yet, when these accents are compared to those in the theology of the author of 1 John, the similarities become so great that many scholars would see the two as intimately related. Consequently, if one works with the distinctive theology of the third edition of John in conjunction with 1 John, one can describe, at least in its main lines, the situation of the Johannine community in its third stage.

The Community as Reflected in the Third Version of the Gospel

Some time after the completion of the second version of John's Gospel,[7] an internal dispute arose in the Johannine community about the interpretation of its tradition. This provoked another crisis, this time within the community. This crisis had two aspects to it.

With Regard to the Dissidents

There is no little debate about the specific nature of the crisis that split the Johannine community, but many scholars see it as centering on divergent opinions about christology and ethics.[8] Also at issue were matters of pneumatology and soteriology. My own view is that the root issue was how to read the Old Testament promises about the eschatological outpouring of the Spirit (pneumatology) in such a way as to preserve fully the soteriological role of Jesus.[9]

This crisis was as serious in its own right as that of the second period. Both sides claimed to be the true embodiment of the Johannine tradition, even though they interpreted it differently. The author insists that the words of Jesus have a permanent validity and are not replaced by the inspiration of the Spirit. Moreover, the members of the community are not so free from sin that proper behavior, symbolized by the love commandment, is unnecessary.

The community was split and some "went out from us" (1 John 2:19). The situation was so desperate that the author depicts it as the "last hour" of apocalyptic expectation. He characterizes the opponents in the harshest of terms, and describes them as "the Antichrist" (1 John 2:18, 22; 4:3) and possessed by "the Spirit of Deception."

Although the author exhorts the community to love one another, such love is not universal in scope but "intra-community" in nature. It strives to strengthen the identity and bonds of the community in the face of the opponents.

With Regard to the Great Church

As we noted, one also finds in the third version of the Gospel the so-called "Beloved Disciple" passages. In these passages, there is explicit or implicit comparison of the Beloved Disciple with Peter, and the Beloved Disciple consistently emerges as superior. Notably, the Beloved Disciple is the only one said to be "loved" by Jesus: at the last supper, he receives special information (13:23–26); at the death of Jesus, he alone of the disciples is at the foot of the cross; it is he who witnesses Jesus' death and receives, and is received by, the mother of Jesus (19:26–27); at the resurrection, he is the first to believe (20:2–10); and even following the resurrection, he possesses greater insight than Peter (21:7). Yet, in chapter 21 Peter, not the Beloved Disciple, is remarkably presented as the one chosen to feed the sheep and to die a martyr's death (21:20–24).

From these passages, two factors become clear: (1) the Johannine community was convinced of its superior spiritual insight and closeness to Jesus; and (2) it not only recognized that authority over "the sheep" had been given to Peter but it also accepted this. Two other passages confirm this. In John 10:16–17, Jesus says that he has other sheep, not of this fold, and that he must bring them together; they will hear his voice, and there will be one fold and one shepherd. And John 11:51 speaks of the death of Jesus as "bringing together the scattered children of God."

It may well be that during the period reflected in the third version of the Gospel, these two factors (conflict with dissidents and movement toward the Great Church) function as correlatives: The community's affirmation of its tradition vis-à-vis opponents was perhaps part of its move toward clearer unity with other communities under the leadership of Peter.

In the second and third epistles of John we find further indications of a change in the community's theology. In the Gospel and 1 John, the common phrase for the message of Jesus is "the *word.*" But in 2 John we hear what seems to be new terminology, as the Presbyter speaks of those who "go beyond" and do not remain in "the teaching of the Christ." What is striking is that here, for the first time, there is a reference to the teaching "of" Jesus that also points to the existence of a body of teaching "about" Jesus. This suggests that the community was moving away from the notion of a spontaneous recollection of the word and toward the notion of a fixed tradition.

In 3 John, the Presbyter addresses Gajus, a member of the community, and urges him to continue to receive the missionaries from the Presbyter's community, even though Diotrephes, "who likes to act as leader," does not accept them. This action on the part of Diotrephes is another "first indication" of the emergence of authoritative figures within the Johannine community. Then, too, we hear for the first time in 3 John of the community's being termed an *ekklesia* (vv. 6, 9), which, elsewhere and most notably in Paul and Acts, is most commonly used to denote the Christian "assembly."

Although this evidence is slight, it nonetheless forms a consistent pattern. This pattern suggests that the Johannine community, once a maverick among early Christian communities, was moving in the direction not of sectarianism but of increased harmony and unity with the Great Church.

The Johannine Community: Some Insights from Social Science

In recent years, various methods of social science have been applied to Johannine materials, granting scholars new insight into the Johannine community.[10] One of these methods is that of cultural anthropologist Mary Douglas. Using theoretical models developed by Douglas, several scholars, most notably Jerome Neyrey, have provided new perspectives on the Johannine community.[11]

Douglas developed a model that measures interaction between a subgroup and its larger social matrix and plots such interaction as a graph with horizontal and vertical axes.[12] The relationship of "power" in which the subgroup stands to the larger group is plotted along the horizontal axis, where positions range from "strong group" (i.e., the larger group is perceived as exerting much pressure to conform) to "weak group" (i.e., the larger group exerts little or no such pressure). The vertical axis is used to locate the correlation between the community's experience and the expectations of the surrounding social group;

here the range is from "low" (little correlation) to "high." When fully graphed, the relationship between pressure exerted by the larger group and the subgroup's experiencing of such pressure is shown to manifest itself in characteristic ways in representative areas of life. Such typical areas of life have to do with ritual, personal identity, the body, sin, and cosmology.[13]

The First Stage. In line with Douglas's model, the "group factor" to be assigned to the larger, Jewish parent body early in the history of the Johannine community would be "strong," which is to say that the Johannine community desired to be identified with its Jewish parent body. The "grid," however, turns out to be low, which means that the values and attitudes ("experience") of the Johannine community would have challenged the traditional understanding of Judaism. Yet, at this stage the Johannine community could still have hoped for the reform of its parent Jewish body.

The Second Stage. However, in the second period of its existence, the Johannine community manifests forms of belief which they recognized as pitting them even more thoroughly over against the traditional group norms. The community finds less and less agreement between their experience and the expectations of the former group (the "grid" continues to lower). The fact that the Johannine group develops in such marked ways in spite of the obvious desires of the larger matrix suggests that the group factor is weakening—the community is affected less and less by the "pressures" of Judaism.

The Third Stage. In the third period of the Johannine community's existence, the plotting of relationships becomes more complex but also more revealing. First, the dissidents within the community itself, who had once strongly conformed to the Johannine tradition, now must be designated as "weak group" and "low grid" vis-à-vis the community. This suggests they had separated from it.

Second, another shift was in the making. The faithful members of the Johannine community, who no longer identified themselves with either the Jewish parent body (=first period) or as an independent Christian group (=second period), increasingly strengthened their relationship to the Great, or Petrine, Church. In Douglas's terms, this means that the Johannine community now became a "strong group" vis-à-vis the Great Church, which then constituted a new social matrix. Moreover, because the Johannine community was also in process of adopting a theology more in keeping with the Great Church, its position on Douglas's grid would move in the direction of "higher."

The real value of Douglas's model becomes apparent when we look at the way in which the relationships just sketched work themselves out in aspects of the Johannine community's life. According to Douglas, communities that are "weak group" and "low grid" have much in common.[14] Generally, they are resistant to the rituals of the communities of which they are offshoots; social control in them is low; personal identity tends to be marked by individualism; greater attention is given to the spiritual than to the material; concerns about purity interest them less; and they sense that they have immediate access to the divine. In contrast, communities that are "strong group" and "high grid" exhibit opposite tendencies. They show greater interest in ritual, social control, and the material; they are more respectful of authority; they concern themselves with matters of purity; and they perceive access to the divine to be more mediate.

Although at its second stage the Johannine community continued to see itself as the true embodiment of Jewish eschatological hopes, its beliefs nonetheless set it against the Jewish tradition. It thought of Jewish rituals as replaced by Jesus: the water of purification by new wine; worship at Gerizim and Jerusalem by worship in the Spirit; the manna of Exodus by the Living Bread; the feast of Tabernacles by the living water of the Spirit; and the temple altar consecrated at Dedication by Jesus himself. At this stage, the Johannine community also demonstrated little concern for material ritual (sacrifice). The community's wisdom is now given directly through Jesus and through the Spirit rather than through the Torah. The Spirit which will be given by Jesus is the source of life and of insight. Indeed, the members of the community regarded themselves as so Spirit-filled that they had need of neither Jewish ethical norms nor an authoritative teacher. Moreover, their worship of Jesus became so exalted that outsiders construed their claims of Jesus' equality with God as blasphemous. All this suggests that the Johannine group saw the historical Jewish community as less and less able to contain the full expression of their beliefs in light of their possession of the eschatological Spirit. Although their expulsion was agony, it could not have been unexpected.

The hallmark of the third stage of the Johannine community is that because it had to deal with dissidents within its own ranks, it acted to strengthen its ties to the Great Church. Nevertheless, its attitude toward major elements of its tradition also changed, the result being that, in Douglas's model, it would have to be described as "strong group" and "rising grid." At this third stage, new interest in ritual arose: rebirth not only of the Spirit but also of water (=baptism; 3:3),[15] the eating of the body and blood of Jesus (6:51–58), and footwashing as symbolic of serving others.

The Johannine community also experienced renewed interest in the importance of the physical as opposed to the spiritual.[16] Before, sin was removed by the Holy Spirit (20:22–23); now it was removed by the atoning death of Jesus (1:29; 1 John 1:7; 2:2; 3:5). The resurrection of the body was likewise stressed (e.g., 5:28–29).

This third stage saw the Johannine community move to control inspiration by the Spirit. It was recalled that the Paraclete will not speak of himself (16:13) but remind disciples of the words of Jesus (14:26; 16:13–14). With an eye toward dissidents, the community characterized its tradition as "that which was from the beginning" (1 John 1:1) and is found in the "teaching" of the Messiah (2 John 9); this was in sharp contrast to its previous notion that tradition is mediated through direct inspiration of the Spirit.

Although at this point the Johannine community neither defined "sin" nor articulated its understanding of what it is to be "perfect" (e.g., 1 John 3:9), one can, if one compares John's Gospel with 1 John, observe a notable shift in its thinking on these matters. Unlike the Gospel, 1 John refers to the need for forgiveness, moral effort, and conduct appropriate to the love commandment. Emphasis on the love commandment, in fact, betokened the rise of an incipient concern for community, the Great Church, and "sheep not of this fold." The same can be said of the new name the Johannine community gave itself: "ecclesia," or "church." Associated with the latter was fresh interest in figures of authority, such as Peter, the shepherd, and Diotrephes.

At stages two and three of its history, the kind of traits the Johannine community appears to have exhibited mark it, in the terms of Douglas, as "weak group" and "low grid" and as "strengthening group" and "rising grid." These terms lend still greater definition to our picture of the community. They confirm that description of the Johannine community at which scholars have already arrived through the use of more traditional methods of interpretation; and they reveal that diverse aspects of the community's theology traceable to different historical phases of development nevertheless fit together to form a discernible and coherent whole. Thus, it is no accident that a community in which the direct influence of the Spirit was highly prized should have venerated the Revealer at the expense of revelation and shown no overweening interest in authority figures and sacraments.

Finally, we are able to see that the relationship between Johannine theology and the community's social situation as we have been examining it was not random. The way the community saw itself theologically was responsible for influencing, if not determining, much of the community's social stance. The Johannine theology, with its emphasis on Spirit, easily led to the kind of individualism and detachment from community evident during the second period — and the kind of problems these entail. At the same time we are able to see how the revaluing of such matters as the sacraments, the role of Peter, and the other elements of the community's theology in the third period could not help but alter the community's relationships in the direction of greater harmony with its larger social and ecclesial context.

Conclusion

As our venture through the materials of the Johannine tradition comes to an end, we are, I think, left with the sense of having witnessed a remarkable theological journey—but also with the sense that this community, which had early in its existence forged such a unique theology and weathered such turbulent times, had begun to move into a period characterized, if not by tranquility, at least by peace and by the assurance that it was among "the scattered children of God" now gathered into one.

NOTES

1. The literature on the composition history of John's Gospel is considerable. Major bibliography can be found in W. Schmithals, *Johannesevangelium und Johannesbriefe: Forschungsgeschichte und Analyse,* BZNW 64 (New York: de Gruyter, 1992).

2. The view of the literary history, theology, and situation of the Johannine community is based on my own work: Urban C. von Wahlde, *The Earliest Version of John's Gospel* (Collegeville, Minn.: Glazier/Liturgical Press, 1989), and *The Johannine Commandments: 1 John and the Struggle for the Johannine Commandments* (New York: Paulist, 1990).

3. The bibliography on this topic is extensive. See, e.g., J. L. Martyn, *History and Theology in the Fourth Gospel,* 2d ed. (Nashville: Abingdon, 1979); R. E. Brown, *The Community of the Beloved Disciple* (New York: Paulist, 1979); and, more recently, John Ashton, *Understanding the Fourth Gospel* (Oxford: Clarendon, 1991), 160–204.

4. See von Wahlde, *Earliest Version,* 26–65, 176–88.

5. The most likely place of composition for the second version of John's Gospel is Palestine. The date is often associated with the Benediction against Heretics, thought to have been enacted about 90 C.E.

6. Von Wahlde, *Johannine Commandments,* outlines several important aspects of the third version of the Gospel from the point of view of the crisis dividing the community (see esp. 74–105, 114–22, 138–85).

7. We know little about the place of composition of the third version of John's Gospel. If the similarity of its dualism to that of Ephesians is any guide, then perhaps the city of Ephesus, which is the location most scholars prefer, is the place. The date was probably about, or soon after, the turn of the century.

8. The most extensive commentary on the Johannine epistles to date is that of R. E. Brown, *The Epistles of John,* AB 30 (Garden City, N.Y.: Doubleday, 1982).

9. Von Wahlde, *Johannine Commandments,* 105–98.

10. A helpful introduction to this field is that of C. Osiek, *What Are They Saying about the Social Setting of the New Testament,* rev. ed. (New York: Paulist, 1992). See also B. Malina, "The Social Sciences and Biblical Interpretation,"

Int 37, no. 3 (1982): 229–42. To cast light on the Johannine tradition, the tools of a variety of fields are being explored, among them sociology, cultural anthropology, and sociolinguistics.

11. See J. Neyrey, *An Ideology of Revolt: John's Christology in Social-Science Perspective* (Philadelphia: Fortress, 1988). Also Bruce Malina et al., *The Gospel of John in Sociolinguistic Perspective,* ed. H. C. Waetjen (Berkeley: Graduate Theological Union, 1984). I am greatly indebted throughout this section to Neyrey's work, which is the most extensive application I have found of Douglas's approach to the Johannine community. However, I have diverged significantly from Neyrey in conclusions regarding the second and third stages of the community. The position I have taken in this essay has the advantage of being supported by a more detailed literary analysis and a view of the final period that is more generally accepted in the scholarly literature.

12. Mary Douglas, *Natural Symbols* (New York: Pantheon, 1973; reprint 1982), 54–64. B. Malina, *Christian Origins and Cultural Anthropology: Practical Models for Biblical Interpretation* (Atlanta: John Knox, 1986), esp. 1–66, is the best general introduction to Douglas's approach and its application to the New Testament.

13. This is, of course, a simplified explanation.

14. This is summarized from Malina, *Christian Origins,* 29–37, 55–61; and Neyrey, *Revolt,* 120.

15. Also, many scholars see 1 John as colored by the community's baptismal ritual (e.g., Brown, *Epistles,* 242–45).

16. Neyrey, *Revolt,* 173.

The Historical JESUS

– 21 –

The "Third Quest" and the Apostolic Faith

M. Eugene Boring

Whether or not one is justified in speaking of a "third quest of the historical Jesus" is open to debate. Any historical quest for Jesus, however, involves three stages of research: (a) establishing a data base of authentic materials; (b) reconstructing a plausible picture of Jesus; and (c) assessing the significance of one's reconstructed Jesus for later history.

THE MAJOR PRESENTATIONS of Jesus vying for attention in the current North American revival of interest in the historical Jesus may be briefly catalogued as follows:

Hellenistic Cynic Sage: Burton L. Mack pictures Jesus as the representative of an urban, cosmopolitan, free-thinking Galilee that sat loose to the imperial claims of the big powers seeking to dominate it. As an individualistic sage on the model of the Cynics, Jesus abandoned the civilized world by becoming a homeless wanderer, mocking the pretensions of society with wit, sarcasm, and charm. Jesus was a Galilean combination of Zorba, Socrates, and Diogenes. He had no eschatology, was not interested in the temple, synagogue, the Torah, or other things Jewish.[1]

Jewish Cynic Peasant: John Dominic Crossan portrays Jesus as a poor, illiterate champion of the oppressed peasant class who challenged the society dominated by elite power structures in the manner of wandering Cynic philosophers. Jesus provided an alternative social vision given concrete impetus by his healings, exorcisms, and breaking down of social barriers by common table fellowship. The kingdom he proclaimed was noneschatological, always available to all who had the courage to adopt his lifestyle.[2]

Jewish "Spirit Person": Marcus Borg portrays Jesus as a subversive sage and social prophet who had visions and mystical experiences. He founded a movement to renew Judaism based on God's compassion rather than on the purity system of the ruling temple elites. Jesus may have believed in the eschatological triumph of God, but it is a this-worldly triumph, it is not imminent, and Jesus plays no role in it himself.[3]

Egalitarian Prophet of Wisdom: Feminist New Testament scholarship has yet to produce a full-scale study of the historical Jesus. The work of Elizabeth Schüssler Fiorenza, while primarily an explication of feminist hermeneutical theory, presupposes a picture of Jesus and Christian origins. This picture presents Jesus as a prophetic sage who understood himself as the child and spokesperson of Divine Sophia. Jesus challenged the patriarchal power structures and founded a radically egalitarian community in which women were the primary leaders. The central symbol of the movement founded by Jesus was the *basileia* (kingdom), which retains its eschatological overtones from its Jewish apocalyptic context. Jesus' overwhelming, if not exclusive, emphasis was on the presence of the *basileia,* not its future advent, imminent or otherwise.[4]

Eschatological Prophet of the Present and Coming Kingdom: John P. Meier's three-volume study is not yet complete. The contours of the picture he has sketched so far present Jesus as an eschatological prophet of the kingdom of God, which was both to come in the immediate future and was somehow present in Jesus' miracles and exorcisms, in his table fellowship offered to all, and in his powerful preaching and teaching. Jesus' role as teacher of the law and his self-understanding vis-à-vis christological titles is to be pursued in volume 3.[5]

Prophet of Imminent Restoration Eschatology: E. P. Sanders pictures Jesus as an eschatological prophet of Jewish restoration: Jesus expected the intervention of God in the near future to bring the present age to an end and to regather the twelve tribes of Israel around Jerusalem. Here a new or renewed temple would form the center of a new social order on an eschatological plane in which Jesus himself would play a key role as God's representative.[6]

A "Third Quest"?

Despite the proliferation of the label, the designation "Third Quest" has been seriously questioned on the grounds there are not enough common distinguishing features in the recent resurgence of "Jesus studies" to warrant the announcement of a New Age.[7] What has occasioned this "renaissance"?

New sources? There have been no sensational new discoveries to fuel the new interest in Jesus studies. What has thrown new light on the world in which Jesus lived, however, is more careful study of Jewish documents already available, such as the Dead Sea Scrolls, and continuing archaeological work in Galilee and Judea. Likewise, Christian documents already available have been reevaluated by a handful of scholars as significant sources for the life of Jesus. The most famous of these is the Coptic Gospel of Thomas, rediscovered in 1945, the English text of which has been commonly available for forty years. None of these sources is new. What is "new" is their reevaluation by a minority of scholars as being early. There is, however, no consensus among "Third Quest" scholars on the new evaluation of sources. Sanders, Meier, and Fiorenza, for example, continue to regard the canonical documents as our most important historical sources. On the other hand, Crossan considers the Gospel of Thomas "very, very early" and includes it along with eight other noncanonical documents and four Pauline letters as representing the earliest sources for the life of Jesus.[8] On this basis, he makes it fundamental for the reconstruction of Jesus' message, arguing that on crucial points such as eschatology and the kingdom of God, Thomas has preserved the original message of Jesus distorted by the canonical Gospels.

New methods? Since the demise of the "New Quest" in the 1960s, many biblical scholars have welcomed and adopted the insights and perspectives of literary criticism and the social sciences. As older methods are refined and new ones adopted and adapted, one would expect continuing research into the life of Jesus and Christian origins to be affected. This is the normal growing edge of scholarship. Some "Third Questers," however, may have made something of a quantum leap in this regard. This reflects the new social setting of much "Third Quest" scholarship in secularized Departments of Religious Studies where the study of religion as a human phenomenon is carried on with interdisciplinary methods.[9] Crossan is the most articulate example of a self-consciously interdisciplinary approach that involves social anthropology, Greco-Roman history, and literary analysis. This relatively new approach in attempting to understand Jesus as a figure embedded in his own social world is potentially very fruitful. It can, however, have the effect of filling in the picture of the reconstructed Jesus with material drawn from cultures and centuries far removed from Jesus' own Galilean setting.

New results? The catalogue above reveals great disparity in the pictures of Jesus resulting from the "Third Quest," yet there are some common characteristics. The birth stories are generally considered unhistorical. There are no "lost years" of Jesus that can be recovered; all attention is focused on the brief ministry of the adult Jesus. Practically all of these scholars agree that Jesus was baptized by John and began his own ministry in continuity with John's apocalypticism. There is, however, no recoverable chronology for Jesus' ministry between his baptism and his final encounter in Jerusalem that led to his death. None of these scholars argues that Jesus understood himself as savior of the world and intended to found an institution such as the church became in a few generations after his death. Jesus was crucified by the Romans under Pontius Pilate, but there is no agreement on the relation between Roman responsibility and that of the Jewish leaders, if any.

Thus, the major disputed issue in the "Third Quest" is what kind of person Jesus was and what the essence of his message, ministry, and intention was. Even here, however, there is considerable agreement that, whatever else Jesus was, he was something of a subversive sage, provocatively challenging the commonsense wisdom of people from the perspective of a new vision of the kingdom of God. In addition, there is agreement that Jesus mediated, in word and deed, the merciful, inclusive presence of God imaged as a loving father and the womb-like compassion he directed especially to outsiders. Further, there is a general shift from emphasizing Jesus' words to emphasizing his deeds, especially his miracles. The rationalist suspicion of the miracle stories in the "Old Quest," and their neglect in favor of Jesus' words in the "New Quest," has been replaced by a focus on Jesus' healings and exorcisms as the enactment of the presence of the kingdom in his own ministry. This does not mean a revival of faith in the "supernatural" on the part of the "Third Questers." It means instead that Jesus' miracles are studied with the same methods and perspectives as the miracles of other religious figures, ancient and modern. In all cases theological truth-claims are bracketed out, and miracles are found to be an indispensable element in understanding Jesus as a historical figure.

Perhaps the most disputed element in the current efforts to reconstruct Jesus' life and message is the question of eschatology. From Weiss and Schweitzer through Bultmann and the "New Quest," Jesus was seen within the context of Jewish apocalypticism as proclaiming the imminent arrival of the Son of Man or the world-transforming kingdom of God: Jesus announced the "end of the world," understood as the dawn of a new age brought about by God that involved the eschatological realities of resurrection, judgment, and dramatic transformation of the conditions of existence any observer could perceive. For Schweitzer, such an apocalyptic Jesus became a stranger to our time who "comes to us as one unknown," but whose challenge continues to motivate us to humanitarian deeds even when we have no conceptual means of translating his message into our own time.[10] Bultmann and the post-Bultmannian "New Quest" exemplify how existential hermeneutics can both allow Jesus to be the apocalyptic figure he was and still be reinterpreted in the New Testament and by contemporary theology as mediating the word of God in a way that addresses later, nonapocalyptic generations. The apocalyptic Jesus continues to be relevant for several streams of contemporary theology no longer dependent on the existential hermeneutic of Bultmann.[11] Some "Third Questers," such as Crossan and Borg, have concluded that the New Testament's picture of Jesus as an apocalyptic prophet is entirely the creation of early Christianity and that Jesus taught and enacted only a present kingdom of God: an inclusive, nonpatriarchal "kingdom" always and everywhere available to those with eyes to see and the courage to live by it. Other scholars, such as Sanders and Meier, continue to advocate imminent future eschatology as a central element of Jesus' message, without (e.g., in the case of Meier) denying that Jesus also saw the kingdom as somehow already present in his life and work. It is incorrect to assume a new noneschatological consensus, or even the dissolution of an older consensus.[12]

New nondogmatic stance over against "the theologians"? The question of the eschatological character of Jesus' message and its potential contemporary relevance brings us to the most important issue presented in the works of the "Third Quest," namely, its variety and ambiguity on the relation of historical to theological issues. Whereas the "Old Quest" was theological (in the sense that it was primarily anti-dogmatic, reacting against an agenda having been set by orthodox Christian theologians), and the "New Quest" was self-consciously theological (in that it was carried on by Christian theologians seeking continuity between the message of the historical Jesus and the church's kerygma), the "Third Quest" uniformly proclaims its separation from the theological enterprise — though it does this in strikingly different ways.

Current Nomenclature

Almost forty years ago Paul Tillich spoke of "the semantic confusion about the meaning of the term historical Jesus."[13] The situation has not improved in the meantime. A wide range of dipolar phrases (e.g., "Jesus of history and Christ of faith"; "historical Jesus and historian's Jesus") has attempted to designate the relation of (1) Jesus as he really was, (2) Jesus as seen in purely historical terms, and (3) Jesus as seen within various perspectives of faith and theology. The variation in terminology is not merely a matter of preference for one label over another, but points to differences in the way the task and results of historical construction are dealt with and how these relate to the faith of the believer.

"That [theology] is another question."[14] The most cogent and consistent claim has been made by E. P. Sanders who, in his historical work on Jesus, explicitly avoids God-talk: "I shall discuss neither what God accomplished or did not accomplish through the life and death of Jesus."[15] Sanders simply accepts as a given the cultural fact that Jesus has been

considered an important figure in human history, without attempting to explain why this has been so. As such a figure, Jesus (like, e.g., Thomas Jefferson) is worthy of the historian's effort, but the historian is not called on to relate history to theology, publicly or privately. "...I am no theologian...I am to be only a historian and an exegete."[16]

"Pre-Easter and Post-Easter Jesus." This is the preferred terminology of Marcus Borg, who speaks easily about "living in two worlds"[17] (the secular academy and the believing, worshiping Christian community), contending that his "Jesus research" is only from within the first world. The pre-Easter Jesus is Jesus as he really was before his death, while the post-Easter Jesus is the Christ of Christian experience. The former is the subject matter of the historian, the latter of the theologian.

"Real Jesus, historical Jesus, and the Jesus of faith." John Meier takes a step forward by distinguishing three aspects of the issue rather than two.[18] Not only is the Jesus apprehended as Lord and Christ by Christian faith to be distinguished from the Jesus reconstructed by historical methods but this latter figure is also not the same as the "real" Jesus, since historical method can apprehend only a part of the person as he really was. As I shall point out below, however, a further distinction must be made as regards the concept of the "real" Jesus.

"The historical Jesus interpreted by faith as a manifestation of God." Crossan does not have an explicit bipolar formula. He explicitly rejects "Jesus of history and Christ of faith."[19] Rather, Crossan contends that when an individual encounters Jesus as he really was, Christian faith can result. This was true of people who actually met Jesus in the 30s of first-century Galilee. It is also true of people who encounter him today through the work of the individual historian's reconstruction. It requires neither resurrection, kerygma, canon, nor creed.

> Here's what I imagine. If you were in Galilee, let's say in the 30s, you would have seen a person called Jesus. Let's imagine three different people responding to that person. One says, "This guy's a bore. Let's leave him." The second one says, "This guy's dangerous. Let's kill him." The third one says, "I see God here. Let's follow this guy." Now each of these, in its own way, is an act of faith....My answer is that Christian faith is to see the historical Jesus as the manifestation of God for me.[20]

Here Crossan runs the danger of placing himself in the apostolic role (see below), with the multitudes of those who are disenchanted with the church but infatuated with a romantic notion of Jesus and are ready to abandon the apostolic church and accept Crossan (or another "Jesus scholar") in this role.

A Proposed Analysis

My own effort to clarify what is actually going on in all of this is to identify three major moves that can be distinguished but not separated: (1) recovering the data base, the results of which can be called "the excavated Jesus"; (2) reconstructing the most plausible picture of Jesus as he really was, the results of which can be called the "reconstructed Jesus"; and (3) a portrayal of the significance of the historical figure thus reconstructed for later human history, culture, thought, life, and faith, which is the "interpreted Jesus." If this interpretation is expressed in terms of ultimate significance, one has made a theological move, whether or not explicit religious or theological language is used. For instance, if, as in the cases of Mack and Crossan, one talks of "following" this reconstructed Jesus, or of somehow adopting him as a norm of what we should do, and regarding him as a paradigm of what human life or society should be, one has entered the arena of theology, regardless of whether or not God-talk is used. The product of such reconstructions can properly be called the "theologized Jesus." In theory, there are thus three stages of the historian's work:

1. *the excavated Jesus* (analytic phase, separating "authentic" from "inauthentic" materials);
2. *the reconstructed Jesus* (descriptive phase, putting the recovered data together into a picture of "the real Jesus");
3. *the theologized Jesus* (normative phase, showing the significance of Jesus for human life).

My own judgment is that whereas these stages can be distinguished in the abstract, they cannot be separated in practice. Theological concerns have been operative (not to say determinative) at every level of the process: in the initial "Jesus movement"; in the church of the ancient world that preserved and interpreted materials from and about Jesus, and in the efforts of modern historians to portray Jesus "as he really was." Hence, while some "Third Questers" claim to work only at levels 1 and 2 of this process, the concerns of level 3 tend to be implicit and inescapable from the beginning.

1. The Excavated Jesus

Even at the level of excavation and data-gathering, one is limited by materials that have preserved only what was considered theologically significant by the early followers of Jesus (e.g., kingdom sayings and miracle stories, but not descriptions of Jesus' education and hobbies).

Likewise, quite apart from this inherent limitation of the available materials, the modern historian will necessarily find the kind of thing for which he or she is looking (e.g., Jesus' words and deeds pertaining to social injustice or eschatological salvation, but not his views on animal rights or gerontology). Already conditioned (not to say determined) by theological perspectives are not only the final hermeneutical step, which is interpreting Jesus' lasting significance or metaphysical status, and the penultimate constructive phase, which assembles a historical portrait of Jesus on the basis of data that survive the criteria of authenticity, but also the "data base" from which all else proceeds.

Just as there is no radical difference between participants in the "Third Quest" and the Bultmannian and post-Bultmannian period of Jesus research concerning the amount of material deemed "authentic," so "Third Questers" do not differ radically among themselves on this score.[21] The real differences that separate the various "data bases" are not quantitative in nature but concern whether one admits particular items to the "data base" such as future eschatological sayings of the canonical Gospels or realized eschatological sayings from the Gospel of Thomas.

2. The Reconstructed Jesus

The excavated Jesus is not yet a historical portrait.[22] After one gets a "data base," there are extremely important moves in fleshing it out into a portrait of a historical figure. It is as though level 1 gives us a number of authentic dots that can be put together into a large number of different pictures—and the dots are not numbered.[23] The goal is to utilize the recovered "authentic" material to reconstruct the profile of a figure that approximates, or at least does not fundamentally distort, the "real" Jesus. But the term "real Jesus" is not univocal, and each author must define what he or she means by it. The term "real Jesus" can be understood in a strictly empirical sense: Jesus-as-he-really-was, regarded entirely in terms of this-worldly reality (the "real empirical Jesus"). Or it can be understood as the Jesus in whom God was present and active in a way that God was not present and active in, say, John the Baptist or Simeon ben Kosiba (the "real transcendent Jesus").[24] Thus, our analysis needs a further distinction, and the outline appears as:

2. The Reconstructed Jesus

    2.1. The "real empirical Jesus"

    2.2. The "real transcendent Jesus"

It is clear that, in principle, the "real Jesus" in this second sense cannot be studied and talked about using the language, categories, and methods of the historian and that only Jesus 2.1 can be the object of the historian's work qua historian, whether the historian claims to be a believer or not. But what is involved in reconstructing the "real empirical Jesus" at level 2.1 is not so simple a matter. Even the "empirical Jesus" is not a univocal term, and another differentiation must be made to distinguish between the real empirical Jesus in the sense of his total personhood (including his internal feelings and motivations, and the network of human relations in which he is involved and apart from which his reality as a human being does not exist) and the empirical Jesus in the sense that he is historically describable, whether by contemporaries or later historians. Consequently, even the "real Jesus" in the empirical, this-worldly sense is more than the historian can handle. This is a truism with regard to any human being, quite apart from Christian, or any other religious, faith. The total personhood of any human being is always a more complex reality than can be perceived even by the person's contemporaries, however thorough and objective they may be, not to speak of later historians, who wish to portray the "real" Julius Caesar or Marie Antoinette.[25] This is why a distinction must be made between the "real empirical Jesus" in his totality and those fragmentary dimensions and aspects of Jesus' life and personhood that can be apprehended by historical method, the "historian's Jesus." A further refinement, therefore, must be made in our analysis, so that the outline appears:

2. The Reconstructed Jesus
    - 2.1. The "real empirical Jesus"
        - 2.1.1. The total person
        - 2.1.2. The "historian's Jesus"
    - 2.2. The "real transcendent Jesus"

In theory, then, it is the best version of the "historian's Jesus" (2.1.2) that the "Third Quest" is after, and the debate should be carried on at this level. Connecting the dots of the data base into a plausible historical reconstruction requires informed historical imagination, and it is precisely at this level that the "Third Quest" has made real advances. But can the dots be connected without introducing the ideals, ideologies, and theologies of the historians making the connections? If historical and theological study could be carried on as neatly as the above outline suggests, one would first reconstruct the historical figure of Jesus in the sense of 2.1.2 (this is all that the historian qua historian can do), and only then, on the basis of this reconstruction and, if one had a mind to do so, raise the level 3 question of Jesus' theological significance.[26] But the more level 3 collapses into level 2, the more the historian assumes the role not only of theologian but of apostle — and this is true whether the historian intends it or not, or is even aware of it.

3. The Theologized Jesus

Interpretation of some kind is necessary to have any picture of Jesus at all; the dots do not connect themselves. Thus, there is a measure of interpretation, including theological interpretation, already at level 2.[27] But when we consciously move past the level of reconstruction to that of theological interpretation, we need to be clear about what we are doing, who is doing it, and who or what validates the interpretation.

Once again, the act of theological interpretation can be thought of in two ways that can be distinguished but not separated:

3.1. *Projection.* One can limit oneself to the "real empirical Jesus" in the sense of 2.1.2 above, the "historian's Jesus," and interpret him as a manifestation of God in the sense that the historian's own sense of values and ultimate meanings recognizes something "divine" in the human being Jesus. In the case of Crossan, "Jesus-as-a-manifestation-of-God-for-me" is acknowledged to be a human construct by the words "for me," that is, I see God here but others may, with their faith, see a bore or a threat to the general welfare. These are, of course, theological issues that require theologically responsible answers beyond the ken of the historian.

3.2. *Confession.* The "real Jesus" can be understood in the sense of 2.2 above, which is the transcendent dimension. In this case, the presence and act of God in Jesus was already there in the pre-Easter figure apart from and prior to anyone's recognition and confession of it in the first or twentieth centuries. From this point of view, when Jesus' disciples use language and imagery confessing the unique and definitive presence of God in the Jesus-event, they are confessing that they have apprehended something really there, though the historian qua historian cannot perceive or study it.

Graphic artists have an analogous difficulty in portraying Jesus. A picture of the empirical Jesus, constructed as carefully as historical study will allow — whether of the baby in Mary's lap, the dying figure on the cross, or Jesus' walking on the water (in this instance, we must assume the historian-artist is convinced the event actually happened) — can be done in such a way that only the empirical Jesus is portrayed, picturing the scene as though photographed with a good camera. Artists who intend to indicate that the figure portrayed is somehow identified with God have traditionally signified this by adding to the figure a halo that no camera would pick up. In verbal communication, this affirmation is made by shifting from what is presumed to be historical description to the language of theological confession, using God-language in some manner of Jesus or the Jesus-event. The historian ceases to be a historian when he or she adds the linguistic equivalent of a halo to the reconstruction. When confessing Christian theologians have used such language of Jesus, they have (or should have) always understood that they were making a confession of faith with regard to the "real transcendent Jesus" in the sense of 2.2 above and that they were claiming to apprehend something real about the pre-Easter Jesus of Nazareth and not merely to give their own projection of the significance of the "real empirical Jesus," which can be partially reconstructed and represented by the historian.

The point here is that to talk about Jesus significantly at all, an interpretation in one or the other of these senses is necessary. Who makes such interpretations? Sanders and Meier acknowledge that the early followers of Jesus and the later church, including the contemporary church, have made such theological interpretations but that they, in their own purely historical reconstructions, do not intend to do so and are relatively successful in their attempt. For Mack, Borg, Crossan, and Schüssler Fiorenza, the early followers of Jesus made such interpretations, but what became Christianity missed the essence of what Jesus was "up to" in the interpretations canonized by the orthodox church. Modern historians not only can recover the real Jesus and give the contemporary world a different option from the Jesus of canonical Christianity but also should do so, since the real Jesus has a message to which we should respond, a message obscured by the church.[28] In varying degrees and ways, with Crossan probably being the most explicit, they call for faith in their reconstruction and theological interpretation of the real Jesus. Whoever makes decisions on these matters is no longer functioning as historian. The interpretation of Jesus as the revelatory act of God that tells us definitively about God and the meaning of our own lives is an apostolic role and function.

Who or what validates such theological interpretations? Since in North America there are no political, religious, or academic authorities to forbid it, anyone can claim to make both reconstructions of what Jesus was really like and to interpret the ultimate significance of his life. But all such reconstructions are not created equal. Should they all simply be left to compete freely in the marketplace of ideas, with each individual free to choose the Jesus of his or her particular taste? In one sense, of course, this must continue to be the case, and the days when the professed followers of Jesus in the dominant church could use political power and punishment to restrain those who offered differing interpretations of Jesus must never be allowed to return. But unless we are to retreat to an isolationistic, monadistic individualism, all claims must be validated by some sort of community. All such claims are accepted only within a community sharing some common presuppositions. With the possible exception of Mack's Jesus, all the current reconstructions present us with a Jesus who opposes such monadistic individualism.

There is a sense in which the community of scholars plays an important and responsible role. The academic community not only filters out bizarre and irresponsible interpretations of Jesus' person and life, but provides a forum in which public discussion and debate by qualified scholars playing by common and examinable rules can get nearer to historical truth. But the academic community as such cannot play the ecclesial role and cannot make theological pronouncements on matters beyond its horizon.[29] It is limited in arbitrating theological differences in a way analogous to the inability of the pure historian to deal with the "real Jesus" at more than the superficial empirical level; that is, the academic community, which is made up of historians, is limited in its area of competence to 2.1.2 above.

The community that validates some theological interpretations as apostolic must be the community that explicitly acknowledges its own faith commitments and takes responsibility for its theological efforts to understand and clarify them. The ancient Christian community did not claim, for instance, that the historical Jesus was transparent to the reality of God. It was the act of God in the resurrection (however this is conceptualized, and there are a number of different conceptions in the New Testament) that reversed all human judgments about the identity of Jesus. The earliest church did not claim that it would have recognized Jesus as the manifestation of God if it had been there, that is, that it was only the bad, oppressive elites that crucified Jesus, but that it would not have done it. Rather, the church confessed its own sinfulness and involvement in the rejection of Jesus, and the resurrection was understood as the act of God that vindicated Jesus and his way of life, that is, as God's act prior to and apart from our own perception of it that reversed pre-Easter perceptions of Jesus by disciples and opponents alike. In this case, "resurrection," however conceptualized, is not a matter of whether we "need" a resurrection to complete or hold together our theological system — if so, some do and some do not, and "resurrection" remains an abstract item necessary in the thought-world of some systems but not others. But those who share the Christian community's faith in the resurrection do not do so because they postulate a resurrection in order to maintain their theological structure. This is not a resurrection at all, not an act of God, but a deus ex machina to salvage an intellectual construct. In the New Testament and Christian faith, resurrection is not our theological act to shore up a faltering intellectual system — an intellectual move that e.g. the Gospel of Thomas can dispense with because not necessary in its system — but an event, prior to and apart from us, that is, God's act for Jesus and not our act for ourselves. The church understood itself to have received the Holy Spirit through the risen Jesus, which enabled it to distinguish true from false apostles, which guided it through the process of forming the canon of authentic interpretations, formulating a living tradition and selecting pastors and teachers to continue leading it in its journey through history.

While canon, creed, tradition, and clergy can and should be studied historically, none of the theological claims inherent in this mode of the Christian community's affirmation of some interpretations as valid and rejection of others is subject to historical validation. Does this mean we must retreat to a pure confessionalism that can ignore or disdain the results of honest historical scholarship? No, it does not mean this. We must not attempt a return to anything like the "No Quest" period in which study of the historical Jesus ("inquiring behind the kerygma") was considered both historically impossible and theologically illegitimate.[30] It is possible to learn something, perhaps a significant amount, about the historical figure of Jesus with considerable probability, and such knowledge cannot be irrelevant to understanding the Christ event as the definitive action and self-revelation of God. Yet the danger persists, especially in an American culture shaped by a combination of individualism, social idealism, and an understanding of truth shaped by the media image of the investigative reporter, that the Christian community called into being by the apostolic testimony and preserved from being "tossed about by every wind of doctrine" on its journey through history by the Holy Spirit operative in its canon, tradition, and ministry, might decide in individual cases to substitute the modern historian for the church of apostles, prophets, and martyrs. In some cases, this exchange is encouraged by historians who project themselves into this apostolic and canonical role.

If, however, one wishes to engage in the perfectly legitimate, perhaps for us in our time even theologically necessary, enterprise of reconstructing a historian's Jesus that can be argued about by historians limiting themselves to historical methods, the Jesus so reconstructed will always be less than the "real Jesus." Even so, there must also be lines of continuity between the reconstructed historian's Jesus and the "real Jesus"—these cannot be utterly discontinuous, or one of them is wrong. Historical study is the necessary risk accepted by a historical faith. Thus we can indeed join in the celebration that there is new vitality in "Jesus research." But when the historian, claiming to disavow theology, usurps the role of theologian, canon, and apostle, one thinks of Barth's response to another kind of attractive natural theology advocated in all sincerity by a respected colleague in the academy: "Nein."[31]

NOTES

1. Burton L. Mack, *A Myth of Innocence: Mark and Christian Origins* (Minneapolis: Fortress, 1988); *The Lost Gospel: The Book of Q and Christian Origins* (San Francisco: HarperSanFrancisco, 1993).

2. John Dominic Crossan, *The Historical Jesus: The Life of a Mediterranean Jewish Peasant* (New York: HarperCollins, 1991); *Jesus: A Revolutionary Biography* (New York: HarperCollins, 1994).

3. Marcus J. Borg, *Jesus: A New Vision* (New York: Harper & Row, 1988); *Meeting Jesus Again for the First Time* (New York: HarperCollins, 1994).

4. Elisabeth Schüssler Fiorenza, *In Memory of Her: A Feminist Theological Reconstruction of Christian Origins* (New York: Crossroad, 1983); *Jesus: Miriam's Child, Sophia's Prophet* (New York: Continuum, 1994).

5. John P. Meier, *A Marginal Jew: Rethinking the Historical Jesus,* vol. 1: *The Roots of the Problem and the Person*; vol. 2: *Mentor, Message, and Miracles* (New York: Doubleday, 1991, 1994).

6. E. P. Sanders, *Jesus and Judaism* (Philadelphia: Fortress Press, 1985); *The Historical Figure of Jesus* (New York: Penguin, 1993).

7. William R. Telford, "Major Trends and Interpretive Issues in the Study of Jesus," in *Studying the Historical Jesus: Evaluations of the State of Current Research,* ed. Bruce Chilton and Craig A. Evans, NTTS (Leiden: Brill, 1994), 57–61.

8. Crossan, *The Historical Jesus,* 427–29.

9. The "New Quest" was carried on almost exclusively within theological faculties, where theological issues were paramount and where scholars were qualified to engage in theological discussion.

10. Albert Schweitzer, *The Quest of the Historical Jesus* (New York: Macmillan, 1910, reprinted 1968), 398–403.

11. E.g., Wolfhart Pannenberg, Eduard Schillebeeckx, Hans Küng, Luise Schottroff.

12. Against Marcus Borg, who has repeatedly spoken of a "major change" in which "in the narrow sense of the term, only a minority of Jesus scholars in North America think that Jesus was eschatological" ("Reflections on a Discipline: A North American Perspective," in Chilton and Evans, *Studying the Historical Jesus,* 21, and often in previous articles). Borg's announcement that the old consensus of an eschatological Jesus no longer exists rests on his informal poll of a small unrepresentative group (thirty-nine American scholars, twenty-one in the Jesus Seminar and eighteen in the Historical Jesus Section of the Society of Biblical Literature). Sixteen of the thirty-nine (41 percent) responded affirmatively to the question "Do you think Jesus expected the end of the world in his generation, i.e., in the lifetime of at least some of his contemporaries?"

13. Paul Tillich, *Systematic Theology* (Chicago: University of Chicago Press, 1957).

14. E. P. Sanders, *The Historical Figure of Jesus* (London: Penguin Books, 1993), 1.

15. Ibid., 2.

16. Ibid., 331, 334.

17. In Hershel Shanks, ed., *The Search for Jesus: Modern Scholarship Looks at the Gospels* (Washington: Biblical Archaeology Society, 1994), 37.

18. Meier, *Marginal Jew,* 1:21–40. Part of the problematic involved in "Jesus of history and Christ of faith" terminology is that it tries to simplify a more complex phenomenon with a neat bipolar slogan.

19. *The Search for Jesus,* 80. "I would never make that distinction."

20. Ibid.

21. Mack's earliest layer of Q, the maximum that could represent Jesus, is seven pages of large print of disconnected sayings attributed to Jesus (*The Lost Gospel,* 73–80). Crossan's data base is thirteen pages of isolated units of material, mostly sayings (*The Historical Jesus,* xiii–xxvi). The Jesus Seminar's *Five Gospels: The Search for the Authentic Words of Jesus,* ed. Robert W. Funk and Roy W. Hoover (New York: Macmillan, 1993) designates 18 percent of Jesus' sayings in the canonical Gospels as authentic. Meier, Borg, and Fiorenza do not give a catalogue of sayings they consider authentic. Sanders rejects the "sayings" approach and presents a list of eight items in Jesus' life he considers authentic.

22. This is the value of Sanders's often-repeated point, e.g., *Jesus and Judaism,* 262.

23. One can also think of the number of different pictures that can be seen in the same constellation of stars: is it a "dipper," a "gourd," a "plow," or a "bear"?

24. These two perspectives on the "real Jesus" have often been designated by the terms "human Jesus" and "divine Christ." It seems to me that these christological categories are not helpful when referring to the pre-Easter Jesus, since they tend to suggest that we possess a conceptual clarity as to the nature(s) of the pre-Easter Jesus in some metaphysical sense that we do not and cannot have. "Transcendent" is here intended to point to the reality of God's presence and act in Jesus as something that transcends our ability to express.

25. The point has been well made in Luke Timothy Johnson, *The Real Jesus: The Misguided Quest for the Historical Jesus and the Truth of the Traditional Gospels* (New York: HarperSanFrancisco, 1996).

26. Sanders and Meier, in different ways, have made the most consistent attempts to do this.

27. That the author of a reconstruction of the "historical Jesus" plays a formative christological role was seen more clearly by Martin Kähler than by most contemporary scholars: "But when Christology appears in the form of a 'Life of Jesus,' there are not many who will perceive the stage manager behind the scenes, manipulating, according to his own dogmatic script, the fascinating spectacle of a colorful biography.... The Jesus of the 'Life-of-Jesus movement' is merely a modern example of human creativity, and not an iota better than the notorious dogmatic Christ of Byzantine Christology." See Martin Kähler, *The So-Called Historical Jesus and the Historic, Biblical Christ,* trans. and ed. Carl E. Braaten (Philadelphia: Fortress, 1964), 43.

28. More precisely, the spectrum of canonical Jesuses, since from the earliest period the church has affirmed a limited variety of authentic representations of the meaning of the Christ event.

29. There are always tendencies in this direction, especially when scholars

are ex- or alienated church members. Cf. Carl Braaten's comment that Martin Kähler was "moved by a deep apologetic concern to preserve the Christian laity from the papacy of scholarship" (introduction to *The So-Called Historical Jesus*).

30. Cf. James M. Robinson, *A New Quest of the Historical Jesus and Other Essays* (Philadelphia: Fortress, 1983), a reissue of his 1959 work with more recent essays, and Carl Braaten and Roy A. Harrisville, *The Historical Jesus and the Kerygmatic Christ: Essays on the New Quest for the Historical Jesus* (Nashville: Abingdon, 1964).

31. Karl Barth, *Nein! Antwort on Emil Brunner* (Munich: Chr. Kaiser Verlag, 1934).

– 22 –

Dividing Lines in Jesus Research Today

THROUGH DIALECTICAL NEGATION TO A POSITIVE SKETCH

John P. Meier

The Jesus of history undertook a prophetic ministry to Israel that involved working miracles. These miracles supported his eschatological message about the kingdom of God. The most adequate way to picture Jesus, therefore, is as the miracle-working, eschatological prophet who cloaked himself in the mantle of Elijah.

PARENTS WHO HAVE CHILDREN going through the "terrible twos" come to dread the word "no." Yet, for all the struggle involved in that painful period of development, parents appreciate that the "terrible twos" are a vital stage of psychological growth. Children begin to define themselves by separating from and negating the significant figures around them. German idealism saw a similar process in the definition of the ego as opposed to the non-ego, and historians regularly describe how early Christianity forged its identity at least in part by negating various aspects of both Judaism and Greco-Roman paganism.[1]

The same sort of "dialectical negation" is necessarily reflected in scholarly research and debate, and certainly the now decade-old "third quest" for the historical Jesus is no exception to the rule.[2] Scholars from different backgrounds and with different views have gradually honed their positions by defining themselves over against their debating partners. Except for cases of intemperate language and *ad hominem* arguments, this definition by negation is a healthy part of the overall development of the third quest—provided that this *via negativa* ultimately leads to the positive goal of a clearer and more carefully reasoned sketch of the historical Jesus.

It is in this spirit that I undertake the following exercise in dialectical negation to clarify my own position within the third quest. This essay will sketch in broad strokes what are the chief points of disagreement, the chief dividing lines, between my own approach in *A Marginal Jew* and the approach taken by certain other authors, especially those associated with the Jesus Seminar.[3] The essay has two parts. First, I shall outline, in roughly logical order, six major areas of disagreement — "major" because the choices one makes in these areas all have a major impact on the portrait of Jesus one paints. Second, after outlining these six areas of dialectical negation, I shall draw together the various positions I have defended into a brief, positive portrait of the historical Jesus.

Areas of Disagreement

1. The Question of Sources

Fundamental to any quest for the historical Jesus is the question of the sources that may and should be used. As one admits or excludes a particular document from the list of relevant sources, one is already beginning to determine the lineaments of one's portrait of Jesus. Perhaps under the pressure of scholarly standards to find as many sources as possible, or perhaps under the pressure of the *National Enquirer* to find as weird a Jesus as possible, scholars have rummaged through the inventory of apocryphal Gospels and the Nag Hammadi library to discover new sources of information about the historical Jesus. Once this tendency was unleashed, apparently no apocryphal Gospel was out of bounds.

To take an extreme example: Richard Bauckham has recently appealed to the second-century apocryphal Gospels known as the *Gospel of Peter,* the *Protevangelium Jacobi,* and the Greek *Infancy Gospel of Thomas* to help establish the precise relationship of Jesus to his supposed brothers and sisters.[4] The fact that the text of the *Gospel of Peter* we possess never mentions these brothers and sisters, the fact that the *Infancy Gospel of Thomas* supplies no direct information about the relationship, and the fact that the *Protevangelium Jacobi* is a hilarious compilation of misinformation about things Jewish mixed together with midrashic expansions on the canonical infancy narratives seem not to have made an impression. To be blunt: I doubt that Bauckham's suggestion will receive wide acceptance, and so his theory need not detain us here.

The *Gospel of Peter,* however, does contain a passion-resurrection narrative. John Dominic Crossan has claimed that this passion narrative is, directly or indirectly, the source of the passion narratives in all four canonical Gospels.[5] Since Crossan also maintains that the narrative in the *Gospel of Peter* is almost entirely the product of Christian meditation on Old Testament texts used to explain the death of Jesus, the historical value of any of the passion narratives is, in his view, next to nil. It is telling that even many of Crossan's colleagues in the Jesus Seminar have been wary of his claims for the *Gospel of Peter.* His theory has met with little acceptance in academic circles, and with good reason. The *Gospel of Peter* shows knowledge of some of the canonical Gospels, most notably Matthew.[6]

There is, however, one apocryphal Gospel from Nag Hammadi that has gained acceptance in some academic circles as an early and reliable source for the historical Jesus. I refer, of course, to the famous Coptic *Gospel of Thomas* (a collection of 114 sayings of Jesus, to be carefully distinguished from the Greek *Infancy Gospel of Thomas*). Members of the Jesus Seminar as well as some other scholars have claimed that in the Coptic *Gospel of Thomas* we have a source of Jesus' sayings that is independent of and perhaps earlier than the canonical Gospels. Other scholars, however, have not been so easily convinced. They point out that *Thomas* contains sayings that have parallels in the Q tradition, the special traditions of both Matthew and Luke, and possibly passages that stem from Mark and John. Such a broad spread of different streams of Gospel traditions all contained in *Thomas* is, to say the least, remarkable if *Thomas* is indeed independent of, and earlier than, all of the canonical Gospels.

More damaging to the theory of independence, though, is the number of times that the sayings in *Thomas* reflect not the form of a saying in Mark but the redactional reworking of the saying in Matthew or Luke. In fact, some of the Matthew-like items in *Thomas* may actually be material created by Matthew when writing his Gospel.[7] If this is the case, then the claim that *Thomas* represents an early and independent source for our knowledge of Jesus must fall to the ground. Moreover, since the portraits of Jesus painted by Crossan and the Jesus Seminar rely heavily on *Thomas,* they likewise must come crashing down. It is risky to prophesy, but I would hazard the guess that, ten years from now, many of the theories proposed by the Jesus Seminar will prove a major embarrassment to most of the academics who once held them. But to return from prophecy to fact: the fact of the matter is that there is no consensus in favor of the independence and early date of *Thomas,* and to claim such a consensus is inaccurate.

2. The Q Document

Along with Jesus research and work on both the Qumran and Nag Hammadi documents, there has been a resurgence of studies over the last decade on the so-called Q document.[8] Since much of this work mimics research done in German in the 1960s and 1970s, one cannot escape a certain sense of déjà vu.[9] Still, the present-day research on Q has helped fuel the "third quest" for the historical Jesus now raging in the United States.

In the name of full disclosure, I have always believed that scholars writing about the Gospels should "come clean" and admit that there have been respectable exegetes throughout the twentieth century who have done fine work while denying the existence of the Q document.[10] In other words, any treatment of Q should begin with the disclaimer that Q is only a hypothesis, a hypothesis not accepted by all scholars. Still, there are reasonable grounds for affirming Q. Most scholars think that Mark was the earliest Gospel, from which both Matthew and Luke drew material. Yet Matthew and Luke — who do not seem to have known each other's Gospels — contain common material, mostly sayings, not derived from Mark. Hence, it is a likely hypothesis that both Matthew and Luke drew on some collection — or collections — of Jesus' sayings now lost to us, a collection arbitrarily labeled "Q."

Personally, I think the arguments in favor of a Q document are more weighty than those against it, but I am becoming increasingly skeptical of ever more refined and detailed theories concerning Q's extent, wording, community, geographical setting, stages of tradition and redaction, and coherent theology. I find myself regularly reciting a reworked version of Ludwig Wittgenstein's famous dictum: Whereof one does not know, thereof one must be silent. Or one might cite the equivalent axiom of Jacob Neusner: What you cannot show, you do not know. I do not see any convincing argument for the baroque theories that are often proposed on the development of Q.

First of all, I have misgivings when scholars speak of "the Q community," as though we could presuppose that one particular Christian community created and carried the Q document as the well-rounded articulation of its particular coherent theology. Actually, I doubt that the Q document had one coherent theology. To be sure, there are a number of dominant theological interests reflected in Q, including prophecy, eschatology, apocalyptic, and wisdom. But this does not in itself make for a coherent theological message. Q is more like a theological "grab bag." We can find sayings of strikingly different, perhaps even contradictory, viewpoints placed next to each other. A prime example is Luke 16:16–18, where verse 16 distinguishes the past age of the law and the prophets from the present time of Jesus' preaching. Verse 17 then proclaims the eternal validity and immutability of the Mosaic law even on minor matters. Verse 18 immediately announces the blanket abrogation of an important institution of the Mosaic law, divorce. These sayings are united in Q by the common theme of the law, but hardly by a coherent theology. Contrary to the overarching redactional tendencies of

Matthew and Luke, there is no attempt in Q to mediate or reconcile the tensions or contradictions among the sayings. Q is indeed a grab bag.

Paradoxically, it is precisely the desire to find coherence in Q, by hook or by crook, that has led some scholars to postulate various strata or stages of redaction in Q. In other words, if we cannot find coherence in Q as it stands, then we shall find it in its varied layers of tradition. A popular theory today is that Q first had a stratum composed of wisdom sayings, to which was added at a later date a stratum containing apocalyptic sayings. We need not be surprised to learn that other scholars hold the exact opposite order of composition.

There are a number of problems with any such suggestion. The most obvious one is that we simply lack the data and criteria to decide what is early and late in Q. Moreover, the idea that Q had distinct strata that could be separated chronologically, theologically, and even geographically should be suspect from the start. A priori, it seems unlikely that the oral and written forms of the sayings tradition of the first Christian generation developed in such a neat, evolutionary fashion as first wisdom, then apocalyptic—or vice versa. It is much more likely that, in the first-flush and excitement of the Jesus movement after Easter, the Q tradition simply grew "like Topsy." Indeed, the suggestion has been made that we should think of Q in terms of a "ring book," a sort of loose-leaf binder, examples of which have been found among parchment remains of the second century C.E.[11] Whether or not Q ever took the form of such a ring book, the ring book can serve as a good metaphor of the fluid state in which Q probably circulated during the first Christian generation. It is not at all improbable that Matthew and Luke worked with variant versions of this fluid Q. Instead of one Q document carried by one community, we should perhaps think of various forms of Q circulating among different Christian communities.

Apart from detailed theories of tradition and redaction, two conclusions often drawn from research on Q need to be examined more closely. (a) Even if we could establish that a particular saying entered the Q document at a late stage, that fact by itself would tell us nothing about whether the saying came from the historical Jesus or was created by the early church. The authenticity of a saying hardly depends on the time of its acceptance into the Q document. (b) It may well be, as is usually claimed, that the Q document had no passion narrative, but that does not prove that the communities that contributed to and used the Q document were ignorant of or uninterested in the passion tradition. If we grant that there was a Q document, the only two communities that we know for certain used it were the churches of Matthew and Luke. Both of those churches obviously knew and valued the passion tradition of Mark, and they may have also known the passion proclamation from the Pauline tradition as well. The idea that some first-generation Christian community proclaimed the sayings of Q without any knowledge of or interest in Jesus' death and resurrection is simply not verified by the data at our disposal. In short, my ability to believe in hypotheses is exhausted by my acceptance of the existence of Q. The further hypotheses about Q developed in recent years leave me a total skeptic.

3. The Eschatology of Jesus' Proclamation

Scholars remain sharply divided on the question of the nature of Jesus' proclamation of the kingdom of God. Did Jesus proclaim that the kingdom was already present in his ministry, or did he see it as a reality soon to come—or both? Crossan and the Jesus Seminar reflect their embrace of the Nag Hammadi documents and the putative wisdom stratum of Q when they champion a Jesus who spoke of a kingdom that was present in his ministry but not of a kingdom still to come on some final day of Israel's history.[12] In contrast, E. P. Sanders has long defended a Jesus proclaiming future eschatology, but Sanders doubts that Jesus ever spoke of the kingdom as already present in his ministry.[13]

I find myself caught between the two positions.[14] On the one hand, there is too much authentic material in various streams of Gospel tradition to deny that Jesus spoke of some future coming of God in his kingly rule. The petition "thy kingdom come" in the Lord's Prayer (Matt. 6:10), Jesus' prophecy at the last supper that he would drink wine again in the kingdom of God (Mark 14:25), his prophecy that many would come from east and west to recline at table with the patriarchs (Matt. 8:11–12), and the future promises in the beatitudes (Matt. 5:3–12)—all these are but a few examples of how the historical Jesus prophesied a definitive coming of God as king beyond the present bounds of Israel's history.

On the other hand, certain authentic sayings of Jesus suggest that he saw his ministry of teaching and healing as somehow mediating and actualizing God's kingdom in the present moment. That Jesus saw his exorcisms in this light is indicated by the famous saying in Luke 11:20, a saying almost all scholars attribute to the historical Jesus: "If by the finger of God I cast out demons, then the kingdom of God has come upon you." Jesus thus claims that, through his exorcisms, God's kingly power is already smashing the opposing power of Satan by liberating Israelites enslaved by demonic possession. Or, to use the metaphor of another saying, Jesus is already entering the house of the strong man Satan and plundering Satan's goods, that is, the persons dominated by the rebellious kingdom of Satan (Mark 3:27). It is in this sense that the kingdom of God "is in your midst" (Luke 17:21). It is in this sense that the audience of Jesus is blessed because they see what "many prophets and kings longed to see" (Luke 10:23–24). Quite logically, then, Jesus forbade his disciples to practice voluntary fasting, since the time of God's joyful wedding feast with Israel had begun (Mark 2:18–20).

I think, then, that the attempt of the Jesus Seminar to see Jesus simply in terms of a Jewish wisdom teacher or even a wandering Cynic philosopher is wrongheaded. Indeed, even the attempt to play off wisdom against apocalyptic is misplaced. Apocalyptic arose at least partially from a convergence of prophecy and wisdom, and Jewish apocalyptic literature around the turn of the era has a fair amount of wisdom tradition within it — and vice versa. Hence Ben Witherington III, in his book *Jesus the Sage,* can affirm the eschatological and apocalyptic elements of Jesus' teaching and yet prefer to use "sage" as "the most all-encompassing and satisfying term."[15] In the Judaism of Jesus' day, there was no necessary opposition between sage and apocalyptic seer. Nevertheless, instead of Witherington's model of the prophetic sage, I prefer to place the emphasis on Jesus as the miracle-working prophet in the mold of Elijah, a prophet who at the same time was a teacher of wisdom. To explain my reason for this choice, we must move to the next major dividing line, the miracles of Jesus.

4. The Miracles of Jesus

The miracles of Jesus provide a dividing line among scholars in more than one way.[16]

(a) In a more traditional vein, a number of reconstructions of the historical Jesus continue the approach that arose during the Enlightenment, namely, to play down or totally eliminate the miracle-working activity of Jesus as an invention of the early church. The sober application of the criteria of historicity to the various Gospel sources makes this approach untenable today. The criterion of the multiple attestation of sources and forms tells especially against it. Every Gospel source (Mark, Q, the special Matthean material, the special Lucan material, and John), every evangelist in his redactional summaries, and the Jewish historian Josephus in Book 18 of his *Jewish Antiquities* — all affirm the miracle-working activity of Jesus.

Besides multiple attestation of sources, the miracles also enjoy multiple attestation of forms, since both narratives about Jesus and sayings of Jesus, two different literary forms that probably had their separate history of development in the oral tradition, testify independently to Jesus' miracle-working activity. Both narratives and sayings speak of major types of Jesus' miracles, such as exorcism, healing the sick, and raising the dead.

Other criteria, such as coherence, confirm what we see from the criterion of multiple attestation. Now, this is not to say that the criteria prove that Jesus actually worked miracles, that is, deeds of power surpassing all human ability and explainable only by God's direct action. Such an affirmation is theological and made possible only by faith. But the criteria of historicity do allow us to make a historical judgment: Jesus performed extraordinary deeds deemed by himself and others to be miracles that proclaimed and partially realized the coming of God's kingdom.

I stress this affirmation not for its possible apologetic value but because I think it holds the key to a basic understanding of how Jesus saw himself and his mission. In the whole of the Old Testament, there are only three Israelites who are noted for performing a whole series of miracles: Moses, Elijah, and Elisha. Of these three, only Elijah and Elisha were said to have raised the dead. And of these two, only Elijah was expected by many Israelites of Jesus' day to return to usher in the restoration of Israel and the final judgment. It would seem, then, that if Jesus consciously chose to embark upon a prophetic ministry to Israel, a ministry that involved working a whole series of miracles that in turn shored up his eschatological message, then he also consciously chose to present himself to his fellow Israelites as the eschatological prophet clothed in the mantle of Elijah. This is why I feel that Ben Witherington's "Jesus the sage" is not the best "umbrella concept" for summing up the historical Jesus. Rather, Jesus was above all the eschatological prophet in the image of Elijah who, like Elijah, worked miracles. If one does not come to terms with this self-chosen portrait, one does not come to terms with the historical Jesus.

(b) In recent years, the miracles of Jesus have proved to be a major point of disagreement in a different sense. Scholars like Morton Smith and John Dominic Crossan have readily emphasized the miracle tradition as going back to the historical Jesus, but for them this only proves that the proper category for Jesus is that of magician. Any attempt to distinguish Jesus' miracles from the deeds of Hellenistic magicians is pure apologetics.

I would argue to the contrary that, if one examines the miracle stories in the Gospels and the collections of magical papyri from the ancient Roman period, one can detect real differences as well as similarities. In volume 2 of *A Marginal Jew,* I suggested that the best way to express the differences and similarities is to draw up a sliding scale or spectrum of characteristics.[17] At one end of the spectrum would lie the "ideal type" of miracle and at the other end the "ideal type" of magic. In reality, individual cases might lie in between the two ideal types, at different points along the spectrum. I think it possible to list the characteristics that, on the whole, distinguish the ideal type of miracle from the ideal type of magic. In my opinion, many of the Gospel miracles tend toward the ideal type of miracle, while most of the Greco-Roman magical papyri tend toward the ideal type of magic.

There are, in my view, seven basic characteristics of the ideal type of miracle in the way in which miracle stories are usually, though not always, depicted in the Gospels.

(i) The usual, overarching context for a religious miracle is that of an interpersonal relationship of faith, trust, or love between a human being and the Deity (or the Deity's representative).

(ii) More specifically in the Gospels, the person in need often seizes the initiative by asking Jesus for a miracle, and this in itself is a tacit expression of faith. Alternately, especially in the Gospel of John, Jesus seizes the initiative and performs a miracle to foster faith. In either case, the overall context in the Gospels is the birth and growth of faith in Jesus.

(iii) Jesus usually grants the miracle with a terse but intelligible set of words spoken in his own language. At times the words are accompanied by a symbolic gesture, at times not. In a few cases there is a gesture and no words. In any case, there are no lengthy incantations or endless lists of esoteric divine names or unintelligible words, charms, or recipes.

(iv) There is no idea that a petitioner can use coercive power to force the miracle worker to perform a miracle against his will. Nor does the miracle worker try to coerce the Deity.

(v) Specifically, Jesus' miracles take place within the context of Jesus' obedience to his Father's will. The overarching context is the prayer of Jesus in Gethsemane: "Not my will but yours be done."

(vi) Jesus' miracles stand in an eschatological and communitarian context. That is to say, they are not just isolated acts of kindness done for isolated individuals. Jesus' miracles are signs and partial realizations of the kingdom of God, the God who comes in power to save his people Israel in the last days through Jesus' ministry.

(vii) Jesus' miracles do not directly punish or hurt anyone. This trait forms a stark contrast with some of the magical papyri, which include spells for causing sickness or getting rid of one's enemies.

At the other end of the spectrum of religious experience, the ideal type of magic, as reflected in the Greco-Roman magical papyri, is practically the reverse mirror image of the ideal type of miracle. Let me simply highlight the most important characteristics of the ideal type of magic:

(i) Magic is the technical manipulation of various (often impersonal) forces or the coercion of a deity to obtain a desired concrete benefit.

(ii) The benefits sought in magic are often surprisingly petty and often obtainable by human means, such as winning a horse race or winning a lover away from a rival.

(iii) The Hellenistic magician does not usually operate with a fairly stable circle of disciples or believers. Between the magician and the individual who consults him, there are no lasting bonds that make them members of some community. The magician has a clientele, not a church.

(iv) Especially important for magic is the secret magical spell, often made up of a string of esoteric divine names and nonsense syllables. The secret spell, known only to the practitioner, is of the essence of Greco-Roman magic. The magician keeps repeating all the secret names and sounds until he hits the right button and gets the desired effect. Efficacy was all that mattered. In a sense, magic was a kind of ancient technology; and so anyone who learned the secrets of the technique could perform the magic. Thus, magic was of its nature a learnable technique, provided one discovered the secret. One simply had to learn the right string of nonsense syllables and esoteric names. The terse, intelligible commands of Jesus, sometimes spoken before an audience, stand in stark contrast.

Admittedly, the two ideal types I have just described are two extremes. There are gray areas in both the Gospels and the Greek magical papyri. For instance, in the Gospel of Mark the story of the hemorrhaging woman who is cured simply by touching Jesus' cloak (Mark 5:24–34) looks very much like magic. And some magical papyri have elements of prayer and personal devotion. But on the whole, the Gospels move in the direction of the ideal type of miracle, while the papyri move in the direction of the ideal type of magic. Hence, I do not agree with Smith or Crossan in identifying miracles with magic and in labeling Jesus a Jewish magician. "Miracle worker" is the more correct label, and that is not just apologetics. It contributes to a more adequate classification of Jesus, namely, a miracle-working eschatological prophet wearing the mantle of Elijah. This is a description that is more specific and fits more closely into Jesus' immediate Jewish context in first-century Palestine.

5. Jesus as Messiah?

Raising the question of an adequate classification of the historical Jesus within the Judaism of his time brings us to our fifth point of disagreement: Is there any indication that the historical Jesus presented himself as in some sense *the* Messiah or *a* messiah? Or is there any indication that he was thought to be *a* or *the* Messiah by his followers during his lifetime? Was he in particular thought to be the Davidic Messiah?

These questions are too vast and complex to answer in detail here, but I would offer a few reasons for holding open the possibility that Jesus was thought by some to be the Davidic Messiah even during his lifetime.

(a) Numerous and varied streams of New Testament tradition affirm Jesus' Davidic lineage or Davidic sonship, including the very early pre-Pauline creedal formula in Romans 1:3–4, another creedal formula in 2 Timothy 2:8, and narratives and sayings found in Mark, Matthew, Luke, and Acts, as well as affirmations in the Book of Revelation and probably the Epistle to the Hebrews.[18] This is a remarkably wide sweep for a relatively minor point. Moreover, it seems that, among early Christians, Jesus' Davidic Messiahship was first proclaimed in order to interpret his resurrection as a royal enthronement, fulfilling Nathan's prophecy to David in 2 Samuel 7:12–14: "I will raise up your seed after you . . . he shall be my son."[19]

Now there is nothing in the Old Testament or in first-century Jewish thought that would have automatically tied belief in the resurrection of some individual within ongoing history to a belief in him as the Davidic Messiah. Nor can one explain the early Christian belief in Jesus' Davidic Messiahship simply by appealing to Jesus' crucifixion owing to the accusation he claimed to be king of the Jews. At the turn of the era, Jews had known a number of kings, both Hasmonean and Herodian, but none Davidic. In the first century B.C.E. or C.E., being king of the Jews was not necessarily connected with being a son of David. Then, too, even if some of Jesus' disciples believed during his public ministry that he was the Messiah, the term "messiah" was open to so many different interpretations at the turn of the era that the disciples' belief would not automatically define Jesus as the Davidic Messiah.[20] In short, that the earliest Christians defined the crucified and risen Jesus as the Davidic Messiah seems bereft of sufficient motivation — *unless* some of his disciples during his earthly life had already accepted a popular belief that he was of Davidic stock. In that case, they would have formed the idea that he was the Davidic Messiah at least partly because of his supposed lineage.

(b) That Jesus' own actions may have fostered such an idea among his followers receives support from the two key symbolic actions he performed as he entered the capital city of Jerusalem at the beginning of the last week of his life. Both actions have undergone massive reinterpretation by the Christian tradition, but a historical core is recoverable in both cases. As Jesus led his disciples up to the "City of David" for the feast of Passover, he consciously chose to perform the provocative action of riding into the capital on a donkey while his disciples acclaimed him — a staged demonstration that would likely have conjured up Zechariah's prophecy of the triumphant yet humble king who comes to Jerusalem riding on a donkey (Zech. 9:9; cf. 1 Kings 1:32–40).[21] One need not think of a Hollywood-scale spectacle; Jesus would probably have staged the prophetic action primarily for the benefit of his own disciples. Jesus then proceeded to act out his authority over the supreme locus of the Jewish religion, the Jerusalem temple, in the so-called cleansing, which may actually have been a prophetic action symbolizing the temple's imminent destruction.[22]

I think there are good arguments for the historicity of both prophetic signs. In brief: Both the triumphant entry and the cleansing of the temple are supported by the criterion of multiple attestation (they appear in quite different presentations in both Mark and John).[23] Moreover, both actions fit neatly into another criterion of historicity, namely, the ultimate explanation of Jesus' crucifixion by the Romans on a political charge. Indeed, without these actions we are hard pressed to explain why Jesus' execution happened exactly when it did and for the precise reason it did ("king of the Jews"). After all, as John's Gospel indicates, Jesus regularly went up to Jerusalem for the great feasts. Why was he arrested and executed this time, at *this* particular feast? The answer may sound strange; but in a sense, Jesus triggered his own tragedy — at least partly by public actions that implied a claim to royal authority over Jerusalem and its temple.

(c) Another kind of action by Jesus during the public ministry may also have fostered his disciples' belief that he was the Son of David, though in a somewhat different sense. Curiously, we find Jesus connected with the title Son of David in the story of the healing of the blind Bartimaeus (Mark 10:47–48) and in allied stories. Now, neither David nor the Davidic Messiah was connected in first-century Jewish thought with such miraculous acts. However, around the time of Jesus, King Solomon, the literal "son of David," was esteemed by many Jews as the exorcist and miracle-worker par excellence. The "Solomon connection" might help explain why Bartimaeus could address Jesus alternately as "Son of David" and "Rabbouni" (teacher). Solomon the Son of David was seen by first-century Jews as both a miracle worker and a wisdom teacher, and so was Jesus the Son of David. It may well be, then, that the exorcising and healing activity of Jesus, joined to the popular belief that he was of Davidic lineage, helped generate the idea among his disciples that he was in one sense or another the Davidic Messiah.[24]

(d) Finally, we might remind ourselves that, if the disciples during the public ministry began to connect Jesus with hopes of a Davidic Messiah, they were not plucking a category out of thin air or retrieving it from the deep freeze. As we can see from Jewish pseudepigrapha and the Qumran documents, the category of Davidic Messiah was alive and well around the time of Jesus. To be sure, as John J. Collins has recently shown, a number of different "models of Messiah" were available to Jews around the turn of the era. The messianic options included a priest-teacher, a prophet-teacher, a "Son of God," and a heavenly being.[25] Yet, Collins maintains that the most common messianic image circulating in Palestine at the time of Jesus was that of the royal Davidic Messiah. Thus, in identifying Jesus as the Davidic Messiah, his disciples, far from engaging in esoteric or unheard-of speculation, may have been reflecting the most pervasive messianic hope of their time.

I would stress that none of these observations proves that the historical Jesus was thought to be the Davidic Messiah by some of his followers during his lifetime. For now, I would be content to have shown that the question should not be dismissed as quickly as some contemporary American questers do.

6. Institutional Elements from the Historical Jesus?

A final line of division between myself and many present-day questers is the nature of Jesus' "charismatic" ministry vis-à-vis what might be described as the emerging institutional elements of the early church. Few would deny that Jesus qualified as a "charismatic" in the sense that he was a powerful personality who derived his authority over an enthusiastic public not from law, tradition, ordination, or any institutional conduit of society but rather from what he claimed was a special, direct relationship to God, manifested in extraordinary words and deeds.[26] What would be very much disputed, though, is whether Jesus' "charismatic" activity paradoxically contained within itself incipient "institutional elements" that were later taken over and developed by the early church. For many questers of the historical Jesus, the very thought of institutional elements proceeding from a charismatic Jesus would be a contradiction in terms, whether they think of Jesus as an anti-establishment Cynic philosopher or as an eschatological prophet announcing the end of Israel's history.

Yet, I would maintain that the neat dichotomy of charismatic versus institutional breaks down before the complex reality of Jesus' ministry, the group(s) he gathered around himself during his lifetime, and the impact that the "Jesus movement," which arose during his ministry, had after his death. Some of the things Jesus said to his disciples and did with his disciples contained within themselves the "seeds" or hints of institutional organization or practice, and many of these "seeds" did in fact "blossom" into institutional elements in the early church. All this may seem paradoxical to us because we too quickly think of eschatological or apocalyptic hopes as necessarily opposed to organized institutions. Nevertheless, the clearest example we have of a Jewish eschatological group around the time of Jesus, namely, the Qumran community, united fiery eschatological hopes with a highly organized hierarchy that was supposed to reach perfection when the final war against evil was won.

Hence, far from rejecting a priori the possibility of incipient institutional elements in Jesus' words and deeds, we should examine the evidence with an open mind. In my opinion, there are a number of things the historical Jesus said and did that tended towards creating a distinct group within Judaism, a group that had its own boundary markers and identity. To list only the most obvious examples:

(a) Multiple attestation of sources indicates that Jesus did create an inner group of disciples. They were exactly twelve in number, with Peter as their shaky leader and Judas Iscariot as their most infamous member.[27] The choice of the number twelve was hardly accidental. Jesus the eschatological, Elijah-like prophet saw at least part of his mission to be the regathering, healing, and purifying of the Israel of the last days. The inner circle of the twelve apparently symbolized the twelve patriarchs or tribes of ancient Israel and were to constitute the core of the Israel of the end time. Intriguingly, Jesus did not count himself as part of this symbolic group of twelve, but rather stood over against it as its creator and teacher.

(b) The circle of the twelve not only spent a great deal of time with Jesus as his quasi-permanent audience; multiple attestation of sources indicates that Jesus also sent the twelve, symbolic of end-time Israel, on a short-term mission to the empirical Israel of his day (Mark 6:6–13; Luke 9:1–6; 10:1–12; cf. Matt. 19:28; Luke 22:30). They thus extended to a wider audience the heralding of the kingdom, the healing of the sick, and the exorcising of the possessed that Jesus himself had undertaken. Hence, for a short time during his public ministry, the twelve shared in Jesus' eschatological ministry to Israel.

(c) No doubt, one of the most influential religious experiences the adult Jesus ever had was his baptism at the hands of John the Baptist. We should not be surprised, therefore, that the Fourth Gospel affirms a number of times that in his own ministry Jesus continued John the Baptist's practice of baptism, even though this created some friction with the Baptist's disciples, to whom Jesus may have once belonged (John 3:22, 26; 4:1). John's practice of baptism was taken over by Jesus just as Jesus' practice of baptism was taken over later by the early church — each time, no doubt, with a notable change in the ritual's meaning.[28]

(d) Baptism was probably not the only concrete, visible practice that marked off Jesus' disciples from most of his fellow Jews. Jesus gave his disciples their own form of prayer — what we call the Lord's Prayer (Luke 11:2–4; Matt. 6:9–13) — and made them stand out among pious Jewish groups of the day by forbidding them to practice fasting (Mark 2:18–20 and parallels).[29] By creating a special form of prayer and praxis for a group he had baptized and was continuing to instruct, Jesus was marking off his disciples as a distinct, discernible religious group within first-century Palestinian Judaism.

(e) Finally, multiple attestation of sources also indicates that Jesus arranged a solemn, final meal with his disciples, complete with prophetic, symbolic words over bread and wine that probably pointed forward to his death (1 Cor. 11:23–26; Mark 14:22–25 and parallels). What, if anything, Jesus expected his disciples to make of this symbolic meal after his death we cannot say. The words "Do this in memory of me" are most likely a Christian cultic addition to Jesus' words over the bread and wine. But simply as a matter of historical fact, Jesus' symbolic words and gestures at the last supper on the night before he died constituted a major source of the Christian Eucharist, a practice we can trace back to the earliest days of the church.[30]

I wish to emphasize that none of these observations aims at denying the deep chasm that lies between Good Friday and Easter Sunday, indeed, the deep chasm that lies between any historian's attempt to reconstruct the historical Jesus and the Christian believer's affirmation that Jesus is risen from the dead as Lord and Savior. Nevertheless, by the same token, any fair-minded historian cannot deny the empirical, historical links that connected a group of Jews for Jesus before Easter with a group of Jews for the risen Lord Jesus after Easter. Disciples who were prominent in the first group, such as Peter and John, became prominent leaders of the second group. From a psychological and sociological point of view, the surprising thing would have been for them not to have carried over some elements of their prayers, practices, and beliefs from one stage of their religious journey to the next.

A Portrait of the Historical Jesus

This concludes our experiment in dialectical negation. The Jesus that results from this process is a complicated combination of a number of different religious types that, theoretically, we would have expected to stay separate in first-century Judaism — but then, Jesus was a rather complicated Jew. What remains to be done is to reduce all the complexity and negativity to a brief, positive sketch of the historical Jesus.

Baptized by John the Baptist around the year 28 C.E., Jesus of Nazareth soon set out on his own ministry to Israel.[31] He presented himself to his people as an eschatological prophet proclaiming the imminent coming of God's definitive rule over Israel, a rule that Jesus had already made palpably present by performing startling deeds of healing reminiscent of the miracles performed by Elijah the prophet. Perhaps equally startling to stringently observant Jews was Jesus' outreach to the religiously and socially marginalized, even to the point of eating with them as a sign that they, too, would be included in the final banquet in the kingdom. Jesus the prophet proclaimed and actualized the kingdom's coming in word as well as deed, most notably in his enigmatic parables, which often challenged the presumed orderly religious world of his hearers and thus opened them to the new world he was heralding. In both his miracle working and his wisdom teaching, Jesus might have been seen as a Solomonic Son of David as well as an Elijah-like prophet of the end time.

Still, for all his fame as a spinner of parables, Jesus the Jewish teacher did not deal just in riddles. He also engaged in straightforward discussion of the proper observance of the Mosaic Torah, sometimes proposing disconcerting changes in its observance — for example, in the matter of divorce. As the end-time prophet wearing the mantle of Elijah, he also began the formation of the end-time Israel, creating the inner group of the Twelve, sending them out on mission to their fellow Israelites, and inculcating various forms of prayer and practice (e.g., the rejection of fasting) that marked out his followers as a special group. Perhaps through a combination of popular belief in his Davidic lineage and his activity of healing and teaching, suggesting a Solomonic Son of David, some of his followers began to identify him with the hoped-for Davidic Messiah. The kingdom of God was to have a visible king.

Jesus brought such hopes to a high point on his last visit to Jerusalem with his two symbolic-prophetic actions, namely, the triumphant entry and the "cleansing" of the temple. Sensing that his clashes with the Jerusalem authorities were reaching a deadly climax and that he might suffer the martyrdom attributed in Jewish thought to a number of the Old Testament prophets, he arranged a final solemn meal with his disciples on a Thursday evening, as the 14th of Nisan began, probably in the year 30 C.E. During this last supper — indeed, the last in a whole series of suppers symbolizing the coming salvation of the kingdom — he used bread and wine as prophetic symbols of his imminent death, a death he accepted as part of God's inscrutable plan to establish his kingdom, a kingdom Jesus still hoped to share. Later on that Thursday night, Jesus was betrayed by Judas, arrested in Gethsemane, denied by Peter, interrogated by the temple authorities, and then handed over to the Roman prefect Pontius Pilate, who had him scourged and crucified on Friday, the 14th of Nisan. He died before sundown and was quickly buried with the help of one Joseph of Arimathea and the assistance of some of his women followers.

With that, one must end a sketch of the historical Jesus — not because Jesus' resurrection is not real, but rather (1) because his resurrection, properly speaking, is not subject to direct historical-empirical investigation[32] and (2) because the experience of resurrection appearances by his disciples and the proclamation thereof properly belong to the faith, theology, and history of the early church rather than to the quest of the historical Jesus. The quest of the historical Jesus is difficult enough as it is; and needless to say, this essay has not spoken the last word. All I can hope is that, through a negative process, it has spoken a positive word to the reader.

NOTES

1. See, e.g., E. P. Sanders et al., eds., *Jewish and Christian Self-Definition,* 3 vols. (Philadelphia: Fortress, 1980–82).

2. For general overviews of aspects of the "third quest," see Ben Witherington III, *The Jesus Quest: The Third Search for the Jew of Nazareth* (Downers Grove, Ill.: InterVarsity, 1995); Luke Timothy Johnson, *The Real Jesus* (San Francisco: Harper, 1996). Both works are highly critical of the Jesus Seminar.

3. For basic statements of the opposing positions, see John P. Meier, *A Marginal Jew: Rethinking the Historical Jesus,* 2 vols., ABRL (New York: Doubleday, 1991, 1994); Robert W. Funk, Roy W. Hoover et al., *The Five Gospels: The Search for the Authentic Words of Jesus* (New York: Macmillan, 1993).

4. Richard Bauckham, "The Brothers and Sisters of Jesus: An Epiphanian Response to John P. Meier," *CBQ* 56 (1994): 686–700. I shall be replying to his article in a future issue of the *CBQ*.

5. John Dominic Crossan, *The Cross That Spoke: The Origins of the Passion Narrative* (San Francisco: Harper & Row, 1988).

6. See Meier, *A Marginal Jew,* 116–18.

7. For these and other arguments against the independence of the *Gospel of Thomas,* see Wolfgang Schrage, *Das Verhältnis des Thomas-Evangeliums zur synoptischen Tradition und zu den koptischen Evangelienübersetzungen,* BZNW 29 (Berlin: Töpelmann, 1964); Boudewijn Dehandschutter, "L'évangile de Thomas comme collection de paroles de Jésus," *Logia — Les Paroles de Jésus — The Sayings of Jesus,* BETL 59 (Leuven: Peeters/Leuven University Press, 1982), 507–15; Craig L. Blomberg, "Tradition and Redaction in the Parables of the Gospel of Thomas," *Gospel Perspectives: The Jesus Tradition outside the Gospels* (Sheffield: JSOT, 1984), 5:177–205; Christopher Tuckett, "Thomas and the Synoptics," *NovT* 30 (1988): 132–57; Jean-Marie Sevrin, "Un groupement de trois paraboles contre les richesses dans l'Evangile selon Thomas. *EvTh* 63, 64, 65," *Les paraboles évangéliques: Perspectives nouvelles* (Paris: Cerf, 1989), 425–39; Michael Fieger, *Das Thomasevangelium,* NTAbh 22 (Münster: Aschendorff, 1991); also Meier, *A Marginal Jew,* 1:123–39.

8. For a sampling, see Ivan Havener, *Q: The Sayings of Jesus,* GNS 19 (Wilmington: Glazier, 1987); John S. Kloppenborg, *The Formation of Q: Trajectories in Ancient Wisdom Collections* (Philadelphia: Fortress, 1987); Migaku Sato, *Q und Prophetie: Studien zur Gattungs und Traditionsgeschichte der Quelle Q,* WUNT 2/29 (Tübingen: Mohr [Siebeck], 1988); John S. Kloppenborg with Leif E. Vaage, eds., *Early Christianity, Q, and Jesus, Semeia* 55 (Atlanta: Scholars Press, 1992); David Catchpole, *The Quest for Q* (Edinburgh: T. & T.

Clark, 1993); Burton L. Mack, *The Lost Gospel: The Book of Q and Christian Origins* (San Francisco: Harper, 1993).

9. See, e.g., Dieter Lührmann, *Die Redaktion der Logienquelle,* WMANT 33 (Neukirchen-Vluyn: Neukirchener Verlag, 1969); Siegfried Schulz, *Q: Die Spruchquelle der Evangelisten* (Zürich: Theologischer Verlag, 1972); Paul Hoffmann, *Studien zur Theologie der Logienquelle,* 2d ed., NTAbh 8 (Münster: Aschendorff, 1975); Athanasius Polag, *Die Christologie der Logienquelle,* WMANT 45 (Neukirchen-Vluyn: Neukirchener Verlag, 1977).

10. Among the many that might be mentioned: A. M. Farrer, Joachim Jeremias, Hans-Theo Wrege, G. Schille, and M. D. Goulder.

11. See Sato, *Q und Prophetie,* 62–68.

12. E.g., John Dominic Crossan, *The Historical Jesus: The Life of a Mediterranean Jewish Peasant* (San Francisco: Harper, 1991), 227–353.

13. E. P. Sanders, *Jesus and Judaism* (Philadelphia: Fortress, 1985), 123–56.

14. Meier, *A Marginal Jew,* 2:289–506. I refer the reader to these pages for detailed arguments defending the authenticity of the sayings listed above.

15. Ben Witherington III, *Jesus the Sage: The Pilgrimage of Wisdom* (Minneapolis: Fortress, 1994), 201.

16. See Meier, *A Marginal Jew,* 2:509–645. For a sampling of various approaches to Jesus' miracles, see Gerd Theissen, *The Miracle Stories of the Early Christian Tradition* (Philadelphia: Fortress, 1983; German original 1974); Morton Smith, *Jesus the Magician* (San Francisco: Harper & Row, 1978); David E. Aune, "Magic in Early Christianity," *Aufstieg und Niedergang der römischen Welt* (New York: de Gruyter, 1980), 1507–57; René Latourelle, *The Miracles of Jesus and the Theology of Miracles* (Mahwah, N.J.: Paulist, 1988); Graham H. Twelftree, *Jesus the Exorcist,* WUNT 2/54 (Tübingen: Mohr [Siebeck], 1993); Werner Kahl, *New Testament Miracle Stories in their Religious-Historical Setting,* FRLANT 163 (Göttingen: Vandenhoeck & Ruprecht, 1994); Craig A. Evans, "Jesus and Jewish Miracle Stories," *Jesus and His Contemporaries: Comparative Studies,* AGJU 25 (Leiden: Brill, 1995), 213–50.

17. Meier, *A Marginal Jew,* 2:535–75.

18. On this, see Meier, *A Marginal Jew,* 1:216–19; for a different view, see Christoph Burger, *Jesus als Davidssohn,* FRLANT 98 (Göttingen: Vandenhoeck & Ruprecht, 1970).

19. See Dennis C. Duling, "The Promises to David and Their Entrance into Christianity—Nailing Down a Likely Hypothesis," *NTS* 20 (1973–74): 55–77.

20. See the various essays in James H. Charlesworth, ed., *The Messiah: Developments in Earliest Judaism and Christianity* (Minneapolis: Fortress, 1992).

21. For the basic historicity of the "triumphal entry" into Jerusalem see Rudolf Pesch, *Das Markusevangelium. II. Teil,* HTKNT II/2 (Freiburg: Herder, 1977), 187–88; Sanders, *Jesus and Judaism,* 306–8 (who considers the historicity of the event probable, but not certain); Joachim Gnilka, *Jesus von Nazaret: Botschaft und Geschichte,* HTKNT Supplementband 3 (Freiburg: Herder, 1990), 273–76. While John J. Collins (*The Scepter and the Star: The Messiahs of the Dead Sea Scrolls and Other Ancient Literature,* ABRL [New York: Doubleday, 1995], 206) acknowledges that the historicity of the event is questionable, he seems to lean toward accepting it as historical. Replying to the

objection that the incident fits the "biblical paradigm" of Zech. 9:9 and therefore might be dismissed as a Christian creation, Collins remarks: "Yet we have seen that the reenactment of biblical paradigms was typical of eschatological prophets, and the incident fits perfectly with Jesus' execution as King of the Jews." Other texts that might have been recalled (either by the original disciples or by the evangelists) include 2 Kings 9:12–13; 1 Macc. 13:51.

22. Sanders, *Jesus and Judaism,* 61–90. For a spirited defense that the "cleansing" was just that, a protest-in-action against what was popularly perceived to be corruption among temple authorities, see Craig A. Evans, "Jesus' Action in the Temple and Evidence of Corruption in the First-Century Temple," *Jesus and His Contemporaries,* Comparative Studies, AGJU 25 (Leiden: Brill, 1995), 319–44. Actually, one interpretation does not logically exclude the other, and both authors argue strenuously for accepting the temple action as historical. In my view, it is not the temple action taken by itself but rather the temple action as performed by an eschatological prophet who is believed by his disciples to be the Son of David and who has just "engineered" a triumphal entry into the Davidic capital that casts the cleansing of the temple in a messianic light.

23. The attempt of David R. Catchpole ("The 'Triumphal' Entry," in *Jesus and the Politics of His Day* [Cambridge: Cambridge University Press, 1984], 319–34) to deny the historicity of the triumphal entry depends to a great degree on Catchpole's denial of an independent tradition in John (321–22). If, with most commentators who have written full-scale commentaries on John in the twentieth century (see, e.g., the treatment in Raymond E. Brown, *The Gospel according to John* (i–xii), AB 29 [Garden City, N.Y.: Doubleday, 1966], 459–61), we hold that John's account goes back to an independent tradition, Catchpole's whole approach is called into question.

24. On all this, see Meier, *A Marginal Jew,* 2:686–90; Dennis C. Duling, "The Eleazar Miracle and Solomon's Magical Wisdom in Flavius Josephus's *Antiquitates Judaicae* 8.42–49," *HTR* 78 (1985): 1–25.

25. Collins, *The Scepter and the Star,* 102–94.

26. Often cited on this question is Martin Hengel, *The Charismatic Leader and His Followers* (New York: Crossroad, 1981; German original, 1968). Yet the whole concept of the "charismatic" is a much disputed one in the sociology of religion. For a critique of Max Weber's groundbreaking work and a careful discussion of how charismatic authority gradually becomes institutionalized, see Bengt Holmberg, *Paul and Power* (Philadelphia: Fortress, 1978), 161–92. Holmberg (174) stresses that, even according to Weber, "charisma is not a type of individual psychological equipment but a social phenomenon, viz., a group of followers attributing charismatic endowment to their leader. Charisma does not exist without a charismatic community, and consequently charisma as a social phenomenon does not exist except in a routinized form!"

27. Sanders, *Jesus and Judaism,* 95–106.

28. For arguments in favor of these claims, see Meier, *A Marginal Jew,* 2: 120–30.

29. For the authenticity of the core of the Lord's Prayer and of Jesus' prohibition of fasting, see Meier, *A Marginal Jew,* 2:291–302, 439–50.

30. See Joachim Jeremias, *The Eucharistic Words of Jesus,* NTL (London:

SCM, 1966); Heinz Schürmann, *Jesu ureigener Tod, Exegetische Besinnungen und Ausblick* (Freiburg: Herder, 1975), 66–96; Helmut Merklein, "Erwägungen zur Überlieferungsgeschichte der neutestamentlichen Abendmahlstraditionen," *BZ* 21 (1977): 88–101, 235–44; Rudolf Pesch, *Das Abendmahl und Jesu Todesverständnis,* QD 80 (Freiburg: Herder, 1978), 69–102; Xavier Léon-Dufour, *Sharing the Eucharistic Bread: The Witness of the New Testament* (Mahwah, N.J.: Paulist, 1987), 157–79; Gnilka, *Jesus von Nazaret,* 280–89.

31. For the justification of the chronology I use, see Meier, *A Marginal Jew,* 1:372–433.

32. On this see Gerald O'Collins, "Is the Resurrection an 'Historical' Event?" *HeyJ* 8 (1967): 381–87.

– 23 –

"I Believe . . . in Jesus Christ, His Only Son, Our Lord"

THE EARTHLY JESUS AND THE CHRIST OF FAITH

John P. Galvin

Christians recognize that the earthly Jesus can never be captured fully by historical scholarship. They recognize as well that Christian faith is not based on historical reconstructions. These recognitions notwithstanding, Christians insist that some elements of Jesus' life, which are open to historical research, are of central concern to Christian faith.

DURING THE PAST DECADE, scholarly and popular interest in the historical figure of Jesus of Nazareth has intensified greatly, especially in North America. Numerous studies, varying widely in religious perspective, evaluation of sources, argumentative rigor, and internal consistency, have sought to present an account of Jesus' life on the basis of modern historical methodology.[1] Recent literature has burgeoned to such an extent that some commentators now speak of a third quest of the historical Jesus as a contemporary sequel to the original quest of the eighteenth and nineteenth centuries[2] and the new quest inaugurated in 1953 by a seminal address of Ernst Käsemann to fellow students of Rudolf Bultmann.[3] In addition to diverging significantly among themselves in their overall portrayals of Jesus of Nazareth, contributors to the third quest also differ in assessing the relationship of their historical reconstructions to classical Christian professions of faith in Jesus Christ.

It has long been clear that few have studied Jesus of Nazareth solely out of detached scholarly interest in a prominent figure of the past. On the one hand, declared foes of Christianity, opposed to Christian faith as such or at least to its traditional christological affirmations, have sought to retrieve the historical Jesus as a tool to be used to undermine Christian faith or to replace its confession of Jesus Christ as risen Lord and Son of God with the memory of a purely human political revolutionary or ethical teacher. The classical instance of the first model is Hermann Samuel Reimarus (1694–1768), a deist who envisioned Jesus as a failed nationalistic messiah whose disciples stole his body after his crucifixion, drastically altered his message, and successfully disseminated falsehoods about his resurrection and ascension;[4] the numerous liberal Protestant practitioners of the nineteenth-century quest who sought, in the words of Albert Schweitzer, to find "the Jesus of history as an ally in the struggle against the tyranny of dogma"[5] are cases in point for the second. On the other hand, such prominent Christian theologians as Eberhard Jüngel, Wolfhart Pannenberg, Karl Rahner, and Edward Schillebeeckx have attributed to the historical study of Jesus a considerable role in their presentations of systematic christology.

While obviously differing in religious beliefs and historical judgments, all these authors share the common conviction that faith in Jesus Christ is intimately connected with the factual events of his life. This conviction is not universal: Rudolf Bultmann, for example, held that Christian faith need concern itself only with the fact of Jesus' existence, not with further details of his life,[6] and Schubert Ogden has more recently argued that Christian faith relates to the "existential-historical Jesus," or Jesus as known through the earliest apostolic witness, not "the so-called historical Jesus."[7] But most authors who investigate the historical Jesus judge that some empirical information about him is, in one way or another, of foundational religious and theological significance. The widespread public interest in such questions, while in part artificially stimulated, reflects a similar presumption on the part of many Christians that the issues under discussion are directly relevant to their religious convictions.

Viewed from the christological perspective suggested by these observations, recent research on the historical Jesus may conveniently be classified into three categories. First, there are authors such as Paul Hollenbach, Burton Mack, and Thomas Sheehan who with varying nuances in detail seek to supplant Christian faith with an alternative conception of who Jesus was. To take but one example, Hollenbach identifies the purpose of research on the historical Jesus as "to overthrow (not just to avoid or to correct) the 'mistake called Christianity,' " an error which "is summed up in the divinization of Jesus as Son of David, Christ, Son of God, Second Person in the Trinity, etc."[8] Here the historical Jesus and the Christ of faith are viewed as antithetical: The faith professed by Christians has no basis in Jesus' actual life. The Christ of faith corresponds to no reality outside the mind of believers, but is rather the figment of deliberate misinterpretation or imaginative flights of fancy on the part of Christians. The accuracy of the historical scholarship of these authors must of course be evaluated on historical grounds, not simply dismissed, but it is clear that their positions are (as they themselves explicitly declare) not compatible with Christian faith.

Second, there are portrayals of the historical Jesus whose content seems irreconcilable with Christian belief, but whose authors nonetheless incorporate professions of faith into their presentations. The writings of John Dominic Crossan are an instance of this type. Crossan portrays Jesus as "a peasant Jewish Cynic," "neither broker nor mediator," but the proclaimer of "the brokerless kingdom of God" in a manner that seems to preclude in principle any mediation of that kingdom and thus any foundation for christological doctrine. Yet Crossan also maintains "that at the heart of any Christianity there is always, covertly or overtly, a dialectic between a historically read Jesus and a theologically read Christ"; he finds "no contradiction between the historical Jesus and the defined Christ, no betrayal whatsoever in the move from Jesus to Christ" because Christians see Jesus as "the unmediated presence of the divine to the human."[9] The internal coherence of this reasoning is open to question but, on the level of explicit affirmation, a distinction exists between Crossan's position and those grouped in the first category.

Third, there are exegetes such as John Meier and Joachim Gnilka who methodologically prescind from faith in their historical research and argumentation but who depict the historical Jesus in a manner open to traditional christological affirmations.[10] Their portrayals of Jesus do not entail Christian faith as a logically necessary consequence of their historical reconstructions — after all, the incommensurability of faith and history, classically expressed in the Pauline dictum that "no one can say, 'Jesus is Lord' except by the Holy Spirit" (1 Cor. 12:3), rules out envisioning faith as an inescapable consequence of historical knowledge. But they do offer an account of Jesus which is compatible with Christian affirmations and which enables Christian faith to be seen as a plausible, though not rationally compelling, interpretation of Jesus and of the events of his public life.

Among other matters, this literature raises forcefully theological questions concerning the relationship of the Jesus of history to the Christ of faith. Are the actual events of Jesus' life important to Christians, or is Christian faith totally oriented toward the resurrection? Is contemporary historical research regarding Jesus of any religious and theological significance to believing Christians? Before pursuing such issues further, it will be helpful to note divergent Christian positions on these topics and to introduce some basic terminological distinctions.

Divergent Christian Positions

Clear examples of alternative assessments of the relationship of the earthly Jesus to the risen Lord may be found — in varying terminology — in writings of Karl Barth and Pope John Paul II. While both authors write in opposition to attempts to replace the Christ of faith with an alternative reconstruction of the historical Jesus, their approaches to the issues reflect different christological conceptions.

(a) Early in the second edition of his commentary on Paul's Epistle to the Romans, Karl Barth comments on Romans 1:4, a text which refers to Jesus Christ as "designated Son of God in power according to the Spirit of holiness by his resurrection from the dead." Barth observes: "This is the significance of Jesus: the installation of the Son of man as *Son of God.* What he is apart from this installation is as important and as unimportant as everything temporal, material, and human can be. 'Even if we have known Christ according to the flesh, we know him that way no longer.' Because he *was,* he *is*; but because he *is,* what he *was* lies behind him."[11] Here the alternative presented by nineteenth-century liberal Protestant research — historical Jesus or Christ of faith — is accepted as a formulation of the issue; Barth's difference from his adversaries lies in his option for the Christ of faith as opposed to theirs for the historical Jesus. It is consistent with this orientation that Barth evinces little interest in the historical study of Jesus' life, and even welcomes what he sees as the meagerness of the results of such research as undercutting what might otherwise provide a temptation to base faith on false foundations.[12]

(b) A different approach to these issues is reflected in brief remarks of Pope John Paul II in "Redemptoris Missio," his encyclical letter on the church's missionary task. In an introductory section on "Jesus Christ, the Only Savior," the pope insists that "the Christ is none other than Jesus of Nazareth" and maintains that "it is not permissible to separate Jesus from the Christ or to speak of the 'historical Jesus' as if he were someone other than the Christ of faith."[13] While these statements do not preclude all distinction between the earthly Jesus and the risen Lord, they strongly accent continuity in the personal identity of Jesus Christ before and after his crucifixion. Formulation of the issue as a choice between the historical Jesus and the risen Christ is rejected as a matter of principle.

These examples represent alternative responses to objections to the Christ of faith in the name of the historical Jesus. Before pursuing the underlying issues, it will be helpful to weigh some ambiguities in the prevalent formulation of the question.

Terminological Distinctions

Reflection on the relationship of the historical Jesus to the Christ of faith is often impeded by ambiguities inherent in the terminology. These difficulties affect not only discussion of the historical Jesus but also references to the Christ of faith.

The one word "history" is commonly used in everyday speech to refer both to actual events of the past and to the academic discipline which studies those events. Drawing on these different meanings, the term "historical Jesus" can be and is used to refer both to Jesus in the period from his birth to his death and to Jesus insofar as he can be reached by the methods of modern historical scholarship. Both usages are in principle legitimate, but confusion results if authors shift abruptly from one meaning to the other. This is especially true when the content of Christian faith is under discussion, for it is one thing to state that faith depends on the events of Jesus' life and another to claim that faith depends on a modern historical reconstruction.

In an effort to keep matters clear, I shall for the remainder of this essay use "earthly Jesus" to refer to the reality of Jesus' life up to and including his crucifixion, and "historical Jesus" to designate information about Jesus (whether isolated pieces of data or a more comprehensive reconstruction) presented by modern authors. In referring to the earthly Jesus, I prescind temporarily from questions about the nature, extent, and reliability of our knowledge of him. This terminological distinction cannot, of course, be imposed on other authors cited in this essay, but it will help to articulate the relationship of Jesus to Christian faith.[14]

Ambiguity is not, however, limited to the term "historical Jesus"; the meaning of "Christ of faith" is also open to different specification. The reference in all cases, by definition, is to Christ as the object of Christian faith. But the term refers directly to Christ, not to faith, and it is in this regard that significant differences underlie its usage. For critics of Christianity, past and present, the Christ of faith is a figment of the Christian imagination, a product of Christian faith, considered real by Christians but in fact lacking existence outside the minds and hearts of its creators. In relationship to the earthly Jesus, the Christ of faith is a misinterpretation or mystification of a mundane human being; in relationship to the historical study of Jesus, it is an ideological concept in the pejorative sense, something to be criticized or at least whittled down to appropriate dimensions. In the judgment of Christians, however, the Christ of faith is a reality not of their making; he is the risen and exalted Lord who lives and reigns personally and eternally with God the Father. According to its own self-understanding, faith does not create its own object, but corresponds to a divinely constituted reality. It is with the relationship of the earthly Jesus to the Christ of faith in this latter sense that this essay is concerned.

The Earthly Jesus and the Christ of Faith

Fundamental to Christianity is not simply adherence to a messianic idea but rather belief "that Jesus is the Christ, the Son of God" (John 20:31). Christian faith attributes decisive revelatory and salvific significance to a specific human being, Jesus of Nazareth, who lived and died in a particular place and time, and whom it confesses as the incarnate Son of God now living eternally as risen and exalted Lord. While further development of christology is beyond the scope of this essay, it is important to insist from the outset that the earthly Jesus is not a matter of indifference to Christians.

The clearest expression of this conviction in the New Testament is to be found in the existence of the four Gospels, which with distinctive emphases and varying literary techniques present the public life and death of Jesus in christological terms.[15] While the Gospels are confessional documents written from a Christian perspective, not neutral reports of uninterpreted data about Jesus, the truth of the evangelists' theological positions depends in part on their having a factual reference point in Jesus and in certain events of his life. While it is important not to exaggerate the scope of faith's necessary reference to events of the past — as did the nineteenth-century theologian who judged the historical character of the flight into Egypt to be as certain as that of the crucifixion[16] — it would be an even more serious error to underestimate the permanent reference to specific past events, which is a basic dimension of Christian faith.

The best illustration of this point — as of many other theological issues — is provided by the crucifixion. In a formulation received and handed on since the time of Paul, Christians profess that "Christ died for our sins in accordance with the Scripture" (1 Cor. 15:3). This belief in the salvific value of Jesus' death far exceeds the simple statement that Jesus was crucified. Anyone who, like Hazel Motes in Flannery O'Connor's novel *Wise Blood,* preaches, "I don't say he wasn't crucified but I say it wasn't for you,"[17] is not a Christian. Nonetheless, although the truth of the Christian profession that Christ died for our sins is not established by the mere fact of the crucifixion, it does presuppose Jesus in fact "suffered under Pontius Pilate."[18] It is for reasons such as this that Nicholas Lash, in a thoughtful essay on the credibility of Christianity, writes: "If I were to become convinced that Jesus did not exist, or that the story told in the New Testament of his life, teaching and death was a fictional construction ungrounded in the facts, or a radical misinterpretation of his character, history and significance, then I should cease to be a Christian."[19]

Because of the relationship of faith to the earthly Jesus, Christian theology has an intrinsic interest in historical research into Jesus' life.

While recognizing that Jesus (like any other historical figure) can never be recaptured fully by historical scholarship, and aware that faith is not based on historical reconstructions, Christians acknowledge that some elements of Jesus' life open in principle to historical investigation are of central concern to Christian faith.[20] Among such items of particular theological importance, I would include Jesus' understanding of his own salvific significance, the coexistence of present and future dimensions in his preaching of the kingdom of God, his personal approach to death, and the relationship of his public life and death to the origin of the church and the Eucharist.[21]

In regard to issues of this sort, a certain imbalance inherent in the relationship of faith to historical research should be noted. Since faith includes a dimension not subject to empirical verification, historical results as such can never ultimately confirm the truth of faith. Yet, since faith includes a relationship to empirical reality, there are some historical judgments that, were they to be definitively established as corresponding to the reality of the past, would make Christian faith untenable. It is for this reason that Lash formulates the statement quoted above in contrary to fact form.

The Theology of the Resurrection

Among the fundamental tenets of Christian faith is the resurrection of Jesus Christ. Essential to this conviction that Christ is risen is the theme of personal continuity, in and through the transformation of death, on Jesus' part because the Christian faith professes, not simply that a resurrection has taken place, but that the crucified Jesus of Nazareth has been raised from the dead.

The theme of continuity is accented strongly in the resurrection narratives of the Gospels.[22] The Gospels make clear, of course, that the crucified and risen Jesus is transformed: In the appearance narratives, even those who had known him intimately during his lifetime often fail to identify him at first and recognize him only after he takes a further initiative (Luke 24:13–35; 24:37; John 20:14–16; 21:1–7). But at least equal stress is placed on the identity of the Risen One with the Crucified. The women at the tomb in Mark are reminded by the young man that they seek "Jesus of Nazareth who was crucified" (16:6), and the heavenly messengers at the tomb in Matthew (28:5) and Luke (24:7) also make reference to the crucifixion. Most dramatically of all, in John 20:24–29 Thomas insists on seeing and touching in the risen Jesus the marks of the nails in his hands and the wound opened in his side by the soldier's lance after his death (see John 19:34); it is only upon being shown these marks that Thomas responds with a solemn profession of faith.

Affirmation of such continuity between the earthly Jesus and the risen Lord is also reflected in some recent theology of the resurrection. The best example is provided by Karl Rahner, who views Jesus' resurrection as the fruit of his individual temporal existence, not a completely heterogeneous period that follows after his death.[23] "The resurrection of Christ is not *another* event *after* his suffering and after his death, but . . . the appearance of what took place in Christ's death: the performed and undergone handing over of the entire reality of the one corporal man to the mystery of the mercifully loving God through Christ's collected freedom, which disposes over his entire life and his entire existence."[24] In this understanding, the resurrection is not an annihilating absorption into God, nor is resurrection language simply an imaginative way of designating the rise of faith among Jesus' disciples. The resurrection means, rather, the full personal life of the crucified Jesus with God. Seen from this perspective, religious and theological interest in the earthly Jesus is not in the least competitive with Christian faith in the risen and exalted Lord.

Two Concluding Remarks

The understanding of the relationship of the earthly Jesus to the risen Lord affects not only the theology of the resurrection but also the understanding of the incarnation. Some descriptions of the risen Christ seem to suggest — perhaps contrary to the intent of their authors — an adoptionist conception of the resurrection, or even the idea that through the resurrection Jesus sheds his humanity in favor of achieving or regaining divine status. If the Christian understanding of the resurrection is articulated by stating of Jesus "that after his death he entered into an entirely new form of existence, one in which he shared the power of God and in which he could share that power with others" and that the resurrection means "the passage of the human Jesus into the power of God" such that "by definition, the resurrection elevates Jesus beyond the merely human,"[25] it is hard to avoid the impression that the earthly Jesus was not, in the words of the Council of Chalcedon, "truly God and truly man." A similar inference could easily be drawn from the statement that through the resurrection "Jesus is placed in *definitive unity with God*."[26] Recognizing Jesus as the Christ requires holding together his incarnation, public life, crucifixion, and resurrection, not opting for any one of the four in opposition to the other three.

Since the inception of modern historical-critical research on the Gospels, christological questions have often been formulated as a choice between the historical Jesus and the Christ of faith, or between the earthly Jesus and the risen Lord. Given this disjunction, critics of Christianity have typically opted for the historical Jesus or the earthly Jesus and against the Christ of faith and risen Lord. It is clear that the church will not and cannot follow them in this choice. But two alternatives remain: Christians can either opt for the risen Christ against the earthly Jesus, or challenge the legitimacy of a dichotomy between Jesus of Nazareth and the Christ of faith. It seems to me crucial for the church's well-being that the latter path be chosen.

NOTES

1. Overviews of this research are provided by M. Eugene Boring (see chapter 21 above), and by Luke Timothy Johnson, *The Real Jesus: The Misguided Quest for the Historical Jesus and the Truth of the Traditional Gospels* (San Francisco: HarperSanFrancisco, 1996).

2. Classically summarized by Albert Schweitzer in *The Quest of the Historical Jesus: A Study of Its Progress from Reimarus to Wrede* (London: Black, 1911). This work, originally published in 1906 under the title *Von Reimarus zu Wrede,* surveys the relevant literature from the posthumous publication of Hermann Samuel Reimarus's *Fragments* (1774–78) to Wilhelm Wrede's study of the messianic secret in the Gospels (1901). The dubious image of a "quest" derives from the title of the English translation.

3. Ernst Käsemann, "The Problem of the Historical Jesus," in *Essays on New Testament Themes* (London: SCM, 1964), 15–47.

4. For an English translation see C. H. Talbert, ed., *Reimarus: Fragments* (Philadelphia: Fortress, 1970).

5. Schweitzer, *The Quest of the Historical Jesus,* 4.

6. "The Primitive Christian Kerygma and the Historical Jesus," in Carl Braaten and Roy Harrisville, eds., *The Historical Jesus and the Kerygmatic Christ* (Nashville: Abingdon, 1964), 20–21, 25.

7. Schubert M. Ogden, *The Point of Christology* (London: SCM, 1982); the citation is from p. 16.

8. Paul Hollenbach, "The Historical Jesus Today," *BTB* 19 (1989): 11–22; the citation is from p. 19. The phrase "mistake called Christianity" is taken from José Porfirio Miranda, *Being and the Messiah* (Maryknoll, N.Y.: Orbis Books, 1977). Cf. also Burton Mack, *The Lost Gospel: The Book of Q and Christian Origins* (San Francisco: HarperSanFrancisco, 1993), and Thomas F. Sheehan, *The First Coming: How the Kingdom of God Became Christianity* (New York: Random House, 1986).

9. John Dominic Crossan, *The Historical Jesus: The Life of a Mediterranean Jewish Peasant* (San Francisco: HarperSanFrancisco, 1991), 421–24.

10. See John P. Meier, *A Marginal Jew: Rethinking the Historical Jesus,* 2 vols. (New York: Doubleday, 1991–94); Joachim Gnilka, *Jesus von Nazaret* (Freiburg: Herder, 1993).

11. Karl Barth, *Der Römerbrief,* 2d ed. (Munich: Kaiser, 1922), 6. My translation; emphasis in original. The Pauline text cited by Barth is 2 Cor. 5:16.

12. Cf. Barth's reply to Adolf von Harnack, in H. Martin Rumscheidt, *Revelation and Theology: An Analysis of the Barth-Harnack Correspondence of 1923* (Cambridge: Cambridge University Press, 1972), 35.

13. "Redemptoris Missio," *Acta Apostolicae Sedis* 83 (1991): 255.

14. Terminological questions are discussed helpfully by Gerhard Ebeling, *Dogmatik des christlichen Glaubens* (Tübingen: Siebeck, 1979), 2:369–81; Karl Lehmann, "Die Frage nach Jesus von Nazaret," in Walter Kern et al., eds., *Handbuch der Fundamentaltheologie,* vol. 2: *Traktat Offenbarung* (Freiburg: Herder, 1985), 122–23; and John P. Meier, "The Historical Jesus: Rethinking Some Concepts," *TS* 51 (1990): 3–24.

15. Cf. Franz Mussner, "Christologische Homologese und evangelische Vita Jesu," in Bernhard Welte, ed., *Zur Frühgeschichte der Christologie,* QD 51 (Freiburg: Herder, 1970), 59–73.

16. Josef Kleutgen, *Die Theologie der Vorzeit,* 2d ed., vol. 1 (Münster: Theissing, 1867), 120.

17. Flannery O'Connor, *Collected Works* (New York: Library of America, 1988), 30. Motes intends "to preach a new church — the church of truth without Jesus Christ Crucified," 31.

18. The same point can be illustrated by a text in which Martin Luther, commenting on Gen. 43:21, criticizes mere *fides historica:* "Historical faith does not rely on the Word or trust in it. No, it says: 'I hear that Christ suffered and died, etc.' But true faith judges as follows: 'I believe that Christ suffered and died for me, etc. About this I have no doubt, and in this faith I find rest. I trust in that Word in opposition to death and sin' " (Jaroslav Pelikan and Walter A. Hansen, eds., *Luther's Works,* vol. 8: *Lectures on Genesis Chapters 45–50* [St. Louis: Concordia, 1966], 193). Despite the insufficiency of historical faith, true faith that Christ died for me does depend on the factual occurrence of Jesus' passion and crucifixion.

19. Nicholas Lash, *Theology on Dover Beach* (New York: Paulist, 1979), 84.

20. For an instructive discussion of these issues, see Avery Dulles, "Historians and the Reality of Christ," *First Things* 28 (December 1992): 20–25.

21. These issues are discussed further in John P. Galvin, "From the Humanity of Christ to the Jesus of History: A Paradigm Shift in Catholic Christology," *TS* 55 (1994): 252–73.

22. I appeal to these stories as expressions of the theological views of the evangelists, not as direct descriptions of actual incidents.

23. Karl Rahner, "Auferstehung Christi," in *Lexikon für Theologie und Kirche,* 2d ed. (Freiburg: Herder, 1957), 1:1038–39.

24. Karl Rahner, "Dogmatische Fragen zur Osterfrömmigkeit," in *Schriften zur Theologie* (Einsiedeln: Benziger, 1960), 4:165–66. My translation; the published English translation is inaccurate.

25. Johnson, *The Real Jesus,* 134, 136.

26. Hans Kessler, "Auferstehung Christi," in *Lexikon für Theologie und Kirche,* 3d ed. (Freiburg: Herder, 1993), 1:1188.

– 24 –

The Social World of Jesus

John K. Riches

The world into which Jesus was born in Galilee was thoroughly Jewish. It was also divided along social and economic lines and by the manner in which Jews dealt with gentiles. This is evident from different ways in which Jewish identity was conceived and differing attitudes toward land and temple. Jesus' teaching reflects this social context and interacts with it.

WHAT DO WE MEAN when we speak of the "social world" of Jesus? Do we mean the social world Jesus inhabited? Or do we mean the social world Jesus helped shape? As a preliminary question, what exactly do we mean by the term, so familiar in biblical studies, namely, "social world"?[1]

The term has its roots in the sociology of knowledge, which is, broadly, a discipline that looks at the social factors affecting the way members of particular groups experience the world in which they live. It is based on the belief that the ways people experience the world around them (people, things, events) can vary significantly between members of different groups and societies. This is so because every person is born into a particular group and learns not only a particular language or languages but a whole range of signs and symbols that may be encountered in a diversity of ceremonial, ritual, social, and artistic forms, as well as in gesture, artifacts, buildings, and even landscape. Thus, we may speak about a world or universe of signs or symbols every person acquires from the society or societies in which he or she lives. The effect of such "symbolic universes," sociologists of knowledge argue, is to create or "construct" a social world for members of the group to inhabit.[2] Religious symbolic universes create a particular kind of world, sometimes referred to as a "sacred cosmos" (though this may beg some important questions about the place of symbols of the sacred and profane symbols in religious symbolic worlds). This function of establishing a particular social world may take different forms: It may be world-constructing or world-maintaining. Religious symbols may be powerful ways of preserving the status quo; they may also be used to disturb the established ways of looking at the world. Inherited symbols may be reworked, discarded, and replaced with others to produce another set of concepts and symbols that will serve to construct different kinds of social world.

If this is the case, then it means that our principal task is to give some account of the symbolic world Jesus was taught and the social world he in consequence inhabited. But that last phrase "in consequence" raises some thorny questions. Is it to be understood that everyone who acquires a particular set of symbols will *therefore* see the world around him or her in a given way, that is to say, the acquired symbols will determine with precision and without exception how they see the world? This would be a bold and surprising claim, which has been recently disputed[3] and would make it difficult to see how changes in social worlds could ever occur.[4] People may resist the categories society proposes. The cantankerousness of old people may be a mark of resistance to the way in which their past, that is, their sense of identity, is being eroded, precisely by those who care for them and who, in caring, reinforce old people's fear that what they are in the eyes of society is no more than that: "people who need to be cared for." People, individuals, and subgroups of people within a particular society may resist the standard readings of the symbols; they may resist the symbols themselves and so, in some cases at least, begin to initiate processes of change and reconstruction. So, in the case of Jesus, we shall need to know what were the dominant symbols and concepts with which he, like other Galilean Jews, was brought up; we shall need to know something about the kinds of social world that such symbols fostered among Jews (different groups) at the time of Jesus. But there will remain a question about the extent to which Jesus himself may have begun to reshape those symbols and to disturb the established social world of his time. In a brief essay, we shall be able to do little more than indicate where such reworking of his inherited symbolic world may have occurred.

The Symbolic Universe of First-Century Judaism

The way religious concepts and symbols are expressed and communicated is wonderfully diverse. It would be a serious mistake to suppose that, just because sociologists of religion are interested in religious symbols, rituals, and artifacts, they should not also be interested in creeds and explicit beliefs. To fully understand Judaism in the first century, we would need to understand the role of beliefs in the oneness of God (expressed daily in the Shema', the most fundamental of Jewish prayers) every bit as much as we would need to understand the significance of the temple and its rituals and of Jewish social institutions like the family and priesthood. Here we shall limit ourselves to some of the basic Jewish beliefs and to a consideration of Jewish attachment to their ethnic group and the land and temple.

Jews in the first century (though, of course, not only then) believed that they had been chosen by God, that God had made a covenant with them, and that the terms of that covenant were to be found in the law. God, out of his mercy, had chosen the Jews, had promised to "bear them up on eagles' wings" (Exod. 19:4) and to give them the land (Deut. 6:1–3); Jews for their part must be faithful to him and obey God's law as revealed to Moses on Sinai and recorded in written form in Torah. God was one and Jews were to have "no other gods but him" (Deut. 6:4, 5:7). He was creator and sovereign over the world.[5]

If these were the main Jewish beliefs of the time, it is clear that many other beliefs and practices flowed from them. If God's law is contained in Torah and Torah prescribes circumcision as a mark of the covenant, then it is clear that circumcision is a central obligation for Jews and an affirmation of their election by God. There would also, however, be other beliefs and practices that would not flow directly from these basic beliefs but from a conjunction of them with other beliefs. Thus if one believed that God's law had been revealed not only in written form but also in oral form, then one might also find, for example, the practice of hand-washing before meals a matter of obligation even though it is not contained in the written Torah. Other beliefs might have arisen that challenged more directly the basic or standard beliefs we have outlined. It would seem to be a corollary of God's promises of the land and those to Abraham that he would also be the father of a great nation and that the benefits (rewards?) of the covenant would extend principally (only?) to this life. But what of those who were faithful but did not enjoy the fruits of their labors, who died horrendously upholding the law in the face of persecution by the Seleucids (1 Macc. 1:60–64)? It is not unreasonable to see the emergence of belief in some future state (Dan. 12:2) or some imminent and dramatic divine intervention to change present trials (Mark 13; Assumption of Moses 10) as a response to such situations. Hence, basic Jewish beliefs were developed, added to, and even modified in the light of experience and history.

Such beliefs are, of course, the bare bones of a religious faith. They need, if they are to move people and to create in them "long-lasting moods and motivations,"[6] further expression, for example, in hymns, narratives, rituals, institutions, common practice and observance, and attachment to particular places and sacred sites. Judaism is rich in these and we can here give only an indication of how they looked in Jesus' day. Let me focus on two aspects: belief in Israel's election, and belief in the land and temple.

Israel's Election

Jews believed that they had been chosen by God as his people and that this set them apart from "the nations" or "the gentiles." What distinguished Jews from gentiles were then two different kinds of thing, one of which they could do little or nothing about, and the other of which they could and did. Precisely because God had chosen a particular people at a particular time, members of the covenant people were such by virtue of their birth; and this fact was specifically marked out in the case of males by the rite of circumcision on the eighth day. Although it was possible (though obviously difficult and painful) for males who were not Jews by birth to be circumcised later and so to become members of the community, it was by no means common and some texts seem to rule it out (*Jub.* 15:26). It would obviously be easier for women to make the transition. Male circumcision was not unique to the Jews in the ancient world; it was also found among the Egyptians. It was a substantial cause of embarrassment to those Jews who wished to move in Hellenized circles: Games in the gymnasium and in public contests were conducted naked and 1 Maccabees 1:14–15 ("They built a sports-stadium in the gentile style in Jerusalem. They removed their marks of circumcision and they repudiated the holy covenant.") records how Jews at the time of Hellenistic reform in Jerusalem underwent a painful operation (epispasm) in order to perform in the games. It is interesting that the rite of circumcision substantially predates the other rite of male initiation into the community (bar mitzvah, which is a product of the late Middle Ages), suggesting strongly the importance of birth into the community.

There were many other ways in which Jews differed from other groups around them that depended not on some physical characteristic but on their patterns of behavior. Foremost among these were the observances of certain days: the Sabbath and the festivals of Passover, Weeks, and Booths (the last two agricultural festivals), and the fast of the Day of Atonement. While the annual festivals and fast were celebrated principally at Jerusalem, Passover was also celebrated elsewhere. Josephus records regulations permitting Jews to sacrifice the Passover in Sardis.[7] Passover recorded God's liberation of the Jews from slavery in Egypt and therefore particularly brought home to Jews their belonging to a chosen people and their sense of God as one who would liberate them from subservience.

Jews were also well known for their observance of purity laws, notably dietary laws. Such regulations, it is suggested, serve to preserve the external and internal boundaries of the group.[8] To Jews, this appears to have been clearly understood. At least Leviticus 20:22–27 makes it clear that avoidance of unclean foods is undertaken to remind Jews that they have been set apart from gentiles and that they are not to act like them, lest God also spew them out of the land. In practice, such regulations have an inhibiting effect on social mixing and serve easily to mark out those who observe them from those among whom they live who do not. Such a sense of distinctiveness would also doubtless help to instill in Jews in the diaspora a sense of alienation they were often keen to overcome.

This is in no sense an exhaustive list of the ways in which Jews reminded themselves of their election by God. The stories of the Hebrew scriptures, together with the Psalms, would recall God's past mercies to the nation. The principal daily prayers, the Shema' and Eighteen Benedictions, would remind them of the hope that God would finally reunite all his people in the land he had given them.

Land and Temple

Belief that God had promised the land to Israel was given clear and powerful expression in the narratives of the Hebrew scriptures. Within the land, the temple was an immensely impressive symbol of God's presence at the heart of his people. However, Roman occupation of the land and humiliating practices like the retention of the high priest's robes by the Roman governor would have served to unsettle such belief.[9]

In one sense, the existence of the temple in Jerusalem creates a polarity between it and the land. The land is divinely promised and given to Israel and therefore itself set apart for them, but not to be abominated or despoiled, lest God vomit them out of it, as he did the gentiles; at the same time, the temple is the holy place in the holy city, itself divided into spheres of increasing sacredness, from the Court of the Gentiles to the Holy of Holies. This is to say that, within the land, there are degrees of holiness, spreading out like circles in a pool from the sanctuary itself.[10] How was this understood? Was the organization of the temple space seen as a map of sacred space in the land, with spheres of decreasing holiness radiating out from the central sanctuary to the border areas with gentile territory? Or was the temple itself seen as marking the boundary between sacred and profane space, such that the purity laws, for example, which related to the washing of hands before meals, properly applied only within the temple? This is clearly a matter of dispute in the first century, with the Pharisees wanting to argue for the washing of hands throughout the land.[11] By the same token, the Sadducees, who were very much a temple-based group (and who disappeared after the destruction of the temple), rejected the custom, wishing presumably to give clear expression to the belief that the true center of the land was in Jerusalem and that it was here that God's presence was centered.

The Social World of Galilee

How did such notions and symbols of descent and attachment to place shape the kind of social world that people in Galilee inhabited?

Descent of the Covenant People

Jews in Galilee will have been as aware as other Jews of their own ethnic identity and of their distinction from gentile neighbors and surrounding territories. Theirs was a territory that had been incorporated into the Jewish state only at the turn of the second century B.C.E. by Alexander Jannaeus.[12] When Pompey carried out his military campaign in the 60s, he "liberated" the coastal cities that, in the main, then remained loyal to Rome. Some have suggested that this will have led to an exodus of Jews from these cities to the Galilean hills, which would explain the apparent density of population in this area.[13] Moreover, in the disturbances after the death of Herod (4 B.C.E.), Galileans rose up in revolt and were put down by the Syrian legate Varus, who destroyed Sepphoris, sold the inhabitants into slavery, and crucified the combatants.[14] Such actions will doubtless not have disposed the population of the hill country particularly well to their gentile neighbors.

It is, then, not surprising that Jews, faced with such foreign overlordship, should long for a restoration of their sovereignty and freedom from foreign rule. Judas the Galilean, so Josephus tells us, stirred up the Jews in Galilee by urging them to reject Roman claims to sovereignty over them.[15] In this way he invoked powerful theocratic ideas rooted in the Hebrew scriptures. Moreover, he linked the idea of obedience to the sovereign God of Israel with ideas of civil disobedience and armed revolt against foreign rulers. This gave a particular twist to the Jewish sense of identity and distinctiveness. No longer was it purely a matter of remaining faithful to certain customs and laws enforcing a sense of separation from gentiles: It was a matter of working for Jewish freedom from foreign control.

This should not be taken to suggest that Jews therefore had no commerce with gentiles. Josephus makes it clear that Galilee was a thriving center of commerce, exporting agricultural and other products. Recent archaeological analysis has shown that pottery from Kefar Hanania was distributed across Galilee and into the surrounding areas of the Golan.[16] In lower Galilee, there is a preponderance of Greek inscriptions over Aramaic and Hebrew ones.[17]

Nor should it be taken to indicate that Jews in Galilee were altogether united against the foreign oppressor. S. Freyne and others have suggested that, under Herod Antipas (who had unsuccessfully made his case to Rome to be made king in succession to his father, Herod the

Great), there was a strong move away from a traditional peasant economy, where all shared in the fruits of the land (which accords broadly with Deuteronomic notions), to a market economy that would concentrate power and wealth in the hands of a few landlords and rulers.[18] The two cities of Sepphoris and Tiberias, which were rebuilt and built, respectively, under Herod Antipas, were centers of commerce between rural and urban populations and clear evidence, and indeed instruments, of the transference of wealth between peasant and landlord classes. Such developments, which were not restricted to Galilee but also embraced the ruling families in Judea and Jerusalem, go some way toward explaining the popular nature of the Jewish revolt and the deposition of the high priest at its beginning.[19] The fierce character of popular resentment against Sepphoris and Tiberias as centers of such aristocratic exploitation of the Galilean peasants is well documented by Josephus.[20]

Consequently, Jews in Galilee by no means agreed about what it was to be a true Jew. At the time of the Jewish War, many Jews regarded those leaders who sided with Agrippa II and the Romans as "traitors of our freedom."[21] Presumably, the same kind of attitudes would have prevailed against those who collected taxes that found their way directly or indirectly to their foreign overlords. But it is by no means clear that those who worked with the Romans or their client rulers would have regarded their cooperation with their overlords as excluding them from membership in the Jewish people. Such people might have had other sticking points as regards what qualified as Jewish and what did not. Josephus, who changed sides in the Jewish War, certainly did not think of himself as having parted company with the Jewish people. But such groups of people viewed the world in very different ways, even while both asserted their Jewishness.

Land and Temple

Again it is interesting to speculate about which different conceptions of the land and the temple may have been entertained by different groups of people in Galilee. To what extent did people in the north of the country feel themselves disadvantaged by the centering of the land on Jerusalem and the temple? The implication was that they inhabited a district in some sense distanced from the sacral heart of the country. Certainly, the Samaritans, who saw themselves as faithful Jews, disputed the claims of Jerusalem (see the echoes of these disputes in John 4) and established their own temple on Mount Gerizim, which was destroyed by John Hyrcanus (the Jewish Hasmonean king, who ruled from 134 to 104 B.C.E.). At the same time, Galilee, which was yet further removed from the center, appears to have been faithful to Jerusalem. The presence of Galilean pilgrims at the festivals, despite their having to run the gauntlet of the Samaritans on their way, is evidence of strong Galilean attachment. The Gospel of Mark also reflects Galilean peasant amazement or possibly estrangement in face of the imposing Hellenistic architecture of Jerusalem: "Look, Teacher, what wonderful stones and what wonderful buildings!" (Mark 13:1).

Still, we have evidence, not always easy to evaluate, of practices in Galilee indicating an interest in trying to assert the sanctity of life in Galilean communities, too. Mark 7, written as it was either shortly before or after the destruction of the temple, is strong evidence of Pharisaic attempts in Galilee to introduce the custom of hand-washing before meals during the time of the temple. This was not prescribed in the written law and was a practice originally restricted to the priests in the temple. Behind such controversies lay in all likelihood an attempt to make a statement about the sanctity of the corporate life of the faithful in Galilee. This, in turn, affirms the continuity between life in Jerusalem and Galilee. There is also a growing body of archaeological evidence of immersion pools (*mikwaoth*) in Galilee. These pools were used for purificatory purposes and would again appear to be a strong expression of a sense of the need to preserve the holiness of Galilean communities. Such evidence, however, is not easy to date and no consensus has yet emerged among archaeologists.[22]

Such concerns about the purity of the community and the land are to be distinguished from the main emphasis of those who, like Judas the Galilean, saw the prime need to be that of reasserting Jewish freedom from foreign rule. It is doubtful whether those who took to the hills to fight would have had time for the finer points of ritual purity. For them, it was necessary to reestablish Jewish independence and to use military means to achieve freedom in order to restore the purity of the temple and the land. For such groups, control over the temple was of central importance, and this indicates that their conception of independence (like that of the Maccabees) was linked to the idea of a renewed temple state in Jewish control. Doubtless there are strong echoes here of Galilee's long history of political separation from Judea.

The Social World of Jesus

Jesus was born into Roman Galilee sometime around the uprising that led to the destruction of the city of Sepphoris, just over the hill from Nazareth. It was a world in which Jewish senses of ethnic identity had been sharpened by the violence of the repression of that uprising. It was also a time of growing tension between the peasant majority of the population and a ruling class that had found new prosperity and power through a developing market economy and through engagement in international politics; such developments are powerfully symbolized by the rebuilding of Sepphoris and its establishment as an important cultural and commercial center. Such economic divisions did not coincide neatly with ethnic divisions and may indeed have, on both sides of the divide, tended to overshadow Jewish ethnic senses of identity and solidarity.

Nevertheless, Jerusalem and the temple would still have provided a powerful center of national unity, which attracted Jewish pilgrims from all over the Mediterranean. At the same time, precisely its power of attraction for Jews could make it an object of struggle, as is shown by the popular election of a high priest during the Jewish revolt.

It is reasonable to suppose that Jesus, like the rest of his Galilean compatriots, would have been aware of these tensions. It is, as Freyne has suggested, striking that Jesus is nowhere recorded as entering Sepphoris and Tiberias, the two main centers of commercial development in Galilee. His parables make it clear he was aware of the economic hardship and social division caused by changing patterns of land ownership and distribution of goods.[23] His advocacy of the poor and the powerless indicates clearly where his sympathies lay.[24] If Jesus identified with those who found themselves economically divided from the powerful and wealthy in Galilee and avoided centers like Sepphoris, it is less easy to know to what extent he identified with the Jewish population and avoided contact with gentiles. Certainly the Gospels record visits to gentile districts and contact with gentiles. His early association with John the Baptist, who according to Matthew 3:9 attacked Jewish reliance on physical descent from Abraham, could suggest a greater openness to the gentile world. On the other hand, the story of the Syro-Phoenician woman attributes strong ethnic views to Jesus (Mark 7:24–30). The question, which we cannot examine here, is how far Jesus may have attempted to refashion the ways his contemporaries viewed these matters. Certainly his meals with tax-collectors and sinners, those in serious breach of the law, would have raised sharp questions about Jewish particularity.

To what extent did Jesus share contemporary Jewish hopes for the restoration of an independent Jewish temple state? Jesus' use of kingship language suggests strongly he was attuned to some such expectations. At the same time, texts like Matthew 5:38–42, 43–48 make it improbable that he espoused the military solutions of leaders like Judas the Galilean. It is more probable that he looked for a divine intervention that would establish God's rule over the land and bring vindication and fulfillment to those who suffered, without their prior engagement in military action. Precisely what his conception of this fulfillment was is difficult to say. His actions in the temple have suggested to some that he predicted its destruction and restoration, but it is an intriguing possibility that his calling of the Twelve indicates that he looked towards a time after the destruction of the temple state when the twelve tribes would be gathered and ruled over by the Twelve.[25] Does such a vision express something of the peasant longing for the return to a state where all could share in the fruits of the land?

Such millennial dreams (if Jesus actually had them) should not be discarded as being without serious moral or religious content. What they express is belief in a God of justice and equity and mercy, "who causes his rain to fall on the just and the unjust" (Matt. 5:45) and who promises that the poor will experience his rule (Luke 6:20). Such beliefs are given powerful expression in his parables as he encourages his hearers to rethink their standard conceptions of God's rule.[26] In this way Jesus encourages his contemporaries to refashion their social world.

NOTES

1. See, e.g., Wayne A. Meeks, *The First Urban Christians: The Social World of Pauline Christianity* (New Haven: Yale University Press, 1983); J. G. Gager, *Kingdom and Community: The Social World of Early Christianity* (Englewood Cliffs, N.J.: Prentice-Hall, 1975), esp. 9–14.

2. See Peter L. Berger and Thomas Luckmann, *The Social Construction of Reality* (London: SCM Press, 1966).

3. A. Cohen, *Self Consciousness: An Alternative Anthropology of Identity* (London: Routledge, 1994), see esp. 134–35.

4. Such a claim is easily suggested by Clifford Geertz's definition of religion as "a system of symbols which acts to establish powerful, pervasive and long-lasting moods and motivations in men," in "Religion as a Cultural System," in *The Interpretation of Cultures: Selected Essays* (London: Hutchinson, 1975), 90. But even Geertz allows that such symbols can be interpreted in a variety of ways.

5. This is broadly the basis of the picture of Judaism put forward by E. P. Sanders under the head of "covenantal nomism" in *Paul and Palestinian Judaism* (London: SCM Press, 1977).

6. See Geertz, "Religion as a Cultural System," 90.

7. Josephus, *Jewish Antiquities* 14.260.

8. See esp. M. Douglas, *Purity and Danger* (London: Routledge and Kegan Paul, 1966).

9. Josephus, *Jewish Antiquities* 15.403–8.

10. For a fascinating discussion of the way in which the symbolization of sacred space in different realizations or depictions of the temple expresses different views of reality, see J. Z. Smith, *To Take Place: Toward Theory in Ritual* (Chicago: University of Chicago Press, 1987).

11. On this view, this is not so much a dispute about observance of these laws by lay people as well as by priests, as about the location of such rituals.

12. It was often held, largely on the basis of E. Schürer's work, that before its reincorporation the population of Galilee had been predominantly gentile.

S. Freyne powerfully challenged this view in his *Galilee from Alexander the Great to Hadrian, 323 BCE to 135 CE* (Wilmington: Glazier, 1980).

13. For evidence of the density of settlement in Galilee, see B. Golomb and Y. Kedar, "Ancient Agriculture in the Galilean Mountains," *IEJ* 21 (1971): 136–40. For reflections on the consequences of the loss of the coastal cities and the Decapolis for the economic and social life of Galilee, see G. Applebaum, "Economic Life in Palestine," in *Compendium Rerum Iudaicarum ad Novum Testamentum* (Assen: von Gorcum, 1974), 631–700.

14. Josephus, *Jewish Antiquities* 17.289.

15. The key texts are *War* 2.118: Judas "incited his countrymen to revolt, upbraiding them as cowards for consenting to pay tribute to the Romans and tolerating mortal masters after having God for their Lord"; and *Jewish Antiquities* 18.23, where we are told that that the fourth philosophy is like the Pharisees in all respects "except that they have a passion for liberty that is almost unconquerable, since they are convinced that God alone is their leader and master."

16. D. Adan-Bayewitz, *Common Pottery in Roman Galilee: A Study of Local Trade* (Ramat Gan: Bar-Ilan University Press, 1993).

17. A. Overman, "Recent Advances in the Archaeology of the Galilee in the Roman Period," *BS* 1 (1993): 35–38.

18. S. Freyne, "Jesus and the Urban Culture of Galilee," in *Texts and Their Contexts: Biblical Texts and Their Textual and Situational Contexts* (Oslo: Scandinavian University Press, 1995), 597–622. "The tensions between these two types of economic system and the increasing dominance of the latter (sc. the market economy) in Herodian Galilee created the social situation that many gospel parables depict—day laborers, debt, resentment of absentee landlords, wealthy estate owners with little concern for tenants' needs, exploitative stewards of estates, family feuds over inheritance etc." (609).

19. M. Goodman, "The First Jewish Revolt: Social Conflict and the Problem of Debt," *JJS* 33 (1982): 417–27.

20. Josephus, *Life,* 66, 376.

21. Ibid., 386. Josephus, in his speech to the Galileans who wish to sack Tiberias, declares that "many of the most eminent men in Galilee have done the same."

22. E. P. Sanders thinks that immersion pools were found across Palestine at this time and that they were used by all levels of the population. He is clearly of the opinion that this is of a piece with the centering of Jewish piety and practice on the worship of the temple, what he calls "common Judaism" (*Judaism: Practice and Belief, 63 BCE–66 CE* [London: SCM, 1992], 222–29). It is not, however, clear how he squares this evidence of widespread practice of purity rites outside the temple sphere with his view that "[p]urity laws affected daily life relatively little; their principal function was to regulate access to the temple" (71).

23. For example, see the references to day-laborers and the labor market, Matt. 20:1–16; to absentee landlords, Mark 12:1–9; to debt and families being sold into slavery, Matt. 18:23–35.

24. Assuming that Luke's form of the beatitudes is closer to Jesus' own for-

mulation than Matthew's (compare Luke 6:20–21 with Matt. 5:1–12) and that Jesus' beatitudes were addressed to those who were literally poor, hungry, and weeping.

25. E. P. Sanders accepts that the symbolism of overturning tables indicates destruction but thinks that any thought of destruction would have brought with it the further thought of its restoration (*Jesus and Judaism* [London: SCM, 1985], 70). For an alternative view, see my "Apocalyptic—Strangely Relevant?" in W. Horbury, ed., *Templum Amicitiae: Essays on the Second Temple Presented to Ernst Bammel* (Sheffield: Sheffield Academic Press, 1991), 237–63.

26. See John Riches, "Parables and the Search for a New Community," in *The Social World of Formative Christianity and Judaism: Essays in Tribute to Howard Clark Kee,* ed. J. Neusner et al. (Philadelphia: Fortress Press, 1988), 235–63.

Index of Scriptural References

OLD TESTAMENT

NEW TESTAMENT